AF480001

I FELL IN LOVE IN A MENTAL INSTITUTION

A MEMOIR OF SORTS

BY NICK JAMESON

Originally published 4.4.24

CONTENTS

"The books that the world calls immoral are
books that show the world its own shame."

- Oscar Wilde

Dedicated to my dear readers, whomever you are.

DISCLAIMER

Before we get to Jess and my recollections of some of the roster of residents at the *Cascade Recovery Center* (CRC), those suffering from SPMI's, or "Severe and Persistent Mental Illnesses," and everything those experiences reveal about the mental health system, and everything even loosely tied to it, and to that wonderful young woman, let's get the caveat lector disclaimer out of the way: If you're a 'woke' slave to political correctness, and blindly conforming to all modern movements, you might as well just 'cancel' me right now. *Seriously*. For what follows is an honest, fearless testament from a natural, progressive provocateur.

No, it's not the testament of an 'edge lord,' in the parlance of the modern nitwit. I don't provoke simply for the sake of provocation, or to be contrarian, or to 'appear edgy,' as a few social media 'trolls' have accused me of doing, or to be iconoclastic, with legions of Christians having condemned my spirituality as being in league with the antichrist, which would be comic if it weren't such a tragic indictment of modern America. Rather, provocation is simply a natural side effect produced by the select few like me who see the inconvenient truths and have the balls to speak them, even in the face of today's appalling self-righteous bullying of everyone into reflexive obedience behind *false* forms of progress. I tell the truth as I see it, even if that risks offending everyone from fake feminists to Me Too mavens to BLM zealots to Trumpers and Bible thumpers. Why? Because 'conventional wisdom' is becoming oxymoronic, and though many of you, dear readers, will hate me for it, *somebody* needs to tell this morally-compromised nation the damn truth. So, without further ado, on to the show.

ME(N) TOO

Allow me to start by saying that though this book is largely critical of my former Bend employers, that, excepting my distaste for corporatism and its parasitic, weakening effect upon the people and planet *generally*, I hold no ill will for PrimaCare. I hold no ill will for the bookstore either, only the way in which a devious clique running rampant within *one* of its locations was permitted to mislead management in a manner that *should've* constituted wrongful termination. Before that, it was one of my favorite places to visit, as it likely is for anyone that knows or senses the value of books. Also, while his mind is that of the perfectly indoctrinated, and his actions are those of the violently insecure, I hold no ill will for Lenny, either, for holding ill will is poisonous. I'd also add that, though I'd do many things differently, PrimaCare and the CRC save some of the most miserable, desperate, disadvantaged people on the planet.

Actually, now that I think of it, though it primarily focuses upon my time working in mental health, this book qualifies as a memoir about all three jobs I've held in Bend, OR. All *four* jobs, actually, if you count Rover, a job that I was considering dramatizing into a semi-fictional novel about a man who, after learning of a certain Bend demographic, uses Rover as a front to meet wealthy widows and divorcees, and ends up becoming a type of prostitute, a la the romantic comedy *Priceless*. I'd call it "The Rover." Okay, so that book would be *almost* entirely fictional.

Ironically, while my jobs in Bend included working with the horribly debilitated and the mentally ill, it was the job set to serve the civilized readers that became the most barbaric. The entirely unacknowledged truth of that experience is that they psychologically abused me, then filed an official report making me out to be the opposite of who I am, then fired me and left me entirely powerless to do anything about it, leaving me with psychological wounds that won't heal. And I can't help but wonder how many others have been similarly victimized and traumatized by colluding covens of conspiring, gossiping witches that've abused the Me Too ethos. Yes, *of course* punish men who wrong women, that should go without saying, but it should also go without saying (but somehow needs to be said) that women who make men appear perpetrators for the power trip and professional benefits of doing so should be equally punished, for their perpetrations are no less devastating.

Finally, I'm compelled to add that my attempts to promote this book and others (including the spiritual but not religious text "The Theosophisutra") through popular channels, including *Facebook* and *Instagram*, have been blocked ('rejected'). In line with the cover warning, *Meta* is owned by self-righteous political correctness. All it takes is for someone to be offended by someone whom thinks for themselves and writes without regard for the prevalent moral code of either the movement-obsessed liberals or the pretentiously-pious Christian conservatives and *Meta* kills the promotion. This, of course, perfectly parallels one of the major premises of this book: that enforcing narrow moral standards is ultimately both irrational and immoral. If *Meta* truly was a meta-force, it would be above such moral policing and would allow freedom of expression pursuant to truth. Alas, this is the age of cancellation, and *Meta* has demonstrated, once again (this is one of *many* run-ins with their political correction police), that it's owned not by truth or freedom of expression, but by the profitable capitulation to the idiocy of popular opinion. When free thinking is censored in the publication and promotion of literature, reading is mind control and truth is burned on the bonfire.

By the way, I could've easily entitled this book "The Purge."

INTRO

A PREJUDICED PLAYER SETS THE SORROWFUL STAGE

Beware all those who would wrong a writer, for not only is writing our foremost form of therapy, no matter what we may say, and is that therapeutic value contingent upon releasing pent up indignation, but we have notoriously long memories; permanent, in fact, as pen is pressed to page.

They say you fall 'madly in love.' So, in a certain sense, it's not just ironic, but apropos, that the only time I've ever fallen in love was in a mental institution. She certainly drove me mad. The irony goes deeper, in fact, for every day I entered the *Cascade Recover Center* it wasn't fear of any mental illness of the residents that gripped me, but my fear of myself in reabsorbing *her*. Because of Jess I know the limits of longing and the depths of despair that may be known when such a love is denied, and when the denied is played with like a toy. I would call my condition at that time, and which I still harbor to a great extent today, a good five years later, *emotionally excruciating*. Every time I lashed out at her, every mistake that I made in what she grossly understated to be "our friendship," was due to my long-standing loneliness finally finding a love that filled me fully, that exposed every inch of my aching internal void, that illumed every speck of the halls of my heart, but which was sucked out of that void at the end of every shift, unleashing an ongoing emotional tumult over which I had little control.

Thus were the heights of my emotional and psychological instability (again, ironically) suffered in a mental institution.

The *Cascade Recovery Center*, or CRC, as it shall henceforth be referred to herein, is a sixteen bed medium security mental health facility in Bend, the nucleus in the high desert nexus of mostly rural 'you blink and you blow by it on the highway' towns comprising Central Oregon. The 'recovery' terminology tells the prima facie tale of the CRC being an institution where those suffering from a recent psychotic break come to *recover*, ideally on the way to proving their stabilization and earning their way out of the civil or criminal commitment declaring them a threat to themselves and others. And we'll arrive at some of their sorrows soon enough; sorrows of such woe that, through their study, one can't help but feel better about one's own lot in life, and ashamed that one ever felt sorry for oneself.

But first, let me describe the place to you, so that you can picture it in your mind whilst I describe all the events, thoughts and feelings which I witnessed, entertained, and which poured out of me therein. The building itself is grey-stoned, the yard surrounded by a high, barbed-wire fence. The lobby is small, and behind the front desk sits Macie, my confidant (I'll have more to say about her later). By legal decree the PrimaCare Corporation must, like all in-resident mental health facilities, post its daily charge for services rendered to its residents somewhere visible near the front entrance where visitors and assessors can easily access the information. Thus, posted in its simple foyer, to the left of Macie, a small framed print presents the fact:

"In-home residential cost: $545 per day."

That's just the base fee, mind you, charged for room, board and twenty-four-hour 'supervision,' and is *far* higher when accounting for 'additional therapeutic services;'

services which we were encouraged to provide and notate, with most such services being grossly exaggerated, if not outright fabricated, in order for the company to make its revenue mark, and for the therapists and 'Recovery Specialists' to make their own marks of services provided by corporate dictate, mostly at the taxpayers' expense. This despite the fact that the position topped out just north of $15/hour, the 'Recovery Specialist' being the term used by PrimaCare for its floor staff; those on the front lines of the mental health war, with no room for increase, and zero 'upward mobility' outside of becoming certified therapists.

Entering through the first electronically locked door to the right of Macie grants you access to the employee lounge area positioned behind her; a small spot with a large printing and copying machine taking up most of the left wall, beneath the window looking out across the street at the massive Department of Corrections building where PrimaCare is permitted to hold its larger meetings. To the right of the printer/copier is a recently installed employee log-in fingerprint scanner, a fridge that always needs to be cleaned, and which is the source of continuous inculpation of those who leave their food in there for too long (I'm sure you know what I mean), a coffee machine that brews ancient residues of coffee as much as it does fresh coffee grounds, and a little reclining seat; one in which I can still see Jess seated, rocking, waiting for the brew that will power the pair of us through yet another overnight shift.

If instead of heading into this employee lounge you go right, through the second electronically-locked door, you enter the resident zone; the area in which the residents daily, and nightly, roam. From here, the office of the chief, Annabelle, is to the right, at the end of this entry hallway. Turning left, on the right as you proceed down the hall into the central space, are the bookkeepers' room, the records room, then the three-desk, three-computer counselors' office, where I had a great many experiences, and was regularly subtly verbally assaulted by Linda, my eventual supervisor after switching to PM shifts post-Jess departure.

Past this you approach 'The Bridge,' an allusion to *Star Trek*, the command center composed of an immense two-computered desk set between the nurse's station on the right and the kitchen on the left, where you find the locked drawer of 'sharps' which, God help you if one is missing at the end of the shift, when the sharps are counted, precipitating all kinds of fear and scandal ("Who let the residents access the sharps? Was it you, Nick?").

These three spots, the kitchen, the nurse's station, and especially The Bridge, form a kind of corner window into the world of observation which was central to our jobs, for they all look out into the Day Room, itself adjoined on both ends by the hallways leading to the residents' bedrooms, eight rooms down each, left and right, typically gender assigned, guys to the left, ladies to the right. Each hallway has a communal bathroom and shower (in addition to the smaller half-baths in the residents' rooms) that would fail even a cursory examination by the Health Department, even as I always wondered if and when such inspections took place. It was, briefly, my job to clean them. I felt like I needed a hazmat suit and one of those high pressure spray washers you see at car washes. It was somehow even more repugnant than during my years working for the *California Parks Department*, cleaning the bathrooms at *Angel Island State Park*. This brings to mind one of what will be many overlaps in my background: I saw as much feces finger-painting in the bathrooms of that park as at the CRC, where a few disgruntled residents creatively employed their waste matter as a combination of realist modern art and rebellious proclamation of discontent.

The Day Room has a large dining table in the middle, where group meals are sometimes provided, and where, through said meals, socialization is encouraged, with a dozen chairs and couches around the outside, a bookcase, a computer for the residents, and, closest to The Bridge and the rest of that corner, a set of couches set in front of the gas fireplace and the common television. At the back of the Day Room is the locked door to the backyard, which itself is, again, ringed in by a high, barbed-wire fence, and is just large enough for me to be able to throw a football from one corner to the other, as one who can throw it a good fifty yards (in fact, retrieving footballs from those playing at the juvenile detention center next to the CRC in our little slice of law enforcement heaven was common; the Department of Corrections, the Sheriff, and both the juvenile detention center and adult prison are neighbors).

Can you picture it? Now, please allow me to put the forthcoming loosely-intertwining chapters into a personal context, for even though I know from *vast* experience that the majority of critiques of any written work reflect the *critic* far more than the creator, I also know that a memoir is about the mind of the *writer*, and that personalization is appreciated by most readers, because it lends an inimitable quality of authenticity. Not that such authenticity shall protect me from the inevitable scorn and ridicule of many of you. And I wouldn't want you to have to work too hard to prevail upon the prejudices that I'll certainly provoke in you (sorry, I meant the 'morality that I'll violate') in prejudging and thereby forming opinions about me on the way to confirming what you already know.

What a horror it is to make the reader uncomfortable! Heaven forbid that you should be challenged, right? That you should be forced to look upon and see your own myopic lens reflecting off of the surface of what you read herein, rather than brave even an *attempt* to put down that lens for now, realizing that truth is *always* on the *other* side of prejudice? Might you accept my challenge, dear reader?

Obviously I possess my own prejudices. This can't be helped. There's no such thing as 'unbiased,' no matter what those subjects relating their 'objectivity' as, and in relation to other subjects, will tell you. And I'll give an example of that bias later, in the active reading of Michael Pollan's rightly respected *The Omnivore's Dilemma*, while also demonstrating my own bias throughout this book. And the heart of this book is my maddening experience of Jess, the magnificent young woman whom so overwhelmed me with a sense of need that I myself nearly mentally cracked, spurring greater inspection of the root causes of psychosis.

When it was clear to me that she had me in the palm of her hand, when I could scarcely think of anything beyond my need to sit beside her on the night shift and listen to her manifold tales of elation and deflation, communicating as much by gesticulation as by articulation, I would tell myself repeatedly before walking into the institution: *Be strong. Don't even talk to her.* But as soon as she would speak, as soon as she pierced me with those mesmerizing eyes, all the hours of self-reinforcement dissolved like a clay wall in the face of a tsunami, and I was the puddy left in the wake.

Despite the resentment that I've been unable to shake, after all these years, of so desperately desiring her, and of that power she possessed being so palpable that even one as good as her couldn't help but wield it against the powerless, me, my own heart her weapon, playing little games, always on *this* side of deniability… despite that resentment, deep down I know that she granted me the invaluable by opening up to me so much. To this day I wonder if that's why I fell so desperately in love with her? Because love is inseparable from understanding, and she told me *everything*, giving me the greatest of gifts: someone to *truly* know, not just someone *said* to be known. As I once told her: *She gave me someone to love when I needed it the most.* I was buried in darkness, and by dropping her guard and letting me all the way in, she filled me with an ecstatic agony that lifted me up into the light, and demonstrated the priceless purpose of the life of every romantic like me: *To be completely conquered.*

When one truly falls in love, it's permanent. It's not some passing fancy. I'll be 90 years old, struggling with the onset of senility, wandering aimlessly around the nursing home mumbling: "Jess? Has anyone seen Jess?" Though we've not spoken nor laid eyes upon one another for years (beyond fleeting seconds of her driving or walking by), by the metaphysical laws of entanglement which connect and govern all as cells of the same eternal body are she and I forever bound, such that, though there may be oceans between us, when her heart calls out its echo resounds within my own, as though she's seated not just beside me, but *within* me, "nearer to me than myself," in Rumi's words.

I miss her not just every day, but every hour of my life. It was like intermittently sitting in the sun three nights a week for eighteen months, then having the sun permanently set and being forced to pretend that I've forgotten its radiant warmth; forgotten that I could see impassioned promise extending past the horizon; forgotten that everything in me reached for that sun as plants thereby reach their leaves, and being forced by social propriety to perpetuate the pretense that, having experienced all of that, I need to 'just get over it;' that I must put on the show that I've forgotten the sun and am completely content with living in the cold night, navigating by soft starlight where once I knew the cynosure; where once there was warmth and brightness.

To this day she's my kryptonite. Before recently deleting my account access (more on this later), I couldn't bring myself to ever check her *Facebook* page because every ounce of love shared therein that I'll never be a part of was like a knife to the heart. It was so bad the first few years after she left the CRC and discarded our friendship that I couldn't even see her face on *Facebook Messenger* without my knees buckling. Eventually I could at least manage *that* much. No, it wasn't a stalking thing. We were *Facebook* 'friends.' I think I still technically have my account, even as I deleted the app on my phone recent to this writing. She may even still think of me as a friend, at least until she reads this, perhaps, or any of the other literary projects in which she's played the muse. They say writers write what they know. Sometimes I think the only thing that I know for certain is that I loved her. The rest is just minutia by comparison; saplings wanting for a forest.

I remember that, when something would touch her deeply, or when she'd connect with a memory of a trauma, her eyes would well up, those gorgeous, bewitching eyes, and that, in those moments, no one and nothing could be more beautiful. This isn't sadism, understand. It's not that I took pleasure in her pain. Far from it. It was that nothing was more true, more of the heart, and thus of God, of love, than *those* moments. And as they set themselves upon her brow I was born again, and given every reason to fight through my own pain, knowing beyond all else that if I could but be the shield for such a perfectly endearing, dorky goddess of goodly grace, all of my pain would be worth it. I would've killed for that woman; *would* kill for that woman, even still. And I'm not so certain that's hyperbole.

You have no idea how many times, dear reader, and with such self-righteous certainty, it was outright said or else strongly insinuated to me that loving a work colleague is wrong. As if my heart gave me any choice in the matter. Love isn't something that you plan, that you map out and sail into upon charted waters, but the overtaking storm that sweeps you out to sea, beyond the horizons of foresight. You don't choose it, just as someone not fully knowing some realm into which they enter in this treacherous, wonderous life doesn't leap, but *falls* into the pit concealed beneath the appearance of but another step in their journey. Besides, it's better to love with reckless abandon, to ache with insatiable longing, to pursue with implacable passion, than to be restrained by trained obedience and ruled by the expectations of the falsely virtuous whom dictate social proprietary to all the corralled lives less lived.

Another of the endlessly recurring thoughts I have about that delightful, life-affirming woman: If I loved her that much, needed her that desperately, without even being physically intimate with her, *God help me if I had been*. I feel like I would've been swallowed by a wave so powerful that, if I'd had her and lost her, I surely would've drowned. Then I think: How can *he* stand it? How can he have as much of her as he wants and survive? How does this not cut him in two? How do his lungs not collapse at the dread of having had such a being, thence living with the chance that someday he may be forced to draw a breath without her? For I myself often thought in those dark days after she left: *Be beside me once more, for it was only then that I could take a full breath.* Does that make me weak, or him strong? Is he clueless that she's the best thing that exists, and that he daily possesses the privilege of the pinnacle of being of which he's oblivious, and so isn't imperiled by?

Perhaps all these things are true. Perhaps we can never have what we value so much that it decimates us with desperation, as such desperation clearly repels what, and whom, we want. Perhaps the more that we want a thing, the more that we know its value from having yearned for it for as long as we can remember that when it finally stares us in the face we're blinded by its full force, that we're thereby precluded from possessing it, owing to entirely knowing the potency that its actual possessor cannot see, and so may successfully attract. It seems so tragic, to be denied a thing by the potency of our desire, whilst those who're immune to its full force thereby attract it. But that's the game, right? What is it that I heard in that film *Ghosts of Girlfriends Past*? "The power in the relationship lies with the one who cares *less*." Don't get me wrong, I know from the endless litany of anecdotes on their relationship spoken by her that he loves her. How could he not? And yet how could he do so without the existential terror that she would surely force any man that so loved her to feel at even the *thought* of losing her? Perhaps he does, but conceals it within that steely stoicism that she spoke of him, and that I saw the couple times I met him. To feel and not show, so the show of the successful must go, for to show what one knows and feels is to bare chest to blade.

The possession of the holy knife came from Jess always having been too close, and too far, for comfort. I knew no comfort in her, only the *promise* of the greatest comfort, always dangled out in front of me, hiding behind the pretense of 'friendship.' And it was this promise, this knowing that she personified a type of completion, a seamless stitching of the sense of separation, a finding and mirroring of the heart held up until one can't tell the source from the reflection, that brought the persistent sense of madness out of me. I called it 'ecstatic agony.'

I've attempted to purge her from my heart and mind, but she's dug in like a tick. So long did I feel so hollow, so long was the void maintained, aching with its constant reminder of my incompletion, and so expansive is that cavern, that when she unwittingly uncovered its entrance through no conscious choice or control of my own, and so violently came rushing in to fill that void, like a high pressure system rushing in to fill the vacuum of zero pressure, that her presence was blasted into every nook and cranny, and remains therein, like everlasting caulk. I can't extricate her, and am not sure that I want to. It's a strange, comforting type of pain; simultaneously expanding and contracting; as if of the concurrent flooding and ebbing of a great spiritual tide; a whisper of what's possible, just audible beneath the taunting cry of what's missing. But is it *her*, or how she made me *feel*? And is there even a difference between the agent and their agency? It's not images of her (I can scarcely see her face in my mind's eye anymore), but more of an ethereal *presence*. It's the *imprint* of her, as if it's been stamped upon the walls of my heart; a cardiac tattoo permanently leaking its ink into my veins, pumped through body and brain as both a tonic for pain, and the pain itself.

It's not her fault. I think she liked me a little, and maybe even cared for me, but she was in love with another, a good young man that she's since married. And she never gave me any indication it could ever be otherwise. In fact, she told me flat out that otherwise was an impossibility. When it became clear that I couldn't completely control my emotions around her, the emanations of the spiritual Self, the intrinsic truth and tremors of love, she painfully spoke of placing and holding 'boundaries' against me. I'll *always* possess an aversion to that word because of her; because it was used as a crushing constriction against my heart; a heart that was so sickened by contraction, and so relieved by the expansion that she offered, that to lasso it and force it *back* into contraction felt like a type of spiritual death.

For the force of the feeling that I had, *have*, for her knows no boundaries. Holding her in my heart feels like a generative force; like a divine furnace firing creation. The sense of her, of the eternal seed she fertilized within, is inseparable from my spiritual awareness. She's my microcosm of Spirit; of the first moment of creation, when the one irreducible energetic thing that was existence in its entirety expanded into infinite possibility, using space, time and matter as the vehicle. The 'Big Bang' was the first act of love, of an instinctive drive to create the illusion of separability for the sake of coming together. Love is the evocation of everyone and everything's interconnectivity, the foremost form of understanding, and we can't discover that interminable inseparability and understanding of one another but through abolishing the illusion of separation and ignorance which the heart always knows is false, for in the heart the all-knowing Spirit resides. I've never felt more connected to anyone, even with the spacetime that has since separated us, and so the memory of her remains my greatest connection to Spirit, my perpetual callback to the first heart-held ember of the spiritual force of pure creation.

True understanding linked to love linked to the subject of that love telling the truth of his or her self. Is this not the aim of *every* life? Is our goal not to learn how to cut through the bullshit designed to deceive and swindle so as to reach the rich reality that only reveals itself when the fabrications are torn away? So much of life seems to come down to the filter. We're so inundated by the unnecessary, all the noise, all the ego and commercialization and artificial fabrication of modern life that when, in those rare moments when it's all cut away and the essential truth is laid bare before us we're shocked and awed in the best way at the irreducible divinity buried beneath the detritus.

That's what that magnificent young woman gave me, as I was passing through some of my darkest hours, fearful that I wouldn't make it through: *The unfiltered truth of her.* And I swear it saved me, and *still* sustains my hope for a brighter future. Why did she believe me deserving of it? And how, in retrospect, can I not believe that I was delivered to the CRC because of her and the salvation she was fatefully bound to give me, as if by more than chance? Randomness is an illusion made by incomplete access to information and insufficient mental and computational means through which 'random' would otherwise be erased.

So while she's not mine in body or mind, she's mine in heart, without any conscious act of so claiming by my mind. From all prevailing perspectives of what constitutes right and wrong, of man's laws, I have no right to speak of her. And yet, speak of her I must, as there are laws which prevail over man without needing man's consent, and any chance of cathartically releasing her, of even somewhat purging her presence painted across the walls and penetrating the cardiac channels circulating through my innermost cloisters, is a chance I have to take. She shall live within me forever, but perhaps I may release some of the pressure that she's unwittingly pressed upon my insides, for the sake of my health. The time spent beside her was suspended, as if nonexistent; they were the fastest fleeting hours I've known, and am likely *to* know.

I'd ached with the hollowed-out absence of love for years before I met her; for *decades*, even. But it wasn't until she providentially came and diabolically departed that I knew the extent of that internal cavern, her power over me simultaneously mapping the void to its furthest reaches and demonstrating the completion that may come should she, or a hoped-for other of equally divine empowerment, come not just to map it, but settle it, and make it her home.

But I'll get back to Jess soon enough. She's easy to write about. The heart wants little more than an outlet for its pulsating pains and pressures, after all, before they manifest their own madness, and shatter their bearer into pieces, producing an internal schism in a place where the most common "SPMI" (again: Severe and Persistent Mental Illness) required to qualify for treatment is one of two diagnoses derived from the word *schism*, either "schizophrenia" or "schizoaffective disorder," the latter of which combines the hallucinations and delusions of the former with a severe mood disorder, the most common of which is "bipolar disorder," what used to be called "manic depressive disorder," a term that has since been denounced as archaic by the political correction police, those paragons of false virtue paramount to this book.

First off, know that when I use the term "madly" in reference to falling in love with Jess, I was well enough trained to know that "madness" or "crazy" or any other such demeaning pejorative are big no-no's within the mental health world. The first lesson coming through the door is: "Someone diagnosed with schizophrenia is *never* to be called 'a schizophrenic,' and thereby reduced to their diagnosis, but *someone who suffers from schizophrenia*."

It's an important lesson, and by no means confined to the mental health world. We're not *only* the labels affixed to us. And, very often, those labels don't stay fixed to us at all, but fall away, the desire to categorize and box us in so that we can be legally 'treated' or otherwise controlled and directed bowing to Oscar Wilde's universally-pertinent, pithy insight: "To define is to limit." The sad truth is that the simpler the mind, the more it requires clear-cut, black and white definitions and parameters within which to think, the more insecure it is about its thoughts, the more it depends upon the approval of others to know that its thoughts are 'appropriate' and 'acceptable,' the more it's driven by fear and conformity, the easier it is to control, the more likely it is to contribute to conservative values and status quo conventions which are typically unjust in both their derivation and their impact upon life. Thus, to be resistant to definition is to pursue the greater truth which is naturally rebellious against all forms of injustice and undue control.

I broke the rules, to be certain. That's the thing about thinking for one's self: it gets you into trouble relative to the institution's reliance upon unquestioning obedience. Trust me, no one knows that better, and has paid more to learn that truth, than I have. It's core to my experience of corporate existence, actually, and became the force that eventually drove me out of this particular institution, when the best supervisor anyone could have, who allowed us freedom of interpretation so long as we remained reliable workers, Ellie, was replaced by the imperious Linda, with whom I butted heads instantly, owing to not immediately, reflexively accepting her confined, officious judgments.

I'll always recall Ellie fondly, even as she appeared to pass judgment against me later. She was the rare person who seemed as beautiful within as without. She organized and promoted those mental illness art therapy showcases of the work of residents at the three PrimaCare locations in town, standing in front of everyone wearing those skirts and white dresses wrapped beckoningly around her svelte form, the attraction softened in lust and amplified in affection by the way her nose wrinkled when she laughed. Her daughter's nose does the same, now halfway across the country, Ellie having moved the family closer to the grandparents. Of all the appealing women of the CRC, Jess was the undisputed queen, but *Ellie* was the princess.

And because of my desire for this CRC royalty I became rather obsessed with an analysis of their mates. And, with all due respect, I was shocked to find them both rather dorky and simple. But at least they were *real*. They weren't the giants whom I imagined would conquer the hearts of this regal CRC pair, but at least they were good guys; reliable men that families and lives could be built upon; rocks; foundations. Not enormities like that underlying the Parthenon, but solid nonetheless. One tires of the assholes taking everything in this world. The dorks deserve some of the best of what the Trumps take for themselves.

Of course, Jess is a total dork herself, and is self-conscious about it, seeming not to realize that her dorkiness is half her appeal; is intrinsic to her charm; is ingrained in her unfailing capacity to so naturally carry around her most defining quality, the word which best captures her for me: *endearing*. *That's* what she is, more than anything. Perfecting flaws. Dominating dorkiness. Conquering self-consciousness. Collected scars of a past transmuted into a resolute determination to build an opposite future, to show her mother what *real* family looks like, thus turning her pain into triumph. Unfortunately COVID would take her mother before she could see the full effect of her daughter's determination, methamphetamine addiction rendering the immune system far too depleted and powerless to defend itself from any great assault to its already ravaged conveyance, like a fortress with holes in it, and too few guards remaining to plug the gaps and repel the invading forces. And speaking of invading forces and insufficient fortresses, unfortunately for me my fond alliance and appreciation for the queen and princess of the CRC ended up being replaced by my battle with its *tyrant*.

Linda's employment of her own allies in her campaign against me seemed to know no end, so much so that the revelation of her machinations reached my ears for years after she effectively forced me out of the CRC. Long after my departure one of my friends amongst the inhouse nursing staff, no doubt feeling at liberty thanks to having moved on herself, informed me that Linda actively sought nurses working overlapping shifts with me to be on the lookout for any inappropriate behavior; anything she could use against me, essentially enlisting spies in her attempt to subvert me. One woman, Bella, with whom I had a brief flirtation, and who openly came onto me therein, and who would become embittered towards me when our interest in one another proved unequal, became Linda's natural ally.

Without getting into all the details, Bella made the workplace near to intolerable for me by her ongoing treatment, turning everything I did into a possible hazard. Subsequently, when Bella and I worked together, with Linda as our supervisor, Linda would come into a room with the two of us and dictate directions solely to Bella, as though I wasn't even there. At one point the two of them, being of my same PM staff (those assigned to the same block of time, though not necessarily working every shift together) organized a 'shift meeting' at a restaurant in Bend, as was the custom, meant to encourage communication and camaraderie, as had worked so effectively with the aforementioned Ellie (back before Jess broke my heart with her own shift change, then her departure), but in this case was used with the *opposite* aim: to disparage me as unprofessionally as possible.

I sat there trying to eat lunch as these two profoundly prejudicial women tag-teamed me with subtle incriminations and sometimes overt, entirely misleading interpretations of past events designed to undermine my confidence and impugn my character. It was the most ridiculous work experience I've ever endured, and *my God*, is that saying something. Bella was so embarrassed by the nature of the 'meeting' that she phoned me half an hour after it had terminated and all but apologized to me for the role she'd played in it, asking for a truce between us.

And if you think *that's* bad, Linda did something even more egregious, something for which, were morality in governance, she would've been fired. In a one-on-one supervisory meeting with a young woman who became my friend, and with whom I'm still friends, and who came to work for the CRC on my recommendation (unbeknownst to Linda, I believe), Linda accused her of being unprofessionally flirtatious with me at work, something reported to Linda by one of her spies on the nursing staff (it was harmless, natural flirtation, nothing overt, and certainly not 'unprofessional' except to those whom, like Linda, might benefit from such a narrow, biased perception being believed). When my friend defended herself, and made mention of a particular incident of such flirtation which had been reported to Linda involving me touching my friend on the shoulder, Linda attempted to convince her that I was sexually harassing her, and should report it as such! *That's* the abuse of power, dear reader, and perhaps the ugliest example of its being wielded that I'd yet faced.

That was, at least, until running into even worse in my subsequent employment (see *Holier Than Thou*), thus cementing for me the fact that I'll do absolutely everything in my power to avoid working for others again. I have, in fact, been wary of going out in Bend for years now for fear of an awkward, painful encounter with the almighty muse or any of the horrible half-dozen: ludicrous Lenny, overlording Linda and her backstabbing spy, Sydney, from the CRC, followed by malicious Miranda, pestilential Libby and ignorantly judgmental Jennifer from *Banned & Ignoble*.

I never go to the nearby *Safeway* during the five o'clock hour *because* of Jennifer, after this fake 'friend' and part-time creative writing teacher whom, before things fell apart, was reading and helping me edit some of my books, condemned me after the official judgment was made against me, turning up her nose at me a couple times therein, when I attempted a greeting. This has fixed for me the fact that free thinkers whose morality is self-dictated and self-enforced simply have no place in corporate America, for to be naturally averse to falling in line, or considerate of what's on that line and where it leads, is to be anti-corporate. Whereas the aforementioned half-dozen are the corporate backbone, toeing the line unto ignobility.

Although I'd like to add, on the rare chance of her reading this (even less likely than Jess reading this), that I'd love to reconcile with Miranda, for I have reason to believe that she was pressured into backstabbing me; she *chose* to plunge the blade into my unprotected back, but I have reason to believe that someone else sharpened it and handed it to her, as was described in *Holier Than Thou*. Not to mention the fact that I loved being around her, and that, before things ran afoul between us, she gave me every reason to believe that the feeling was mutual, at least until the stabbing. All in all, my work experiences in Bend have been so disturbing and disheartening that they've ingrained in me the need to avoid the conventional workforce at all costs, so plagued is it by cold-blooded exploitation, manipulation and prejudicial, internal politics, and so concealed are those abuses behind the façade of politically correct propriety and care for the patron. Then, of course, there's the fact that every second I work for others, playing some unnatural pre-programmed part outside of my calling, I feel myself drawing nearer to death. I know a lot of people, even most, feel this way, but I think I feel it more acutely than most, for the nature of a creator and free thinker, especially one whom has reached counter-cultural conclusions, is to be most naturally averse to corporatism.

I challenged Linda, and thereafter became an enemy to be driven out. I've since come to learn that Ellie, who was an artist at heart and used art and love and consideration in the attempt to ameliorate the pain endured by our residents, was the *exception* in the corporate environment. Linda is the rule. In fact, I think that the more that the institution depends upon such demanded, unquestioning obedience, the more likely it is to possess policies and practices of a dubious ethical and rational nature. The Church and the corporation are not unlike one another in this regard. In fact, the more you're contented by the "because I said so" and "doubt and questions are akin to a lack of faith" rationale for the discouragement of inquiry, the more likely you are to be content operating within the ecclesiastical and corporate spheres. Hence my conflating them in *Holier Than Thou*, based upon my position of employment post-CRC. I know, I know, if it's a recurring issue with me, it must be *me* that's the problem, right? Well, yes, you're right. Those who naturally provoke the insecurity and irrationality of others, especially their 'superiors,' and who possess a level of conviction that creates, in turn, an automatic type of 'seek and destroy' arsenal against immorality, are a problem in *all* hierarchical institutions. *That's* the problem. And I honestly believe that only the most fearful, deferential nitwits live professional lives free from politicized conflict, being so afraid to tell the truth and 'jeopardize their careers' that they become the mouse begging for morsels of cheese to take back to their secure confines buried in the baseboards of their masters.

I broke rules that the sheep parroted as though absolute ethical truths, failing to realize that most of those truths aren't true at all, and aren't about 'ethics' so much as corporate liability mitigation. They failed to realize that the very thing which the corporate model counts on to keep their liability low, 'boundaries' set between employee and employee, and between employee and resident, are walls erected to *prevent human connection*, denying our very humanity and obstructing the most direct, natural paths to healing. Jess and I walked just such a path together, not coincidentally. Of course, we would've expanded upon our natural practice of these sacred, healing arts if I'd had my way, and, frankly, if nature had been permitted to take its course (wink wink). But endlessly persisting fantasies of Jess aside, the larger point that I'm making is that it's innate to the secret, primary corporate directive to *never* allow anything to undermine profits, which *always* includes the natural gifts bequeathed by Mother Nature, and not just via 'food is medicine' displacing pharmaceuticals with always less toxic, typically equally or *more* effective herbal medicines, but with *anything* freely endowed by nature, including simply listening to one another on equal footing, or doing *anything* in nature, of which the possibilities are endless (with many such options explored later herein).

This, in fact, explains the practices of almost every corporate entity in the 'health and wellness industry,' as well as the unholy alliance between Big Pharma and every conventional health treatment. Relative to the healing power of listening, it was clear to me early on that the resident knows the difference between being treated like a mental health patient and being treated like a friend, or, better, like a co-embodiment of Spirit, on equal terms, and that this difference is often what separates psychological healing and growth from continued disease and suffering. Many residents essentially said as much to me, emotionally attesting to how good it felt to be listened to *without* it seeming like the listener wasn't *really* listening so much as preparing a written report in their minds on matters which may compromise them. They desperately needed *not* to be treated with the veiled contempt and condescension that was, and I'm assuming still is, all too common in the shady world of mental health treatment.

To the obedient member of the herd, there is, in fact, no difference between 'ethics' and 'liability;' it's a part of the invisible propaganda pervading all institutions, unseen but by the discerning few. And we few often face the firing squad for seeing it, especially if we possess the integrity and courage to openly speak of it. And that immediately makes us a threat to the continuity of the status quo, the popular pretense of propriety dominated by mob mentality. What was it Machiavelli said? Something like: "Everyone sees what you appear to be, few see what you truly are, and those few dare not oppose the opinion of the many," and thereby face the wrath of the politically correct mob.

So what were my egregious offenses, you might ask? My rebellious refusal to simply, mindlessly agree with everything that Linda said, for one. Generally, as just mentioned, I believed in protecting the residents by *not* recording or reporting absolutely everything that they said and did. Like the time that Amy, this poor women on whom psychiatric drugs were the *least* effective, and whom I would always drive to the same convenience mart, and be hit up by her for extra cash (there's another penalty against me: I sometimes gave residents money) to buy cigarettes, and drive to the same park, *River Bend*, where she'd chain smoke them and ignore my entreaties for her to save some for later, in a vain attempt to prevent the cycle of no funds leading to 'lending' her funds… We'd always take the long way back to the CRC, over Aubrey Butte via Mount Washington Drive, and one time on the drive back she propositioned me; she asked me to take her to a hotel room. I was foolish enough at that time, early in my experience of her stifling reign, to tell Linda about it. My refusal to "write Amy up" was soon enfolded into our war.

Honestly, my most-recurrent offense was being anti-hierarchal and, therefore, upsetting of corporate control mechanisms, essentially being more apt to be a human being building level bridges where the policy was always to keep them obstructed, and built across unlevel ground. This was, as you may already sense, and shall soon see, a major issue with Jess and I as well. But with regards to the residents and my employment at the CRC, in parallel to my refusal to document everything that might even be *construed* as a sign of symptomatic escalation, I was also admittedly *horrible* at enforcement. This too is discussed elsewhere herein. Then there was my closeness with Cain, and the fact that my encouragement of his art naturally led to my breaking corporate policy by commissioning him to do a painting on a theme which we'd discussed at length: the Ancient Greek 'modes of persuasion,' *logos, pathos and ethos*. That is, persuasion through the respective appeal to mind (reason and logic), heart (emotion and empathy) and the semblance of credibility and authority, the last of these being the foremost method of modern persuasion, and most likely to be leveraged by the Lindas.

The *pretend* Godfather's of the world are ruled by insecurity and the need for absolute, unquestioning obedience, leaning on pretentious, distracting shows of authority to conceal their deviousness, lack of honor and limited intellect. They depend upon the hollow, gleaming, towering façade of ethos set upon unstable foundations, just waiting to be toppled by someone more devious, with a grander show and a greater semblance of authority. These pretend Godfather's rely very little on logos, which they mostly fail to grasp the value of, and their reliance upon pathos extends little further than fomenting fear. They *force* obedience upon their underlings by the threat of termination, of one type or another, and are sticklers for a simple set of rules that may never, *ever* be questioned.

They are the Linda's of the world. The *real* Godfather's, on the other hand, you don't even know are there most of the time. But they know that *you're* there. They grasp the power of their anonymity; that they may observe and act without being observed and acted upon. Thus their reticence to take up positions of power, and their insistence upon delegation, minimizing the possibility of being targeted by their enemies, both within and without.

They enlist ethos mostly to mislead those enemies into thinking that they are, or think of themselves, in ways that they aren't, or don't. Their persuasions are the cunning, stratagem and principles of logos. Their followers are inspired by their minds and words towards *willingly* granting them power over them, knowing that they'll thereby be empowered in turn, naturally building a paired pathos of inspiration, respect, and, ultimately, a platonic love of authentic connection. Things of which the Linda's of the world know next to nothing, those over whom they rule thereby granting them feeble fealty but by convenience, and the fear underlying conformity; lambs led into a sycophantic herd only until they generate hearts of courage, minds of conviction and claws of resistance.

As you no doubt have already guessed, when Linda caught sight of Cain's 'modes of persuasion' canvas and learned of its provenance, which I saw as supporting the self-therapeutic work of a resident artist, she immediately tattled on me (I mean 'dutifully reported my violation') to Annabelle, and I was called into a disciplinary meeting in which it was explained to me that this constituted taking a gift over a certain value (a bribe promoting a conflict of interest), even though, as I of course didn't bother to report, I'd actually *paid* Cain for the work, as I thought fair.

I still have the painting. I should gift it to the CRC in Linda's name. And it's not the only original work by Cain that I possess. I hesitate to share all the details of my relationship with him here, but I will say that, upon his second incarceration for the double homicide, after everyone but his father washed their hands of him, I became his primary point of contact 'on the outside.' Amongst other responsibilities this entailed meeting his father on several occasions, in discussion of his unfolding case at the time, as well as helping him gather and secure personal belongings from an eye-opening trip to his property in Christmas Valley. 'The Manic Hoard' would be a good title for that acreage. A dusty slice of the middle of nowhere that looks like a cross between an incoherently organized dumpsite and a used automotive lot, with more stuff than most people would be capable of compiling in *three* lifetimes. Between what I collected there and what he's sent me from behind bars I have more than enough content to compile a 'Prophet of Death Art Collection' of original works by his bloody hand, including many that the general public would regard in, let's just say, poor taste.

But, with regard to my relationship with Cain before all this, while we were both at the CRC, and while I supported his artistic therapy in ways that Linda condemned, I'd argue that the main area in which I diverged from the central herd of Recovery Specialists is that I actually *thought* about the policies and their application, and was ready to absorb the assaults of the imperious enforcers in order to do what I thought might relieve the residents of pressures which not only prevented healing, but which often were the causes of their institutionalization in the first place. Obedience to something beyond and greater than the corporate dictate and oxymoronic 'business ethics' is, sadly, *extremely* rare, both because it's more difficult, and because it risks termination, or at least the unpopularity of most resistance.

Try to exercise your likely atrophied empathy muscles for a moment, dear reader (not a criticism of you, only the knowledge that empathy is unprofitable and, thus, un-American), and attempt to imagine what it would do to your self-esteem to even be *considered* for a severe mental health diagnosis, or worse, to be forced to concur with that diagnosis and have it communicated to your family by the pressuring psychiatrist, or worse, to have your physical freedom taken from you and be locked into a mental health facility, or worse, being essentially forced into taking medications like megadose lithium that turns you into a zombie and completely curtails all of your highest capacities such that you're nothing near your natural self, a 'medicine' that eventually fries your kidneys and forces you to have at least one organ transplant on the way to an early demise, all so that you can be deemed 'stable,' all the while with the threat hanging over you that should you fail to agree with this course of action and comply with that treatment *for life*, an even fouler fate may befall you. The devastation is *permanently* psychologically wrecking. I escaped that fate by the skin of my teeth (more on this extensive personal case insight soon), but I know the psychological wreckage from exercising my own empathy in the face of numerous residents at the CRC, many of them 'discovering' their illness through a trauma that would crack *any* psyche, the diagnosis communicated to them as though it was just a matter of time before it was unleashed, like they've *always* been hiding their latent sub-humanity.

Whilst in employment at the CRC, based upon my own past experiences, my reasoning, and a mound of anecdotal and case evidence gleaned and studied therein, I came to the conclusion that, though many take comfort in their 'sanity' and 'normality' and look with condescending fear and contempt upon the mentally ill, *everyone possesses the latent capacity for psychosis*. It's simply a matter of pressure, of stress and trauma, and *how* the mind breaks. It isn't a matter of whether or not this is a possibility for any particular person; that possibility is a *certainty*. The same can be said for criminality, in fact, and the ubiquitous latency of becoming a criminal (more on this pressure/stress-based overlap later). And though it may be argued that many possess a greater predisposition for the development of psychotic symptoms, and some may, indeed, develop, or else innately possess, a greater resiliency to such a devolution of their mental state, it's even more reasonable to assert that not one person on this planet is impervious to such a fate, and to having to carry the lifelong stigma and resultant severe reduction in personal and professional opportunity that go with it. *You* can become mentally ill; it's all a matter of pressure, and most pressure is (sorry ye capitalist titans we're trained to revere, but you're most to blame) *socioeconomic* in origin.

Certainly the residents of the CRC supported this conclusion, for nine of ten possessed backgrounds of horrid abuse, neglect and other forms of stress and suffering through which their psychosis was induced. And to a handful of such sad stories shall you be delivered herein. But before those come, and before I interweave them with the tales told to me by she whom is the adored muse behind this book, and with memories of she whom was permanently pressed into my heart, let me allude to how I know the aforementioned to be true by my experience alone, an experience I'll relate in greater detail soon; how I'm *certain* from personal experience that sufficient stress can, and perhaps *must*, induce psychosis, for all pressure eventually finds a way through. If the diagnosis had stuck, my entry into the employment of mental health services would've been *not* as a 'Recovery Specialist,' the official designation of most CRC floor staff (as opposed to therapists and prescribers), but as a 'Peer Support Specialist,' those possessing of precisely the same responsibilities as a Recovery Specialist, yet distinguished by their carrying of a severe mental illness diagnosis. The purpose of the Peer Support Specialist position was clear: lend greater understanding to and ability to treat severe mental illness, as well as role models for those receiving treatment, by including amongst the ranks of the therapeutic providers those whom understand that therapeutic value from *direct* personal experience.

Again, I would've been a Peer Support Specialist myself had my own trauma-induced manic break, and my parents' love and concern sending me to a psychiatrist, and his subsequent diagnosis, resulted in my acceptance and signing of a document giving him legal permission to discuss my 'condition' with my parents. Loud alarm bells rang in my head at the time: "Don't sign it!" If I had, I would've been marked with the lifelong stigma of being bipolar, all so the psychiatrist could force me to take lithium for life (which, at high doses, destroys the kidneys) and be a walking zombie in order to increase his profitable patron list. But by the time I'd reached him and reported the symptoms, which (again, I'll get into the details later) certainly qualified, I'd already begun to come out of it, and haven't experienced a manic state since. Yet, if I'd signed the document, and fallen under his dark wing, I'm certain that, with all the other crap I've had to wade through in my life, most of it self-imposed, I wouldn't be alive to write this.

And yet, all of my defeats, and all the wrongs which I've myself committed, shall ultimately contribute to *our* victory. For every evil that I've suffered, and caused, has been the goodness of my growth. And the same is true for you. On the surface of things the obstacles that stand between where we are and where we want to be seem cruel tricks of fate, as though absolute encumbrances upon our personal progress. But, in truth, they are the very means of our *advancement.* There isn't a pain that I've endured, an indignation that I've been seemingly endlessly embattled by, or an apparent misfortune that's befallen me that *hasn't* led, in addition to all the invisible inroads of personal progress, to a writing spree that's bound to free both myself and the committed reader from the restraints of our respective circumstances. Indeed, what is this book but a transmutation of assorted agonies? But a reformulated repository of heartache and hope, of disappointment, dread and dreamed salvation? With every denial is my own weakness denied, my spurned satisfaction the fertilization of my flowering. All that which, at first, we fear to be our downfall are the feathers of the wings upon which we'll fly. Now knowing what's possible, denial was the opposite of stifling. It spurred me to fly towards the glimpsed horizon.

The difference between my desire for Jess and my desire for every other woman that I've ever wanted, and there have been countless, seems to be the difference between the subjective and the objective, between the metaphysical and the physical. Love, it seems to me, once it enters and permanently transforms you, turns the object into the subject; makes the objective aspects seem extensions of the grandness of the beloved, subject being. Those aspects become more beautiful, become irreplaceably exquisite, not innately, not separately, not as mere objects, but *because they're a part of her,* because they're inseparable from the love, and so become magically imbued. So, while I found her physically attractive, that part of the attraction faded into the background, the animalistic being overshadowed, even subsumed, by the spiritual being. For my attraction to her *person* was infinitely greater. My innumerable fantasies of her were, *are*, almost always of intimacy and rescue, of an affectionate, heroic nature, seldom of a sexual nature. And even when they involve(d) sex, it was *affectionate* sexuality. The fantasies were never base. The beauty of her being was retained.

And the best thing about beauty, inside and out, is that it's simultaneously ubiquitous and perfectly unique; it's absolutely everywhere, but never takes the same form twice. And love makes beauty shine, its every form only coming into its fullest form *through* love. This makes of our adorations a type of inimitable holy reverence, for never, ever again can adoration take the exact same form, or render beauty in a purer, more potent, life-affirming light.

To the true, full-hearted romantic there's no difference between love and adoration; between that which is adored and the act and subject of worship. Do we not live for the rare moments when our vision is wiped clean of all occlusion, and the immeasurable is set before our eyes? And do those few whom are able to cleanse our vision not automatically hold for us an inimitable sacredness? And do we not enshrine them in a permanent state of adoration because of such inimitable power? I mean, how can a man watch Kate Mara in *Happythankyoumoreplease* (a great flick, by the way, and not just because of her, but because it delves into the dirty crevices from which truth invariably springs, like those dandelions that grow through the cracks of city sidewalks) and *not* thank God that he's a man? How can such vicariousness not elicit a fullness of heart, a tingling of testicles, an engrossment of spirit and manhood at the sense that her wonderment represents but one of an infinite number of forms of the Divine Feminine proving the God-given provenance of every man's masculine function?

Some 'philosophically-minded' men are disposed to believe that man being bewildered by the beauty of women is the same as being victims of our biological programming, like it renders us doomed puppets strung up by God, or by fate. But I'm disposed to believe much the opposite. Not that women are here to serve men, as the self-righteous reader is no doubt already interpreting this. But that man is predestined with the good fortune of having the chance to be bewildered by women; that the duping design of beauty isn't a sign of our being victimized by predestination, but our being bequeathed the ideal fortune of finding ourselves able to be, and blessed by, a naturally programmed bewilderment designed by the divine Source.

Even now, I don't think I'm capable of experiencing any greater ecstasy than of saving Jess in some way; than taking from her some misery, or adding to her life in some immeasurable, invaluable manner. "I'm *always* here for you," I imagine saying to her, "no matter how far I have to come. No matter what it is, no matter what it takes, just ask." In such imaginings, and they continue to this day, I'm like the knight of old, boldly driving away all of her assailing evils while, and this seems the most important part, making sure she knows that I need nothing in return, only the heart-ballooning, spiritually-levitating internal reward innate to all right action, exponentially magnified in this case by knowing that I'd helped someone whom I love completely.

Attaching strings is for cowards and villains, not for such a holy thing as this. In the greatest of contrasts, every other desire I've had for a woman was, once the effect wore off and I could see it with clarity, like having a spell cast against my biology, like a demonstration of the aforementioned biological victimization, enforcing the line between objective trickery and subjective revelation; the lustful illusion of desire and the real, romantic thing. Not that I couldn't fall in love with those other women, and not that I'm not romantically-inclined, for, again, I think few are so inclined as I am. But what baited the hook in every other case, so to speak, was their physical allurement. Beauty in sexual relations blinds us to reality, and, one may argue, does so by design, for the continuation of our existence, and, again, as an invaluable gift to that existence, but not without a cost, and not without a sense of having been deceived. It's like a thin, biologically-manipulative patina that can be painted over any woman, even the most monstrous. In fact, one is often drawn towards the beauty only to be bitten, as though the physical attraction is akin to the web of a spider. When I behold a beautiful woman, I can scarcely think straight, my biology possessing me.

The great pleasure produced by beatific visions often belies a great risk, and one that, the greater the spell, the lesser our ability to see it. Stars in our eyes can easily disguise black holes of doom. And this weakness, of which I believe I suffer more than most, has driven me towards a great many mistakes; has dropped me into the clutches of more than a few bewilderingly gorgeous egomaniacs not only lacking the qualities of a compatible mate, but, once the patina is removed, seemingly lacking character and integrity altogether. But with Jess it wasn't like that. *At all.*

Again, I found her attractive, but not in a way that immediately inspired lust. And it wasn't love at first sight, either; not bewitching stars in my eyes nor an instant adoration. It was more like the gradual mounting of some alien sense of my own transfiguration; like the substance of my being was being transformed by her presence, until it seemed that I'd been made into something else entirely; something that was greater than any sense of myself I'd ever known, with that fuller form of myself only able to be sustained by *her*. The bewitchment snuck up on me, until it was total and consuming, going well beyond the sensual, superseded by something more akin to the supernatural.

She was no common spell-caster; not a maker of lust-provoking potions, but a master sorceress rendering all others feeble by comparison. A bewitcher of the innermost self. And while I'm considering the idea of transmutation, let me add that Jess represents the concept not just for me, but for herself. In fact, it may well be that the force by which she was being transfigured was inseparable from my own transfiguration. Rather than be conquered by the pains and deprivations of her past, she transmuted them into an empowering pride and fierce determination to produce an opposite future for herself and her family. "The past is never dead," Faulkner said, "it's not even the past." Jess embodies this insight as much as anyone, her past producing her resiliently prideful present producing her fruitful future, with no temporal separation to be found. It's a philosophical first principle that *separation is an illusion*.

And when I speak of her pride, I mean it less as an emblem of ego than as a leveraging of self-love; not a vestige of vanity so much as loving life and its potential so much that one refuses to capitulate to the pressures which conspire to reduce it. For are there not two forms of pride? One rooted in the ego, one born of love? When I say that I'm proud of her for the qualities of her character which produced the aforementioned transmutation, which I am, I'm really saying that *I love her*, that it's inseparable from my loving memories of her. This is far different, and stands in stark contrast, to the pride she often seemed to exhibit to me of egotistic enlargement built by my engulfing desire

for her. But I don't blame her for that. Honestly. We all
have egos, and how could hers not be burgeoned by my
inability to control my feelings for her? An inability that was
so overwhelming in force that it verged upon omnipotence.
No ego can avoid being enlarged by wielding such a force.

01

NOTES FROM THE FIELD

The following chapter is comprised of a selection of the notes and documents that I made during my time at the CRC, with names changed to protect the innocent, and sometimes not so innocent, just as names are changed throughout this book. This is to give you a sense of the clinical and bureaucratic nature of the Recovery Specialist position, as well as some insight into attempts at progress.

CRC Lessons For A Future Mental Health Retreat

Some lessons and ideas derived from my time at the CRC:

(1)   A weekly or monthly meeting is needed during which ideas for improving the program are openly and constructively discussed, making it clear that no negative repercussions will be delivered upon those whom are *constructively* critical of the system, and, in so doing, creating a humble environment in which it's made clear that the best systems are *always* bent on perpetual improvement. Feigning perfection, on the other hand, is hubris.

(2)   More direct one-on-one care and greater empowering of advocates working more directly with therapists as dedicated therapeutic teams – less generalized work and 'floating' of staff (not as effective), more pointed dedication and specialization of staff.

(3)   There're no consistent rules, having only guidelines that staff may or may not follow, and without a strong position set by leadership. This creates *constant* inconsistency of policy and enforcement leading to resentment and both staff and patients not

possessing a sense of structure or continuity that increases stress and makes battles recurrent. This, in turn, diminishes morale and encourages residents to seek out the 'weaker' staff members to get what they want. Leadership must teach and support *clear* directives.

(4)   We didn't feel like our voices were heard as RS's, especially *NOC* RS's (NOC = 'nocturnal' = 11pm-7am shifts). I've had many ideas with great potential value given mere lip service 'good job's,' but not taken seriously – the monthly therapist updates on all residents for one – the consolidated Resident Info for another.

(5)   *All* records should be kept through a digital file management system – when derived from paper, scanned into an accessible online system. *Far* too many CRC records are *only* paper.

(6)   *Everything* should be electronic, including passes, as well as residents/guests signing in and out, both of which are currently exclusively manual, paper-based operations here at the CRC.

(7)   The use of naturopathic remedies should be utilized to decrease symptoms and impart other benefits; to revitalize, nourish, reduce stress, help with sleep etc. Pharmaceuticals should be used as a last resort, and at the lowest possible effective dosage – they're essentially unnatural, and the costs are exorbitant on *many* levels.

(8)   It's an incentive-based world; people do what they do because they desire the benefits, or else fear the repercussions. If your program isn't driven by this reality of human nature and behavior your program is wrong, and you're doing those you're mandated to serve a disservice, as they discharge from your program without having learned this lesson; learning instead things like how to be helpless, how to make people pity you, and how to gain attention. These lessons instill disadvantages in most 'real world' situations, outside of institutions. And though you may believe that you're being progressive and supportive, in the end it's the *result* that matters. Showing love, compassion and patience is essential, but, at the same time, I've found that you can go *way* too far with this. I've seen it. Be careful what you teach and what you're preparing people for. I've found that *much* of what is chalked up to symptoms of mental illness at the CRC is actually *learned behavior.*

(9)   The 'Recovery Based Clinical System' (RBCS) that's said to govern the actions of CRC employees is overly invested in and emphasized in the oversight of administration, even as the employees themselves can recite almost none of it; not even the contents of page *one*, much less the fiftieth page of the handbook. When *actually* applied, the RBCS has *many* virtues, including showing patience and compassion and helping our residents with building their skills and self-esteem etc., but it has *many* flaws as well. For example, I've realized that patience is actually only a virtue when it's *necessary*; otherwise it's closer to laziness, justification and a lack of courage and proactivity. And *far* too much of this occurs at the CRC. *No* emphasis is placed upon the value of discipline and the creation of self-sufficiency and operating based upon the incontrovertible truth of reward and punishment; of incentive and disincentive. *Far* too much is permitted that shouldn't be, and, thus, far too many behaviors are explicitly or implicitly condoned that're stultifying, if not regressive, for CRC residents. Also, the administration and top counselors and anyone with seeming 'skin in the game' at the CRC are *so* invested in this proprietary, nationally-promoted clinical mental health system that they're *completely* closed off to any and all constructive criticism; to *any* suggestion that the system is imperfect and that there's room for improvement, thus losing sight of the fact that the *outcome* is what matters. Whatever leads to the most self-improvement for the residents *should* be the focus, and there are *so* many residents that *don't* progress because certain potential improvements are prohibited from being promoted because they conflict with RBCS. Thus, as you climb the company ladder the governing philosophy becomes mired in ego, greed, insecurity and arrogance. *No* admission of any form of improvement which in any way implies that the RCBS is imperfect is permitted.

(10)   More 'tough love' and incentive-based reward and punishment systems are needed, so long as they're within the law. Yes, recognize and be compassionate and understanding regarding histories and obstacles, but *don't* allow this to become an excuse/justification for not pushing clients to progress; to challenge themselves and become stronger and more self-sufficient. I have this

continually recurring thought whilst working at the CRC that there's a disservice being done when residents aren't being prepared for more self-sufficiency and the 'real world' consequences post discharge (less coddling is needed). *When it's behavioral, tough love is what's needed; when it's psychiatric, soft love is what's needed.*

(11)　Make the entire treatment system more fluid, dynamic and flexible, less obstinately, rigidly fixed. Customize the progressive system to the specific resident, relative to their needs and abilities.

(12)　From a respected coworker, I'd add: Don't make the safety net *too* effective due to learned helplessness; make it more productive/progressive so to provide just as much as they need, and no more, and thereby motivate and even *require* them to progress.

(13)　Therapist-led staff meetings on the progress of residents should be held. The therapists have insights that RS staff can use.

(14)　A cleaner summation document should be relied upon for anyone with any interest in any of the residents, including the resident themselves. There are too many documents too heavily relied upon at the CRC, many of them poorly organized and loaded with repetitive, superfluous information. Assign someone this task of constantly distilling, updating and disseminating a summation doc.

(15)　Do away with separate therapist offices for LMP's (Licensed Medical Professionals) and QMHP's (Qualified Mental Health Professionals; i.e. RS's and PSS's) etc. Shoot for complete integration. Remove the psychological and logistical division of power and position etc. Make the program wide open and integrated.

(16)　More efficient, better-distilled communication between shifts. Communicate out of the ordinary resident actions *only*. We spend half of shift change meetings talking about baseline incidents.

(17)　Emphasize the importance of the *therapeutic environment*. Make nature immersion and cultivation core to the program, but also focus on sensorially-pleasing aspects, like the lighting and the flow/layout of the facility and yard, and other touches that have a long term, cumulative effect with the residents and staff when continually experienced. *Healing is far more likely to occur in healing environments.* With this in mind, make the facility specialize in *nature-based therapy* – tapping into the restorative power of nature and nurturing – nature immersion therapy, animal therapy (domesticated and wild), agricultural cultivation, music, exercise (like hiking and working the land growing residents' food), nutritional practice, environmental consciousness etc. Place the facility in the country, in an idyllic setting not far from (or ideally bordering) a state or national park. Research the benefits of these forms of therapy – studies etc. that back it up. Cite studies in the mission statement.

    (18)   Incorporate treatment of the mentally ill, the homeless and those with severe substance abuse issues, or those needing a healing retreat from other forms of abuse (like spousal abuse), into the mandate of the facility, allowing better study, prediction and prevention and more efficient treatment of overlapping populations.

    (19)   Have dedicated case managers assigned to each resident or patient for legal, health, SSI etc. (SUPER ADVOCATES).

    (20)   *More focused, one-on-one attention is clearly needed!*

Example Resident Summary

Scooter admitted to the CRC on 5/10/16 from the Salem Mental Health Hospital (SMHH) in Salem, OR, to receive secure residential treatment services. Scooter is in immediate need of services because he is unable to maintain his safety and wellbeing in the community. He is under the jurisdiction of the PSRB (the Psychiatric Security Review Board) which has deemed him to be in need of the level of care provided by the CRC. We will collaborate with the Department of Behavioral Health and his PSRB liaison to determine community safety and provide appropriate treatment. Scooter has been at SMHH for the past 7 years. He admitted to SMHH under a 920 hold for crimes in the community. While at SMHH he was violent and assaultive towards peers and staff. This culminated in his severely assaulting an SMHH staff person resulting in assault charges and an eventual NGI (Not Guilty for Reasons of Insanity) adjudication. Scooter was experiencing persecutory and paranoid thoughts and beliefs. He thought he was being harmed and mocked by the staff member to whom he was violent. After investigation, it was concluded that Scooter was experiencing symptoms of psychosis, and that the staff he'd targeted was not mistreating him.

Following this assault, Scooter continued to struggle with violence towards others until he was able to be stabilized on a significant regimen of antipsychotic medications to address strong symptoms of psychosis. Scooter has not been violent towards others since starting on this regimen. He does, however, continue to struggle with paranoia and suspicion, but is able to reality check this and use skills to work through his anger and suspiciousness without being violent towards others. It is also noted that while residing at SMHH, Scooter was the target of harassment and threats by fellow residents. Scooter has a history of self-harm, including suicide attempts (cutting and overdose) and poor self-care including episodes of homelessness. Scooter has a significant history of substance abuse and dependence including marijuana, alcohol, and nicotine which reportedly started at the age of 12. Historical reports indicate a history of using or trying a majority of both controlled and illegal substances, all of which heighten his associated aggression related to psychosis. Records indicate that he would smoke "a pound a day of marijuana", snorted Wellbutrin while at SMHH, and has cheeked medications.

Since being under the PSRB, Scooter has struggled with symptoms of schizophrenia. He experiences periods of thought disorganization and can struggle with suspicion and paranoia. Scooter has four years remaining on his current jurisdiction under the PSRB. Scooter will benefit from a supported and structured environment that can help him manage his symptoms more successfully, reintegrate into his community, improve his health decision-making skills, and improve self-care skills such as budgeting, hygiene, medication administration, and nutrition. Scooter presents with an ongoing need for structured, secure living to rehabilitate his capacity for independence as he continues on his path towards mental health recovery.

It is the goal of the CRC that, through our treatment, Scooter will experience reduced impulsive behaviors, episodes of threats or violence, paranoia, and internal stimulation while maintaining his sobriety. Ideally he will expand his knowledge and self-awareness about his paranoia and substance use history and urges, as well as increase his social and support connections with family and in the community. We will do this by providing skills training services which will focus on helping him learn and practice symptom management, healthy decision making, and relaxation. We will provide community psychiatric services where he can explore community resources and opportunities for social interactions that support a sober lifestyle. CRC staff will provide activity therapy services which will allow him to explore meaningful activities that increase his self-esteem, promote positivity, and encourage healthy interpersonal relationships. Based on his history of medication non-compliance, staff will provide ongoing medication education services to help Scooter maintain stability and increase his understanding of his illness and how the taking of meds is in his best interest.

Recovery Specialist Orientation Notes

PrimaCare Corp and CRC Basic Information:

- Approximately 50 years in business
- 9 facilities in Oregon, 3 in the Bend area (Annabelle oversees all of these local operations)
- Most of the company's 99 programs are located in California, where the company was founded
- Corporate HQ in Oakland, CA
- Programs focus on individuals diagnosed with a severe and persistent mental illness
- CRC is a 16 bed facility, with half of the beds generally reserved for PSRB clients/residents
- CRC is a level one secure facility, whereas other 2 Bend-area facilities are less secure/restrictive, which means that the CRC is licensed to use physical restraints in the 'seclusion room' that is sometimes used as a safe and secure place for residents per their request; restraint against the wishes of the resident is a last resort and is considered a clinical failure; physical restraint by the staff is not attempted unless at least a 3 to 1 height and weight ratio is available – because this is not usually available during NOC shifts it is not attempted, and law enforcement is called instead
  - Difference between facility types sometimes referred to the difference between an RTC (Residential Treatment Center) and an RTH (Residential Treatment Home)
- **Residents' Legal Classifications**
  - **PSRB – Psychiatric Security Review Board**
    - Held for NGI – not guilty for reasons of insanity (mental disease or defect)

- CRC is usually a 'step-down' facility for PSRB clients who are very often stabilized at SMHH (Salem Mental Health Hospital) or other facility first
      - Under more strict supervision, security and other guidelines
      - Automatically receive the longest possible sentence in lieu of prison
      - Avg. stay at CRC approx. 2 years
  - **Civil Commitment**
      - Committed by civil court because considered a public nuisance (disturbing the peace) and/or deemed to be a potential danger to themselves or others
  - **Guardianship**
      - Clients do not have the legal authority to make their own decisions and are usually under the legal guardianship of a relative or relatives (such as their parents)
  - **Voluntary**
      - Client/resident has voluntarily checked themselves into the CRC for treatment

Client/Resident Interactions and Guiding Principles

- Build rapport with the clients/residents, as it facilitates everything
- Crisis Mode exists on a bell curve
- Be aware of what 'triggers' clients – those things that cause mental distress and potentially elicit outbreaks of mental illness (where knowledge of patient charts is valuable) – examples provided of law enforcement and those wearing formal attire reminiscent of legal authorities (dress informally)

- Be aware of the 'baseline' of clients/residents –
  what is their personal 'normal;' allows you to predict
  when a 'break' or 'episode' is likely to occur upon
  deviation from this understood baseline
- Every resident is treated differently and encouraged
  towards internal motivation, is treated with respect
  and has a customized treatment plan

General Position Duties/Expectations and Protocol

- HIPPA – Health Information Portability and Privacy
  Act – governs when and how client's personal
  health information can be accessed, saved and
  shared – do not disclose information to others
  except on a need to know basis (agreements of
  disclosure are kept in the client's charts)
    - clients/residents own their own information
      (need permission to release)
- When someone calls asking for a resident you
  "cannot confirm or deny" that someone by that
  name resides here (CRC), but "I will transfer you to
  the resident line and you can leave a message"
- Minimize or logout of your computer when you're
  not attending it to avoid privacy violations
- Press CTRL-ALT-DELETE and then click "Lock this
  computer" to prevent access to your desktop
- **Pass Types (various time allotments per type)**
    - Staff Outings
    - Peer Passes
    - Solo Passes
    - Family Passes
        - Clients pre-approved to use a
          certain number of passes of different
          types per day depending upon their
          status and prior approval (of the
          PSRB and their therapists)

- - - - - Clients fill-out pass requests that they're allowed to use and approved by QMHP's (admin and the therapists authorized to do so)
- **Tracking of Passes**
  - o Pass pre-approval information kept on white board in Day Room (central room)
  - o PSRB clients must take a GPS unit with them when they leave; information is uploaded and added (the map using download software) to a Word doc by NOC shift and stapled to the pass the next day
  - o Used passes then hole punched and filed in file room (black cabinet)
  - o Passes used also noted on an Excel document in the Shared Drive
- **Shift Change Binder**
  - o New document printed with new date at beginning of NOC shift (for a new day)
  - o Notes as to the next day's health appointments and those scheduled to work plus main notes on the front page then information pertaining to residents on subsequent pages, with such notations more involved for the day shifts but often simply 'slept through night' for NOC shifts
  - o Pertinent information passed into next days – old information in back – judgment call
- **Hourly Rounds Log**
  - o New document printed with new date at beginning of NOC shift (for a new day)
  - o Contains a list of all the residents that must be accounted for (and where based upon provided code) every hour (unless under close observation for certain reasons, like

having recently been AWOLD) using quiet
entry and check with red light
- o Other essential duties, like sharps count,
  GPS downloads and cell phone charging
- o RS or other employee must initial each
  relevant cell, then initial and sign at the right

Not "What's Wrong?,"
But "What's *Missing*?"

It occurs to me that, after reflecting upon my interactions with others, especially with those whom I disagree, as well as working in the mental health field for a while now (and especially after taking courses having to do with Peer Support and Trauma-Informed Care), that so many of the ills and hostilities in the world can be drastically curtailed with a simple change in attitude. That change in attitude must be that when we see ourselves or others suffering or doing wrong, rather than judging us or them as inherently weak, mentally ill or incompetent or applying some other reductively derogatory label (which, when applied to others, is usually an egotistic response done to make ourselves feel better about ourselves), instead keep in mind that *all suffering and wrong-doing is based upon deficiency*. Don't label and ask "What's wrong with you?," listen and attempt to discover what it is that's *causing* the suffering or leading them to commit wrongs. Ask: "What're they missing that I can help them find, or help them build?"

They are *many* possible answers to this depending upon the person and their situation, but some of the most common deficiencies that I've seen while at the CRC are:

- Lacking a sense of trust, safety and basic comfort, often as a result of past traumatic experiences
- Not feeling loved, respected or listened to
- Lacking health and experiencing the lowered quality of life/existence and reduced capacity, confidence etc. that results from the pressures of the poorly functioning, ill-at-ease body and mind
- Lacking self-esteem (having a negative self-perception, i.e. a deflated ego)

- Having too much self-esteem (an overinflated ego) that blinds them to their own limitations and causes them to treat others unfairly, or as exploitable tools (lacking accurate self-awareness)
- Lacking knowledge (ignorance, which we *all* suffer from to various degrees)
- Undergoing too much stress of one kind or another
- Lacking the resources necessary (money, shelter, food) to live a healthy, happy life free from too much daily stress/worry
- Lacking connection to the outdoors and exercise
- Feeling disconnected from people and the world

It's the job of not just the mental health provider, but the moral, progressive human being to, instead of labelling and condemning ourselves and others, identify the deficiency and do our best to fill it; to fill the gaps that are causing ourselves or others to suffer or to act unjustly towards others. Provide that which, when missing, is the source of the wrongdoing, rather than condemning the wrongdoers. The more we do this, the more value we create, the greater our contribution to total quality of life.

Note: Scooter's Concerning Behavior

NOC staff is concerned that Scooter may be becoming increasingly symptomatic and at-risk for escalated and unstable behavior based upon a series of incidents over the past couple weeks. Due to these shared trepidations we felt it prudent to note the pertaining incidents, such that staff is aware of the rising risk and may act to counter it.

Concerning observations by NOC staff, as well as those communicated to NOC staff by staff from other shifts:

- Scooter approaching NOC staff and asking on several occasions if we'd heard anything indicating that a certain resident does not like him. He has been continually reassured that said resident is going through her own things which she is processing mentally and that her non-response to him when he asks her about it is in no way indicative of her possessing any dislike toward him.
- As reported by the nursing staff, following the series of intimacies shared between two other residents, including one female resident, said female resident shared her feelings of shame to the nursing staff in the nurse's station, and soon thereafter was seated in the Day Room. During this time her body language and demeanor exhibited extreme vulnerability. Scooter was then observed by nursing staff to approach this female resident in a manner suggesting he was 'coming onto' her. Nursing staff reports that he was very likely aware of her interactions with another male resident and felt that Scooter's actions were not gentlemanly.
- On numerous occasions during NOC shifts Scooter has approached staff and expressed the belief that other residents mean him harm and have been

looming in his doorway at night. He has made several requests that staff watch for those walking down his hallway and make sure that they don't enter his room. He has specifically targeted two residents in these urgent entreaties to staff, saying that each of them have verbally threatened to enter his room and harm him during the night. He has partially blocked his doorway on several occasions during NOC in the attempt to bar their entry, which, of course, violates safety and monitoring protocol.

- On successive nights Scooter has attempted to convince NOC staff to let him into the cigarette drawer to rearrange 'his' cigarettes. He was permitted access on one occasion during which he acted in a suspicious manner, both while trying to convince staff of the need and while moving cigarettes from one bag to another. Staff suspects he is attempting to take cigarettes from peers. He has requested access since this occasion and staff has politely denied him any continued access.

- Last week Scooter reported to NOC staff that a particular staff member was saying exactly what was being said on the television. He believes that he heard exactly what staff was saying *through* the television, even though staff assured him that what this particular female staff member was saying had no correlation to the content of the television, because we, ourselves, were involved in the subject discourse. He was not receptive to this.

- PM staff reports that he has requested that staff not serve him his food. Considering his history this is a possible indication of escalating fear-based paranoia, which is of particular concern in correlation to his assault at SMHH against a staff member whom he believed was spitting in his food.

Jess Asks for My Recommendation

To whom it may concern –

I highly recommend Jess Hollenbeck, my fellow Recovery Specialist here at the Cascade Recovery Center, for the *Ben McCloud Scholarship.* I have worked with Jess for a year and a half now and could not have a higher opinion of her. She is exceedingly bright, very hard working, highly conscientious and is very generous with the time that she spends lending empathetic, thoughtful service to the residents here at the CRC. I find her to be one of the few people that I have met and gotten to know whom balances all the qualities you'd wish for in an employee and a friend, including humility and confidence. I feel very privileged to work with her several nights a week. There is no doubt in my mind that she is an incredibly valuable asset to our team and that the value that she provides will only increase as her confidence and experience increases. Anything invested in her ability to add further value to the service that she provides here would be repaid to the quality of care which our residents would receive many times over.

Sincerely –

Nicholas (Nick) A. Jameson

Recovery Specialist II

Cascade Recovery Center

02

THE PROPHET OF DEATH

Monsters are made by the merger of the sickened psyche and the insecure ego, that sickness and insecurity exacerbated by the pressures and unnaturalities endemic to capitalist society. Their monstrosity is an extension of their imbalance, a lashing out at anything and anyone that threatens to further imbalance them, and a spreading of the pestilence which they possess in their attempt to purge it. Thus are the greatest champions not those whom slay the monsters, vanquishing evil with evil, as in the old tales of knights, but those pacifying and palliating the monsters by giving them what they need to balance out, absorbing their assaults without retaliating, which only makes the monsters more monstrous. To tame the dragon without becoming one is how the truly heroic champions are made.

"Snakes, gophers and hawks," Cain says under his breath.

It's 5:50 am. I've been up all night, per my position, and can scarcely keep my eyes open, much less give him the attention he needs. Cain and I are seated on the couch in the Day Room, the couch you can't take too long a look at if you want to retain your own sanity. He's looking at the movie on the television hung over the gas fireplace in front of us, speaking in a far off voice, as if to no one in particular. I might add that he's requested that I become his advocate; his prime point of staff contact at the CRC. And that means listening with patience. Looking at me with

those wild jade green eyes, the spittle in his handlebar
mustache leading up to his shaven head with a green viper
tattooed on the back, knowing that he's always on the
brink of a furious, blindingly rapid speech, I can't say I'm
without my reservations in taking him on as the staff 'lead.'

Cain is anything but a cakewalk, even though he's 'come
down' quite a bit since the hyper-manic state he was in
upon arrival, mitigating his mania not by chemical
correction, but of his own free will, refusing pharmaceutical
intervention, as I once had. He arrived not long after
burning down the logging museum on the Metolius River,
the one-time headquarters of the logging company that
was core to the early history of Sisters, about half an
hour's drive northwest of Bend, which he asserts the
company stole from the natives; those aboriginals whom
he claims, entirely without evidence, to share blood with.

"What?," I ask, afraid of the reply, knowing that to posit any
question to Cain is to be on the brink of opening Pandora's
Box, and thereby being forced to face the consequences.

"Snakes, gophers and hawks," he repeats, a bit more
forcefully this time, looking at me like *I'm* psychotic for not
following what he's saying; like *I* should be the resident.

"C'mon, Nick... You know. All women are snakes, and men
are either the gopher or the hawk. Prey or predator. That's
the way it'll always be, a war of the sexes, regardless of
the romantics who like to paint everything in a shiny sheen,
as though the blood we're all bleeding onto the canvas is
something harmless and pretty, calling it, like... *vermilion.*"

I look around the Day Room. Thankfully no one can hear
us but Jess, doing her homework for the Central Oregon
Community College (COCC) biology course she's taking
whilst seated nearby at 'The Bridge,' which is, again, a
term borrowed from *Star Trek* for the large two-computered
desk representing the 'command center' set in the ideal

position to see as much as possible of the CRC at any one time, across the Day Room and into the kitchen and down both hallways, and thus the base position for the 'NOC shifters.' As the only two staff members on duty overnight, aside from the nurse, we have to be aware of as much as possible at any one time. Luckily for me that means sitting next to Jess at The Bridge for most of the night. She's used to Cain's diatribes, and knows better than to challenge him, especially since she's struggling as much as I am to make good use of the remaining hours of the shift. On the computer screen in front of my vacated seat my screensaver bounces around: "*Nick and the NOCers.*"

"If I was still in my past life as Hitchcock I'd make a film about it, filled with metaphors and symbols about how men and women are in an eternal war for primacy, and are *always* the animals that they pretend not to be. I mean, look at my dad and I, once proud men, reduced to… *this*," he adds, looking around him, alluding to his circumstances.

"*What* about your father?," I utter through my listlessness.

He's looking *through* the television now, as if peering through a time portal into a reimagined part of the past.

"There are a few pictures of my dad that I've seen from his youth, just before he was married to my mother. He was beaming with pride and unassailable confidence, like a conqueror just setting foot upon an unexplored paradise stretched out endlessly before him. Two all-strings-attached relationships later, to an uptight defeatist and an imperious bitch, the first of whom will never get over the superseding encroachments of the second that I'm not supposed to know about, much less be bothered by, and look at him now! He's the paragon of practicality. He's retreated from the frontier and built two imprisoning castles in lands of tradition overlorded by emasculating matriarchs.

And all for the sake of not being alone, of being able to mate, and so he can say he did the 'responsible thing.'"

"Hmmm..." I slowly eject. "You blame his mates for that?"

"Yes! Fucking feminism! I mean, yeah, the past sucked for women, but how far do we have to suspend our disbelief and still retain our own manhood, know what I mean?"

"*Maybe...*"

"All these over-empowered women pretending progressivism, forcing us to accept falsities for fear of politically correct, irrational backlash. I mean, look at this stupid fucking film that we're watching! How many times do I have to watch a movie based upon a little 140 pound girl beating up legions of 200 pound, expertly trained men before someone with his balls still attached stands up and screams: *Biology, bitches!* Men evolved to be more physically formidable. That's science, not sexism! Just like, how many times do I have to listen on *Sports Center* to these women whining about the poor attendance of WNBA games before one of the shameful, head-hanging half-men seated beside them pull their head up and ask: Why watch the little leagues when you can watch the big leagues?"

"I don't know man," I challenge him, thinking back to my undergrad days at UCSB, when I was so self-deluded I thought that I was going to go into business. "I remember when I was in college and working event staff, which usually meant overseeing *sporting* events. Our women's basketball team was really good; they competed nationally. And I got really into it. I looked forward to working games."

"Did you watch the *men's* games?"

"Yeah, but our men's basketball team wasn't very good..."

"There you go. It was the thrill of the competition you liked; the fact that the women contended for the title. Otherwise, why spend our limited time and money watching those who are literally less physically capable when we can watch Lebron do what no woman will ever come close to doing? Dude can probably beat a whole team of WNBA bitches!"

I can't help but let out a little snort of encouraging laughter. The 'Third Wheel,' as I call her in my head, the nurse that usually works with Jess and I, and is always stepping between us when we're on the verge of the connection I so desperately need, steps aggressively out of her hole, the nurse's station, set behind The Bridge, her face saying the same as Jess's, but ruthlessly. 'Ready that tranquilizing PRN!,' I think, knowing that most nurses are too lazy to resort to actual *listening* when chemical quietude is so close at hand, all with a quick little justifying note in the log (PRN, by the way, is acronymous nursing shorthand for the Latin phrase "pro re nata," or "as the situation demands").

"Men need to conquer life almost as much as women need to conquer men! And how, I ask you, can a man even know that he's a man if everything that he does isn't for himself, isn't a part of his self-creation, but is done to please and attract women? That's how I ended up here! Doing everything that I could to keep Katherine in love with me, and the stress of it drove me nuts, and she was the first to abandon me for it! Fuck man, if she thinks she had nothing to do with setting fire to that place to set the native spirits trapped in the basement free, she's a fucking idiot! *She* lit the match, I just chose where to drop it, you know?"

"I..."

"I mean, what *is* a man if he isn't free to say what he thinks? To speak *his* truth? All because he's afraid of what these so-called 'woke' women, and the men whose balls they wear around their necks like those big-beaded Buddhist necklaces, will do to them with their misplaced empowerment? Fuck man, the hot ones like Katherine make emasculating collections of testicles just like those beaded necklaces, wearing their vanity around their necks like the natives used to do with the scalps of their defeated enemies, regaling in the glory of their conquest of the male sex, just like the old trope of men collecting notches in their belts. As if women don't do the same thing! They're just sly about it! They get away with it because they're good at pretending like they're innocent as they quietly cut 'em off!"

"Everything okay over there, Nick?," the Third Wheel asks, speaking to me as though Cain isn't there, or the subject.

I nod my head, and she slinks back into her hole. To this day I can't even look at an *image* of a nurse without thinking about the Third Wheel; sorry, about *Laura*. About how badly I wanted our tricycle to be a bicycle. And about how she lectured me on *Facebook* about what I was allowed to say to Jess. She already *had* a husband, for Chrissakes. Why couldn't she let me have the little bit of one-sided love that may prove to be my only experience of it? Why did she always have to scurry out of her hole at the most inopportune moments, like she sensed that I wanted her *not* to, and so did. Speaking of her husband, I still can't see a nurse without also thinking of the time when Laura told us about how she was once giving oral pleasure to her husband, and how he finished in her mouth, and, suddenly having to sneeze and not being able to stop, she blew more than snot out of her nose. Proof of the nose to throat connection. But somehow that's not the memory of the Third Wheel that most stands out: she stole one of the most poignant opportunities to connect with Jess from me.

One night Jess was spilling her guts to me, as had become common, even as I had little sense at that time of how valuable those guts would eventually become to me, and how much I'd come to miss their spillage. She was describing her constantly contentious relationship with her drug-addicted mother, and how this, in turn, placed tension upon her relationship with Brady, her then boyfriend, now husband, who tended to take a colder, more unforgiving stance on the subject, thinking Jess needed to avoid her outright until such time as she changed her ways, with Jess no doubt knowing that that would never happen, and that, therefore, the only possible result of his strategy would be estrangement from her mother. And as Jess was describing this interpersonal warfare, the dam broke and she began to cry. And *that's* when I fucked up. My instinct was to comfort her; to put my hand on her back or shoulder; to do something, *anything*. But my nerves and anxiety, and fear of her potential recoil, stopped me. I'll *always* regret that. For, in the intervening moments, Laura came out of her station and lent her succor instead. I remember being furious, thinking something like: *Goddamnit, go back in your hole! That's my role to play!* I never hated my nerves and anxiety and sense of never being whole, stable or confident more than when I felt it precluded me from connecting to and gaining *her* interest.

The war of self-restraint, and the unjust sense of self-*constraint* that it created, was *constant*. It was an ongoing struggle not to tell Jess what I was thinking; to bottle up my emotions and keep the drawbridge up between my heart and mind. Like when she was briefly hospitalized after one of her many surgeries on her shattered ankle, and the CRC employees put together a 'get well soon' card for her. I wrote something a little too honest in it, and when the Third Wheel came around and started getting nosy, and I remembered, once again, that the dictates of propriety cared not for the natural outpourings of my heart, I ended up using whiteout over what I'd written. I even had this little fantasy of Jess eventually scratching it off and revealing the true sentiments scrawled beneath, as though it would be some sort of poetic truth, some metaphorical wiping away of concealing facades to reveal the loving truth beneath. We all hide our true emotions for the sake of some advantage, in the face of one fear or another. Would the whiteout remain forever? Not if this book has anything to say about it. As if she needed another testament to the truth of how I felt, and will likely *always* feel, about her. So much of my life was then forced into an immanent fight to withhold the feelings that Jess's boundaries, coupled with corporate policy, killed in the crib. But back to Cain...

"Bitch!," he whispers, boring lasers into the back of Laura's head as she reenters her large-closet-sized station behind The Bridge. "See what I mean? What stands for progress today is testicle-wearing women. Just like you said the other day, Nick: The popular thing tends to be the wrong thing, for the two simple reasons that it's easier to be in the wrong than to be in the right, and because it's easier to give into the mindless, sheepish herd baaing their own self-approval than to stand in front of their bleating and scream: *Fuck you and your herd!* You go on sniffing one another's assholes and repeating your reflexive affirmations! I'm keeping my manhood, because I'm the only one among you who knows its true qualifications! I'm the only one who knows that real men have the courage to stand up to fake women, no matter how popular their fakeness becomes! I mean, if it were up to half of these bitches we'd be rewriting not just history, but *biology*, like some twisted neo-feminist Big Sister version of *1984*."

This time I resist the temptation to add fuel to the fire, for even then, even *before* working for *Banned & Ignoble*, I sensed truth in what he said. I also knew that, if I *did* pour fuel on the fire, the ramifications for Cain could be greater than my satisfaction at irritating Laura. So I resisted, even as I was tempted to add to his argument the fact that the institution in which we were sitting was a bit of a girls club, and that I was often aware of the sociopolitical power games at play in the middle of it, and of the irritation of several of the conservative-minded men that the 'smart girls' were in charge, and the sly satisfaction the ladies clearly received from this, smiling at one another and socializing in cliquish, insider manners that spoke far more to interoffice politics than to any authenticity of friendship.

I'll never forget the day after Trump stole the election from Hillary, thanks to the archaic electoral college (I still have a meme in the pictures folder of my laptop from my CRC days depicting Trump in the Oval Office captioned with: "Dear World: We are so fucking embarrassed about this. Love: all of the sane Americans."). I remember how impossible it was for said consistently emasculated men to contain their glee in the face of women who weren't just their *professional* superiors, but their *intellectual* superiors as well, and how some of said women had to be reminded that wearing one's heart on one's sleeve at work when it came to politics was 'unprofessional,' like every other corporate policy reducing people to robots for the sake of not rocking the profit-producing conveyor belt. Of the top five positions at the CRC, consisting of three full-time therapists, the head nurse and the foremost alpha, Annabelle, the head administrator, four were women.

Which, you may not believe me, dear reader, actually didn't bother me at all. In fact, the mischievous side of me *prefers* to have women ordering me around, knowing that most women tend to like me, at least until I express my opinions honestly, rather than simply nodding my head when, for example, women hypocritically make sexist comments whilst nailing men to the cross for doing the same thing, in an era that I honestly believe from *vast* experience has leaned too far in one direction to compensate for the obviously patriarchal past. Eve is Adam's rib, for Chrissakes, and only a fool falls for the idea that God is *male* – what need the all-encompassing, pure energy of Holy Spirit for *gender*? Gender is a byproduct of *material* existence, and its procreative needs and fetters.

At the same time nature isn't skin deep, and gender has gone from denoting a quality bequeathed by nature to being entangled in identity issues and related confusions, insecurities and depression, but that's a whole other ball of wax that this 'woke' world isn't ready to melt down, frankly.

Despite the constant stats thrown around about unequal pay and position, and the number of women I meet who canalize their frustrations in life as hatred of male versus female inequality, I believe the present era to be prejudiced *for* women; an era that's ignorant of the fact that everyone knows what misogyny is, and is happy, even over-eager, to apply it to men, but almost no one has even heard the equally pertinent term *misandry*; *more* pertinent, considering the same modern sociopolitical climate. Please allow me to clarify that for a second, ye whom are already reaching for your pitchforks: Yes, I'm sure the *numbers* still reflect an inequality of pay and position suggesting an unfairness towards women, even though I'm sure even *that* is narrowing drastically. Those numbers, however, fail to reflect not only my personal experience, but the politically correct zeitgeist that empowers women over men in almost every conflict that forms between them, including their competition for the same positions, as I witnessed at *all* of my jobs in Bend, excepting, perhaps, as a *Rover* dogsitter.

At *Banned & Ignoble*, for example, the 'boss' *was* a man, but three-quarters of the remaining posts were occupied by women who, I swear to Christ, had that man so under their thumbs that his position at the top was only *ostensible*. It was the women who were *actually* in command; two separate factions of women, in fact: the older faction whom saw themselves as the mature, rational leaders, and the younger faction with whom they perpetually bickered, and for good reason, for that younger faction embodied, as a group, the cliché gossiping girls group forever vying for popularity within their faction, and ever pursuing power over the aforementioned older faction whom had the balls of the 'boss' forever in their squeezing grip. Do you think that an older man who has a conflict with any of the gossiping girls has even a *chance* to have his side of the story heard in such an environment, much less a chance of prevailing in the conflict which those girls thrust upon me?

Nope. Admittedly my indifference, even preference, for having the *right* women in charge is partially due to the imp in me *wanting* women to be pleased and empowered, and not just at work. No lover who's even decent fails to find satisfaction in the satisfaction of his/her partner. But my professional gender indifference, even my *preference* for empowering the *right* women, is also due to the fact that, in contrast to the aforementioned men, I'm not only *never* emasculated by a woman having more power than me, I can honestly say that I'm not intellectually intimidated by anyone. *Ever.* Regardless of sex, and no matter how many acronymous credentials they append to their name or title.

I have my insecurities, like anyone, to be sure, but as arrogant as it may sound, they're never related to my mental capacities. Besides, I quite liked Annabelle. And one of the female therapists, Ellie (the CRC 'princess' cited in the intro), my former supervisor before she switched responsibilities and was replaced by her complete opposite (the secret Stalin, Linda), was a sweetheart art therapist that used the invaluable nature of artistic release to help the residents healthfully reflect upon and cathartically purge the pains of their past. And Leslie, the head nurse in charge, has become a friend since I was compelled to leave the CRC, and reintroduced me to the sacred mushroom, which, I don't think it's out of place to say, will revolutionize mental healthcare, and likely force another propagandist wave of rebuttal from the greed compelling the grotesque profitability of Big Pharma, and conventional healthcare in general, harkening back to the early days of marijuana and psychedelic criminalization in this country, a history which buried boatloads of data demonstrating the medicinal benefits of these substances before absurdly legally classifying them via the narcotics 'scheduling,' labeling them dangerous, addictive 'drugs' offering no medicinal benefits, when, in truth, cannabinoids and psilocybin are perhaps the *most* potent medicines in existence (see *How to Change Your Mind*). Leslie, who was a rather maniacal cannabis and mushroom consumer during her own manic break, which I witnessed, and which demonstrated that these medicines can be abused, once said to me: "I *love* the way you talk about women, Nick."

Reverence, loneliness and self-doubt conspire to turn women, even those regarded as silly little girls in retrospect, into persecutorial behemoths. And the more one approaches a type of enormity oneself, frankly, of the mind, of intellectualism and conceptual consideration, of awareness that others don't possess, and, through those qualities, accidentally invents obstacles which the simple minds will never know, and will thus never be forced to fight, the more the aforementioned qualities, boons in the academic and professional arenas, become immovable burdens in the arena of heart-rending, stifled romance. And so the dim-witted man, sure of himself in his basic egotistic self-conceptions, charges forward with the blind boon of self-faith, continually taking shots that the thinker finds himself too befuddled to even *consider* taking. Gretzky said: "You miss 100% of the shots you *don't* take."

And, for the same reason, the one who fails by fear to take his shots is starved, and values any nibble he gets more than the all-you-can-eat meals served to the unworthy. Guys like me (though I *am* occasionally overcome with a transcendent streak of confidence) generally flit from tree to tree, bush to bush, flower to fruit, seeking but a sustaining morsel that never wants to come, simply because we haven't the entitlement to reach out and take it. We wane beneath the bush, waiting for a berry to fall, whilst the assholes eat their fill above us, gobbling whole bushes of berries in one rapacious wolfing after another. And it's not just the romance we miss, due to our failure to summon the inner 'grab her by the pussy' Trump that this shameful world honors with towers rising as high as their integrity is buried equally deep beneath the basement.

As with women, I have similar thoughts about jobs; about 'career opportunities.' "*How* much do you make?," I find myself repeating in my head when a braggart puffs up his chest in shameless self-aggrandizement, name-dropping and salary-citing around women. Chalk it up to undervaluing myself, and/or being morally offended by the difference in compensation creating the deplorably vast and forever growing disparity between those who have more than they can ever use and those they prey upon who can't even afford to take a family trip, or to a dozen other factors relevant to morality, but I can't conceive of being 'compensated' on that level, even knowing how much more capable I am than most of these preening peacocks who, put a book in his hands or attempt a meaningful conversation, you'll find can scarcely fly; who can't even *find* the thermals, much less rise to where I am. Alas, capacity isn't directly compensated in this world, especially when it's bound to the conviction forgoing profit. The rapists of planet and people prevail over progressives.

Nice guys really do finish last, even as legions of jaded, gorgeous, egomaniacal women conflate the 'take every shot you can' Gretzky's of the world with men in general, such that, should I finally *find* the nerve to take a shot, I'm treated with the disgust and disdain owing to, and owed to, the Trumps. And, adding *immense* insult to injury, being forced to absorb such falsely targeted disdain is getting off easy. Many an aforementioned type of woman will, heaving with their own egotistic enormity, turn the conflation of men and beasts, and having to face uncivilized monsters amongst overgrown boys, into a type of aggressively empowered, concealed entitlement of their own; namely, that they're entitled to destroy men for their present and past abuses, real and imagined; *all* men, even those whom don't fly anywhere near to the ground-feeding flock of preening peacocks; men who fly solo, and with the best intentions, far overhead of those who eat *everything*.

If you think male birds and beasts are the only animals to put on elaborate shows in front of females and violently claim and defend their breeding grounds, think again. They have their watering holes, and we have ours, and both brim with such showboating, compensatory, concealing behavior. There's not as much distance between people and 'creatures' as you might think, dear reader. It's only the particular forms of that game that are different, not their function, nor their motivation. But in most of these games, all those pertaining to on-the-spot performance, at least, the mind tends to get in the way; as much representing a roadblock as an opener of avenues. Most people are relatively good at the things that they're predisposed to do when they're not wondering whether or not they're predisposed to doing them. This is true with sports, with women, even with writing. In fact, my favorite written passages and poems occur when I'm channeling and reflexively reacting to some force which feels like it's being conducted from elsewhere, passing *through* me to the page. I'm not its source, not its provenance, but its *path of providence*; like I'm simply the avenue that *it* has chosen; the targeted translator of something that, if not divine, is at least *necessary*; essential, unforced, not reduced to or convoluted by *thoughts* that can only muddy the water. And yet, the more one possesses anything even *nearing* such thoughts, the less likely he is to even *want* to play.

Most men simply aren't smart enough to accidentally take themselves out of the game. And the sports metaphor is more fitting than you might think. Again, I've long been aware of the fact (as are most, in this case, I'm sure) that my best athletic performances occur when I'm *not* thinking. Whereas that game is typically played *for* women. "Why do men do *anything*?" George rhetorically responds to Seinfeld. "*For women.*" Even nitwit women are acutely aware of this, especially when they're recipients of a constant barrage of such shameless displays. Nor are those shameless self-showcases of absolute benefit to those they're meant to attract. I'm not afraid to say, as I've said elsewhere, that there tends to be an inverse relationship between the growth of the ego and the growth of the character; that the inflation of the former tends to coincide with the atrophy and ensuing stunting of the latter.

Only when the mind of the recipient is well enough developed *not* to have her ego thusly broadened and befouled may this deleterious effect be mitigated. And so the shameless shows go on, neither the men nor the women who perpetrate their respective egomaniacal acts paying the true price for their disgraceful displays and reactions, the unacknowledged bill-payers being the loveless lingering on the sidelines, wondering how to enter the arena without becoming a buffoon in a country where a clown plays president; where an adult was replaced by a temperamental toddler as petty as the Old Testament God.

To this day I feel like Leslie (again, the former head nurse at the CRC) is the only woman who ever saw the fact that my reverence towards and weakness for women is inseparable from the pains I've experienced in my relationships with them. Where most women to whom I might risk honestly expressing my thoughts, feelings and indignations in relation to 'their gender' will dismiss them under insinuations of misogyny, especially since my honest semi-fictional retelling of the worst work experience of my life in *Holier Than Thou*, Leslie recognized that I love women even more than I hate them, and that the latter doesn't only *not* preclude the former, but that they're typically interdependent. Leslie would eventually be forced from the CRC herself, after losing control of her own bipolar predispositions. Actually, I'd come to find out that she subsequently sued PrimaCare for, ironically, treating her prejudicially with regards to her bipolar disorder, leading to what she'd consider her wrongful termination. I should've asked her who her lawyer was, and inquired as to the possibility of a case against *Banned & Ignoble*, suing for sexism. Alas, when it comes to professional positioning, I'm *meritocratic*, like any just person. Give the job to the best person for the job, regardless of *anything* else. I don't even care if they *are* a person. They can be an alien from outer space. If they add the most value to the position, it's there's. Universal rights, protections, privileges and opportunities constitute the only *true* form of progressivism.

Back at the CRC, in the intervening quiet, as my thoughts flow tangentially to a reflection upon the fact that *none* of us have more of an innate right to anything than anyone else, and how *everyone* in America is an immigrant, *including* the 'natives,' who are only the nearest to being native, having crossed the Beiring Straight from Asia as but the *oldest* North Americans, the dawn ekes through the glass of the back windows and door, protected by electronic key, leading out to the barbwire-fenced-in yard. The only sounds that can be heard are Jess's occasional taps of the keyboard on her lazily-entitled "Evolution Paper," and the hushed thwacks of the wispy feme fatale killing another ex-Marine on the television in front of me, turned to the highest volume allowed during quiet hours.

Sensing her writing her paper at the periphery of my perception, I think of my own undergrad paper-writing days; how most students would be intimidated by the requisite word counts that I felt *restricted* by; how I always felt that I could wax poetic on *any* subject for *any* length of time; how the difficulty isn't filling space, but narrowing it, astutely summarized in that line by Cicero, or Twain: "If only I'd had more time, I would've written a shorter letter." Or that scene in *A River Runs Through It*, where the father of the future editor of a paper, the older brother, brings his work to his father, who reads it and promptly commands something like: "Now write it again, in a hundred fewer words." The challenge is to make it *more* concise, not less. The difficulty is in whittling the wood down to the sparest sculpture, not adding to its amorphous mass. The difficulty is distilling the ideas into their essence; into their most fundamental, most unambiguously expressed forms so that *anyone* may understand even the most abstruse concepts. Einstein once said: "If you can't explain it to a five year old, then you don't understand it yourself." Soon Cain's restless energy overtakes him again, and he continues his rant...

"I remember visiting my mother, just after Katherine had sliced me from stem to sternum, and torn out my heart and eaten it in front of me, and strung my shrunken balls from her throat. I was as low as I'd ever been. And I remember my mom saying to me: "I'm almost embarrassed to say that I like you like this." In retrospect I realized what she was *really* saying: I like you in this reduced state. Too weak to fight, to argue with me, like you normally do. Too little to challenge me or threaten my ego. *That's* what I think all women secretly want: for men to be reduced to little boys, conquered, utterly docile, perfectly passive, ready to bend to their every whim and desire. They *say* that they want men, but what they *really* want is to turn men into boys. They want their own egos to remember that a self-confident man walked through their front door, ready to take on the world, and that, when he left, crawling and crying, on his knees, having faced the power and glory of the *true* conqueror, he was like a little boy with a pacifier in his mouth, whimpering to his mommy, begging for a sip from the baby bottle filled with the self-worth *she* controls."

As I may've already mentioned, one of the reasons that I had a stronger affinity for Cain than most of the other residents is that our journey shared not just a fearless awareness of politically incorrect truth, but a major mental health overlap: *self-correcting a manic psychosis*. Of course, I corrected mine under *very* different circumstances, *before* the evidence could present itself, and the argument could be made, that I'd become a danger to myself and others. I'll never forget that night. Like being unable to forget one's only time falling in love, it's impossible to forget the two times that I've felt the peril of a grisly death descend upon me. Care for some obvious advice, dear reader? Don't become indebted to drug dealers. Their collection agencies can be a bit... *harsh.*

But a little more context first... so, yea, okay, they banned me from *Deschutes Brewery* (where Cain himself worked, and where, from his telling, the stresses they put him through became the catalyst of his psychosis) because I was going through a phase of showing up drunk and stoned at bars, and making obscure comments that made perfect sense to me but which made the middling patrons "uncomfortable," which is bad for profits. So the manager took me outside to politely insult and promptly ban me. But how about some compassion, for Chrissakes? Let a few patrons be "uncomfortable." And yea, they also booted me from *Astro Lounge*, when they cut me off, and that barely articulate kid they had bartending tried to correct my grammar on top of it, and I called him a moron. So what? And there might be one other place in Bend. I can't recall.

But let me say this: I'm sure many of you, dear readers, don't approve of me already, but if you haven't been booted from a bar or two in your life let me suggest that you stop being so damned well behaved all the time, so afraid to respond to the nonsense of another patron out of fear of 'causing a scene,' and that you grow a pair, man or woman, and speak your mind and get in a little trouble, instead of personifying Thoreau's "most men lead lives of quiet desperation." Hey, I'm no stranger to desperation, I'm sure you can tell. And Jess, that poor, glorious queen of my heart, I'm sure she felt it seeping out of my unrequited pores every night. But at least my desperation isn't quiet!

At least I yawp from time to time, in paraphrase of Whitman, and in a bow to one of the greatest films of all time: *Dead Poets Society*. And I *have* read *Walden*, by the way, a book that I couldn't recommend more highly; a book that's not only brilliant but that's even more relevant today than it was when he wrote it. My first book, *Infinite of One*, written long before reading Thoreau's treatise on purposeful living, ran in close parallel to it, in fact, at least in terms of what compelled us to write our respective works. So, yes, I'm familiar with what drives my type into the woods, seeking not just the marrow of life, but *rescue*.

For all the variety of personage and its principles and pursuits, the secret truth is that there's only one goal of us all, mostly unrecognized and, thus, unacknowledged: *To be at peace within ourselves. To need nothing more than true necessity, right where and when we are.* All the rest is a vain, unsustainable attempt to drown the disquiet; an egotistic delusion which we escape in moments of clarity. And yet, as rare as this basic knowledge is, escaping the pains and pressures of contemporary society is easier said than done, for so ensnared are we by our lives, and by other peoples' expectations of those lives, that escape can feel impossible, and many people perish in pursuit of it.

As I write this in late February, in the intemperate high desert of Central Oregon, the wild winds of the previous night (which besieged the senses of my charge, Finnegan, the most lovable of canines, sparking a continuity of growls and barks through most of the evening) brought on their heels yet another burst of snowfall. And I think of Jess, and her fondness for the cold, once telling me how it makes the indoor warmth all that more warming. I recall that, as she made this one of an innumerable number of endearing comments, she gave accentuating life to the remark by *enacting* it. As the master gesticulator, with a movement that further laid claim to my already conquered heart, she gave herself a hug whilst describing the warmth of the winter fire, blanket and covers. I bought her an electric blanket to plug in and keep her warm during the overnight winter shifts at the CRC once, and she rewarded me with an embrace that was worth a thousand electric blankets.

And I recall that paralleling comment of hers about how, once she's at home, she *has* to put her pajamas on. The most adorable damn thing to say, and which made me that much more desperate to cuddle up with her after she's adorned said PJ's. It just kills me, to this day, how perfectly she brought out the deepest internal desire for intimacy. How it seemed that cuddling with her, under a blanket, beside a fire, a snowstorm outside, an emotional movie on the screen bringing out her own sublime swings from sorrow to joy, would be Heaven on Earth. I don't think it would be possible for me to want to be closer to anyone else. At the same time, Jess, I'm compelled to say: Anyone can rock the PJ's at home, but it takes a true OG like me to rock them everywhere you go. I have them on as I write this, in the midst of radiant sunshine but minutes removed from the former snow flurry, proving the Bend cliche: "If you don't like the weather in Bend, wait fifteen minutes." Nothing long settles in the high desert, where the meteorological equivalent of bipolar disorder reigns supreme, the weather swinging with violent caprice from one extreme to the next, and where 'shoulder seasons' are mostly skipped. It makes it difficult to lay down roots and grow with any stable continuity, and not just for the flora. The weather patterns accentuate my own unsettled sense.

I remember how badly I wanted to buy Jess things; to spoil she who wasn't mine to spoil. Any excuse to get her a gift. Her birthday, when I bought her the electric blanket, and a book of interest... When she hugged me for the first time. Every time I went anywhere, I wanted to buy remembrances of the place not for me, not for the one there actually having the experience, but for the one there with me in heart, but never in body; for the one lording over me from within. It's like I needed to bring a piece of the place I was in body back to the place I *always* resided in heart. I wanted to give her *everything*. To carry a part of every place through which I passed to the altar at which I prayed, regardless of time and place. I never *said* these things to Jess, obviously, but felt them *all the time*. And I ask you, dear reader: Is not the truest love inseparable from obsession? Does not the muse *want* to be obsessed over, just not in the dangerous manner that the former Nick did, but in the manner that I do, physically removed from her? Wait, I haven't mentioned the former Nick yet... soon.

And my desire to purchase her things, to feel the joyful lifting of my heart from her appreciative reception, wasn't limited to my trips out of town. She possessed an eclectic set of interests, as all intelligent people do, I believe, for intelligence, and inquisitiveness, and exploration, and experimentation all go hand in hand. Thus it was with joy that I vicariously experienced *her* joy at exploring and enlisting things which few come to. For example, Jess knew about *Whole 30* when it had yet to come into prominence as a dietary strategy; when I, myself, was early in my research and personal experimentation with the 'exclusionary diets;' that is, nutritional strategies built upon excluding the inflammatory substances which lead to the chronic bodily distress (i.e. dis-ease) precipitating disease. This led to my offer to buy her the books, but we actually ended up discovering them on the CRC bookshelf sometime soon thereafter, donated by a staff member whose intentions proved inadequate to the required effort.

Or when I purchased her a trip to the sensory deprivation tank here in town, a practice all but unknown back then. Considering that this book is largely about mental health, I'm compelled to add that both *Whole 30* and sensory deprivation, or 'dark retreats,' as they're becoming known through the use of caves around the world, show promise in relieving the symptoms, and potentially even targeting the causes, of some forms of mental illness, especially those of the overlapping anxiety and depression cluster. Dark retreats even have some parallels with psychonautic substances (like P. cubensis) in the treatment of mental illness, in that both help induce changes to consciousness and offer accompanying benefits of reduction in the severity of stress, anxiety and depression. I even reached out to the owner of the sensory deprivation chamber services here in town and suggested that, as the use of cubensis is rising into accepted treatment status for mental illness, with Oregon leading the way, that he consider integrating the two. He seemed intrigued by the idea.

Psilocybe cubensis relieves the weight of the self through a more seamless merger with the Self. Adding sensory deprivation would likely heighten this relief of the bodily self, it seems to me. Actually, my experiences floating the river here in Bend (an iconic Bend experience) leave me with a weightlessness that I sense is conducive to healing, through an opening up of and depressurization of the nervous system. When I get off the river, I feel lighter, and more at peace, and I instinctively sense that this feeling is conducive to the greater efficacy of other therapeutic modalities with which it may beneficially combine. Thus, I plan to combine my floats with my 'trips' this coming summer, and with other forms of therapy, and look forward to the results. I'm guessing that it'll seem a highly valuable therapeutic practice conducive to healing and rejuvenation, in addition to the anxiety-and-depression reduction, and the invaluable experience of the sense of expanded consciousness and connectivity with the Everything; something that's impossible to quantify or qualify, and which, as already predicted herein, will revolutionize mental health itself, in a rediscovery of what's been known to silenced scientists and psychonauts for a long time (see *How to Change Your Mind* and *Fantastic Fungi*).

Generally speaking, I'm more and more coming to the realization in my own practice that health treatments, whether considered to be targeting mental illness, or simply efforts at improving health in general, are effective commensurate to their *holism*. That is, they're the most effective when they're not standalone, but, rather, represent a synergistic constellation of treatments hitting the ills from myriad directions, each form of treatment representing its unique, inimitable contribution to treatment *as a whole*. Not a new concept, I realize, but a critical one, and one that modern medicine is clueless about, or simply resistant to because it tends not to be profitable, and to involve naturalistic, free treatments it dismisses behind the 'alternative medicine' umbrella insult, and the nonsensical 'not enough scientific evidence' justification, forgetting to tell sufferers *why* there's not enough evidence, hoping they won't figure out that 'no major medical corporation wanted to pay to generate the scientific evidence which would only serve to reduce its profits' is different from 'not effective.' Anyway, *all* forms of 'alternative health practice' were of interest to she whom I loved, even as I remain aware that to have actually *been* with Jess during our exploration of such treatments would likely have ended up hampering such exploration, and kept not just me, but both of us, from finding our best fit in life.

There seems an inescapable aspect of being a detainee of destiny whereby the creator is afflicted with a conflicting desire to transform the muse into lover, and the lover into partner. Your heart wants it, yearns for it as though it's the only thing there is, but blindly… blind to the fact that birds can't soar when tethered to one another; that hunting for the food and shelter of survival and all the comforting signs and accoutrements of modern 'success' is largely mutually exclusive with the deeper hungering of the ardent mood; that the greatness of the artist is in their *refusal* to give into 'reality,' to *not* dwell upon the Earth so as to remain free to explore the heavens. Isolated we're pained by our loneliness, and yet only alone and in pain, suffused with suffering, alienated from the world, can we best hone our alchemical gifts; can we purposefully make of them a Philosopher's Stone that may transmute the ordinary world into the extraordinary possibility that all of humankind may be bettered by reaching for, in their imagination and imitation of. The problem, of course, is that the alchemical artist is *also* a human being, and his dwelling in various states of dissatisfaction and deprivation leaves him, at his lows, to make such notes as the following in his journal:

Is it possible to be so unhappy for so long, to live such a loveless life for such a length of time, that you don't know how to be happy when the opportunity presents itself? Like love could fall right in front of you, but is so alienated from you that you don't recognize it, or don't believe it's actually there, like it's a hallucination? Or you're so used to your unhappiness that when happiness presents itself you convince yourself that you don't need it, or don't deserve it, so you don't bother to reach for it? Or, perhaps most twisted of all, you're so afraid of it, and so accustomed to your misery, that you confuse unhappiness with happiness, and, mounting misery, ride away from happiness as quickly as your assorted sorrows can carry you? And is it possible to become so dependent upon dependencies from decades of self-abuse that you become dependent upon dependency in general, in the abstract sense? Like you could emancipate yourself from every particular instance of unhealthy dependency in your life yet still feel enslaved by its imprint upon your psyche, doomed to loneliness and unhappiness because you can no longer conceive of anything else, and are thereby incapable of manifesting freedom from dependency, much less of creating the prerequisites positioning you to truly pursue happiness?

And yet, as much as my knowledge of unhappiness is informed by loveless loneliness, it may be even better informed by my contempt for modern society, and all the sickness it spreads, accepted by the invisibly infected as 'normal;' as effects of the one inescapable 'reality.' In fact, as I type this on my phone, sitting at a picnic bench beside the Deschutes River in a miniature escape from that artificial reality, I'm reminded that this is one of the parks wherein, at the heights of my disgust with the world delivering me into the depths of depression, and losing the will to continue producing the income required of survival, I explored the periphery of this aspen-populated park. Why?

I was ready to give up. I was preparing to give into the disgust and despair and build a shelter in the woods and live there as long as I could. I remember discovering a circular mound of rocks near the crest of a hill over which I'd planned to lay large limbs in the production of said shelter. And I was honestly considering walking away from it all, going Lao Tzu on everyone, and delivering myself to the primal forces to sustain or consume me at will. The only thing that reigned-in this impulse were thoughts of what my disappearance might do to my immediate family, for I'd never be able to inform them of such a 'plan.' The pain and miserable mystery of finding my car parked in some inconspicuous spot outside the park, wondering what horror I may have succumbed to, imagining me falling into a ravine or accidentally stepping between a black bear mother and her cub, or slipping and hitting my head whilst crossing the Deschutes in an exploration of the mountains.

Thoughts of what this would do to my already emotionally ravaged, perpetually vulnerable mother was an especially prevalent force for this restraint. And, of course, I'm glad I reigned myself in, for hope, the last shred of sanity, yet remains within me somehow. Hope that people might someday value what I have to say, despite all possible evidence of the contrary yet prevailing. Hope that I might thereby be afforded the opportunity to buy my freedom, and purchase property beyond the clutches of the parasitic overlords. And, perhaps especially, hope that someone whom made me feel any significant portion of what Jess did may someday find me worthy of reciprocation of the feelings that make every other sense seem insubstantial.

And just in case you're wondering about the other places where I'd considered disappearing, it was either going to be here, near Shevlin Park, or somewhere on the outskirts of the Metolius River, also scouted for that sad purpose. *Actually*, the real leader in the contest was my town of birth, Fort Bragg, CA, beside the Pacific, enshrouded in fog, carpeted in fern, reigned over by the mighty redwood.

I would've walked from my father's property, on a redwooded hill near the Noyo River, ten miles inland from the coast, surrounded by logging land and the largest

State Forest in California, *Jackson State Forest* (which my father had managed at the heights of his career working for the *California Department of Forestry and Fire Protection*), and simply disappeared. In my imagination I become some sort of holy man in the painful, chrysalis-shedding process, though, most likely, I'd starve to death after eating the wrong mushroom, my body found, buried there, memorialized with a plaque reading: "Here lies a spiritual philosopher of a modern age that cares even less about philosophy than about any insight into God being bigger than religion." Truth be told I was far closer to actually doing it when I lived on that property, before moving to Oregon. In fact, I was only saved by a DUI.

I'd already procured what I'd then thought to be all necessary supplies and was driving back to the property on Oak Street, heading towards its extension into Company Ranch Road, when I decided to stop at a bar. I drank too much and ran a concealed stop sign; concealed by a tree that has since been cut down, I might add. But in the ensuing period of familial assistance I was relieved of the mindset of what may, indeed, have ultimately become a fatal course of action. For, before the DUI, I was resolved to take that course, and ended up having the sixth sense later that I'd barely escaped what would've been my death. Because, of course, I was ill-prepared for such a course, despite my resolve. It felt less spiritual then, and more a test of manhood; of feeling emasculated by modernity, and envious of all the 'men's men' who possessed practical skills of survival. I still have the precipitating document on my laptop, entitled: "The One Year Plan to be a Man."

And speaking of *Walden*, I honestly believe that the smarter you are, the greater your spiritual instinct, the more you see the fabricated bars and chains that entrap and entangle and confine and, finally, *enslave* common bourgeoisie society, the greater your drive to defy it, to rebel against it, and ultimately to seek to destroy it. It's like an impulse to run away from it and annihilate it at the same time. Like you want to free everyone in the cage, your blinded brethren that can't even see that they're in a cage, whilst simultaneously fleeing from and purifying yourself of it before it squeezes more of the precious life-force out of you. To fight or to flee, the question seems to be. Perhaps both. Fight from a place of purified remove from the toxins. This was, in fact, the basis of my first book, *Infinite of One*.

And I'm definitely not alone. What is it, dear reader, that drives a person to abandon the world and disappear *Into the Wild*? Even short of this, what makes the plan to leave everything behind and hike the whole of the Appalachian or Pacific Crest Trails, a la Cheryl Strayed, and the resolve to reset one's life such a popular focus of many a memoir? Certainly it's a multitude of factors. The desire for purification; to live a natural life outside of the artificiality, noise, greed and pervasive egotism of society. The *Walden*-esque desire to connect to something real and grounded. To reintegrate with the wonderous, pagan part of ourselves that senses magic and spirituality in nature, mostly lost to modern day humankind, but forever inextricably buried deep down in our blood and bones. To possess a life and purpose beyond consumerism and production for profit. To develop hands-on skills and abilities. But also, of course, anxiety and depression; already feeling isolated and alienated; a combination of mental and physical health ills inseparable from mental illness which, absent the rescue of loved ones which some don't possess, leaves one feeling desperate to escape their misery, often driving them from one form of it to another. But at least, you tell yourself, you'll be in the *natural* world. At least you'll escape the persecution of unnatural addictions, a motive that I share with Cheryl.

I'm *intimately* familiar with Hell, dear reader. *One* of its innumerable forms, at least. And it may well surprise you to hear me say that it's not some fiery torment. It's much the opposite. It's a pleasure of such unspeakable bliss that it wrecks your brain for the thought of it, burying itself deep down in your psyche with sensations of such overwrought, absolute ecstasy that you sign over your entire future and every ounce of the potential with which God bids you to serve your brethren. And the Devil is the one handing you the pen; beckoning you, in fact, to just reach out and take it. Sign here, and be troubled no more. The same Devil that took Cobain, and countless others; not in terms of the same substance, but the type of lure. The seemingly inescapable pull of the memory of the feelings amounting to selling your life. And all it seems to take for me is to drink or smoke too much, and I forget everything God has told me, and sneak away to seek out the Devil once again.

The thing is, it's part of the Devil's deception that you typically don't know, else don't care, that you're in his den when you're actually *in* it. It's only when you escape the binds and put some distance between you and him that you're truly aware of the extent of the debauchery (some would say the *depravity*) that exists within it. And for a time following satiation of my demonically-costly vice, I'm fine. Largely inactive, the beast hibernates in the depths of my psyche, yet persists in wending its way through the pleasure centers of my brain and body, whispering its sinister forget-me-nots. But, with sufficient discipline, those whispers can be successfully ignored, for I'm not on the short leash as seen in the sufferers whom I sometimes share the evil ecstasy with, whom have tragically accepted their relationship with the Devil as a lasting dependency in their languishing lives. Luckily, with my fortitude and conviction ever waging war with the corrupted parts of myself, I'm able to remain on the relatively *long* leash.

I've been able to stretch that leash for almost two months in the years since the servant of Satan first wrapped his arm around me, having been invited into that hotel room, at the *Hilton Airport Hotel*, by that deceitful demon. But I haven't been able to cut that leash. Around the one month mark my loveless life of perpetual loneliness, isolation and dissatisfaction catches up to me, like an army from hell pulling my guard all the way down, at which point all it takes is for me to drink too much, and I awake in the Devil's den, after a day and night of wanton debauchery, and wonder how I got there, and assault myself with self-recriminations of such magnitude that it's a wonder that I yet retain even the scantiness of self-esteem that I do.

That afternoon at the *Hilton Airport Hotel*, and full until the dwindling hours of the next day, the Devil filled the aching void within me *not* with the only thing that can truly fill it and keep it full, the sustainable satisfactions of good health, purpose and the requited love of one like Jess, but with an insidious, illusory shadow of sensuous satisfaction so enormous in stature, so simplistically gratifying in grip, it *seems* to one starving for satisfaction to be its greatest embodiment. And it took root, digging down into its insidious corruption of my body and brain. And I've been unable to extricate it, like those plants you think are dead that sprout from some tiny part of their buried root system, concealed beneath the visible surface of apparent non-life, just waiting for the circumstances to be right to thrust them into the light once more, where they enwrap themselves around their hosts like a pernicious, virulently-vining weed.

That is the corruptive vulnerability of body and mind; of the mental (especially egotistic) and material forms of the self: to be capable of being so owned by the illusory needs of debilitating dependency, of addling addiction, that the incorruptible aspect of heart is left unheeded, and the manacled mind and unnaturally-burdened body are willing to sell everything that's best in life, all love and purpose and higher calling, to slate their artificial thirsts. *This* is the provenance of evil, too. The Church is wrong. *Again.* You're not 'born into sin.' That's Christian, mind-controlling propaganda; one element amongst many in the wicked playbook of impious priests. They sell you a false affliction in order to sell you the 'cure.' You're not 'born evil,' but born *capable* of evil. And yes, there's an *immense* difference between the two; between being inherently evil and inherently possessing of the innate limitations and vulnerabilities of body and mind which *potentiate* evil. The Church wants you to believe in their equivalency to keep you enchained to its will, but they're definitely *not* the same. Again, evil isn't an innate quality of body and mind, and comes not from the invulnerable Spirit residing within the heart, but is born of and borne by the *corruptibility* innate to the vulnerability of mental and material limitation.

Allow me to state a connected secret, dear reader: *Every war between good and evil is first fought within yourself.* It's the battle between the incorruptible heart and the corruptible body and mind. It's a war of fortifying body and mind against its innate vulnerability, and thereby repelling the corruptibility that gives rise to the *potential* for evil. It's about strengthening body and mind *towards* incorruptibility, through the interconnected virtues of love, knowledge, discipline, wisdom, service, purpose, and especially good health. For the better one's health, the less vulnerable they are to becoming subject to the false needs that're planted into the undefended furrows laid across body and psyche.

I'm speaking, of course, of *positive freedom*; of the purposeful erection of fortifications, or 'boundaries,' against the corruptibility that gives rise to evil. I'd add that, though Jess's use of the concept has rendered the word forever sour in my mouth, for I was *not* the evil against which a boundary must be raised (only a threat to the largely false virtue of monogamous love and its control of all 'acceptable' modern romantic relations), I nevertheless acknowledge the truth asserted by many philosophers that positive freedom is the only *true* freedom, towering above the form that most Americans believe to be absolute: the *negative* form of being free to do whatever one wishes.

This negative form is, of course, favored by the tyrannical conquerors and subjugators of conservative America whom learned from their aristocratic and imperial forebears in crafting the prevailing conservative value system built to advance the evils of greed and ego whilst concealing them with propaganda. That value system was built around a simple objective: *to enable them to do anything within their power*, to fully exploit their inordinate power disparity relative to non-equity-holders, so their workers and buyers, and the resource-rich areas of the planet, would remain as unprotected (i.e. remain as positively *unfree*) as possible.

Thus it is that America is the hub of positive slavery hidden behind lies like democracy (it's a plutocratic republic in which those we vote for typically represent the interests of the wealthy first) and there being but one form of freedom. America is the foremost land in the world in which even the few who free themselves from the weaker sides of themselves first, and thereby become the few to win the war within, still remain mired by immense positive slavery *without*; the slavery of being 'free' to work to enrich the already wealthy, and to vote for one of a handful or pre-selected (i.e. already corrupted) 'representatives of the people.' For even amongst the few who come to fight the oppressors, no person may be *truly* free when subject to the evils springing from the insufficiently fortified vulnerabilities of his/her inner self, and can only thus remain a slave to them; to the debilitating dependencies of the egotistic shadow self and the body burdened by false needs. You cannot win the wars that your heart bids you to

fight in the world without first winning the wars waged
within. This, in turn, reminds me of a maxim that I heard
often whilst at the CRC, about the invaluable nature of
what's called 'self-care:' *You cannot serve others from an
empty vessel.* Recently I've come to expand this metaphor
a bit: *Don't try to serve others from a vessel that's cracked,
unclean, empty or filled with sickening, befouled fluids.*
That is, having the desire to serve others, and connecting
this to one's purpose in life, is inseparable from honor, and
denotes one of the virtues remaining from the Church's
corruption of Christ's teachings. But first you must patch up
and clean the vessel, and purify the contents to be poured.

And it's only from having so long carried around a cracked
vessel carrying impure fluids that I know this. It's only from
so long being buried by the evils sprung from my
corruptible self, and by harnessing my contemplative mind,
that I know the battle of good versus evil better than most.
And it's only from suffering so much loss to that war that
I'm so resolved to win my freedom from it, and to thereby
earn my way to becoming a champion in the eternal
squabble between the corruptibility born of mortal construct
and the incorruptible aspect of the divine force that bids
me to fight back, in the hope of winning my own freedom,
and the freedom of as many others whose own wars I may
contribute to. This is the One War behind every war. And,
again, we must win the wars within ourselves before we
may win the wars without ourselves. For without this we
remain far too vulnerable to outer corruptions. It's in the
failure of the former, in our inability or refusal to win the
wars within, that all the latter wars are lost, and that evil
may prevail in the world. Until recently, I'd lost for decades.

I don't have to tell you, dear reader, that when one carries
around a hole inside oneself one is compelled to fill it, by
any means necessary. Does this not define and drive us
all, to some degree? And does not the success of

---

capitalism depend upon focusing on and artificially broadening that hole until it's so big that it fits every damn useless product its profiteers can conceive of? Damn, there I go again, being tangential! Well, anyway, my hole just happens to be more gaping and persistent than most, and conventional consumerism doesn't fill it. And I'm more aware than most not only of how large a hole can be dug, but what one is compelled to fill it with when it reaches a certain magnitude of size and depth, and when the one hosting that hole is too long assailed by the burden of it. There's a reason that two women whom I briefly dated in Bend both ended up deciding that I was a "mess," and not worth the effort. Long have I had the sense that most people are simply not strong enough, or open, considerate and compassionate enough, to be my friend, much less my 'significant other.' I have to clean and repair my vessel first.

"I cannot give myself to another until becoming myself," I'd reflected in my journal recent to writing this book. "Absent that I do only dishonor to the Divine Feminine by crawling to Her as a beast of burden borne by the shadow of self."

I wrote some poetry on the subject recently:

Corrupted Cathedral

My cathedral has been corrupted, take the drug away from me. For the crystalline creature worms its way through the fissures of my history. Luckily the body knows the mind, so the demon is interrupted, yet the victim is caught in the cage, and by the prisoner instructed. For my heart nears its failure, and by the wanton has been waning. The prisoner well knows his doom, but by compulsion lacks refraining.

And:

Beast of Burden

The demon comes, and hiding, lies in wait

Will the tethered and tormented take the bait?

Kilned, its keen eyes converge upon all

In unguarded capture, upon my sword I fall

For this beast well I know, its claws surround

Yet it's only within me that its burrow may be found

Extricate this evil, not a one may do

And yet try, I must, and so folly I accrue

Thus assailed and railed, the savage storm rages on

What angel of mercy may my missing deliverance spawn?

In fact, one of the many notions that I'd had for this book was for it to be a play on the idea of *Beauty and the Beast*, written by one who knows both with equal fervor, immense, ardent passion on one side versus inescapable torture and despair on the other. And I'm not just referring to drug addiction, but to another, far more ravaging, far deeper-dug-in addiction I've spoken of to very few, for so outside typical experience does it lie that it's nearly impossible for others to understand it, much less offer me any salvation I've yet to consider. Some of the notes from that outline:

These are some of the thoughts and memories within the man buried by The Beast. The man who yet survives on the memory of the love that he held for her there, in his deepest recesses, where even The Beast can never touch them. The memories that yet sustain him, that let him know how great life could be were he ever to escape the clutches of The Beast and chase such a love towards a warmth in which he'd never before basked. And therein were the battlelines drawn between the corrupted and the incorruptible waging war within. The war tearing him in two.

The Beast keeps him in the dark; consumes him with constant unnatural stress; stealing his energy and ability to focus with its constantly distracting clawing at his tormented body and brain. It suffocates his hope, precludes all the best connections, eliminates all the best relationships. It tells him that sensory gratification is all that matters, even as it prevents him from having any fulfilling measure of it; from having the opportunity to come together with anything and everything that might reciprocate the pleasure. It growls: "Have sex with anyone, fulfill every bodily craving, even as your heart perpetually aches for true connection, love, meaning, fulfillment; for everything that I'll never allow you to have." It owns him.

It sends its messages to his brain at every moment of every day, corrupting his thoughts and making his nerves the preeminent power of his being. It makes him always uncomfortable. It takes away all coolness, all confidence, all level-headedness. It tortures him relentlessly, yet can't kill him. "You have two options," it ceaselessly growls: "You can kill yourself, forcing me out of the host, or you can let me drive you to an early grave, having never known yourself, who you really are, what you could have and have ached for since you were a tortured teenager. You'll die a semblance of self; a hollowed-out, fractured shadow of what you were born to be, and there's nothing you can do about it. Your mother, father, brother, your few true friends that stick around, you yourself… none of them know you." People speak of suffering. They lament certain parts of their lives. They think sometimes that they have it hard. They think that they know what it is to live a life of struggle; of misery. Yet they've never known The Beast.

The love says: "Protect and honor her and the memories of her." The Beast says: "She destroyed then discarded you, absorbed your need for her into her ego, and now lives in happiness with the one she could never leave, and has always preferred to you. How can she do that to you? Pretend to care, suck up everything good in you that you felt for her, then cast you out? Kill your love, for I cannot."

Beside it in my journal I wrote: *When the hope leaves you, there's nothing left standing between you and destruction.* Later, in the effort to preserve that hope, bolster my confidence and define my challenge, I wrote: *There's not a single person on this planet better set to serve Spirit whilst being simultaneously and equally enslaved to the service of Satan. For every sword may cut both ways with equal sharpness, and so may you penetrate the firmament as easily as you may slice into the underworld. Thus must you summon the strength to emerge from the beastly den armed with the knowledge of how to cut The Beast down, and pass that knowledge to any who will listen, and thereby save as many as possible from being ravaged.*

Yes, I have issues, including issues with substance abuse, that continue to this day, though not like before. I was addicted to oxycontin for a year before the aforementioned meeting of the demon in the *Hilton Airport Hotel*, which came *after* the episode I'm soon to relate. With the oxycontin, I had just enough money for one 80mg pill per day. I'd buy it from a drug dealer whom, like most of the drug dealers I've dealt with, I knew from high school, bring it home, chop it into four pieces, and crush those pieces into 4 daily lines. Then: *bliss.* See, the trouble with opiates, similar to cocaine and ecstasy, is that it makes it such that you're okay doing just about *anything*, for you're floating in a state of euphoria regardless of where you are and what you're doing. Thus the danger of drifting into an oblivion indistinguishable from bliss. I'd play the Tiger Woods golfing game for hours on end, thinking it near to nirvana.

Cut to late in my oxycontin addiction, and I've traded drug dealers, the new one having a connection with a hit man who's offered to 'rub out' the perpetrators of the anecdote I'm getting to… But I remember walking down the stairs leading out of the apartment after this killer had made his offer in front of my new supplier, and I had declined, and had immediately been hit with the sense that the killer was considering killing *me* now, owing to that denial, and, of course, to the fact that I could now identify him, and was walking behind me, and the terror I felt imagining that he was reaching for a gun in his bag and would, at any final moment of my existence, pull it out, shoot me in the back of the head, watch my body tumble to the bottom of the closed-in staircase of that sprawling apartment complex in Rincon Valley, CA, half a mile from where I'd attended high school five years earlier, step over my body and walk out.

Okay, so that's actually at least *three* times that I've almost been murdered by black market denizens. In fact, this, for me, represents one of the best arguments for opening up the 'self-medicating' markets, taxing and regulating them *for the safety of addicts whom otherwise risk their lives*. So, before this new supplier, the younger brother of a friend from high school who thought *he* was the drug dealer, but dealt only in weed, and had *nothing* on his younger brother, who'd move anything he could, and who became seduced by the lifestyle of the drug dealer after following his older brother's lead, though to far greater heights (or is it deeper depths?)… Before he took the wheel of my 1998 Honda Civic LX painted in "Cyclone Blue Metallic (I'll never forget that color description!)" and drove it from Santa Rosa, CA, into some shady area of San Francisco whilst I was coming down off the oxycontin, and he'd promised me a discount if he could borrow my car and go with me to pick up a new supply from a supplier he'd not yet met, driving my little four cylinder faster than I knew it could go, weaving through Hwy 101 traffic at 90 mph to meet this guy on the street who had this *massive* canister of the stuff, and who was looking around paranoidly the entire time, talking about how much of a risk he was taking selling to my dealer without knowing us, his hand under his coat on a weapon the entire time… so maybe *four* times.

Afterwards my dealer spoke of himself as though he was *Scarface* and had just made the connection that was going to make him rich. All I cared about, of course, was that my skin had stopped crawling, the dark clouds of choking despair displaced by clouds of an ideal ivory sheen, surreal and heavenly soaring. My parents thought *I* was the addict, eventually sending me to an opiate addiction doctor who put me on something that was *much* more difficult, and uglier, to get through than the opiates themselves, *Suboxone*, which combines a mild opiate 'fix' effect with a substance that blocks the uptake of opiates themselves, thereby making them ineffective and lacking in appeal. But just as my friend from high school had nothing on his younger brother's drug dealing scale, my addiction was nothing compared to his. He should've paid more attention to *Scarface*: *don't get high on your own supply.* An oxycontin addition on *his* level was scary, for he wasn't subject to the same self-regulation or financial restrictions that rendered my addiction mild by comparison. He'd do so much of it so regularly that he'd literally drift into and out of conscious awareness *all the time*, including whilst you were talking with him, coming back into the conversation as though nothing had happened. *And then drive home.* But before all that, going back to the first time I knew for certain that my life was imperiled, I was only a marijuana addict. And yes, it *is* addictive, just little league addictive.

If you doubt its addiction deny THC to a hardcore stoner, and see what happens. The difference is they won't offer to go down on you to alleviate the relative discomfort of the come down. But the underestimated, and in some ways far *greater* danger alluded to by the idea of the 'gateway drug' isn't just that marijuana opens one up to the world of narcotics and the risks of becoming fond of the harder, more addictive, more self-destructive substances, but, as recently referenced, that (at least before its more recent decriminalization) it's a gateway to the perilous *people* in the drug world. Thus, mostly because narcotics have yet to go from the black light of awarding criminality and cartels at the paid-for risk of the consumer and the sacrificed, taxable proceeds of public benefit to the red light of regulated, taxed areas of safe use, marijuana is/was a gateway to an escalating endangerment of *associations*.

To get my marijuana fix for as low a cost as possible back then, in my mid-twenties, and also because I sometimes dabbled in its distribution in the early days of 'medical marijuana,' when you'd see a specialist who'd secretly urge you to come up with *any* seemingly plausible justification for the prescription, else he'd risk losing the $200 that went with the writing of said prescription, and when grams of the best product sold for $20 a pop, and the economics of the business essentially empowered the criminal element (again, I'll resist the temptation to get into why the black markets should be red-marketed for the protection of everyone, and for the revenue given over to the public good, instead of going to the hoodlums)... back then I befriended a couple of growers, and the common arrangement was, and often still is, one of paying stoners to trim in exchange for some portion of their trimmings. And when I say 'trim,' to those not down on the lingo, I mean using a pair of small, sharp shears to turn the plant into the crystal-laden, sticky buds that are then dried and distributed as the 'flower' once profitable enough to finance legions of criminals under the narcotics scheduling lie.

One of said growers was a *true* thug. The other of these growers was another friend from high school, one of my best receivers when I was the varsity quarterback (I still have football dreams; I could've been so much better), and who, before this night, and the invitation that would follow, I remembered most for his propensity to suffer dislocated shoulders during practice and games. I thought it was the most gruesome thing imaginable, excepting that dislocated knee and the bending of the leg in the wrong direction that one time (another player, during practice). But this friend of mine was so used to suffering these dislocated shoulders that he'd just pop them back into place and be back on the field five minutes later. And like the *Scarface* wanna be I mentioned before, who nevertheless really did embody certain elements of that iconic, some may say *infamous* character (surely no character in film history has had a greater impact on cocaine addiction and drug-related homicides; but don't get me wrong, Pacino is one of the best actors of all time), this friend of mine was a type of sidekick to an individual as amoral as Scarface himself. When they advanced me a quarter pound of their product and I was unable to sell it quickly, leading to a confession to and an offer of rescue from my mother, the resulting peril would propel me into PTSD-induced psychosis.

My mom wrote me a check for what I owed this person, who, to this day, was, I swear, the closest thing to pure evil I've ever felt the presence of. I went to this psychopath's (I don't use that term lightly) house the night she gave me the check, a home I'd never been to before, with a big, shadowy backyard overhanging with mature trees, and centered around a chipping-green-paint shed; a backyard

I'll never forget, for I was almost buried there. Handing this guy, Aaron, the check from my mom turned out to be a mistake. I just wanted to clear my debt, because I sensed he wasn't someone to trifle with, and would suffer little compunction in hurting me. And I couldn't have been more right. For handing him the check from my mother that night, I realized in hindsight, was a type of 'tell' that I feared him, and this fear made him paranoid, which made him dangerous. He started wondering *why*, exactly, I was afraid of him? Afraid enough to 'borrow' the money from my mom, rather than do what most distributors in my then position do: gradually pay it off through their distribution.

Aaron thought I knew something that imperiled him. Or perhaps he thought that I was an actual informant. He tested me that entire night, always standing between me and the door. He talked about having done time for attempted murder, looking at my face when he said it in such a way as to read my reaction; to discern whether I knew about it or not. The fact that it was clear to him that I *wasn't* surprised that he'd served time for attempted murder (for his character, or lack thereof, was also clear) didn't bode well for me. I remember my friend widening his eyes at me when Aaron wasn't looking, and putting his index finger over his lips, enacting the 'shhhh!,' and I realized then that I was in danger, and had imperiled myself by what I was doing and saying. We were playing darts at one point, and I had the distinct, instinctive sense that I shouldn't turn my back on them, for they might kill me. I think they noticed this, and my death grew more imminent. I expressed the desire to leave *many* times after that, but they always blocked me, pretending like they *weren't* blocking me at the same time, and I knew that, had I pressed the matter, had I panicked and tried to flee, they would've killed me then and there. It's near impossible for me to describe what transpired the rest of that night, for my psyche essentially fractured for the sake of my survival.

Something deep inside me took over; something that refused to die. I experienced a type of psychological leap, like information was given to me that would preserve me, but that wasn't coming *from* me; like God wanted me to live. After Aaron showing me his gun, after forcing me in the car to drive and pick up cocaine, Aaron never letting me more than an arm's length from him, after implications that the backyard would be an easy place to put a body, and that, perhaps, I wouldn't be the first... when the walls were closing in the thought jumped into my head and I said something about a *listening device*. I implied that the necklace I was wearing could hear. Now, you might think that this would be the last straw, bringing my life to an end, but that wasn't the case. Somehow I knew that if I could plant even a sliver of a doubt in his mind that he *wouldn't* get away with killing me, for the evidence was being recorded as we spoke, that he wouldn't go through with it. But before that successful salvation of my life would be ratified, so to speak, I'd take another psychological leap.

There's something so animalistically resonant about keeping the threat in one's field of vision. Everyone instinctively knows not to turn their backs on the threat. I sincerely empathize with women and the disparity of their strength in relation to men on this front; on the fact that people (if you're generous enough to apply such a word) like Aaron are out there. God, the horrible things I heard him say about women, including his girlfriend, and the stripper he wanted to go see... But the turning the back thing... I couldn't do it when we were playing darts, and that 'tell' of my awareness of the danger I was in was almost the final straw for me, I'd sensed. But the same phenomenon came into even more terrifying focus near the end of the ordeal, when my friend, Matt, went to bed in a bedroom whilst I was forced to sleep on the floor not far from where Aaron lay on the couch, gun in hand. Just like the preceding leap hours before, the invention of the listening device, it entered into me that I had to prove to him that I wasn't a threat, despite being truly terrified. I lay for almost an hour facing him, pretending to be asleep. It was, ironically, only when I found a level of courage that most never feel, and turned over on the floor, showing him my back, that I relieved him of his paranoia and saved myself. When I finally walked out the door the next morning, shortly after Aaron left, having not slept a wink, my entire body was quaking. PTSD soon swept over me.

I recall that just before going over to that house I watched *Alpha Dog* at the *Airport Theatre* (not far from my mother's house, and across from the *Hilton Airport Hotel*), a film centered around the abduction and murder of a young man in order to satisfy a drug debt, and that immediately after escaping my plight, as my PTSD was taking hold and my mania was ramping up, I was realizing the irony of that viewing, and soon considering it to have been a signaling warning that I'd failed to recognize in the moment. I'll forever associate that film with that particular trauma (and with Sharon Stone's masterful performance in playing the inconsolably-bereaved mother in the interview at the end, which was so good that, at the time, I thought it was an interview of the actual mom of the slain boy that the film is based upon). As soon as I quietly crept out of that house after that sleepless night, momentarily saved, my psyche started to reset itself around the trauma, giving me insight into a future of working at the CRC and seeing similar psychological resets stamped into its residents' histories.

For weeks thereafter I was a different person. After making reports to the police, and seeing them parked out front of our house on and off for a few days, and my mom being embarrassed that "the police had to come to the house," my mind wasn't my own. I wrote in gibberish; ideas and codes that only made sense to me, scrawled enigmatically across countless pages, then printed in rainbows of different colors from my home printer, like it was in a code that only *I* could decipher, because I was the only one brilliant enough to do so. When I looked at this writing later, I suffered cognitive dissonance. *This* came from me? And I had energy *all the time*; too much of it. I would hike for hours, or jog for miles, and return home still feeling wired, ready to go out again. At one point I went to the *Banned & Ignoble* in downtown Santa Rosa and soon had the manager visiting me at my upstairs reading table because, in my mania, I'd walked around the store for an hour, feeling as though *everything* was interesting, collecting books and stacking them into a mountain upon the table.

A couple weeks later my family, out of concern, and whom I was afraid of by then (I'll never forget the look on my brother's face when he saw that I was afraid of him and my mother when they entered my room – a mix of heartbreak and terror), because I feared that they wanted to have me committed, compelled me to see the aforementioned psychiatrist, who wanted to make me one of his patients on the spot, even though I was coming out of my mania by then. It lasted about a month in total. If I'd signed the paper giving him permission to treat me as his patient and talk to my parents about "my illness," I would've been officially diagnosed then and there, and the stigma would've stuck; a stigma that, like being 'a convict,' grossly inhibits at best, outright denies at worst, most opportunities in life. But my instinct told me not to. I didn't sign it, and I never saw him again. I'm thus compelled to wonder: for all the good that he and his ilk do, what does his failed coercion of me say about the psychiatric profession and all the unnecessary costs it forces the disadvantaged to pay in order to fit the profitability paradigm? For I had the mind and strength to refuse such payment where most others surely capitulate.

Around the same time this high school friend of mine, Matt (a different Matt than the two I speak briefly of later herein), invited me to a party on the pretext of missing me and wanting to hang out. But he wasn't the 'missing me' type. The intuition entered my mind that he was inviting me into a trap. I had the inescapable feeling that Aaron would be wherever he was attempting to bait me to go. Needless to say I didn't go, and for a long time thereafter I went through a psychological cycle that I can only relate to the stages of grief. I was afraid for a while, but eventually found a way to rationalize myself out of my fear, as the palpable sense of the terror slowly receded, and eventually delivered me to anger, even fury. I wanted revenge. *Badly*.

In my own life I can only really compare that feeling to what happened to me in my employment *after* the CRC, at the bookstore in Bend, precipitating the project *Holier Than Thou*. I'll admit that I fantasied about burning that bookstore to the ground *many* times, just as I fantasized about going all *Scarface* on my would-be killers, seeing the shock on their faces before unloading my pistol in those same faces, burying their bodies in the big, dark backyard. For the wronged, revenge is but a side-effect of the pursuit of justice. Of course, for me that revenge doesn't *actually* look like setting the bookstore aflame, or getting CRC coworkers Lenny or James fired for their reprobation (more on that later). What it *actually* looks like is burning the bookstore up from within with the sales of, say, a rather incendiary memoir, the colluding perpetrators forced to sell it. And, when it comes to the less searing psychological scars taken from the CRC, it looks like exposing the likeness of Linda, Lenny and James in a manner which might prevent even *one* of their like from being hired into the mental health treatment world in the future, for those such as Cain are sitting right on the precipice, and can't handle the shoves that these workers are bound to give. Now that I think of it, Cain represents another mortal fright. But before I get to that, let me back up to his CRC arrival.

Adjacent to the nurse's station, just behind and to the left of The Bridge, at one end of the Day Room, is the Media Room. A small room of fifteen by ten feet, with soiled furniture and a TV suspended in the far corner, it's where some of the shift change meetings are held; where the Recovery Specialists and shift-leading counselors can keep their eyes on the residents meandering in and out of the communal spaces, grumbling that another resident has already taken control of the main TV, the waking hope of watching morning cartoons having been dashed by another half-awake residents' watching something barely worth glancing at, near to where, still rubbing their eyes, they begrudgingly oblige the nurses with the intake of their morning meds (in my case, at least, when the meetings were at 7am, at the transition from the NOC shift to the AM shift), and where some ask about breakfast, hoping Mindy, the cantankerous, gruff, old-fashioned housekeeper and sometime cook, has prepared one of her absurdly greasy morning meals of factory eggs, cheap cheese and nitrate-laden processed meat. It was in this Media Room, door closed in the wee hours of the night to keep from waking the other residents, of course, that I got to know Cain. Assuming, of course, that you can really know anyone, especially when they're as hyper-manic as he was then.

Is the manic Cain the real Cain, or is the real one he who, for fear of a lifetime of institutionalization, snapped himself out of his mania, as I had after escaping my own death a decade or so before, just before the psychiatrist imposed a similar threat of a lifetime of stigmatization coupled with minimized opportunity and self-esteem? The words of R&B-esque rap artist *The Weeknd* come to mind (no, that's not a misspelling, but the common 'cool guy' technique of butchering the English language to demonstrate that they're too cool to give a fuck about proper spelling), he having risen to popularity when I was at the CRC: "When I'm fucked up, that's the real me." So true, it seems to me.

In vino veritas. In wine there's truth. For it, arguably like many other substances, removes the nervous inhibitions blocking the expression of true, underlying sentiment and instinctive awareness. Are manic expressions inherently false? Certainly not. Just another form of truth, I say, even as the majority would dismiss them as 'the ravings of a lunatic,' in the common, prejudicial parlance. Cain raved, certainly, and was 'unhinged,' still borderline psychotic, definitely. *But untrue? Inherently false? Certainly not.* No, he was tapping into something that most people never know; some endlessly-unfurling form of twisted truth buried somewhere beneath his sounder mind, bound between his entirely-unhindered, fully-unhinged, psychosis-associated intertwining of addled psyche and unrestricted imagination.

I can't recall even a tenth of what he told me that night, often shouting, expressing himself in a rapidity and with a force that I'm quite certain would have driven most, if not all, other Recovery Specialists from the room, seeking support from others, including possible chemical sedation. Whatever faults I may've had in my role at the CRC, I know I was better than most at a great many things, including a certain confluence of curiosity, patience and willingness to listen. And my God did I listen in those hours. What did he say? Or, maybe I should say, what was violently ejected from his being, from a mind brimming with such conception that it would overwhelm and frighten the vast majority?

Well, there was a tale of 'Spirit Lake,' once set atop Mt. St. Helen, trapping his spirit; of being sucked down and intermixing with the buried blood and bones of ancient ancestral natives, and exploding out upon its famous eruption in biblically-renewed form. There was an assertion of being Alfred Hitchcock in a past life, and endless tales of how and why he came up with the stories that he did.

And there was a retelling of everything that had landed him in his position at that time. Of the police arriving at his rural property in the Prineville area, of his making connections with their names on a deep level of prophetic meaning, of their finding evidence that he had killed and eaten his dogs, some of them puppies, which they, of course, misunderstood. It wasn't cruelty, he insists. It was a ritualistic cleansing of sickened beings. These discoveries coming after law enforcement sought him for having set fire to the aforementioned historic structure, a blaze that began in the basement where the witch had dwelled, his having stood testament to a battle between good and evil intrinsically tied to the white settlers' theft of the lands and desecrated remains of his native brethren, all of the dishonor and foul energy thereby trapped therein, ending in his forcing the spirit of the witch into hell and the release of the spirits of his brethren in the fiery cleansing of white man's evil. Did I mention that Cain is as white as can be?

The association with Native Americans, the continually demonstrated delusion of his being of the same blood, reflects, I believe, a feeling that I and *many* others share, and which was innate to my writing *Old Blood*: he, *we*, would rather identify with the nature-revering natives than the white race that conquers and enslaves and oppresses everything it touches. I've done this myself, in my self-identifying more with my Greek heritage than my English heritage, associating the former with the philosophers and creators whom founded the best of western civilization, the latter with the corruption and imperialism that has since dominated that civilization. Cain's latching onto the Native American identity is, in other words, an example of 'appropriation,' something which the bullying, politically correct associate with evil and white entitlement, but which is actually nothing more than a biased, selective absorption of all the forces of history with which we're all continually exposed, especially in the era of globalization, turning everything into a melting pot from which we selectively feed. Modern culture is, in fact, *built* by appropriation, and so are our personal identities. They're not innate to you, but *crafted*. We're exposed to beliefs and practices that originated elsewhere, from some other people, and we appropriate those that make sense to us.

That said, he *did* marry a Native American woman. And sire offspring with her. And live with her on the Warm Springs Reservation about an hour north of Bend. That much I *can* verify. As can I verify the fact that much of the book I helped him publish pertaining to the events leading to his initial incarceration at the CRC is based at the Reservation, and upon his personal anecdotes folded into Native American lore. This highlights one of Cain's consistent 'personality traits:' there's always enough of a basis to what he says for most to at least think it *feasible*. And *that's* what empowers him, toying with the line set between possibility and probability, his favorite playground.

About three years after this witch burning ritual, and a year or so after his double-homicide, whilst 'level-headed,' on his weekly call to me from the Eastern Oregon Correctional Facility (after having been sentenced to life in prison for killing that young couple whom he worked and sexually experimented with two years after his release from the CRC), he would tell me how and why he'd first cracked. Per his report, it was the pressures of life, of his wife Katherine's demands for all the accoutrements of the well-provided-for existence, that had finally become too much for him. His story of his breakdown begins with the accumulation of these stresses, and all the pent up frustration that they produced, all of which eventually manifested as boiling-over anger. Ultimately, this accretion of pressurized emotions gave way to a series of strokes;

strokes that damaged his brain, especially the areas in and around his amygdala (which he says was confirmed later via CT scans), thereby drastically reducing his capacity for compassion and empathy. Early on, this produced synesthesia; the scrambling of sensory experiences, like 'seeing emotions,' in his case. For him, this meant *literally* seeing red for rage, blue for sorrow. At this point in his telling he offers me his translation of those experiences.

Similar to my own understanding of *everyone* carrying around the latent capacity for 'madness,' i.e. mental illness, he believes that everyone carries around the pure force of wrath within them. Most just learn how to keep it bottled up. After his series of strokes he popped-off and lost the cork, so to speak, and thereby gave himself over fully to what he calls "the universal power." When I ask him if this universal power is something that he was struggling against *before* losing control, he assures me that *everyone* does so. Referencing Mark Booth's *The Secret History of the World*, a book which I'd sent him, and which was recommended to me by the lost friend, Vince, mentioned later herein, Cain parallels the writer's assertions that the advance of human mind and culture has closed us off from the divine forces which were once *far* more prevalent in guiding our thought and action. We've lost our connection to the divine, he insists, and this struggle accounts for everything from the rise of the ego to modern man's desperately clutching to religion; desperately reaching for and attempting to hold onto the part of ourselves that we've lost to 'progress,' and are attempting to recapture.

But he doesn't believe in *God*, he tells me. That's not what he means by "universal power" and "divine force." When I press him for a meaning, he reflectively pauses before replying: "Picture personifying time. That's as close I can come to describing it." There's no good or evil involved, he insists, only *necessity*. This, in turn, reminds me a lot of Nietzsche's love for the Latin phrase "amor fati," or "love thy fate;" how fate is simply a form of necessity playing itself out. In Cain's telling, his own role in the collective fate of humanity was to be freed from everything that had kept him bottled up, his 'evolved mind' and all the expectations and pressures of modern life, and to eventually violently release them in giving over to the necessary march of this force of divine temporality. Through this atavistic reversion he became "rudimentarily animalistic," letting go of all conscious thought, releasing the illusion of free will that plagues individuals, thereby returning to man's hive mind.

By the time of his second sentencing, I was one of the few people who would still talk to him. You may scoff, but I feel like I'm providing a humanitarian service by doing so. He's already been judged and convicted, and is facing a lifetime of imprisonment, and is currently being held in isolation owing to certain family members of the slain couple, reputed members of a local gang with apparent contacts 'on the inside,' seeking vengeance. What good would my ostracizing and refusing to speak to him do at this point? I faced ridicule and attacks for doing so, including by a couple self-righteous former colleagues at the CRC, and for helping him print a book he'd written while at the CRC; a book related to the *arson*, not the double-homicide that had yet to occur. A book which, by the way, his mother, having learned of the book and acquiring my contact information through my website, texted me about on multiple occasions, threatening action against me if I didn't remove it from my site. Why? Not out of any concern for *him*, for she'd already washed her hands of him, but because it made her look like a bad parent; like she had something to do with what had become of him. I eventually had to block her. Deciding to self-righteously enact my condemnation through silent ostracization, like the *vast* majority who knew him, including everyone from his ex-wife and mother to every purported friend, didn't feel right.

But, you may be realizing, my thought patterns don't typically align with those of the majority. *I think for myself.* And often in terms, and within paradigms, and through the harnessing of deep spiritual instinct and insights, that I find near impossible to accurately convey. And those thoughts and feelings didn't dictate a turning up of my nose and turning away from him. In fact, I came to befriend a number of residents post-CRC. I even dated one former resident, briefly, before my drinking freaked her out. And I traveled to Portland with another, and still have an occasional drink and meal with him to this day. Why? Because they're *people first,* patients second, regardless of what most of the drone-esque former colleagues of mine say, sheepishly bowing to liability-fear-and-profit-protection-based corporate policy as though it reflects some absolute, righteous truth. People are so easy to train, for the most part; so easy to condition and peer pressure and shame into conforming obedience. *It's pathetic.* And it explains, sadly, far too much of all that which prevents progress, including the right-wing parroting of the paradigms of, and building their values around, the cross-sectional history of Empire and its aristocracy, and the disturbingly successful propaganda innate to everything from Naziism to the Bible. But anyway, back to the CRC and Cain's life imprisonment.

As mentioned earlier, one of the things that Linda hated about me the most was my resistance to the 'record and report everything' manner of mental illness 'treatment;' that I didn't record and report absolutely everything that the residents said to me, as protocol dictated. The reason is simple: I was keenly aware of the fact that the residents guarded against any form of judgment which might further reduce their self-esteem and independent volition; anything which might worsen their psychological and living circumstances. Not only that, but as I speak of several times herein, the only way I believe that one can play an effective role in the healing of another is through building a level bridge between you and them, over which they may unburden themselves of the dis-ease leading to disease.

And this bridge is blocked at the least, if not burned down permanently, as soon as they feel like they can't tell you the unrestricted truth of themselves without some sort of negative repercussion. My perception of this self-protection of the residents, and the fact that I was *always* the most effective as a psychological healer when I was listening to someone on equal footing, the bridge between us complete and unobstructed, and the fact that most of the Recovery Specialists were ineffective because they were perpetually rebounding off of a boundary-laden bridge set between unlevel spaces, with themselves standing taller on one side, speaking down to the un-advancing resident... it all dictated a *different* approach than the one Linda kept futilely trying to hammer into me. That said, there were a few times, and one in particular, where, in retrospect, I think it might've been better to have recorded the incident.

Early in his stay at the CRC, shortly after the arrest, and not long after his manic purge in the Media Room recently described herein, I was with Cain in the counselor's office, which we Recovery Specialists sometimes used, such as when the main computers at The Bridge were occupied, or when we needed privacy for the sake of the resident confiding confidential information. I can't recall exactly what drew us into the room that night, but it was just the two of us therein. And on one of the therapists' shelves was an object that probably shouldn't have been there, were all safeguards in place: a large, round obsidian stone, the size of a small basketball. It must've weighed thirty pounds, at least. And it happened in the blink of an eye. While I was looking at something on one of the computers he grabbed it off the shelf and mockingly bashed me over the head with it, stopping so close to my skull that I felt it touch the tips of my hairs. *That could've been my end.*

From his prison cell years later, the automated voice sporadically cutting in to inform us he has "one minute remaining" before he promptly calls me back, he informs me that, despite serving life for murdering two people, that he's actually killed *eighteen* people, most of their flesh fed to his dogs, twice fed to his ex-wife and her friends. He also claims to have smuggled the flesh of one of his human victims into the CRC in the guise of an ice cream container and cooked it into the communal dinner on one of my days off, as the residents were often involved in meal preparations, making it a rather simple task. And he speaks of how easy it is to get away with murder, and that he was only caught for killing the young couple because he *wanted* to be. But don't believe these grandly grotesque claims, dear reader. It's my firm belief, as one who has heard him wax demonic countless times, that he's merely playing a persona; that he's entertaining himself in a way that most anyone else would consider verboten, but which pleases him in the sense of matching what others would be eager to believe about him, in the same way that we all, to one degree or another, find ourselves playing a role when enough others attempt to force it onto us, believing things about ourselves, and acting the part, perceived by others.

I tell him he's full of shit, and that he's but playing a part, and, furthermore, likely taking advantage of the fact that, as the monotone voice of the facility intones at the beginning of our conversation, "this call will be monitored and recorded." It's attention seeking behavior to stave off boredom, in other words, while also supplying an ego boost in the bolstering of the persona, a characteristic of which is to believe he's outfoxing everyone around him.

I tell him he likely imagines that he'll receive extra attention from law enforcement for making such claims, and is getting off on the idea of their listening intently for any information that may lead to closing old homicide cases, hoping they'll be foolish enough to visit him in person, and that he can experience the power trip of having them chasing their tails over murders that never actually happened. I can tell from his reaction to this that I'm right. I wonder if, when I challenge him this way, he behind bars, my sitting safely in my apartment 260 miles away, if he ever regrets not having made me supposed victim #19.

He still talks about his mock murder of me today, when he calls me from his prison cell. He assures me that he didn't *want* to kill me, or even harm me. It wasn't *that* which compelled the mock murder. Rather, it was his having then given himself over to "the universal power." The "rudimentary animal" was what wanted to kill me. And he says that he almost wasn't able to stop himself. Of course, these weren't his explanations back when it happened. Honestly, I was kind of a dumb animal about it; like a deer in the crosshairs that never even knew that he was in the crosshairs. I remember that when it had happened, that I'd laughed it off as though he was kidding, even though, on some level, it creeped me out that he'd even be instinctively urged to such an action. And no, I didn't record the incident. And I can't help but wonder if my having not recorded it, and, later, after his release from the CRC, if my having criticized his character when he was being a dick to me during a drunk phone call, makes me slightly responsible for the deaths of that couple. Perhaps if I'd been the dutiful employee, or if I'd been more self-secure and less critical of him, there'd be no "Prophet of Death."

03

HOW A HOLY MARY WAS MADE

I wish I'd had more time, listening to you speak your mind. I've been thinking about her, every day, on my mind in an atypical way. Are you a lifeforce?

-   From "By and By," by Caamp

Thank God for the law that says that in-resident mental health institutions are required to have at least three staff members on duty, including a nurse, at all times. I'm more indebted to that law, and to whatever stars aligned to seat Jess next to me, making us a paired captive audience, than any other blessing ever bestowed upon my life. For it was these stars, as they intersected with that law, and with all the pain, passion, beauty and intelligence that made Jess the most wonderful of young women that she is, that I owe for the most powerful series of emotions I've felt my entire life, still with me today. Nothing else comes close.

Normally a guy saying "she's got a great personality" means that he's unattracted to her, but is trying to be kind and find something positive to say about her. With Jess it's different. On the surface, in pictures and online profiles, she's not *bad* looking, but isn't likely to provoke the guys to yell "dammmmnnn!" It sounds cliché, but she has a beauty that radiates far more from within than from without, and isn't so much photogenic as *ardency*-genic. For, in person, with those images enlivened by her personality, she becomes absolutely *gorgeous*; the most endearing, beautiful young woman that one could ever hope to know. For I swear to you, dear reader, that I'd sooner take Jess for my own than the most breathtaking of beauties known to the human race! And that, in the endless absence of that greatest of treasures, it's now the requirement of my continued breath only that I know that she's out there in the world somewhere, continuing to draw breath herself.

The combination of warmth, sincerity, playfulness and persistent well-meaning intention inherent to her presence makes you ache, and feel the need to cultivate more of the same within yourself. It's like you become a better person when you're around her out of necessity, as not to try to pull yourself up closer to her level is unendurable for a good person, and can only make you feel unworthy of being around her. When you're within her radius it feels as if she was born to purify you; like she embodies the baptism, washing you clean and purifying you through her presence. Perhaps this is why her ex didn't want to have sex with her, and compared her to the Virgin Mary, imagining her at the center of his religion; the religion that she inspired him to invent, in his insanity. I think her eyes alone are enough to drive any man insane whom stares into them for long, as I did; as though she's some form of the Medusa, turning the gazer not into stone, but clay, ready and waiting to be molded into whatever she wills.

Jess was born and raised in Coos Bay, on the southwestern coast of Oregon. Many of those hailing from the area call it simply 'The Bay Area,' triggering a burst of pride from someone like me, raised near the California Bay Area. *The Bay Area, please*! Ya'll are small time next to the *real* Bay Area! Similar to my own upbringing in Fort Bragg, California, the Coos Bay region was once a thriving blue collar town replete with well-paying careers in fishing and logging. Alas, also like Fort Bragg, it fell on hard times following shifts in the economies of both industries, with most of the best-paying jobs drying up. This had a cascading socioeconomic impact, as it's bound to, reducing property values, increasing unemployment and inviting an influx in the supply of cheap narcotics to sell to those finding it hard to cope with their downtrodden lives. Eventually it would be called "The Meth Capital of Oregon."

Jess's mother was herself a methamphetamine addict, and it eventually led to her death. There's no way to describe the extent to which this addiction, and its financial and social ramifications, penetrated into Jess's young, developing psyche, forever coloring her outlook. There's a cruel repeating pattern within the socio-spheres of neglect, deprivation and abuse. Whether it's self-abuse or abuse of others, those raising children under such circumstances imprint a type of pattern upon the impressionable young mind. It takes a very strong person to extricate themselves from that pattern; to, out of strength and love for one's self, one's partner and one's future children and life, shout "No more!," and leave that world as far behind as possible. Jess is just such a person. So is her now husband, Brady.

Out of guilt and prideful insecurity, those attributes of the wobbly ego, her mother could never admit what she'd done to Jess in her youth. The addicts that would frequent their unstable homes. The boyfriends that would treat Jess like a nuisance. All the time spent not being able to take anything for granted, even the place they called home. How likely it seemed that, at any moment, that home could be taken away. The cops could come bursting through the door and find the cocaine and meth that her mother and boyfriend had hidden onsite, and that would be the end.

There was one particular time period that, though she was young, Jess remembers well. One of her mother's especially troubled, addicted boyfriends was more psychologically and sometimes physically abusive than the others. He'd manipulate her mother to join forces with him in his emotional and psychological abuse of her. They'd condition her as to what to say if the police arrived, or if a schoolteacher or counselor were to question her as to her missed time at school, or the bruises she carried, being consistently, violently 'moved out of the way,' or the trouble she had controlling her resultant anxiety and occasional fits intermixing sorrow and anger. He locked her in the closet once when she was insufficiently compliant. And every day, before school, she was interrogated: How will you react to this? To that? And upon her return the interrogation would resume. What did you say? Are you sure?! You know what will happen to you if they call here, right? If they come here, you're not going to like the outcome! It'll just hurt your mom! Throughout the rest of her time at school she'd get cold sweats approaching campus, and still got them when I knew her, when she'd enter COCC. When she'd approach the grounds, when she'd take her seat and survey the other students, when the teachers approached to pass out assignments. Will they question you?, the psychological wounds inquired.

Eventually Jess would be diagnosed with an anxiety disorder, lending credence to the belief held by many within the mental health world that mental illness is largely a matter of some form of broken nurture thence breaking nature. Numerous times whilst sitting beside me at the CRC, Jess would be brought to tears from interactions with her mother via text or social media messaging apps. It would be two or three in the morning, and she'd receive strings of semi-coherent text messages; clear indications that her mother was using methamphetamine. She'd always deny it, of course, just like she'd deny that Jess was ever subject to any form of psychological or physical abuse as a result of her lifestyle and boyfriends, or as a direct result of her inability to hold down a job, or a home.

For many people growing up, 'camping' can be an incredible, positive experience filled with the wonder of nature, the sense of adventure and the irreplaceability of 'getting away.' Canoe rides on the lakes, hikes into the mountains, hot dogs and smores and ghost stories in the dusk under the swaying, towering trees reflecting the flickering light of the warming campfire. When it becomes a substitute for a safe, secure home, however, 'camping' takes on a very different meaning, turning a great potential positive into a euphemism for an equally potent negative.

'Camping' is underdevelopment. Hiding homelessness under the guise of constant camping trips was a part of Jess's upbringing; a part of the cycle that must cease. And, as with most cases, in Jess's family that cycle started before her, and came from deeper, darker depths. While it's near impossible to trace a cycle of abuse and deprivation to its root, from where it sprouted and first shot its suffocating vines up and through and around, squeezing every limb of the family tree, and while its perpetuation by victims turned into perpetrators can't be merely excused and accepted, sexually abusing a child places a 'pox upon the house' that's near impossible to eradicate, carried forward by the victim throughout their lives. Her mother carried this, through addiction, to death.

Jess spoke of the horror of finding out that her mother had been sexually abused by her grandfather for years similar to how one might speak of the ghost stories around the aforementioned campfires. Like it was a horror she could scarcely believe, and didn't *want* to, for already had she absorbed her share of such psychological destructions. And that horror turned into anger toward her grandmother, for surely she *must* have known about it. She loved her grandmother more than anyone, and spoke of her reverently all the way until her death (which I found out about through *Facebook* posts after Jess had left the

CRC), even as the question persisted: How could she permit such an evil? Versions of such a question plagued Jess. How could her mother, to the day of *her* death, deny what had happened to Jess herself, adding the ugliest insult to injury by essentially gaslighting her about the abuses she delivered upon her, else failed to fight against?

My answer: *the insecure ego*. In fact, nothing illuminates the motive of human action more than the ego. Her mom's already minimized self-esteem at living an impoverished life of intermittent homelessness, and everything that led to her hollowed-out adulthood, the spreading neglects and abuses of her own childhood that sought and latched onto the sickening cycle through her ravaged psyche, simply couldn't allow for any more reduction in self-esteem by admitting her own part in Jess's precarious upbringing. Not many in her mother's position can find the strength to say: "Sorry, my love, for needing you to become *my* mother."

As a continuation of this theme of the minimized ego defending any vestige of pride it yet clings to, and becoming a master of justification, in overlap with the life of a drug addict, Jess's mother took Jess's desire to study social work and help children in need, and those living in states of constant fear, abuse and neglect, as a judgment of *her*, and everything that she refused to admit to doing, or at least being complicit to. By her experience and immense natural capacity for empathy, Jess became a further persecutor of her mother's pride by following what she'd learned towards her calling, especially the need of the abused and neglected youth for advocates such as her. To this day I've never met anyone whom I believe, by the combination of her background and the qualities of her heart and mind, to possess a greater ability to help disadvantaged families. It's a silver lining *very* hard earned.

Jess's *father* is a long-haul truck driver. Whilst once fond of drugs and alcohol himself, he was, unlike Jess's mother, able to escape the hard drugs, even as the alcohol remains a crutch, as it is for *many* of us. While her mother and father are *logistically* split, and while her death during COVID mooted the point, he never bothered seeking a divorce, as he "doesn't believe in divorce," and yet also worried about being with another woman "out of wedlock," a seeming contradiction, and yet another reminder, to me at least, of the befuddlement of Christian conditioning, especially amongst the uneducated constituting the majority of its constituents. Since unofficially breaking ties with her mother, he's entered into a long-term, stable relationship with a woman whom had supplanted Jess's recently deceased, biological mother in many ways *long* before her death, including in terms of her worry and support. And yet Jess harbors ongoing resentment of her father's mate in a manner which I'm all too familiar with.

That is, Jess and her father are close. So much so that they're more like best friends than the conventional 'father and daughter,' such that he treats her like a confidant, telling her things he doesn't even tell his mate, likely owing to Jess's intellect and capacity for empathy. This, in turn, creates a constant tension between Jess and her unofficial 'stepmother,' whom, thereby threatened, looks upon their relationship with jealousy and suspicion, to a degree that she actually once told her father that his relationship with Jess was "inappropriate." When word of this reached Jess, it created a deep resentment which she still harbors, and which prevents her 'stepmother' from stepping into Jess's inner circle, a circle which, dear reader, you no doubt already know that I think the most radiant of radiuses.

I'll never forget the way Jess spoke of those "in my life," the purely emotive force of the expression passing into me in such a way where, even today, some five years later, I'm aggrieved at no longer being inside that warming sphere. I was unceremoniously, blithely booted after she left our shared shift, rendering her use of the phrase 'our friendship' mostly false. And it should go without saying that being repelled from the radius of the only woman I've ever loved created some serious psychological wreckage. *Within* that radius stands her half-sister, begotten by her father and her 'stepmother.' As close to her as she is to her father, Jess's relationship with her half-sister is plagued much the way as it is with her 'stepmother.' That is, Jess has been forced into a continuously tumultuous position of attempting to balance her own development and self-protections (which, reading this book, you'll find to be *well* developed; *over*-developed, from my prejudicial perspective) against her connection with her half-sister.

Throughout their time in school, and, in many ways continuing to this day, they're in a constant competition, as many siblings are, for academic, athletic and professional reward and recognition. But that's not the worst of it. The worst of it is that her half-sister has drug addictions and other "risky habits" paralleling her biological mother, putting Jess in the sticky, tricky position of constantly having to decide between 'tough love,' like communicating her struggles to her father and 'stepmother,' and being the close, compassionate friend that permits her her freedom. As tough as that sounds to me, her relationship with her biological brother actually seems much more difficult.

I *try* to remain on the progressive side of things, dear reader, I truly do. And that often means going against what popularly *stands* for progress. As reflected throughout this book, I *vehemently* believe that political correctness has run amok in this country, and enforces its will in ways presented as progressive, even when they're often not. Sometimes this means that tradition is truth, and that the pretense of progress is just that: a *pretense*. And, I'm sorry, but sex changes often fall within this category. Hey, you can think of yourself any way you wish, and I would never deny you any rights, protections, privileges or opportunities because of how you wish to identify. At the same time I retain my own right to use my own pronouns, and I believe in nature, and think that gender isn't some superficial, skin-deep thing. Yes, there may be rare cases where biological mishap produces a 'woman trapped in a man's body,' but I also know from certain experiences and viewings and readings of the testimony of others that the confusion and depression of still-developing minds can lead to identity crises. Irreversible surgeries can result.

A friend of mine on *Instagram* once confided in me that a 'boob job' she'd had in her insecure youth, when she was in her twenties, resulted in suicidal ideation. It's not just that it doesn't look or feel right (your bodies are yours to determine, but *please*, ladies, leave nature in place), it's that the implanted material, which was sold to her as 'inert,' has since been determined to be toxic. She's seen countless doctors seeking ways to mitigate the resultant effects. One of her messages to me: "It took years of being bedridden before I found out it was the implants. By then my gut and hormones were destroyed. I was eventually able to get rid of the persistent brain fog and joint pain and fatigue, but I still have chronic pain in my vagina. Any virus I contract is experienced far more severely than with most people. I can't even eat citrus without everything burning."

Jess's brother took a step far beyond this, one that you've likely already guessed: he's now her *sister*. And, again, it's your body, but it's clear from what she told me that he was severely depressed and struggling with his identity when he made the decision. So what happens down the road when he realizes that road has been paved over, and there's nowhere to make a U-turn? Adding insult to the horrendous injury (in my mind, at least): he's not the only one in that car. Jess says that, post-operation, his two kids feel like they've lost their father. Similar to Jess's role reversal with her mother before her death, and in some ways to her relationship with her father, and speaking, as a general insight, to the long-term psychological effects of growing up in an unstable environment in which various threats and abuses linger around every corner, the interpersonal ties binding her whole family together are frayed, to say the least. Jess fears that she and her now husband, Brady, will be forced to raise those kids, as their flight from her now *sister's* house seems an inevitability. And so it is that Jess's past stalks her future, and not just in terms of her family, but in terms of romance as well.

For, while Jess would, again, eventually lose her mother during the COVID epidemic, with her now husband, Brady, having lost his as well (the shared understanding of trauma that may tie them together more than anything else), Jess's traumas would continue, even after she'd gained the young adulthood that allowed her to free herself from being dependent upon the abusive and irresponsible. Many a night of our shared shifts were filled with tales of how her most serious relationship *before* Brady was with a highly intelligent, artistic young man who was both manipulative and borderline schizophrenic, like his mother.

And while most might be disposed to paint that ex, also named Nick, like yours truly (a 'coincidence' that, you'll see, possesses the type of depth that makes those like me scoff at the word), as a type of villain, or at least a perpetrator, in Jess's story, I can't help but feel for him, and identify with his position. In fact, the extent to which I reminded her of him frightened Jess. I saw it in her eyes when she spoke with me sometimes, especially when I'd theologically theorize; flashbacks paired with flashes of recognizing the past in the present. Like him, I'm a contemplative person, and can be very emotional and imaginative. And, as recently related, I, myself, had a short-lived psychotic break once, after a night being held captive sent me into a PTSD-triggered manic tailspin.

Speaking of my mental health, and the critical question of whether or not my, or *anyone's*, state of mental health should be considered a 'disorder' deserving of pharmacological correction, you may've already noticed that all of my paragraphs in this book are perfect monolithic blocks. They're justified, in a sense, and not by *Microsoft Word*. Rather, it's a reflection of my undiagnosed OCPD (which is different from OCD) that I need my paragraphs to present as well as possible upon the page. That inborn need has since become a type of ongoing spatial awareness exercise in which I match what I'm writing to the space of the paragraph, which itself means vacillating between concision and verbosity, pulling up on the lingual reins else letting the horse run free to fill the next, lower line, so to speak. And I honestly don't think that the quality of the writing in any way suffers because of it, speaking to the fact that there are endless ways to skin a cat; that you can accurately express the same idea, story or sentiment innumerable ways, even as concision tends to be best.

And in case you're wondering, OCPD is defined as "a personality disorder that causes an obsession with order, perfectionism, control and specific ways of doing things," and is considered to be innate to the personality, so deeply ingrained as to be persistently inseparable from the person, whereas OCD is "marked by recurrent, intrusive, unwanted thoughts and repetitive behaviors" and tends to symptomatically fluctuate relative to the stress and anxiety of the sufferer. But here's the part that bothers me: *I like my OCPD.* A counselor at the CRC suggested that I suffer from it, to some degree, and the aforementioned list of symptoms suggests that this is so, as I've exhibited such behavior for as long as I can remember. I often recall how my younger brother would tease me about it, coming into my room and seemingly innocently setting the books and CD's and other items on my shelves slightly askew, knowing that I'd be compulsively compelled to put them all back at perfect right angles, everything perpendicularly oriented and in its right place. But let me say this: calling it a personality *disorder* I find to be both insulting and incorrect. In fact, I joke that it's more like a *super*-order.

Calling it a disorder and suggesting that it be 'treated' with pharmacology reflects both my contempt for our overmedicated modern health paradigm of treatment in America (one that just happens to make Big Pharma filthy rich directly, and doctors and psychiatrists dirty rich indirectly), as well as my disdain for conventional society's need for everyone to fit some arbitrary norm, for the sake of the conforming comfort of the 'average individual.' You see this play out in consistently disturbing ways in borderline cases in the mental health world, as reflected in the aforementioned anecdote from my past: the individual in question isn't necessarily unable to function in society (the inability to function being the barometer of mental illness, especially when it leads to their endangerment, or the endangerment of those with whom they come into contact), they just have more internal stress and struggle to fit the expected mold more than most. Alas, this is often a reflection of their *gifts* more than anything; of what sets them apart in ways making them both 'abnormal' and uniquely capable of doing and creating what others can't.

And rather than supporting them and their gifts, finding ways for them to contribute to the world which might not be a part of the statistical average contribution, the societal reflex, spurred by Big Pharma and conventional medicine, is to chemically 'correct their abnormality,' acting like they're some sort of deviant (which, in a sense, they are; they *deviate* from the norm, which is, in my opinion, very often a good thing, even as these 'deviants' make *others* uncomfortable, the so-called 'normies,' and even as the word 'deviant' is rife with negative connotations reflecting society's need for conformity). It's like society, especially its conventional health practitioners, are compelled to drug everyone into killing what makes them unique whilst retaining their ability to be good, obedient little consumers and producers. The irony, of course, is that such forced conformity, and the overvaluation of 'normality,' is the common critique historically used by conservative interests to condition us against *communism*, and even socialism.

The truth, of course, for those few of you, dear readers, ready to receive it, is that a society can be backed by socialistic virtues whilst leaving *plenty* of room for individual uniqueness, just as a society can be run by a system of laissez faire capitalism that depends upon the majority of the population conforming to the drone-like consumer/producer paradigm of existence, even if, in a nod to Huxley's *Brave New World*, that dependency is facilitated by narcotics, loveless sex and other meaningless sensory gratifications. Not to mention the fact that, in the case of my OCPD, it's as much a strength as a weakness. I'm *far* more organized and assiduous than most. And the need for order, and the striving for perfection ingrained in my person, make me more capable of success than the vast majority of people on many levels, even if they also come with the cost of greater stress. Like anything, it's a double-edged sword, not some absolute 'disorder' simply because it's uncommon. In fact, it's a sword that I'm happy I wield, even as it often cuts me, and, in combination with other attributes, makes me appear a threat, granting me greater ability to cut through to others' insecurity and making love hard for me to find, for few can handle such swords without sometimes slicing themselves.

Speaking of the medical community inventing disorders so that it can turn you into a paying patron and sell you 'cures,' a trick which reminds me of religions selling you afflictions like sins and Hell so that they can sell you lies (like doubt equaling a lack of faith) and Heaven, the most recent health documentary that I watched, on the ever-growing study of microbiotic health and its connection to health disorders generally, including mental illness (*Hack Your Health: The Secrets of Your Gut*), taught me a new word, one sharing the suffix of anorexia, as though they're anywhere near to being in the same league: *orthorexia*. Get this: Orthorexia is a 'disorder' in which the eater is obsessed with only taking healthy foods into their body whilst cultivating an equal obsession with avoiding unhealthy foods. That's a 'disorder' needing treatment!

How many people hear that, like me, and are like: Wait a minute! You want to convince people that doing the one thing most linked to the *well*-ordered health of the body and brain, and thus most responsible for promoting peak capacity and potential for best pursuing their purpose and finding happiness in their lives is an 'unhealthy disorder?!' Now *that's* some fucked up shit! I mean, even considering the possibility that one could be *too* focused on 'food is medicine,' certainly the *last* thing you want to do in the modern 'food is chronic poison' world, in which the aware see pure misleading evil propaganda overwhelming ignorant obese customers every time they walk through the grocery store, is to give them further justifications to be ignorant and unhealthy and suffer innumerable *true* health disorders by calling a steadfast focus on the direct link between consumption and health a *disorder*! Yet another example of propaganda placed in the dictionary to the

gross disservice of the best interests of the people!
Convince people to follow their long-conditioned impulse to
purchase their fleeting satisfaction by selling their health!
Alas, I must admit that impulsivity isn't always the absolute
evil that, like so much conventional wisdom, it's thought to
be by those following the misleading conservative lead.

I find common criticisms of impulsivity alarming, actually;
they come with connotations of recklessness and
irresponsibility. In the mental health world, in fact, behavior
perceived as 'impulsive' is seen as a sign of mental illness
itself. The word was often used in the reports that I read in
justification of diagnoses and behavior deemed 'unstable'
by the professional observer. But I ask you to consider the
possibility, dear reader, that an 'impulse' can come from
something, or someplace, deeper than some desperate
flight of unanchored fancy; that it often can, in fact, come
from an instinct as primal as life itself; a life unbound by the
conventional analyses and judgments we've been
conditioned to consider rational and 'proper.' Certainly
most of the most talented creators are impulsive, as are
the best lovers, as are all those so alluringly uncontained.

Sometimes, in fact, I think impulse, like instinct, comes
from the deepest, best-informed part of ourselves; the
truest self desperate to break out of the confines which the
conventional world traps us in; that it comes from some
whisper of a greater understanding linked to spiritual
awareness and those stored up, deeply buried conclusions
of our subconscious which are dying to surface. As a
corollary, I often feel like my 'following my gut' puts me at
risk, and pushes me into conflict with others, and denies
me love, for the sake of some greater good that I only
sense, but could never explain to any of you 'realists,'
much less to any woman requiring stability or wherewithal.

I must freely admit here that I've had more than my share of trouble with women, and that the bipolar manner of my experience of women generally, my effortless swings from experiencing them as goddesses to demons, from their being both the boon and the bane of my existence, matches my experience of myself and the human race in general. One might say that I'm an *extremist*. I spend very little time in the temperate center. This matches not just what the psychiatrist would attempt to define me as during my aforementioned PTSD manic period years before, and Jess's reductive description in front of our colleagues of my being "moody," but also, in retrospect, the peculiar role I found I played in Jess's own psychological development.

For, as already mentioned, she freely admitted that I uncomfortably reminded her of her ex-boyfriend, a young man whom she said used his intellect to manipulate her, who had theological conceptions similar to mine, who demonstrated a borderline schizophrenic disposition, and who refused to be physically affectionate with her because he believed it would tarnish the sacred purpose of their relationship, which he saw as paralleling that between Christ and Mary. In a cruel twist of nature, such predispositions as his are very often inherited family legacies. For Nick's mother suffered from a mental illness to which Jess was often exposed and felt an imperative to help alleviate. This, like her own anxiety disorder, may've been what drove her to work at the CRC (though I'd prefer to believe that it was a saving overlapping of our fates, as I honestly believe that I *needed* to know her), just as my own experience with PTSD-triggered mania made me a better CRC employee. But these same forces which pushed us together also made me a trigger for Jess, even as I sense that, unlike her relationship with the *other* Nick, physical intimacy would never have been a problem between us, and even as my own dispositions were less extreme from a mental illness perspective, and would *never* have become abusive, no matter their extremity.

Yet, often would I say things that produced a troubling reaction from Jess when they too much mirrored the spirit and content of her memories of Nick. A wild look of borderline terror would then fall upon her beautiful face. And the fact that her current boyfriend at the time, Brady, a man whom has been the object of more envy in me than anyone else can ever be, a man she's since married and had at least one child by (again, it's still too painful for me to follow her too closely), is the exact *opposite* of her ex, and me, in many critical respects, is no accident, of course. In fact, I'm tempted to call it a certainty of causality of her psychological formation. That he's described by her as being the epitome of stability, the embodiment of stoicism, ever supportive and affectionate, never controlling or emotionally unhinged, couldn't better fit her psychological profile. Of course, I'm not unlike Brady in *some* ways. For, again, I remember her describing him as "affectionate." My incessant retroactive, imagined, idealized responses to the things she's said to me include my reaction: "Of course he's affectionate! What halfway decent guy *wouldn't* be with you? Do you have any idea how God-damn endearing you are Jess? I'd gobble you up if given half the chance!"

I think that my so closely paralleling her ex, without the abusive tendencies, permitted her a safe means to make some peace with that part of her past, while also making me a convenient target for acts of remote revenge against him. I sometimes think, in our mutually-provided therapy, I became *his* vicarious target; a natural outlet for her pent-up enmity towards him, attached to my own resentment at having to remain on guard against the inevitable effects of her overwhelmingly-entrancing nature. That he couldn't get over her, that she was constantly forced to defend against his ongoing stalking of her, was something that, though I would never be reduced to taking the same sad, threatening tact, I nevertheless feel I understood better than anyone else could be *capable* of understanding. Yet, somehow it sounds like the other Nick suffered a worse fate than my own, both in his dispositions and the fact that he now has to live with having had and lost the Holy Mary.

Nick saw and heard things (that is, he suffered from visual and auditory hallucinations), and imagined that he was at the heart of a new religion; like he was its first prophet and was tasked with canonizing and proselytizing it. Honestly, I'm familiar with such thoughts, and have recorded many of them, both here and elsewhere (we all have a prophet in our hearts, dear reader, some of us just have matching minds better able to translate the messages received in heart). The 'other Nick' believing Jess to be a type of reincarnation of the Holy Mary I'm referencing here *half-jokingly*, for, after she told me about it, it became an insider joke between us which she mostly took as a good sport, but which she was never fully comfortable with, owing to my mirroring him so closely. Alas, I can't imagine taking my conceptions to the extent of not wanting to have sex with her because it would tarnish the purity of the relationship.

Sex needn't be a dirty act. That itself is a byproduct of Christian brainwashing; to associate sex with impurity so that the Church may further control its followers through the programmed need to have their romantic relationships rubber-stamped with false propriety. I've seen this particular lie, one of many in the Christian playbook, create a ton of destruction, both in its prohibition of healthy relations and in its concealment of unhealthy relations. If the heart condones the sex, it's a pure extension of love, and, in fact, one may argue that there's no greater worship.

In effect, Nick's attitude towards sex only ended up making Jess feel unwanted, unattractive and starved for affection.

She left the relationship, entirely against *his* desires, with a built-up anxiety about her blossoming sexuality, not dissimilar to her anxieties about going to school, and not, I think, again, dissimilar to the anxieties which Christianity, and especially Catholicism, ingrains in the minds of its fear-governed adherents. Later, when I worked with her, and would speak to her about some of my own spiritual revelations, about how I felt like I had insight into certain metaphysical truths, I could see that it frightened her, so I started to avoid anything that might seem too close a parallel to him. Both Nick and I were, or *are*, highly creative, intelligent people, though our forms of artistic expression differed, he expressing himself more by crafts and canvas, whilst I stick with the written word and the exploration of ideas. But where I identify with him the most, of course, is the fact that he fell in love with Jess. The main difference, and, again, the difference defining my greatest empathy for him, is that he was actually *with* her, and lost her. I think that would've killed me, honestly. But for the *other* Nick, the overwhelming grief made him a stalker.

When Jess decided that she wanted out, he couldn't accept it, and did anything he could to stop it. He'd make her feel small so that he could control her, and confine her physical movements. And she was subject to all of his outpourings, including those that felt delusional, and sometimes even dangerous. Anytime she attempted to enforce her independence, he'd drive around town looking for her. She'd hear about it from one of their shared friends, and subsequently feel compelled to flee. He'd contact her all the time at the CRC, even years after their break, and even after she blocked his number. He'd find her through other means, like *Facebook*, or through the phones of mutual acquaintances, and lean upon their long-established ties in the attempt to emotionally blackmail her. He'd follow every social media account that she'd start, forcing her to keep blocking him, and sometimes to cancel accounts and start new ones. The messages came in through every form of communication that he could find.

He found her at a bar in Coos Bay once, when she was with Brady, her future husband. He approached her, and demanded to talk long past the point of comfort, eventually resulting in Brady and his friends forcing him to leave the bar. He just couldn't let her go. And, in my experience, it's hard to blame him, for my heart can't let her go either, even as I'd *never* be inclined towards stalking. I don't know what it is in a person that makes them even *want* to keep a connection that the other person clearly *doesn't* want. Some combination of desperate need and zero self-esteem, perhaps. She delivered me the first, but to lose the second entirely, so as to force oneself into another's life? *That's* hard to imagine. Alas, having experienced all that, and felt the parallels with me, is it any wonder that she saw me as she did, and that the result of it was needing *Brady*?

In reflection upon not just her relationship with Nick, but her past in general, I wonder: Is Jess's marriage to Brady perfect proof of determinism? Is it pure cause and effect that someone as sweet as she, someone with such a big, beautiful heart and emotive being that has experienced these things, the unstable, abusive upbringing, the unhinged, punishing, psychotic first love, the anxiety disorder, the formative years of every manner of financial and emotional insecurity being raised in a place of persistent poverty and drug addiction, ends up falling in love with and marrying the equal opposition to these chaotic forces, one whom embodies perfect *order*? Is it deterministic to such a degree as to disprove free will that Jess ended up with someone stoic, perfectly stable, and nearly impossible to throw out of emotional balance? Someone unforgiving of anyone and anything resembling the abuses that she, and to a large extent he as well, experienced growing up? The perfect shield. The ultimate counterweight. Is there choice, or psychological *certainty*?

There was clear evidence of a completion of opposites element in their relationship. She the worried, anxious planner driven by a need for control, clearly rooted not just in her nature, but in the nurture, or lack thereof, of formative years in which she felt entirely dispossessed of control. Brady, on the other hand, was the 'happy go lucky' balancing point, the 'fly by the seat of his pants, everything will work out' rock ever tempering her anxiety. Two parts of a completing spectrum. I actually had the audacity to comment on his seeming normality to her after the first of two times meeting him, at a company function, implying that he's not very impressive; that I'd expected more. She responded by threatening to "punch me in the nose" for my mild disparagement. *Lucky fucking bastard.* Some guys have it all, likely obliviously. I was even irritated by her descriptions of Brady's relationship with his best friend.

It was irksome to listen to Jess speak of how she and Brady's best friend, Darren, would compete with one another for his time, like a divorced couple fighting for more time with their shared child. What immense fortune to have such a woman as her fighting to spend time with you... I can scarcely imagine such a priceless privilege. Listening to her talk about it, I found myself annoyed at the ease with which the 'happy go lucky' type constructs connections. Brady would no doubt find it humorous how much a part of my psychology he's become, considering he only knows me through our two brief interactions during company events, and through he and Jess likely having a few fleeting discussions about me as 'someone she cares about,' something I gathered by implication, and that I primarily know him through her constant descriptions of the guy "who isn't even my type" whom she nevertheless fell in love with (which, again, seems like inevitable determinism).

My understanding of him is part mythical, like a giant whom conquered Aphrodite, even as he seemed all too normal and unimpressive to me. Though I suppose any man would have seemed as such considering on how high and ornately, grandly designed a pedestal I had her. Ringing in the back of my mind during those days was that line from *40 Year Old Virgin*: "You know what your problem is? You put the pussy on a pedestal!" My sense of Brady was based mostly upon the heights of vicarious envy and ego-driven comparison. For how can one listen to the only person that they've ever fallen in love with describing the characteristics of the person whom it was clear, even then, that she was going to dedicate her life to loving, and *not* make comparisons? How could I *not* ask every version of the question: How does that description compare and contrast with me? Or wonder: What will I do without you?

When it was confirmed that she was leaving our shared shift, I called in sick to work. I didn't eat for four days. Not a bite. I'd been reading about the ability of fasting to heal intractable health conditions. So I thought: Since I've lost my appetite anyway, since I feel like the life has been sucked out of me, I might as well try the fasting method now. So I stayed in bed. It was the weakest and saddest I've ever felt. But the fasting was easy. I had no desire for food, for anything but the fantasy that she'd change her mind. But I knew she wouldn't. She has *far* too much pride to make and announce a decision only to then backpedal.

So she switched shifts for a time, from our shared NOC 'graveyard' 11pm to 7am shift to what they call the 'PM shift' in the three segment 24 hour daily cycle. What did this mean? For me, it meant going from working alongside her three nights a week, a full 24 hours a week, to seeing her during a couple shift changes a week. There are no words to express how painful that was. It would've been better for me had she left completely. But no. Instead, I was to exchange the most cursory of formal niceties with her as she passed by. *God it was awful.* The most painful transition I've ever known, from seeing her all the time, from feeling an overlapping of heart and mind with the only woman that I've ever loved, to spending a few minutes with her during shift change meetings a couple times a week during which I was forced by 'professionalism' and decorum to pretend that I wasn't in agony, all the while feeling like I was about to split in half. I remember at one point that she acknowledged "it'll be hard," not saying *for you*, as if implicitly admitting she'd have a hard time letting go of me as well. How badly I wanted to believe it was so.

She teased me a little bit during this particularly painful period. She'd occasionally throw me little playful flirtations on the way out the door, like seeing a short story that I'd left in the break room and, after exiting the main area of the CRC, reenter and torturously ask me about it. Thinking of even that one fleeting incident reminds me, once again, that the love that I felt for her, the love that remains with me *still*, really was indistinguishable from the best parts of chivalrous knighthood. That's not hyperbole or grandiosity. That's a truth recognized by my heart. She'd call me at the CRC and I'd come running. Not the way I ran to a boss or a coworker, out of jaded obligation, but the way one runs to the holder of his heart, pulled by an indomitable force, figurative sword in hand, ready to cut down any threat.

Stepping in front of her upon being summoned was like something out of a myth or legend for me, in terms of how it *felt*, as a versified veracity of inner ardency, regardless of how prosaic it likely *appeared.* For me, in answering her call, I might as well have knelt before her, as knights once did when honor yet prevailed, when they swore fealty to what they loved most and pledged to protect it unto death. That was me in heart, on one knee, head bowed, waiting for her to knight me, taps of the sword thrice upon my shoulders, my honor thus bound to her by divine decree. Even as this most honorable of dictates existed in constant contrasting conflict with the petty playground ego wars.

On several occasions after she'd switched shifts, during these agonizing renditions of 'ships passing in the night,' she'd pretend that she didn't notice that I was there, and then suddenly see me. But she knew I was there the entire time. She'd act as though she didn't know I was hovering, saying hello, trying to get her attention, then pretend like 'oh, hi, I didn't see you there.' But she knew I was there. It was all so gratifying to her ego, I'm sure. Don't get me wrong. She's a most excellent person. But there's no way to be aware of possessing that much power over a person and *not* relish it, at least a little bit. And she did. Often, in fact, and long before this. It started to occur around the time you'd think it would: *when she realized I loved her.* It would surface quite frequently, actually. What does it say about the cold power of the psyche that even the warmest people can't help but play to the advantages that the love of another grants them, even when it means putting the heart of someone they claim to care about in a vice? The unavoidable ugliness of sentience: Once one becomes aware of a 'self,' one is driven to enlarge it by any means. This isn't pessimism; this is awareness backed by *tons* of empirical evidence that even the good enlist ego for evil.

Towards the end of her time at the CRC we had this sad thing with one of the whiteboards at work... The board was a record of who was scheduled to come into work the following day, and the graveyard workers would be tasked to fill it, ending the schedule with a message meant to be motivational, or at least of insightful use, to the residents, workers, and anyone else that might read it. I *always* had something to say; always felt I had some insight to offer.

But, being in pain then, after she left our overlapping shift, and knowing she'd come in later and read it, I found it difficult not to leave a little hidden message for her; a reminder that her dusting me off her boots and just walking away was emotionally excruciating for me. One of the messages I left was about the difference between healthy and unhealthy relationships; how healthy relationships are balanced in their power and benefits, being symbiotic in nature, and unhealthy relationships are out of balance, with those having more power, or all the power, exploiting the powerless, and with the benefits had being lopsidedly delivered to the one with power. They're *parasitic*. I admit that the message was left under the pretense of being for the *residents*, to encourage them to develop healthy relationships. But I knew she was coming in and would read it. And, honestly, when you're in that much emotional and psychological anguish it seems impossible to keep it entirely to yourself. You may be inclined to chalk it up to 'misery loves company,' and there's a lot of truth to that, but for me, at the time, it was more like: *If I don't find a way to unload some of this misery, it'll be the death of me.*

A coworker she was confiding in called my messages 'passive-aggressive.' When I heard this, I remember thinking: Yea, because I can't be *aggressive*. It's all I can do, to release it a little, to keep from cracking. Who are you to judge me for wanting her to know my pain, and my sense of injustice? Who are you to dismiss such crushing heartbreak with such a cold psychological term, condescendingly condemning me, wiping away my shattered heart with a flick of your wrist? Another coworker admonished me long after she'd left: "You know you'll never be with her, right? You have to let her go." Like it's so simple. Like you can just snap the heart out of it based upon *logic*. Like you can make someone accept the unacceptable. Like you can make the mind realize some truth, some incontrovertible reality, that supersedes love. No. *The heart owns the mind. Your logic is meaningless, powerless, no matter how true, for the power of any truth held by the mind pales in comparison to the power of any heart-held truth.* The first is feeble, a mere translation and attempted reflection of the second *source* truth. Thus is trying to eradicate a heart-held truth with a mere mental truth akin to trying to knock down a mountain by throwing pebbles at it, a mirroring of modern materialist madness.

Speaking of associating that beloved young woman with the Holy Mary, it makes me think of the story that she told me of the collision that almost claimed her life, but instead resulted only in such a severe shattering of her ankle that she almost had to have her foot amputated. I can't recall where she was driving, but I believe she was going through one of the passes separating the high desert of Bend from the Willamette River Valley. She hit a patch of water or black ice (and would later learn that her car at that time was particularly prone to such losses of control) and veered off the road whilst going 60mph, and plummeted through a copse of trees, the last, largest of which stopped her so suddenly that it forced the lower front of her car into the cabin and smashed her lower left leg. Surviving that immediate collision wasn't even the miraculous, Holy Mary part of the story, however, but what happened afterwards.

Going in and out of consciousness, her vehicle filling with smoke and about to go up in flames, she was pinned inside, and certain that she was about to die a horrible death. Alas, from her unconsciousness she somehow suddenly regained consciousness and found that she was

some yards away from the collision, just before it was
engulfed in an inferno that *would've* excruciatingly ended
her life. Obviously the official explanation was that, even in
her severely debilitated, vulnerable state, she'd harnessed
an instinctive survival mechanism to pull her shattered leg
free and crawl to safety. But I think she may well have
been *drug* from the wreckage, perhaps by an angel
preserving her entire future family line, and, in her saving
me from the depths of my own despair through my love for
her, mine as well. I know, it's ironic that I write this in a
book about a mental institution, but I swear to you, dear
reader, that metaphysical forces drive physical forces.

I remember her limping up and down the two CRC resident
hallways during her checks and 'counts' of the residents,
and teasingly calling her 'hop along.' And I remember her
shedding tears after my describing my enjoyment at taking
up jogging, an activity that she was once fond of. And I
remember her insecure need to explain away the unsightly
scars she carried on a few places on her body after
surviving the collision and the subsequent surgeries, and
all her anatomical descriptions of her ankle and surgical
options and potential amputation. I remember her trying to
reinforce her confidence by claiming that she wasn't so
vain as to be threatened by amputation, and saying "scars
are beautiful," no doubt repeating something she'd heard
somewhere, and my many unspoken reflections on the
comment, like: "The scars themselves aren't beautiful, but
when worn by someone who embodies the beauty of
perceived flaws, they're fitting, and certainly aren't capable
of degrading the loveliness that you so effortlessly exude."

I thank God for saving her, for she saved me in turn, even
as that salvation was very often experienced as torture.
Our last words were kind, as were our words to one
another in general, in our few brief interchanges since

speaking to one another for hours every week for eighteen months before that, even as I continually struggle *not* to reach out and share a thought or a feeling, always knowing that all it takes is for me to share too much emotion even once, and she'll cut me off, her 'boundaries' like the rock-hard, precipitous faces of mythical mountains; the contrast between the ice-cold, impenetrable fortress walls and the softest, warmest, most uplifting of all forces they fortify.

I tell myself she'd rather avoid me, especially when she's with her family, because they represent her ground, and, especially owing to her past, she *needs* to stay grounded, and avoid those of us living with our heads in the clouds; clouds that could carry storms as easily as they carry the soft comforts of soaring sentiments. He's like the rock that you build your foolproof home on, whereas I'm more like the air that only the fools build upon, or at least so sayeth conventional wisdom. I'm that force which may shine with the sun in one moment, and call in the hurricane the next. Better to keep me as a lukewarm memory, as a supporting prop for self-love, than to deal with my actual presence. It's too risky a proposition to integrate the two, especially considering that she never *really* saw me, but defined me in slight terms reflecting her self-image. Such agony when the one you love decides you're only of value to her ego.

I've seen her a few times since being shattered by her blithe departure. She pretends not to see me; ignoring me in the park whilst seeing to her wailing daughter in the stroller, even though I *know* that she saw me; swiftly skating behind her shopping cart to the other end of *Safeway* after seeing me in the produce section; looking away when she drives by me walking down the road. Love is all that gives life meaning, and when you've been in love but once, and when that subject of adoration sees you as an uncomfortable reminder of what you're unwilling to give or admit, well... let's just say it's a difficult thing to live with.

But why flee from me? Does she imagine me a danger? Would she rather forget the guy who fell in love with her at work, our mutual affection making it impossible for her to retain the pretense that monogamy is the only right way?

Maybe. That, and/or she's aware of the pedestal that I had her on, one that's impossible to live up to, and she'd rather remain there in my heart and mind than be forced into a present moment where she'd feel the psychological and egotistic need to live up to that impossibility. It's better, in other words, to keep the ethereal realm in which I had her, and I'll likely forever keep her, segregated from the all too real realm of the mother and wife in which she now resides. As alluded to earlier, the muse of the poet is incompatible with the everyday family woman. To an extent I imagine that's true of *every* woman that's *ever* inspired an artist, which likely leads to issues if muse becomes mate.

It reminds me of a passage from Rumi I recently read:

I choose to love you in silence
For in silence I find no rejection

I choose to love you in loneliness
For in loneliness no one owns you but me

I choose to adore you from a distance
For distance will shield me from pain

I choose to kiss you in the wind
For the wind is gentler than my lips

I choose to hold you in my dreams
For in my dreams you have no end

In confirmation of this ode of Rumi to loving from afar, I must admit that a big part of *me*, too, wants to keep Jess in that sublime state of adoration; that it's not just *she* who likely feels the need to segregate the past from the present, the surreal romanticism of memory from its incompatibility with reality. As much as I'd love to see her, there's no way to match the Jess whom reigns in my heart with the mother and wife whom reigns over a far less grand, but, to her, far more significant domestic kingdom. Thus, I may never visit her again except in my dreams.

The dreams... countless dreams of Jess. Most of them have involved feeling ignored by her, or not being able to reach her. Like the one where she was seated at the opposite corner of a classroom, speaking to all the students around her, and never even turned around. Or the one where she was at the far end of a party, surrounded by friends, laughing with everyone but me, my feeling both literally and figuratively outside her circle; a circle that I so desperately wish I was still within, recalling, again, how she'd talk of those "in my life." But every rare once in a while the feeling flips, and she's beside me, and *warm* to me. Why? Was I just in a better mood when I fell asleep? Did I feel better? Healthier, stronger and more confident? Or is there more at play? A recent dream of her surprised me, and made me question my assumption about dreams as being what they typically seem to be for me; that is, as manifestations of fears and psychological wreckage constructed entirely by and within my own psyche and imagination, with me as their *only* source.

For in this particular recent dream I found myself near her, and fully expected her to ignore or spurn or otherwise be cold to me per my typical self-fulfilling prophecies. But, instead, she took me entirely off-guard and embraced me, warmly. It's the first time I remember feeling truly surprised by a dream, as though it was a true interaction between us; as though it represented an actual meeting on another plane of being. For how can one be genuinely surprised in a dream if the experience is entirely created by and within oneself? How can I surprise myself if it's entirely my own creation, as though shocked by a film fully of my own making? Expecting to be spurned but instead being lovingly hugged and leaned into, expecting to be violently repelled by her notorious boundaries (notorious to me), yet again facing a confirmation of the fear of rejection, made the ensuing embrace all that more overwhelming. It made the dream feel far more authentic than most, because it involved the type of genuine surprise and feeling of good fortune that seems almost exclusively the realm of reality.

What's the meaning? Was she there with me, truly, like a spiritual embrace? Or is it my psyche suggesting, or my deep instinctive awareness informing me, that she cares about me more, and regards me far better, than I realize, and more than my riddled psyche and reduced ego can allow my conscious mind to even consider? Was she, or my subconscious, informing me that my fear of her indifference towards me, or, worse, her distaste for me, is entirely unfounded in reality, and that these feelings are entirely byproducts of the aforementioned states of my psyche and ego? Is she telling me, in the dream state lying beneath and ever belying the limits of perceivable reality, that she actually *loves* me, but is forced to deny that truth? Is she telling me that I can let her go and still love her?

Tell me, dear reader, when you've felt your heart fill with someone, how can anyone else ever be brought into the filled space? There's no room for anyone else. No one else will fit. Certainly no one near as immense as her. I just can't imagine Jess being expelled from the sacred sanctum. Even if I *had* the ability to do so. Even if I *was* the exorcist of my own heart, which I'm not. No, it's governed by a force far greater than me. Its presiding priests hail from some realm beyond the human capacity to identify, much less control. Besides, I think a successful exorcism would kill me. Holding on to the memory of how much she filled me is, in and of itself, a type of defense mechanism.

Because *actually* expelling her would mean bringing back the absolute emptiness that preceded her, and was gradually killing me. Having the hollow instantly replace whatever part of her lingers within, opening myself back up to the vacuum, to the eternal void, to the black hole of loveless life, and being immediately forced into that bottomless abyss, would likely be lethal for me. Better to keep someone I'll never have within me, whose phantom yet fills the space, than nothing at all. The only possibility, my only possible salvation, is finding a force of equal or greater power, as impossible as that seems, and such a seemingly mythical woman displacing Jess for me, by her own force, a force far beyond anything that I can summon. I can't go back to the emptiness. I can only accept the possibility of a divine displacement that's unlikely to come.

When she officially announced that she was leaving the NOC shift, I suffered true grief. The losing of a loved one. It literally made me physically ill. You want a weight loss technique? Heartbreak is unbeatable. "It'll be hard," she'd warned. Such a feeble word. *Hard*. To go from carrying around a vacuum for the preceding decades of one's life, embodying a black hole of being, to finally finding one with the capacity to fill the unfathomable, feeling her trace every inch of it with her presence, to having it vacated yet again, the black hole engulfing me once more. *Hard*. And when I got angry at her for not calling or texting to see if I was okay that week, missing some of our last shifts together, she said: "Don't challenge our friendship like that." The prideful power games persisted even at the end of that 'friendship;' another feeble, pedestrian term entirely failing to reflect reality. For me especially. Still, I'd give anything at this moment to sit beside her at The Bridge for one more night; to redeem one of those lost shifts right now, so as to be regaled with but a few more of her gesticulated tales. I'd give anything to have one more night before the ending of that shift that spelled the permanent end of our proximity.

For I remember, after we started our cars together that final time, how I pulled out of the parking lot of the CRC just in front of her in my 1998 Honda Civic painted in "Cyclone Blue Metallic (marketing is everything, dear reader)," and how she followed me in her newer compact red Hyundai all the way across town towards my apartment complex, because we lived so near to one another back then, before she left our shared shift, then the company, then my life, forever. There was something about the *way* that she followed me towards our respective homes. So close. Like the closeness was symbolic. Like the proximity wasn't just physical, but emotional. Like her following me was a secret wish. I could feel it through the rearview. And I swear it was as if she was saying: *If only. Maybe in the next life. Maybe when we've outgrown archaic monogamy.*

04

RIVERS, DAMS, FENCES & TABLES

If you have more than you need,
build a longer table, not a higher fence.

The ego is the very embodiment of barbarism, dear reader. It drove even the most wonderful woman in the world to, in her keen awareness of our power disparity, and her knowing beyond any doubt that she'd been lodged deep down in the most vulnerable part of my heart, knife in hand, to jab and twist almost on impulse. It led her to call me 'buddy.' To say 'I care about you' when she knew that only a confession of love, even Platonic, would do. It made certain that she refused to contact me for any reason whatsoever, knowing how badly I wanted her to; how I'd have killed for even a word, for but an ounce of consideration, even as she oft insisted that we were 'friends.' I think that if she'd ever said anything that I desperately needed to hear (a desperation she slyly fomented), like "I believe in you," I would've squirted in my pants, and soared aloft to such great heights that I'd still be suspended there today. Alas, that would've reduced her power, so why do it? She'd say it was about protecting herself, about boundaries; euphemisms, dear reader, for the infliction of pain and the controlling of territory for the one on the wrong side of the overfortified self-fortification, a fortification built not just to protect, but for the fact that barring entry to one so desiring of it was hugely gratifying.

I'm well aware that it flies in the face of conventional judgments of propriety, especially in 'professional environments,' but in terms of how it *feels*, one person's boundary is usually another person's exclusion; the self-protection of the stronger and well-provisioned the knife to the gut, defenselessness and deprivation of the weaker. For it's not like I was an invading force. I *never* hit on her. I don't think I've ever hit on anyone, honestly, which might be my problem. Certainly the 'man's man' would say so. And so the power disparity was the omnipresent 'elephant in the room' sitting upon my chest, as was the constant subtle messaging system keeping me in my place; keeping me small and weak and starving, begging for any morsel I could get. Morsels she refused to drop, even as she *always* fed upon a bounty of love. One such as her, one who's always had love in her life, can never know the torture of having it seem to never come before suddenly sitting beside you, night after night, talking of all the love shared with someone who was allowed through the fence.

While she's not the only woman who informed the concept for me, for I've had a crush on many a married woman, including two of her colleagues whilst at the CRC, Jess, as the only one of them I was in love with, best embodies the informant of the following: *Marriage turns the most natural, universally-empowering force for connection and inclusion, love, into the most unnatural, universally-restricting force for division and exclusion.* She wasn't married then, but she was so clearly on that path, and so possessed by its mentality, that she might as well have been. For the violated principle is the same, regardless of whether or not the vows have been taken yet: *Love is polyamorous, not monogamous.* The power and truth of love is in 'free love,' not in *possessive* love. *Everyone* has something to teach us about love, yet conventional wisdom restricts us to a single teacher. The 'soulmate' concept is a lie, regardless of how you feel about the one person that you're bound to.

For me, all of life's problems are solved first by knowing God, and thereafter developing the discipline to follow that knowledge and its true faith, despite the fact that society and everything it teaches us reinforces the conflicting lies. For what's a 'soulmate' but an extension of the belief in an absolute self with a soul separate from everyone else, *including* God, that belief perpetuating, in turn, the belief that we're isolated 'selves' with one other 'self' that we're meant for? And what happens when that belief ends in breakup? *Disaster.* So much so that suicidality falls on the heels of this form of identity and possession: oneself and the possessed 'soulmate.' For the two-headed monster of modernity is *identity and possessiveness*, and those heads are congenital twins, like the two faces of the same hideous head of human evil. As soon as we believe that we're some certain, absolute thing, we become insecure relative to that believed definition of ourselves which we thereafter defend, the ego forever fighting for its survival.

Anything threatening that sense of self is attacked, and the ugliness of these self-defenses is always commensurate with the insecurity of our egoist conceptions, as it's the vulnerability engendered by the illusions held by the insecure self that are the source of its self-defenses. So it is that *possessiveness* means not just the traditional notion of material and financial possession, but possession of the ideas of ourselves, and even the possession of our defined and defended 'committed relationships.' The 'single man' is made to feel isolated, vulnerable, ashamed and aberrant when he remains 'single' for too long, even as, from a spiritual perspective, he's never *actually* isolated, which is *not* beside the point that I'm making. Through socially-conforming peer pressure he becomes the 'boyfriend,' then the 'husband,' clinging to those possessed self-definitions along with everything else that he believes that he is, like the philosopher and the writer. And it's not a matter of how true those definitions are, but that they create a *constant clutching and clinging that blinds him to greater truths while also perpetuating the conflicts that he has with anyone and anything that threatens those individualized possessions.*

And capitalism, and the law defining us and what we own, only exacerbates this tendency towards identification and possessiveness. I'm in no way immune to this struggle, of course. In fact, my spiritual practice is inseparable from all the pains I've absorbed and inflicted through this shadow war, slicing at and exacerbating divisive delusions when, if I'd been more disciplined and self-secure, I would've left my sword in its sheath. After a recent bad breakup with a woman I briefly dated whilst doing a final edit of this book, a woman whose psyche was cracked and ego corroded and who desperately clung to anything seemingly secure in order to compensate for her imbalance and resultant rampant 'self-medicating' that only made things worse, and whom triggered my own regrettable egoist self-defenses, I'm more sure than ever that most people are so wrapped up in what they believe that they possess, in their self-possessions, their relational possessions and their material and financial possessions, that it all *becomes* them. And when it turns out it's not *actually* them, all hell breaks loose, eroding the illusive boundaries of self-possession.

We live our entire life in this deluded state relative to the extent which we believe that we've accurately defined and thereafter possess ourselves, others and the world at large. This is the wisdom at the heart of Buddhist teaching: *everything that we believe that we possess shall inevitably fall free of our clutching grasp, including our sense of self.* Only that which never began has no end, the infinite Source, God, of which we're all a finite individualization.

Everything else is doomed to oblivion, even as we latch onto it all for dear life. From ongoing observation I've come to realize that *everyone*, no matter their egoist conceptions and political affiliations, seeks something stout and true to cling onto, like our personal life rafts as we float upon the imperiling existential sea, braving its storms. It's different for everyone, even as, for most people, that raft is composed of *other people*, especially what we identify as our family and tribes, the 'my people' designation at the root of human discord, for 'my people' is inherently divisive.

Most commonly we cling to one other person, the center of most rafts, the every-egg-in-one-basket 'soulmate.' Jess represented this 'family and mate is everything' tendency as much as anyone, not because she's common, but because her perpetually-imperiled upbringing informed her as to the indispensability of the leakless raft, so to speak. And she certainly represented that raft for me, as I clung onto what she offered for dear life, in a time when that life was rife with depression. I'm still clinging to it, though not quite as desperately. But no matter the composition of the raft, the component(s) have one thing in common: *they end*. The composition degrades. The raft deflates, sinking to the bottom of the sea. So be careful how you compose that raft, or better yet, *don't*; have faith that the sea shall deliver you to providential shores; that the current shall carry you home. For there's only *one* exception to the rule of the sinking raft: the Sea of Source. We must have faith in the *only* permanence, the One Ceaseless Self. And this is where the modern mores of 'acceptable behavior' and 'proper relationships' rears its ugly head: *propriety means clinging to every fleeting, eroding possession*. Capitalism, materialism, classism, realism, egotism, conservatism, even, arguably, monogamy: these are swatches in the blindfold of a modern man whom sees only the possibilities that he's defined and believed about himself, others, and the world, wasting limitless potential value in the process.

Ideally, we come to an understanding of God as being our inseparable, imperishable essence, and only to *that* do we cling, letting the raft go and simply allowing anything and anyone in that collides into us on its overlapping current. For we can all love limitless many, each a little differently, and every single such love has something invaluable to offer. I'm not saying monogamy doesn't have its value, but what of its unrecognized *cost*? What of the cost of the corruption of the institution of marriage, inextricable from the controls of Church and State? Can you imagine, dear reader, what may've become of me had I *not* fallen in love with Jess? To have been denied even that one paramount unrequited love for one who craves love as much as any man on Earth, and thereby knows its value by its ongoing denial? And do you not see that conventional propriety dictates that she *not* have the opportunity to be connected to another man, and that our tethered rafts circumvented this unwise conventional wisdom due only to the 'captive audience' aspect of our own overlapping NOC currents?

I can't imagine being deprived of everything that I experienced through her. The loss would be incalculably immense. And yet, if the Christian conservative majority had had their way, that connection would've been denied us both, to inconceivably devastating effect for me, and to her loss as well, regardless of her pride's prohibition of such an admission. And if nature is a whore, as Kurt Cobain and *Animal Planet* reminds us, is there not something decidedly unnatural about not only monogamy, but about building our 'most sacred of institutions' upon it?

When a coworker commented that Jess and I should "just get together already," Jess's response was: "I can't." Not 'I don't want to,' but "I can't." Can't is the real c-word, as they say. And like all exclusionary institutions, marriage has *can't* written all over it. Then there's the fact that marriage tends to motivate couples for the wrong reasons, like

staying together in their misery and shared distaste
because they're too intricately intertwined financially,
legally and logistically to attempt disentanglement; or
giving up their independent lives and pleasures because
'compromise is what marriage is all about,' failing to realize
that they're thereby actually compromising *themselves*
whilst barring everyone from their lives that even has the
potential of getting close enough to threaten them with
love. They set their table, and by the time they realize that
it needs to be reset, or that there should be another space
set, or that some flexibility in its arrangement would be
more beneficial for everyone, *it's too late*. Dinner is served.
The banished are eating elsewhere, at another table,
wondering why the tables can't be pushed together, and,
for that matter, why they were separated in the first place.

Monogamy, especially marriage, is the high fence. Open
love, that which honors all the love that can be shared
between people, is the long table. I allude here to the line
introducing this chapter, one that Jess herself had posted
to her *Facebook* page years ago: *If you have more than
you need, build a longer table, not a higher fence.* Like
anything of an axiomatic nature, the line applies to more
than the usual context of wealth and resources. It connects
to the concept of connection itself; to union, to love, to
what I consider the inexhaustible spiritual currency that's
meant to be given and received freely, and yet buys all the
best in life; everything that can save us. *The long table.*

Centuries ago the British poet Percy Shelley put it thus:

I never was attached to that great sect,
Whose doctrine is, that each one should select
Out of the crowd a mistress or a friend
And all the rest, though fair and wise commend
To cold oblivion, though it is the code
Of modern morals, and the beaten road
Which those poor slaves with weary footsteps tread,

Who travel to their home among the dead
By the broad highway of the world, and so
With one chained friend, perhaps a jealous foe
The dreariest and the longest journey go.

All the rest, though fair and wise, commend to cold oblivion. *That* is what you've done to me, Jess. All to chain yourself to one, for it seems more secure than the possibility of being chained to and drawn and quartered by the uncontrollable many, thus wasting a great fortune, for:

True Love in this differs from gold and clay,
That to divide is not to take away.

That is, love grows by being shared, not hoarded like capital, its inestimable value short-sold by monogamy. Is it not at least *possible* that the secure-most, non-possessive love is that which is free to be beyond the confines of monogamy, and not have the love of another risk the one? Is this the future of the human race, as the hippies believed, as the modern 'open relationship' permits, or is this but a delusion? I wish it to be true, selfishly, even as I know that were I *actually* to be with Jess, there's no fucking way I'd be able to share her with another man, much less other *men*. Not without some sort of drastic psychological reconstruction, at least. Maybe never, honestly. Why must the love we may possess for the committed so imperil their commitment? Does this reflect a spiritual truth, as the 'soulmate' Christians have been conditioned to believe and conform to, or is Shelley correct in assuming it's amongst the foolish, anachronistic mores of even his early nineteenth century form of modernity?

Waiting on pins and needles for my conclusion on this subject, dear reader? Let me venture one. I think the answer to the riddle of exclusive love versus inclusive love, to 'committed' versus 'uncommitted' (which feels like propagandist terminology, as if implying that only monogamy is correct), to Church-sanctioned versus heart-sanctioned, is that most, including myself, simply aren't self-secure enough to allow a hypothetical significant other to be with anyone else intimately, even in non-physical forms of intimacy such as Jess and I had, without feeling threatened by it at the least, betrayed by it more likely.

Even if I *had* been with Jess, 'sharing her' on that level (as if anyone is rightfully possessed by anyone else on the level of 'sharing' them being morally correct) would've felt impossible, *but that doesn't make it wrong*, and doesn't necessitate a threat to anything but the insecure ego. For I would've loved her as one who has so long been deprived of love that I would've been desperate to preserve it, and likely would've felt even her fleeting fancy for another guy threatening, even as I would've done everything I could to hide that insecurity (and am here thinking of her attraction to Brady being largely based upon his steely self-security).

What I'm trying to say, in other words, is that we're generally not yet evolved enough as a race, or freed enough from religiosity and its grip upon our antiquated notions of propriety, to securely share love with more than one person, even as literally every single one of us *can*, and likely should, love far more than one person, each of those loves felt and expressed in its own special way. It is, in fact, arguably the absence of, and boundaries set against, *inclusive* love that's largely responsible for the division, discord, evil and suffering of the world. Not that I'd ever expect *Jess* to understand or agree with that, especially considering her personal background and its imparted imperative to produce stability in every possible facet of her life, especially a 'stable family unit' that likely seems everything to her. Yet I know that this doesn't seem everything to anyone who's lived for so long under such a stable family unit that they see its downside, and know that to live within it can eventually seem as much like living behind bars as to her it seems essential to happiness.

Put another way: *Love is the river. Marriage is the dam.* To me, this metaphor is inseparable from the aforementioned: "If you have more than you need, build a longer table, not a higher fence." In retrospect, I find that to be an ironic quote for her to utilize, not because she isn't generous and loving, for she's these things in spades, as much as anyone I've ever known, in fact, but because she, more than anyone, taught me about how the protection one believes one is granted from a 'boundary' acts to cut off the love of, and is painfully slammed into by, anyone on the *other* side of it. Metaphorically, longer tables, higher walls, rivers and dams, these are revelatory ideas and images.

The river and dam metaphor, in fact, is inseparable from my ardent, core moral belief that what we possess only has value if we pass it along to others; if we share it and make it a passage of love between us; if our waters flow freely out of us, and connect us, one acre of identity to another, so to speak, as by a river, carrying fertilizing nutrients to all of the interconnected realms of humanity, no matter how separate they seem to be to us at first. Even between 'enemies' who're more likely undiscovered friends awaiting the right circumstances for a riparian connection.

Actually, it's my fervent belief that any excess of *anything* which we possess, including, of course, the spiritual currency that we call love, but also including *every* form of wherewithal, we shouldn't dam up and allow to languish, unused, unvalued, unapplied to life (the sin of capitalism and consolidated wealth at the heart of most modern evil and suffering, by the way), but permit to freely flow through and out of us, and on to those whom may best make use of it. So, of course, I'm referring not just to monogamy and marriage, and to tiny, perfectly divided tribes and tribalist beliefs, and to small, staunchly divided familial and social circles, but to social and economic policy (more socialistic, or communitarian policy and practice), to financial arrangements (more collective investment and shared equity), to charity over miserliness; to the *awakened* Scrooge, and all that he may do to improve *all* of our lives.

"Evil is the accentuation of division," says Huxley at the end of *Eyeless in Gaza*, "good, whatever makes for unity with other lives and other beings." The sense of the separateness of physical being and the ego presiding over it versus the sense of shared spiritual being, Spirit (God), presiding over *It*. That, dear reader, is the heart of it all; the *only* war, everything called and recognized as warfare being but a microcosm of that metaphysical macrocosm. In fact, it's my belief that all of human evil stems from the *actual* Original Sin: *Man's belief is his separation from God*. Not his *actual* separation from God, but his *belief* in his separation from God. In actuality humanity cannot be absolutely separated from God, for through Mother Nature does the eternal One give birth to infinite mortal forms of Itself upon the Earth. We all share the same essential, eternal Self of pure conscious energy: *God*. Yet, through man's corruption, and greedy need for power over his fellow man, and especially his individualist ego identities, he has, with the help of religion, then science, sold the now dominant idea of our separation from the One Source Self.

Only when we believe this lie, and when we suffer from the illusion of separation, may evil result. Only through the belief in our separation from one another, from life as a whole, from *anything,* in fact, from the whole of the universe and existence (as 'new-agey' as that sounds), is evil duly spread across civilization, through every sphere of social existence, theologically, politically, economically, personally, professionally and otherwise. Separation is the very source of evil, both our belief in it, spiritually and within the aforementioned social spheres, and our perpetuation and expansion of it through most prevalent social practices. Only this belief allows for idolatry, hierarchy, warfare, egotism (belief in a self separate from God) and all forms of concentration of resources, including wealth, which create all misery and injustice. All the evils of religion and capitalism have the illusion of separation at their heart. For when we operate from the perspective of divine revelation, in the holy illumination of perfect non-separation, in our perfect spiritual equality and unity with all things made up of the irreducible energy of the One, then none of the evils stemming from Original Sin are possible.

Generally speaking, inclusion and symbiosis and universalism are just, exclusion, parasitism and specificity are unjust. Which is why MLK is the *far* greater leader in comparison to Malcom X. And why 'spiritual but not religious,' the ability to explore theology without the constraints inextricably tied to the history of Empire, is greater than religiosity. And why there's no possibility for socioeconomic justice under laissez faire capitalism, in denial of socialistic virtues. And why *any* law or principle which doesn't apply to everyone *equally*, regardless of race, creed, color or any other form of distinction and segregation, promotes injustice, regardless of how it's sold to a gullible public. And the monopolization of love is no different. We must "build longer tables, not higher fences."

It reminds me how Jess once said: "We click, but don't connect." I think that may've been the most absurd thing she ever said. In retrospect, at least to my ears, what she was *really* saying was: "I know that we have a connection, but we can't be together (or, maybe, I don't want to be with you), so I need a way to rationalize it. Saying we 'click,' i.e. get along well naturally, is easier to embrace without the connotations of saying we have a *connection*." In fact, most everyone we worked with commented on our connection at one point or another, either to both of us, or to me alone when she wasn't present. Everything from the new coworker saying "I was *sure* you two were together," to the long-time coworker saying "you two are like brother and sister, or maybe boyfriend and girlfriend." Those are two incidences that stand out, but such comments were common. Of course, speaking of it to her was strictly out of the question; a boundary violation. Nothing could be permitted to imperil her relationship, the foundation upon which a finally stable future was to be built for her and her family, *regardless* of who might have to be run roughshod over along the way, forever turning round, trying to figure out how the seemingly innocent trampled him underfoot.

Years later, shortly after the birth of her first daughter (I think she has more now; I can't bring myself to check), she would come to admit our connection via *Facebook Messenger*, perhaps as a way of saying goodbye, for now there was *no* chance for us to share a future, and perhaps because the change in her circumstances (marriage and childbirth) permitted her the ability to admit connection without any threat to her relationship, that score having been settled, so to speak, by the lawful contract of marriage. I'll *always* be suspicious of marriage for a great multitude of reasons, *especially* its preclusion of the free admissions of the heart and the unnatural monopolization of affections that go with it, informed by my love for her.

What price in wasted love is paid by the human race, especially those constrained by conservatism's false proprieties, for its enforcement of monopolized affections? At least the French have the reputation of being able to see the natural human practicality of possessing a legal partnership that needn't be the whole of expressed emotional and physical intimacies between bound parties. We Americans, on the other hand, remain overlorded by Christian 'virtues' whose design, though invisible to all but the studied and truly sighted, were based upon the perpetuation of the power of Church and State through the sanctioned control of personal relations, those control measures themselves predicated upon the conditioning of the morality of its gullible victims; sorry, its 'parishioners.'

There's something wrong in a society ruled by sociological paradigms dictating that we're not allowed to acknowledge that we all may love people outside of our closed family units, admissions met with the reflexive condemnation 'inappropriate,' and where the personal connections inherent to our humanity and inseparable spiritual natures, and inseparable from our growth and healing, are labeled 'unprofessional' when they occur within work settings, where they'll inevitably continue to occur, and remain undernourished, as though aberrant beasts to be starved, and where anything that involves coming together with others for mutual advantage in overcoming the exploitations of the extreme minority of major shareholders of corporatism forever keeping us divided and conquered is condemned as 'communism.' All traditionalists whom 'lean right' reflexively label such things as 'evil,' even as they're actually inseparable from justice and progress, and even as what's *actually* evil is everything springing from the unnatural divisions that their 'propriety' preserves. Similarly, speaking of spirituality in ways expanding the narrow, disempowering, hierarchal, constraining scope of religion is considered an exhibition of the heresies of a heathen, if it's not outright decried as 'devil worship (as countless Christians have condemned my spirituality).'

How many of you, dear readers, are capable of seeing that all of these false equivalencies are byproducts of the divide and conquer imperialism inherited by and inherent to the conservatism that culturally and politically dominates this nation, and ever more of the world? How many of you are mentally strong enough to resist the evils that they sell as goods, teaching us from the time that we're able to think that any form of connection outside the sanctioning of Church, State and Corporation, all run by the plutocracy for greedy, controlling purposes, is wrong? Do you not see *why* this is so? Do you not recognize the fact that restraining, if not killing, the connective drive that makes us social and spiritual human beings is core to the ever-evolving divide and conquer playbook passed down from Caesar to his modern ilk, the Nixons, Reagans, Bush's and Trumps that run the government on behalf of the aristocracy? Do you not see that the 'propriety' of conventional relationships is just another of these cages?

I mean, how fucked up is it that the very thing that most makes life worth living, the tightening of the interconnecting spiritual tissue that we call 'love,' is what prohibits me from being a part of Jess's life, because her monogamy, and then marriage, the relationship standards, render that love 'inappropriate?' Not necessarily inappropriate to feel, for that can't be helped, but inappropriate to admit, much less to speak of, much less to explore. *That would be immoral.*

It's simply cut off, the rule being that the only appropriate communication remain at surface level, entirely devoid of emotional content, and, thus, entirely discarding of any truth or honesty. And after the love is undeniable, even *that* must remain denied, else the potential of it being misconstrued, either by the accepted or unaccepted love. It's inseparable from conventional corporate workplace policy, and divide and conquer Americanism in general, honestly. Just be a wife and a husband sanctioned by the Church, or a tool in the corporate machine making profits for the rich; anything else is too messy, too risky, and jeopardizes profit and control. *Kill the truth before it threatens the profitable falsehood.* That's conservative America in a nutshell. Just keep scarfing-down chronic

poison sold to keep you weak and on a leash, ye 'patriots'
living in the land of the free, where freedom = *dependency*.

05

THE KITCHEN IS NEAR
THE NURSE'S STATION

"To eat with a fuller consciousness of all that is at stake might sound like a burden, but in practice few things in life can afford quite as much satisfaction. By comparison, the pleasures of eating industrially, which is to say eating in ignorance, are fleeting."

- Michael Pollan, from *The Omnivore's Dilemma*

As a topic that will be expounded upon in greater detail later, using Pollan's work as an example, there's no such thing as 'unbiased' or 'non-prejudicial,' for even a non-editorialized mere 'reporting of fact' is biased by way of the facts *chosen* to be reported, before any 'objective interpretation' of those facts. It reminds me of the absurd 'the science says' preludes to the pretense of objective reporting in the endless research I've done on various natural nutritional compounds over the years, as if all the science is known, and without the least bit of regard for how and why scientific studies are financed, or *not*, and the interested parties' influence over the interpretations.

Do you think it's Mother Nature pushing the 'science says' narrative? Or every ridiculous report concluding 'there's no scientific evidence to support' such and such anecdotal treasure trove of benefit derived from literally *millennia* of unofficial studies by legions of medicine men, Ayuverdics and Traditional Chinese Medicine doctors? Might it be that the use of scientific evidence to control consumers and steer them away from nature and towards chemicals has something to do with the difficulty of turning a naturally occurring medicine into a profitable proprietary product? Might it be that Mother Nature isn't financing scientific studies, and offers Her healing to one and all, by natural *right*? What would happen if those financing medicinal studies did so *without* the profit motive, driven instead by an *actual* Hippocratic desire to reduce human suffering?

Might these also be the reasons that the nurses of the CRC, and the psychiatrist-slash-primary-prescriber who makes a quarter million dollars a year peddling the same profitable chemicals, sorry, the same 'medicine,' never reach for Mother Nature's salubrious medicine chest when treating the residents? Nah, I must be a 'cynic.' A foolish hippie. A tree hugger. I swear to Christ that to this day I'm certain that I can heal, or at least substantially alleviate the symptoms, of most patrons ineffectually dependent upon their primary care physicians, simply by trading their fast food for food is medicine, and their pharmaceutical bottles for judicially-selected twigs, leaves, berries and roots! And as an *amateur* naturopath barely scratching the surface!

Speaking of which, I'm fairly certain that the true purpose of *WebMD* isn't to provide accurate, unbiased medical advice as it purports, but to convince the gullible market that "no scientific evidence" or "not enough research" and the like are the same thing as "no proof" and "not enough validity," failing to inform the consumer seeking ways to improve his or her health that such a dearth of evidence and research is due to a lack of *financial motive* and interest in seeking truth and proof that will only undermine the profits of their clients in the conventional medical and pharmaceutical industries. This, in fact, runs parallel to the scientific bias in general, one that turns a blind eye to any force or truth of nature or spirituality which doesn't register on their instruments and in their cash registers, and which risks undermining their authority as profiting 'truth-tellers.'

There isn't a naturopath alive that doesn't grimace at the fact that poison that's only effective in rare, acute cases is regarded as 'primary treatment' whilst *true* medicine that's the only thing that's effective in the vast majority of cases, i.e. in the 'chronic illnesses' or 'lifestyle cases' *representing literally three-quarters of the profits of the medical industry*, is regarded as 'alternative treatment.' And yet the leeching primary caregivers are the 'doctors,' and *we're* the quacks!

If only that were the only insult. The heaving injury heaped atop it, to the extreme disservice of humanity: *An herbalist can't give advice that sounds medical without facing legal censure*. Hear me plainly: The only real doctors, those working with the guidance and providence of Mother Nature, with the only true, ancient apothecary at their disposal, aren't legally allowed to give medical advice! That is, we must speak of health benefits without it *sounding* like we're talking about medicinal benefits. We have to suggest it without saying it, whispering our advice in the dark like we're criminals. So perfectly have the perfidiously-spent yields of Big Pharma been invested in buying the allegiance of the law and pulling the teeth of the regulators *meant* to be serving the public's best interests that *real* healers are forced to hide in the shadows, reduced to the entrenched conflation of herbalism and 'witchcraft' that the Church made of earlier corruptions of authority, pretending like the medicine known by medicine men and woman for *millennia* isn't medicine, but something between idealistic, superstitious nonsense and irresponsible danger. Thus have the modern, *true* Hippocrates' been turned to grey market practitioners of what today's world has been conditioned to consider nonsense or poor sense so they can be chained to dependencies by glorified drug dealers.

For the same reason one should be very wary of taking nutritional advice from an FDA-backed dietitian, as the FDA is severely compromised by its relationships with food and pharmaceutical corporations. I've had discussions with dietitians claiming (thanks to, you know, all that training of theirs) that pizza represents a 'complete meal.' Ummm, have you read the literature on the *Whole 30*, *Paleo*, or *Wahls* protocols? Complete meal! Yea, *macro*nutriently, perhaps. I mean, even more basically, you have heard of *micro*nutrients, yes, Mr. 'Dietary Specialist?' And inflammatory compounds, yes? And heart disease, and diabetes, and gluten sensitivity, and the endless forms of autoimmune disorder that are more and more being linked to depression and most other mental illnesses, including CRC-prevalent schizophrenia? "All health begins in the gut," Hippocrates warned us over two *millennia* ago.

Maybe it's time to update the 'Hippocratic Oath,' huh? Maybe 'do no harm' needs another look? By the way, what are they serving for dinner at the CRC today? I'll give you a hint. They cut it into slices first before 'thoughtfully' dishing it out at this 'mental health facility.' Pizza is one of the best examples of a 'food' that seems designed to reduce the quality and longevity of human life; of a food *product* (for calling it a food is an insult to the real thing; to, you know, anything with any density of micronutrients in it) with a big profit margin (owing to cheap processed constituents) that's almost entirely devoid of life-guarding, vitality-increasing micronutrients whilst bombarding its consumers with massive amounts of inflammatory compounds through wheat, dairy and carcinogenic processed meats. But, hey, traditionally trained dietitians love it, so go for it you self-destructive glutton (don't get me wrong, I love the *taste* of pizza as much as anyone)! These FDA-rubber-stamped 'professional dietitians' are the same people whom, secretly in bed with Big Ag, their pants down, bent over the barrel of profit with Big Pharma standing behind them, whole-heartedly backed a food pyramid that any uncompromised student of nutrition laughed at; a pyramid that has since been turned on its head. Be very careful where you source your 'facts' from, dear reader. Medicine comes from one place, and one place only, and it sure as hell isn't the laboratories producing profitable dependency.

There is, by the way, a very creditable theory of disease that contradicts the conventional paradigm, and mirrors the mental health theory of every mind cracking under sufficient pressure, always in a manner best befitting that mind. The theory states that chronic dis-ease, the ongoing absorption of unnatural stresses, is eventually embodied, or *manifested*, at the weak point in the body, as disease relative to that particular part of the body. The theory reflects the law of nature related to the path of least resistance. That is, like a river of rancidity, the foul fluid of dis-ease flows through the cracks of your body and mind before settling at the lowest, weakest, least-fortified point, and there mounts into disease. Chronic dis-ease into disease. This as opposed to the conventional wisdom of health treatment as perfectly divided diseases, instead testifying to the truth that two people can face the exact same causal culprit, the same chronic source of stress and pressure (the same dis-ease, that is), and that it can, and usually will, manifest itself as a different disease. The revelation of this theory is, of course, that conventional treatment tailored to the effect isn't nearly as ethical and efficacious as rooting-out the weakness, damming the aforementioned path of least resistance that the foul fluids are taking, and fortifying the weak points against invasion.

If you're a moral person, you should, at this point, be asking yourself: If this paradigm of disease and treatment is legitimate, why haven't I heard of it? Or: Why isn't it a part of the conventional paradigm? Alas, you should also know the answer already: *it's not profitable*. Instead of selling you a drug for every particular manifestation of chronic dis-ease, one that you'll thereafter be perpetually dependent upon, to the endless profit of the manufacturer and prescription writers, it bids you to understand and fortify against the *causes*. And treating in terms of causality is almost always a matter of strengthening body and mind through nutrition, natural medicine, exercise in nature, meditation, practicing gratitude etc. *The free, far more effective forms of disease prevention*; a holistic, synergistic set of fortifications and recuperations requiring effort and education, typically sourced from Mother Nature, rather than quick fix 'throw money and chemical concoctions at the issue.' All efficacious healthcare is about *changing your life*. Your entire lifestyle must become one big holistic treatment. Knowledge, effort and nature against ignorance, laziness and profit. *There's* your battlefield, dear reader.

Where are you upon it? And have you any concept of how much of our limited means, and how much of our highest quality lifeblood, we'd prevent the parasitic leeches from draining out of us should we supplant their oppressive 'conventional medicine' with what they disparagingly dismiss as 'alternative medicine?' Or are you so well-conditioned, and so readily conforming, as to be blind to these caging, controlling bars, and the fact that I'm here referring to but one such cage within the larger cage of convention and conformity dictating the contemporary human condition? I know, I know, you're likely throwing up your hands at this point, decrying me as a wanna-be soothsayer, saying: "Stop preaching to me!" I'd pretend to be sorry, yet a tiger bears his stripes when left to the jungle, and only conceals them in the face of the poacher. And this book is *my* jungle. I refuse to hide my stripes, or to run from the fact that the *jungle* is precisely where the medicine is, crushed underfoot by conventional wisdom.

Shit, I'm convinced from *vast* experience that the sacred-*most* medicine, the resurgent Psilocybe cubensis, the lifter of the occluding veil, the great emancipator of the rutted form of self, could replace half the chemical cornucopia *by itself*, and with greater efficacy, and with no side-effects, and minimal potential for addiction and abuse. And that's before considering the fact that there are literally *thousands* of plants that've 'randomly' co-evolved with us animals to produce their own uniquely-beneficial-to-fauna medicinal compounds, most of which appear in only the most esoterically-obscure medical literature. Random my hairy Greek ass! The new nursery rhyme: *Do you know the mushroom man? The mushroom man? The mushroom man! The one that lives at the end of Enlightenment Lane?* And yet, despite knowing where the medicine is, the prevailing standard continues to be to simply conceal and perpetuate all forms of disease, treating illness with poison.

To this day I remain flabbergasted that the official, conventional medicinal policy when it comes to Type 2 Diabetes, caused by insulin resistance due mostly to excess carbohydrate consumption, isn't to reduce and strictly control carbohydrate consumption so that the body can counteract the cause, but to exacerbate it through the lifelong chemical leash of adding more insulin. I mean, I get that it fits the 'a patient cured is a customer lost' conventional corporate leeching primary care paradigm, but this case of pretending to fight a fire by throwing fuel on it is so overtly wrong that it's hard to believe it was, and maybe still is, the conventional treatment method. In fact, most chronic conditions, especially neurological and autoimmunity issues, have been linked to excess carbohydrate consumption and metabolic dysfunction, and the only sustainable treatment involves intermittent fasting and carbohydrate reduction, and reduction of consumption in general, something known and applied in those more liberal nations of the world where corporate greed isn't the *only* factor dictating how patrons-not-people are treated. The chemical leash and gradual tightening of the connected collar unto strangulation and death in *Killers of the Flower Moon* isn't so anachronistic as one might think. To me that film is as much an allegory of the evils of the modern pharmaceutical industry as it is a cousin of my previous book, *Old Blood*, on the corruption of nativism.

We evolved for scarcity, for our brains to equate sugar and fat with the preeminent drive: *survival*. In the modern age this ingrained evolutionary dictate is an anachronism for most of us, with the seemingly tragic, ironic result being that what once compelled our salvation now compels our sickness and demise, as the health conditions associated with overconsumption of simple carbohydrates and the sick, toxic, CAFO-raised animals that displaced the natural ruminants we once fed upon on the *rare* occasion when we were lucky enough to procure them now constitute the vast majority of our health ills, and, not coincidentally, most of the profits of the disturbingly profitable medical and pharmaceutical industries that do little to nothing to educate their victimized patrons as to the *actual* cause of most of their suffering: the unnatural 'foods' they consume.

That's 'business ethics' for you, where it's *unethical* to educate your patrons in any manner which reduces profitability. There should be a banner hanging over every doctor's office, hospital and pharmacy that reads: *Profits Over People.* This would be the case were *truth* the dictate of 'business ethics,' rather than profit-protecting propaganda. The same banner should fly over most every business, for that matter. But, hey, disregard us 'cynics,' that's just the 'free market,' right? *More propaganda.* Free to do, and from, what, exactly? Free from protection against exploitation, and free to live your entire life helping the rich get richer, both professionally and as a consumer, all while consuming for dysfunction, disease and disability.

My God, dear reader, if we could but *Erin Brockovich* the correlation between incidences of human disease and the food industry, and the collusion between those corporations and the toothless FDA, and the human cost of the medical industry refusing to identify and treat the causality of disease for the sake of their own profits, and the environmental ruin and planetary warming treated like inevitable collateral damage because of it all, and hold corporations financially responsible for what they *actually* cost the human race, the planet and life at large for their 'profits for us at any cost to anyone and everything else' dishonorable driving ethic, and expand and further empower a white collar crimes investigation division of some federal policing body, as *true* morality and ethics dictate, I'm quite certain we could bankrupt all of them and give food and medicine back to nature. Maybe then we'd actually cure people, instead of hiding disease with the incurring of ceaseless side effects from concealing chemicals and even more gluttonous, distracting, artificial 'foods' for the forever victimized, secretly-enslaved public.

With a wider application, considerate of what constitutes the full human cost, and considering even the oppression of lost opportunities and every manner of reduced quality of life, and accounting for the unaccounted for responsibilities of the 'business community,' the whole consortium of American (and global) corporations would likely face bankruptcy. This is certainly an angle for the socialistic revolutionaries to consider, at the least. Maybe what we really need is a consortium of moral lawyers driven to use the legal system and political correctness against the parasites for whom the law was mostly written. If we can't change the medical practice, and give it back to the true healers, maybe we can take on parasitism through legal channels, using nonprofits to finance lawsuits that benefit the *people*, rather than the parasites, for a change.

Every nutritional documentary that I've ever watched on *Netflix* or *Amazon* (and I must be damn near the century mark at this point) has had one or more medical professionals saying something like: "I was never trained on the connection between consumption and health," and various forms of "if I'd only known" and "now my life is dedicated to such and such form of treating the *actual* cause of disease." So it's not that doctors are actively conspiring to undermine the health of the human race, but that the conspiracy is built into the biased education constituting the medical degree, and that 'medical professionals' are conditioned not only to turn a blind eye, but to dismiss anything they hear that wasn't covered by their prejudicial training as being the baseless claims of the 'alternative medicine' morons. Scientists do the same to philosophers. Christians do the same to the 'spiritual but not religious.' Confirmation bias abounds in *all* states of ignorance and injustice, in fact. But you'll be hard-pressed to find a form more damaging to humanity than what primary care practitioners and their colluding chemical craftsman, Big Pharma, deliver upon the human race, or the fact that they're doing so to treat 'food is poison.' If you really want to 'make a killing,' invest in this industry trio, profiting off of all of the lives reduced by and lost to what the vast majority calls 'healthcare, medicine and food.'

As a corollary, the most underestimated skill on the planet is *grocery shopping*. It's the primary means by which any person or family may be freed from constantly paying the price of reduced quality and longevity of life incurred by the aforementioned Unholy Trinity. Why? Because you can't be good at grocery shopping without possessing a solid knowledge of nutrition (and *not* the knowledge possessed by most professional dieticians), and you can't possess such a solid knowledge of nutrition without understanding that it's the foremost constituent of good health, and you can't understand what it is to possess good health without knowing, or at least sensing, that health means nothing less than *the quality of the experience of existence*, and you can't well feed that quality and deny the Unholy Trinity but through well-knowing how to navigate the grocery store. And after extensive research and a treasure trove of empirical evidence gathered from my own shopping and consumption, and from recording the results, I've come to the conclusion that the pinnacle of nutrition is what I call the 'Super Paleo Protocol.' The Paleo approach to eating is commonly misunderstood. In truth, it's not meat-forward, but *produce*-forward, and (in divergence from Paleo), *it's starch-free and only consumes animals that themselves ate naturally* (non-CAFO). We evolved to gather *first*, *including* from the water, to *fish* second, and to hunt *last*, mostly due to the risks and challenges entailed in these respective activities, and to the fact that we evolved along waters bequeathing a *broad* array of animals *and* plants.

And I say this whilst well aware of the modern popularity of approaches like Atkins and the Carnivore Diet that sell people what they want to hear (*eat only animal products!*) in confusion of and conflation with the very real dangers and disruptions of grain, sugar and starch dependency. Alas, *all* nutrients start with plants and microorganisms, not animals (macro-organisms), *including* the Omega 3 Fatty Acids that come from the grasses consumed by ruminants and the aquatic plants consumed by seafood. The density of those nutrients are paltry in the consuming animals compared to the source produce, as little of it survives in the tissue of the consuming animals, at least on any level of bioavailability whereby those nutrients are passed into us upon consuming the consuming animal. Even the B12 that meat-eaters like to cite as proof of the deficiency of veganism actually comes from microorganic activity. An occasional glass of kombucha alone kills that argument. Actually, we could reduce this whole guiding principle to a single nutrient, *fiber,* and its critical nature in protecting cardiovascular health (soluble fiber) and gut health, where most neurotransmitters are produced that protect against every mental health disorder (insoluble fiber), and it would *still* be an irrefutable principle, even *after* dispensing with the *thousands* of other indispensable plant micronutrients.

Long have I imagined how I would rescue the chronically ill, given sufficient resources. A retreat in the midst of nature, entirely removed from the choking corruptions and uncleanliness of modern society. That's the indispensable starting point. Then a strictly purifying diet for at least a month; smoothies of organic fruits and veggies, with only wild seafood and spirulina for protein, and its myriad other benefits. Moderate coffee, tea and kombucha. Only natural medicinal compounds as medicine, and in alleviation of any and all symptoms. Micro-to-macro doses of Psilocybe cubensis, monitored, especially with beginning users. Hikes around the property, with accompanying wild harvesting and gardening of the cultivated portions of said property. Artistic expression; music, painting, sculpting, writing and the like, enlisting the critical fact known by the freely-thinking and the *true* healers that humanity is creative by its holy nature, and that the more that this nature is denied to us by unnatural society the more unnatural, i.e. distressed and diseased, we become. Communal fires at night, as a part of the 'return to nature' core of the healing process. Massage and meditation and aromatherapy and water therapy, including bathing in a river, and hot baths, as optional activities. Reading books. Sunbathing. Nothing electronic; no phones or televisions. Actual human connection, listening, healing. A one month commitment to this lifestyle, in a truly natural setting, as a *minimum.* My 'Revitalization Retreat.' I honestly believe that there's very little this simple set of synergistic treatments couldn't heal, *especially* if taken away from the retreat and made into the visitors' ongoing holistic *lifestyle*.

My pitch for the dietary core of the Revitalization Retreat:

The Superhuman Reset

Aka "Medicinal, Raw and Wild Pesca-Paleo (MRWPP)"

- 30 days of consuming entirely raw, organic fruits and vegetables plus strictly wild seafood (not 'wild caught' and definitely not farmed - only the real, natural thing) mixed into fiber-dense smoothies and salads using only select cold-pressed plant oils (primarily olive and avocado), vinegars, salt and spices for flavor. The added sauces and dressings are a *major* culprit in the Standard American Diet, as they're almost uniformly based upon cheap, inflammatory oils, especially soybean oil, and packed with high fructose corn syrup and unnatural preservatives. Initially, consume as much as you want per day. There's no counting of calories, only a strict *quality* maximization, allowing absolutely nothing linked to chronic inflammation and disease.

- Big mixed salads containing only raw organic fruits and vegetables and wild seafood ('Super Salads') plus smoothies and snacking on raw fruit is the whole diet, with only water, coffee, tea and low sugar kombucha allowed as drinks. My favorite strategy, especially for breakfast, when I can best utilize the resulting relatively high blood sugar, is to pair such a salad, with greens and mixed veggies and satiating wild seafood, with a smoothie based upon bananas and other fruits, and sometimes spirulina powder, raw ginger, turmeric and other 'superfoods.' It's a "Smoothie and Salad" version of Superhuman, or "SS" for short. In fact, I sometimes abbreviate this entire dietary strategy as 'SSS' in my health journal: Seafood, Smoothies and Salads.

- No drugs or alcohol permitted the first month of the reset, with moderate wine allowed after (I don't recommend consuming grain-based alcohols). And I don't consider P. cubensis a drug, but *medicine*.

- Once you're comfortable with *what* you're eating, and can sustain it, begin introducing the benefits of intermittent fasting, which have been *well* studied and documented (see, for example, Longo's work at USC). While seemingly counterintuitive, the fact is that when you eat less often your body is given the opportunity to commit its limited energy and resources normally expended through digestion and all associated physiological processes, like waste elimination and energy shuffling and storage, to activities of healing, fortification and rejuvenation. The potential benefits are too numerous to list here, but intermittent fasting has been connected to improved metabolic and neurological functioning, as well as staving off disease risk (including cancer) and improved results in illness recovery.

- It's a sad but necessary truth to learn that the only way to become your fullest self and guard against all disease and dependency and protect the planet and eat morally is to be the slimmest of customers, 'just saying no' to all conventional industry foods (and to primary care doctors - go to *naturopaths*) that cost us our lives, forcing us to forfeit our true, natural selves. For the truth is that the entirely unscrupulous, greed-is-God nature of the industrial food supply is such that their goal is *always* to amplify and sell to your weakness, to your gluttony and impulsivity (chemical flavor enhancers that artificially exaggerate your appetite are standard additives in all prepackaged and fast foods), whilst simultaneously misleading you with the sales scheme of the packaging, designed to make you focus on the wrong thing and make the 'food' seem better for you than it is. *Ignore everything but the list of ingredients*. Better yet, only buy food that isn't packaged or pre-prepared, and is entirely unprocessed. The sad, albeit unavoidable truth is that if you want to really be your complete self you MUST go to war with convention (and not just when it comes to diet), and that, largely because the standard food supply is predicated upon rampant propaganda amounting to making you miserable for profit, that this requires an extraordinary level of education and discipline that, tragically, less than 1% of the population will be able to muster, leaving 99% of people unaware of their fullest forms of self. This is NOT hyperbole, this is incontrovertible fact.

- The Superhuman Reset is a 'food is medicine,' 'all health begins in the gut,' maximum micronutrients per calorie, gut health rehabilitation model, with absolutely no inflammatory compounds, and high ethics owing to its low carbon footprint and no allowing of suffering foods produced in toxic environments. The vast majority of meat is CAFO and toxic, and most of what constitutes SAD (the Standard American Diet) is in some way unnatural to the human body, with unnatural cause always leading to unnatural effect. 'Return to nature' is the wisest creed, and is reflected herein by the recommendations not only of this dietary template, but of using natural medicines in lieu of toxic pharmaceuticals, as well as incorporating as many activities in nature as possible, including cultivation.

- Raw organic foods are the focus for many interconnected reasons, including the toxic skin layer and agricultural run-off produced by non-organic produce, the nutrient and enzyme loss caused by cooking (especially at higher temps without water), and that cooking is the primary means by which food is denatured, and by which a fattening condensing of calories is created, and, through gastrointestinal leukocytosis, by which the body's immune system is activated during digestion, triggering cascading inflammation. Generally speaking, if it can't be consumed without cooking or other forms of processing, through a pure, evolutionarily-grounded, pre-agriculture, gatherer-fisher approach, it probably shouldn't be consumed at all. That said, you may add select cooked foods back into the diet post-reset, and most of the benefits of this reset will be sustained.

- Daily administration of herbal medicines in the alleviation of stress and symptoms is not *required*, but is *highly* advisable, as it mitigates stress and puts the body and the mind in a state conducive to revitalization. Incalculable quality of life improvements may be garnered by leaning on herbal medicines as a shield against the common contemporary contagions of stress, anxiety and depression *instead* of leaning on alcohol, recreational narcotics, prescribed pharmaceuticals and 'comfort feeding.' The difference between these two general forms of treatment is, of course, that the former is sustainable, and achieves its benefits free from deleterious side-effects, whilst the latter, more common forms of 'self-treatment' trade their short-term reductions in stress, anxiety and depression for the *worsening* of these symptoms in the long run, by the cause of gradually degrading bodily function and capacity. But to successfully employ the former you must commit yourself to a course of exploring and experimenting with the cornucopia. I tend to have at least a dozen such medicines in capsule form alone at any one time (before teas and tinctures etc.) that I mix and match, and consider that to be a rather miniscule number considering what's available. I also make what I call a "Restorative Tea," simmering in a non-dairy 'milk' for an hour a rotating mix of whole organic medicines, such as (in but one version): Oat Straw, Skullcap, Damiana, Bacopa Monnieri, St. John's Wort, Gotu Kola and Maca + honey to taste, filtering out and composting all the solids. This is, of course, but one of an endless number of combinations of the *thousands* of medicinal plants whose combination, dosage and means of administration should constitute an ongoing basis of experimentation and self-improvement for the evolved modern human being freed from doctors.

- And when it comes to animal products, especially meat itself, toxicity, carcinogens, environmental ruin and inhumanity run rampant. Watch a single film on CAFO's. Eating their 'food' is supporting evil. But even for the amoral consumer caring nothing for the hell his/her consumption unleashes upon these feeling animals, the stress hormones and toxicity especially concentrated in the fat cells of CAFO animals raised in such feces-and-urine-stewing environments *will* increase all risks of contracting disease for those whom ingest it. In stark contrast, wild seafood is *far* superior in that its fat is not only *far* less likely to be toxic (depending upon the waters where the seafood was sourced, and, when it comes to mercury risk, to how high it is on the food chain) but brimming with the highly salubrious Omega 3's sourced from the aquatic plant base of the marine food chain, plus the environmental cost is *far* lower, both in that it has a much lower carbon footprint than CAFO animals *and* that it doesn't produce the toxic waste and cascading, polluting, riparian-poisoning runoff of evil CAFO operations.

- Simply stated, this one month reset (ideally leading to a longer term approach; keep reading) maximizes all the beneficial elements of true, evolutionarily-sound food, and takes a strict exclusionary approach to all of the detrimental false 'foods' inextricably linked to every form of 'lifestyle disease' by which primary care providers and Big Pharma are enriched through human misery. You'd be hard pressed to find any form of disease that isn't greatly alleviated, or even healed, by this diet.

- Necessary fat is provided by avocado, olive (both the oils and the whole fruits) and wild seafood. Necessary protein is provided by the wild seafood, the spirulina, and what's naturally in produce. And functional energy is provided by the fruit you snack on, in addition to your body learning to more efficiently convert fat into energy through such a lower-carb approach (relative to SAD). Keep in mind that the protein 'requirements' of conventional recommendations are *grossly* exaggerated, and that high animal protein diets are linked to many diseases, especially when that protein is derived from concentrated animal feeding operations.

- It's not a perspective, but a fact, that whatever satisfaction you sacrifice in terms of food enjoyment to make your food more healthful/medicinal will be delivered back to you *many* times over in terms of the far longer-lasting satisfactions of greater vitality, energy and personal ability. So, as a part of the practice, rather than thinking about the short-term satisfaction sacrificed by the diet as a loss, as something you're 'missing out on,' think of it as a savings and reinvestment that rewards massive dividends. Satisfaction isn't wasted, it's *invested* in something *far* more satisfying over time: *a true you!*

- Don't focus on what you can't have, focus on what you *can*. Exploring the near boundless realm of fresh organic produce is invaluable to anyone the least bit experimental whom really dives into it, and represents the best possible gateway into the culinary arts; arts that begin with sourcing, knowing and appreciating the best *ingredients*, which, of course, means *the plant world*. With practice, you'll find that the enjoyment of fresh fruits, vegetables, herbs, spices, vinegars and select cold-pressed oils exceeds any other dietary modality; that is, when you're cognizant enough to notice and add together both the direct enjoyment of natural foods *and* the sustained enjoyment of feeling better, and being more capable, than at any other time in your life.

- All you need is the strength to stick with this plan for 30 days, with zero justifications or excuses for going off of it, and you'll be effectively reborn. Keep in mind that the *only* thing that *all* human beings are experts in is unjustifiably justifying their bad habits. If you can overcome this 'expertise,' you'll be rewarded with what few know: *their complete self.*

- After the first reset month, you can add in eggs if you can find actual free range eggs (not just 'cage free,' or any other misleading term; most egg operations are the most unnatural and unethical of all CAFO operations), as well as nuts and seeds, as long as they're not flavored with anything problematic, like soy and preservatives, and select Paleo-approved sauces (the *Primal* brand is a good choice). You may also begin cooking some of your produce, but it remains highly recommended that, in order to avoid leukocytosis, that you keep at least half of every bowl or plate as consisting of raw food. Finding local(ish) suppliers of wild seafood and true free range eggs is highly recommended. You can also add back controlled quantities of red wine at this point, but, again, I don't recommend drinking more inflammatory grain-based alcohols.

- Note that while I reference this dietary approach as 'superhuman,' this term is only relative to the way in which most people living in the 'advanced nations' of overabundance eat. The sad reality, of course, is that this approach is actually the *Human Diet*; the way that human beings naturally evolved to eat for peak vitality and capacity, and is only 'superhuman' in the sense that most modern humans living in said 'advanced nations' eat *so* unnaturally as for their diets to gradually render them *subhuman*; chronically-compromised versions of themselves.

- As a final note, please take heed of the fact that this dietary approach is based upon decades of intermittent academic study and TONS of personal empirical data, and includes principles sourced from and shared with innumerable books and documentaries, including work that's classified under the *Paleo*, *Whole 30* and *Wahls* protocols.

- P.S.: If you *really* want to clean house, follow this with what I call the "TranscenDance Purification:" A 1 to 3 week cleanse in which you ONLY consume:
  - Water
  - Matcha
  - Kombucha
  - Fire Cider (medicinal-plant-infused ACV)
  - Fresh-squeezed citrus
  - Blended plant powders (like spirulina, maca, and beet powders)
  - Medicinal teas (infused spices and herbs)
  - P. cubensis: opening and closing 2g, with micro dosing in between (0.25-0.5 g daily)

- o With lots of music, dancing, singing, hiking, wildcrafting and, if possible, lots of sex as well. And ideally on a property surrounded by the majesty of nature, with nightly fires
  - o Also highly recommended during this: cultivate, study and develop a relationship with plants, generally, but especially those with known medicinal qualities (i.e. those with known, established human relations)

"Too extreme!" the mindless minions shout. Just before they say "Everything in moderation!," as if uttering some great, divine wisdom. That maxim cracks me up. First of all, *everything*? Murder? Crack? Rape? Incest? Pedophilia? No? Okay, so not *everything*. Second of all, you'll never learn anything about yourself remaining in the unchallenged center, baaing with the herd. Self-knowledge requires measures which most people dismiss as 'too extreme.' How can you know who you are and what you're capable of if you remain safely set near the center of obligation and expectation, without pushing yourself towards the margins? How many explorers were renowned for staying inside their home bays? How much of anything of value falls into the lap of anyone too timid and pretentious to push themselves beyond what the majority considers appropriate, or normal, or acceptable, or any other middling, everyone-pat-your-groupthink-pals-on-the-back description of the 'proper' person. *Fuck normality.* Be the weird one beyond the standard deviation from the norm. Third of all, as, actually, an extension of the second point, you'll never meet an inspiring, or even, I would suppose, an *intelligent* moderate. Not only all the great people, but even someone qualifying as truly *interesting*, will possess beliefs and practices that the glut of humanity dismisses as 'extreme.' Progress, personal or societal, is set at the extremes, beyond the caging comfort zone.

In the case of consumption, it seems like most people think of eating as though anything *but* maximizing immediate satisfaction is 'extreme;' that any policy but gluttony or epicureanism is nonsense. My contemplations, however, suggest that the *indirect* satisfaction only achievable by honoring what food represents to body and brain, a strengthening of an ultra-complex set of biochemical systems, is the *far* greater satisfaction; a satisfaction that's wasted when the 'non-extreme' is the practice. At the same time, if you reach the point where you can cultivate a healthful form of highly *selective* epicureanism, then the culinary arts can provide an invaluable addition of mental and sensory satisfaction to the holistic health practice.

Anything that similarly focuses our feeling of presence, in league with enhanced sensory awareness, makes a valuable addition to holism, in fact. But since food is so integral to our evolved sensory experience, its benefits may be *particularly* pronounced, especially, again, when its conspicuous contents fortify and strengthen us, rather than constituting SADly careless contents that imperil and weaken us. Epicureanism must evolve to reflect human evolution and its overlap with the healthy human body and brain, else the idea of maximizing food indulgence becomes destructive. SADly, most never know who and what they could be, how good they could feel, how much they would be capable of, and how attainable the higher satisfactions approaching true happiness are *because* they treat food as a type of slowly self-compromising gratuity rather than a type of gradually self-actualizing annuity.

This is also why a healthy, fully capacious body is the cornerstone of peace and wisdom. For when our bodies are burdened by unnaturalities, by one or more forms of disease and its dis-ease, how can the mind be free to be where it is, without being beleaguered by bodily burden? When your body is at peace, it's *far* more likely that your mind shall be as well; it makes it *possible*. But when your body is distressed, by the inseparability of body and brain, so shall be your mind. In fact, while anxiety and depression and many other afflictions are listed as 'mental diseases,' the truth is that they live in the body *before* the mind; the mental aspects of such diseases are but extensions of *physical* disease. It's inconvenient to psychiatrists, and to institutions such as the CRC, but little true healing comes from psychological treatment alone, and *none* comes from pharmaceutical masking; these modalities offer little more than alleviation, and usually come with considerable concealed financial, physiological and psychological costs that almost everyone fails to accurately account for. Get to the root of the *physiological* distress first, and often this will be sufficient in itself, and will negate the need for what the 'head doctors' and institutions such as the CRC are ready to sell you. *Build from the ground up. Start with the foundation. For the ground is the body, and the foundation upon which we build is food. The cure is 'food is medicine.'*

Most people, especially SAD Americans, are at least a little bit sick their entire adult lives, they're just not aware of it because *it's their normal*; there's no revelatory contrast, only insidiously developed debilitation and dependency. The only ones who come to know this through the Great Teacher, Experience, are those with the rare combined qualities of sufficient knowledge and discipline to apply Hippocratic principles in a world that's more likely to apply Hippocrates to an oath that *every* doctor breaks when they use concealing chemicals instead of 'food is medicine.' The result of relying upon them is an erosion of every part of our experience of existence, including our very thoughts.

I find that the foremost predictor of my thoughts is how I *feel*; and the foremost predictor of how I feel is my health; and the foremost predictor of my health is my diet. It's an

unbreakable, incontrovertible chain. It's the inseparability
of past, present and future; Faulkner in physiological
microcosm. Thus, when we pick up the apple instead of
the fast food we're *literally* changing our thoughts,
cascading across every avenue of existence affected by
thought processes; which, of course, includes *every*
avenue of existence. Produce precipitates peace, fast food
triggers dis-ease and disease. There's no way around it,
no matter how much belligerent blowhard petty presidents
stand at their pitiful pulpits and brag about their SAD diets.
If anything he's a demonstration of why *not* to eat his way.

And capitalism, meanwhile, counts upon our lacking this
wisdom, and our dispossession of the discipline to practice
it. Its parasitic profiteers depend upon stoking our dis-ease
and the dependency that it causes. Its commercialism drills
dissatisfaction into our heads. Its consumerism consumes
the countless un-lived lives of its common conformists. Its
bourgeoisie is the quintessence of classist comparisons,
conditioned to *never* be at peace, to never be satisfactorily
aligned with the artificial lines that society draws between
its forever divided and conquered socioeconomic sectors.
These, by the way, are also the cornerstones by which the
crooks that run this country, that reign over the plutocratic
republic (*not* a democracy, people, sorry - read my
book *Cultural Cornerstones, Recarved*), build and maintain
their crookery. That's not conspiracy theory, that's *fact*.

"Let me make you a PROMIS," said every Cheney to every
Bush, "that this will never come back to bite you, only our
(self-defending) terrorist enemies." And yes, I left the E out
of PROMIS on purpose, for the many-tentacled truth of the
conspiratorial *nature* of capitalism requires that you see
that a conspiracy is innate to every illegal expansion of
power and greed in history. In fact, with an open, liberal
enough application of that word, 'conspiracy,' it's clear that

all expansions of profit and power are the results of some form of conspiring, and that this is the very nature of capitalism. Hey now, duped, delusional Republicans, don't *Kill the Messenger* for having the brains and balls to speak the truth! Your leeching lords and masters will still be *Filthy Rich*. If anything goes wrong with their conspiracies they can simply claim it was an *Inside Job* with no connective tentacles, and that WMD's really were uncovered in the *Green Zone*, for surely such crimes are easily concealed within the mindless modern *Zeitgeist*.

If anything they'll be forced to pay fines amounting only to *Loose Change*. Of course, if I ever *am* listened to, dear reader, is it really such a stretch to imagine that I could be targeted as an *Enemy of the State*, as is everyone whom shines too bright a light on the concealed crooks that run this compromised country? Just keep in mind that those predisposed to committing these big league crimes *depend* upon you reflexively associating all conspiracy theories and their theorists with lunatics, and that, as the last aforementioned film reminds us, "credibility is the only currency on this playing field." Not that there aren't mentally unstable, deluded types giving us theorists a bad name (the CRC was replete with them, and not just among the residents), but for every ten stories of bug-eyed alien overlords living on moon bases there's at least one *Pelican Brief*, its writer often too terrified to publish it. It's simply a matter of having the intelligence and information to connect the detecting dots between motive, means and opportunity. Not to mention the fact that countless amongst the self-righteous and 'respectable' openly endorse beliefs involving resurrection, messiahs making voyages to the New World and science fiction stories taken as gospel.

Frankly, if you're even the least bit aware of the grand scheme of things, that awareness includes the fact that those whom should be hung for their crimes against humanity instead hang high above it, running the country, and ever more the world at large, ever raping people and planet with impunity. Actions that *should* condemn them to eternal ignobility instead grant them nobility, their heinous machinations rewarded by the compromised systems and purchased public institutions underpinning the planet. And every single one of them is empowered by the obese, reflexive, conservative consumers of not just unnecessary, unhealthy products and services, but propaganda taken as truth. You really want to 'stick it to the man?' *Need not what he sells. Be the slim customer forever practicing presence.* And start by procuring food from *Mother Nature.*

But it's not just diet that's misunderstood and abused in a manner that fractures our foundation, but most any habit which trades a long term accruing of vital force, of a quality experience of existence, for a large quantity of dissipating pleasures. I'm not advocating for a non-pleasing existence here, but, in fact, for a superior form of pleasure which most shall never know: the pleasure of becoming what one may become *absent* self-reductive habits. These are the pleasures attained in the persistent state of not needing what delusion and contemporary conditioning dictates that we need, but which are, in reality, part of the unnecessary cage of capitalism and consumerism; the dictates of the gratuitous and diseased; being chained to fleeting pleasures costing us our long term happiness, the unnatural pleasures enriching the crooks at the top of the entirely unstable pyramid scheme that shall inevitably collapse, the free market that keeps extracting in order to sustain its unsustainability. I'm referring here to the possibility of trading their invisible chains for the greatest pleasures, for they're the pleasures of your complete self; pleasures that're only possible by disciplining ourselves against the corruptive forces which cost us the truly anomalous 'extreme' in the United States: *happiness itself.*

Corruption is the sullying of the source signal, the perversion of a purity of purpose. There are endless examples, of course. Sex losing its connection to love and spirituality. Arousal requiring pornography. Masturbation displacing the mate. (The corruption of one's sex drive is, unfortunately, something that I'm all too familiar with.) Drugs superimposing themselves upon our neural pathways until dependency is confused with need. Politicians turning the law into a means of injustice on behalf of plutocratic puppet masters. But the most common is the conflation of satisfaction and carb-stoked 'hunger,' and the often false, conventional wisdom of 'listening to your body.' Yes, the body should be listened to *at times*, for its sophisticated mechanisms and your instinctive and studied awareness of them offer a bounty of useful information. But don't forget that, at the same time, the body can be, and usually is, corrupted by unhealthy habits producing relative unnaturalities within it, and that this unnaturality, in turn, sends signals of its own. This is something that every drug addict knows, and that all addicts of unnatural types of foodstuffs, and degrees of their consumption, should know as well. Just because an addiction to an unnaturality is common doesn't mean that it isn't an unhealthy addiction, and that its unnaturality won't hijack and corrupt our neurochemical signaling systems.

In fact, for the vast majority of people hunger is a liar. And it's at its worst with metabolic dysfunction and insulin resistance. Anyone that's gone from SAD (Standard American Diet) to low carb, or, more extreme in transition, to Keto, knows the 'jonesing' of the most common form of addiction: to *carbohydrates*. To the carb addict, going from floods of blood sugar to a trickle is agonizing. You'll experience withdrawals. Trust me, I know, as I'm sure many of you, dear readers, know as well. You'll literally dream about sweets, as I did. Even as it's known that the actual carbohydrate necessity is *zero*. That's right. A person can go their entire long lives without consuming a *single* carb, regardless of what your box of cereal says. The risk is one of *micro*nutrient deficiency, like the scurvy of insufficient Vitamin C, *never macro*nutrient deficiency (deficiency of carbohydrates, fat and protein). For the body is adept at adapting to the circumstances forced upon it, and can make of fat, and even protein, the energy necessary for survival, both by converting it into blood sugar via a process known as gluconeogenesis, and by more directly translating lipid energy into ketone bodies.

By paving the path to hunger with sensory gratification, we hijack a signal of self-preservation and turn it into a downhill path of gradual self-reduction. That's the first thing that I notice when I force myself into a 'cleanse;' that my corrupted neurology is telling me that I'm hungry because I'm feeding myself substantial, salubrious calories instead of empty, deleterious calories. Every time I undergo such a transition I'm forced to go to war with these hijacked neurochemical signals; to experience an incessant false sense of hunger until I realize that I'm not *actually* hungry, I'm just not getting the neurochemical fix formed by my dependency upon greasy, unhealthy, sweet, inflammatory foods. My stomach could be full, and yet the hunger signal persists; is doing so as I type this, in fact, on day one of my own Superhuman Reset. You see, there's an undeniable, invisibly-insidious, gradually-gripping corruption of the neurochemical apparatus that occurs when consumption is driven purely by gratification, as opposed to diet being driven by true hunger and nutrient density. And this corruption can only be revealed by the knowledge and discipline required to see the contrast that most people haven't the strength of will to bring to illuminating light.

The corruptive influence and the short-term physiological and psychological discomfort of the contrast is similar to what a drug addict experiences upon his/her withdrawal, and, indeed, involves the same neurochemical pathways. When, for example, fresh fruit doesn't qualify in the brain as 'dessert,' or when an avocado doesn't qualify as rich and decadent, you've got a problem, and are most likely suffering from being overweight and metabolically dysfunctional, else are well on your way there, and to the possession of connected disease. Again, just because this problem is so common as to be considered normal doesn't make it non-problematic. If you share the conventional standards, that's another problem. "Thank you for your patronage!," secretly shouts your doctor and pharmacist.

In fact, I firmly believe that one's relative ability to achieve food-based satisfaction from raw produce to be a barometer of their overall healthfulness, for it measures the relative extent of their neurochemically-linked gastronomic corruption, or the rare lack thereof, which itself is inextricably tied to what contributed to that relative corruption, which, in turn, is a measure of what they have, and haven't, put into their bodies. As a corollary, during a recent mushroom trip, as I was contemplating the unhealthy habits that've produced my own insidious health conditions, I heard in my head: *Habits are trained dogs*.

Most people have heard the Native American proverb about everyone having two dogs within them, and that these dogs, in the simplified version, represent the duality of good and evil, and what the individual makes of his or her self is based upon the relative extent to which he or she feeds these two dogs. Well, without getting too much into the philosophical quandary that this simplistic dichotomy unearths in the contemplative mind, and the fact that good and evil are actually inseparable, like two sides of the same coin, rather than absolutely separated enemies, as typically depicted... that God and the Devil are secret, intimately-connected *allies*... that contrast is the revelation of truth, and that this truth is the revelation of the purpose of the two-sided coin... without delving deeper into that 'offensive to Christianity' secret stash of truth, I *will* say that within the context of the aforementioned Native American proverb that these two dogs are actually a *pack*.

We ourselves are akin to the alpha dog, the head of a pack that constitutes our total self, and anything and everything that we not only do, but that we *think*, with any repetition whatsoever, is akin to training one of our many composing canines. And those canines, every single one of them, no matter how set he or she is in its ways, no matter the extent of its conditioning and feeding, can be reconditioned, starved, or fed something else entirely. You *can* recondition *any* member of your pack, no matter how dominating he or she may be, and cut or increase the slack on the leash that binds you to them, and thereby remake the force flowing through them to the alpha that energetically and spiritually feeds upon, and leads them through, all of your leashed-together lives. For every member of the pack feeds off of every other member, and the better our relationship with any one of them, the better our relationship tends to be with the others, and vice versa, proving that the snowball effect rolls as readily up as down.

And speaking of 'leashed lives,' and of snowballs being composed of what they roll through, it's also incumbent upon the observant, moral and progressive to note that the *rampant* mental illness delivered upon the American public must be considered an indictment of American Life; of constant unnatural degrees and forms of stress on the front end, and a dearth of sufficiently countering support on the back end (a point made by my favorite book during my MA study, Mark Fisher's *Capitalist Realism*, a work that still rises up to my conscious mind years later, and was integral to the novel I wrote whilst studying for my MA, *Avant Garde*). Not to mention the fact that pharmaceutical companies and prescribers pull inordinately exorbitant bounties from the suffering on a daily basis to conceal and never heal their afflictions, all treatments of which are toxic to the body, and that the vast majority of providers fail to prescribe, or even *consider*, natural forms of treatment that come with a low-to-no price tag, far superior long-term sustainability and often greater efficacy, and are the only potential true 'healers.' Mother Nature heals for free, Big Pharma conceals whilst leashing and tapping the patron for as much of their limited wherewithal as possible. This is but one of a seemingly limitless number of proofs of the parasitism of capitalism versus the symbiosis of nature.

As alluded to previously, the primary prescriber for Cascade Recovery Center and, indeed, for Deschutes County at large, made the local paper for 'earning' north of a quarter million dollars annually for prescribing a profusion of chemical cocktails to 'stabilize' mental health patients who, in turn, are so internally ravaged by this 'medicine' that most recurrent 'recoverees' are lucky to see the age of forty. Looking at the list of pharmaceuticals absorbed by some of their beleaguered bodies and brutalized brains, in many instances numbering a dozen or more different daily medications, one wondered how some of them could *stand up*, much less function. "Were all other avenues exhausted *before* resorting to such extreme measures!?," I oft wanted to scream, "or is nature's non-proprietary cornucopia of *actual* medicine too cost-effective a treatment modality to consider on behalf of those regarded as the easily sacrificed refuse of society!?" Yes, chemicals can well conceal and thus shortsightedly reduce the appearance of symptoms, but at what cost? And then walk into the kitchen, and if thee be trained in nutrition (free from the FDA corruption of the dietician) gaze in horror at the total rejection of Hippocrates' "food is medicine" revelation, and

the fact that innumerable mental and neurological and
autoimmune issues are intertwined to the point of
inseparability, and that everything from fasting to including
more probiotics to lowering carbohydrate consumption to
eliminating known inflammatory agents of the Standard
American Diet usually constitute *more* effective treatments.

Yes, I must admit, *some* efforts were made at the CRC,
including bringing in one of the aforementioned dieticians
(Gretchen was hot), but those efforts folded to the comfort-
feeding demands of the residents almost as soon as they
were enlisted. 'At least we tried,' I imagine the
administrators consoling themselves. 'We can't *force* good
health upon them, just as we can't force them to clean their
rooms or the bathroom or acknowledge the fact that living
in filth undermines everything we purport to represent.'
How, I ask, can someone make progress in mental and
physiological health when daily feasting on enough carbs
and saturated and hydrogenated fat to kill a pig, then go to
bed in a room that so badly reeks of urine and feces that
many Recovery Specialists can't bear to enter it in order to
administer him/her their exorbitant daily treatments? And
this from a "leader in the progress of the mental health
field." To me, and as attested to by the emergence of the
'integrative health practitioner,' it's long been clear that a
paradigm-shift in the way that we view health is absolutely
necessary for the wellbeing of not just those suffering from
diagnosed mental health issues, but for the entire
population. And, ironically, this shift represents *reversion*.

The secret base of the human being has always been:
Body *is* mind. Reason *is* emotion. Matter *is* energy. In my
final days of editing this book I'm reading *Stealing Fire*. In it
the 'emerging field' of 'embodied cognition' is discussed.
An expert in the field, Guy Claxton, says: "The body, the
gut, the senses, the immune system, the lymphatic system,
are so instantaneously and complicatedly interacting that

you can't draw a line across the neck and say 'above this line it's smart and below the line it's menial.'" The same section of the book goes on to say: "The heart has about 40,000 neurons that play a central role in shaping emotion, perception, and decision making. The stomach and intestines complete this network, containing more than 500 million nerve cells, 100 million neurons, 30 different neurotransmitters, and 90 percent of the body's supply of serotonin." Perfect interconnection wins again, and here demonstrates the foolish scientific dismissal of feelings as being irrational and beneath our reason, for, in truth, they *inform* our reasoning. This also abolishes the conventional western medicinal and materialistic assumptions about the body-mind separation, and the mind's superiority. Taken a step further, my experience and ruminations suggest that there's no separation between *anything*; that what 'health' *actually* represents is a clearer bridge between us and Everything; that what we're *really* trying to do is make ourselves cleaner conduits of Spirit, the Self upon which every self sits, and more effective conductors of every other such form of self, plant and animal, by which we're surrounded, and likely communicating with on a level that most will dismiss, and will never be able to acknowledge.

Reflecting the fundamental philosophical precept that separation is an illusion, health is, again, *holistic*, not compartmentalistic (a valid neologism, I think). Excepting acute cases it's about *interactions*, not isolations. And even then the acute case isn't perfectly isolated, but more likely represents the path of least resistance through which a multi-sourced, compounding issue manifested. That is, the more that we examine health, the more connections that we find, the more that symptom-oriented healthcare appears foolishly limited in scope and efficacy compared to a holistic approach that dutifully digs for and attempts to rectify the underlying disorder(s). The closer that we look, the more that mental health is gut health, the more that stress, anxiety and depression are three heads on the same monster, the more that autoimmunity and mental illness are curiously correlated, the more that metabolic dysfunction becomes neurological dysfunction, the more that all dis-ease leading to disease is catalyzed by cascading forms of chronic inflammation, the more that every single one of these separately classified conditions is so intertwined with all the others that we realize that we've been spending our time pulling on separate threads in the same spool, the more that naturalizing the body and brain is the answer. How then can pharmaceuticals and surgery, the primary, and sometimes *only*, products and services offered by conventional healthcare, ever be the answer? How can they naturalize us, and keep us naturalized?

Yes, a surgical removal of an unnaturality is sometimes invaluable, and sometimes pharmacology feels like the only resort, but generally these are outlier cases. And yet we treat all *inlier* cases the same way, as if the costly doctor and pharmacist should provide the treatment (costly both financially *and* in the cost of concealing the cause and perpetual suffering without resolution, and with complete dependency upon continued doctor patronage), when really it's, again, about developing the knowledge, discipline, awareness and appreciation to take Mother Nature up on *Her* medicine chest; a chest absolutely jam-packed with an endless multitude of medicinal wonders, and not only those which you're likely familiar with, or may immediately connect with naturalization. As reemphasized numerous times in this text, the true, underemphasized human qualities of connection, listening and reciprocation of healing are naturally-evolved forms of medicine, as a core example; the best of what we call social and sex lives. And that's just the tip of the melting iceberg. Sunshine on our face, hearing wind in the trees and the river flowing by, walking or working in nature, cultivating and wildcrafting plants, learning and applying Mother Nature's cornucopia;

anything 'outdoorsy,' essentially, offers an invaluable form of natural treatment improving virtually every condition.

Upon inspection, nature teaches recurring lessons of symbiosis and interconnection eroding our sense of individualism and pointing to the cure of connection. It's true for the wide-angle as much as for the narrowing lens, equal to the macrocosm and the innumerable microcosms which constitute it. For what is nature but one immense symbiotic entity so inseparably intertwined in force, function, form and phenomena as to eradicate the pervasive illusion of individualism relative to our inspection? The same may be said of God. And the same may be said of the health of every human body, of the symbiotic interdependence of what conventional medicine foolishly treats through isolation, separation and symptom. So yes, most of the CRC residents arguably required pharmacological intervention, but it was so eagerly and exclusively and excessively applied that not a single one of them will ever know even the *possibility* of actually healing, and will instead live their entire lives under the yoke of not just their illness and the costs of its popular stigmatization, but the fact that the yoke is largely held in place by the forces of evil hiding behind clean white coats of credibility.

The Holy Communion of the Golden Teacher

The Master Therapist is Psilocybe cubensis. Why? Because its effect upon the individual consciousness transceiving the Universal Consciousness is to increase the frequency of transmission between the self and the Self to such a degree where anything once seemingly fixed and finite in the consciousness becomes unfixed and can't cling to it, because it's vibrating at the higher frequency nearing the unfixed and infinite. By doing so, it inoculates the local, singular self with a greater sense of the divine state of the non-localized Universal Self that's like the mycelium underlying and interconnecting all of Life; the entirely inseparable interbeing that's the metaphysical foundation of physical and mental being. Thereby relatively removed from the body and the fixations of the ego and psyche and their delusional impacts upon the consciousness, that consciousness experiences a peeling away of fixed forms of identity, sensing more from the unfixed position of the Universal Self. And by thereby peeling the small self, the individualistic ego identity, from the Big Self, the universal spiritual identity, one gains a massively beneficial perspective upon themselves and their existence and the totality of universal interbeing. This experience thereby grants them an invaluable reprieve from every form of suffering bound to the self-conceptions of their individualization. And through this experience they're gifted the more direct awareness of their egos as being that which is experienced BY the spiritual Self, better sensing the Observer, or Self, versus the self it observes *through*. This is The Holy Communion of the Golden Teacher.

[Added during the (hopefully) final read-through, October '25]

06

LUCY(FER)

If I were to write an entire book about a single CRC resident, Mazie would probably be the one. I'd intermix the true life details which she imparted to me (that one night in particular) with the creative license of the fiction writer such that the reader couldn't separate fact from fiction. Which is kind of the definition of good fiction, right? Telling truth through fiction and fiction through fact until the reader can't only *not* disentangle the two, but senses that the fiction is adding greater, revelatory substance to the fact. And I almost don't even need to go *that* far with her, so fantastically well were Mazie's facts merged with what everyone *assumes* to have been her fictions, making for a profound testament to the philosophical wealth tied between the two, in the often impossible quest to sift the truth from the delusion, the immanent fantasy from the unbelievable fact. From a marketing perspective, the book would have appeal considering that Christianity, and tales of its demonically-possessed adversaries, sell almost as well as sex. Maybe I could just turn Mazie into a sex addict when she satanically-succumbs to Lucy, for that matter, and kill two massive markets with the same mountain-sized stone. She certainly didn't lack sex appeal, after all.

Excepting the ravages of time, abuse and mental illness, Mazie was a beautiful woman. In her late-thirties, with sandy brown hair, a freckled face and stunning hazel eyes, she created a natural gravitational pull of a man's gaze.

And considering portions of her past that she alluded to, I can't help but think of something that I heard in a film once, about how beauty isn't always a benefit, for it attracts the bad as much as the good. And, in Mazie, those attractions, and everything that she's been forced to fight, have produced *Lucy*. That is, the female embodiment of Lucifer.

It was the most convincing form of the alter-ego I've ever seen; a monumental manifestation of the defense mechanism that was so richly-infused that it gave over to some of her previous psychiatrists actually considering the diagnosis of 'Dissociative Identity Disorder,' DID for short; what was once called 'Multiple Personality Disorder;' a diagnosis seldom used in the field today, thought by many in the profession to be a myth. And hers is *freaky*. And it makes sense, this embodiment. For if one feels that one is *constantly* being forced to defend oneself, what better defender than Lucifer? "What is God without love?," Lucy rhetorically asks. "*Fury*." So embodied fury was her shield.

The voice had an affected rasp to it; a deep guttural displacement of her natural voice when freed of possession. I remember what precipitated my getting to know her, or *it*. I was working at The Bridge in the Day Room, typing a report on a service that I'd provided to one of the other residents, when she came out of her room and started screaming in that voice of masculine rage, agitating other residents who were up late, and calling the nurse to prepare and offer her a calming PRN. This only infuriated her further, as did the fact that no one else would consent to her demand to be called Lucy. She refused to answer to Mazie. In order to allay the escalation I offered to talk to her, if she'd follow me into the backyard. The encounter that would follow is hard to forget, and reminds me of what I reported earlier herein, of my early experience of Cain whilst he was in the throes of mania, and the fact that I *still* believe that I possess a unique combination of empathy, patience, understanding and curiosity that, in her case, as well as his, served to make them *heard*, thereby 'talking them down' from their escalation, rather than their being further injured by what likely would've otherwise unfolded.

To this day what sticks with me most are the *details*; how richly thought-out the alter-ego of Lucy was. It wasn't some passing, mindless fancy. This character had a depth to her that almost made me believe that Mazie was summoning, if not Satan, then some primal force of fractured, infuriated psyche. She made me wonder about the truth underlying symbolism. And I must admit that, after passing through the electronically-locked back door into the barbed-wire-fenced-in backyard, my own years of contemplation of theology and the development of my own spiritual theories, in close parallel with 'non-dualism,' Gnosticism and the 'spiritual but not religious' category of spiritual thought, led me to explore the character and ask questions of legitimate interest that no other CRC staff member, either then on duty, or in general, could've matched. And, again, there's my patience and self-control. For 'Lucy' was in my face almost as soon as we exited the building and entered the backyard, scream and spittle upon my brow, staff and a couple residents watching us from within, wondering if they'd have to place a call to the mental health wing of the local police department, the CIT, or 'Crisis Intervention Team;' the cavalry whom are called in when a resident loses control and requires containment. But, honestly, I wasn't afraid of her. Maybe partly because I'm a relatively strong guy, and knew I could overcome her if necessary. But also because I sensed that she was simply purging.

Lucy fights fire with fire. I don't know what, exactly, had brought the fire out in this particular instance. Perhaps something that she'd heard or watched in her room. Lucy doesn't deny the existence of Mazie, but simply says that she's not, in this moment, in control. She's buried in there,

unable to cope with the resurfacing evil and suffering, and
so has run and hid, like a frightened child. Children at risk,
I'll soon find out, is a theme of Lucy's; maybe Lucy's very
genesis. Perhaps the deepest of her psychological wounds
is rooted in, in one of the few times she lowered her voice,
her whispered fear of killing her own children, and her own
son saying: "I see the Devil in you." Is this the source of
Lucy? Is this why, of all she says, she seems most revolted
by her reminiscences of gazing upon her own reflection?

Unlike Mazie, Lucy *welcomes* the suffering, and keeps it
from reaching Mazie. Lucy *wants* to feel it, and has no
need to run from it, because it's not a threat to her, for
she's the very, enraged embodiment of suffering. She
wants to be uncomfortable; is, in fact, comfortable with
discomfort, and *desires* the pain and confusion of the
world. 'What an ingenious defense mechanism,' I thought,
'to use identity to flip the threat into a desire in the mind,'
like an ingenious form of reverse-psychology embedded in
the ego. Later, as Mazie, she'd tell me that she couldn't
believe that I'd withstood Lucy's full force; that it was
Christ-like, and made her cry when Mazie had momentarily
risen to the surface (I remember the tears leaking through
those wild eyes, dropping down cheeks reddened with
rage); that the way I'd handled the situation had made her
want to be intimate with me, "which is a *big* deal for me."

By the way, if you'll take some advice from a perennial
bachelor, dear reader, taken as much from my time in
mental health as from my observations of men and their
'making moves:' leave sex out of it until you just can't take
it anymore, and watch what blossoms in the unforced fold.
Trust me. Nothing has greater capacity to fuck things up,
and unnecessarily string strings, than sex. Second is
money. If, therefore, sex and money aren't extensions of
love and natural, symbiotic partnership, please, dearest
reader, leave them out. Don't pervert truth with transaction.

Listen. Forge the bonding bridge. Even if what crosses it is someone so burned by unmanly men that they play the Devil. For, in truth, Lucifer is a horned form of vulnerability.

She speaks of Mazie having been abused in the past, as a separate entity from her, but being keenly aware *through* Mazie of what men did to her, and how long Mazie was afraid of men and physical contact as a consequence. It's a tragic, fascinating relationship between the personas. The one underneath, Mazie, is sweet and trusting and wants to be good to people and to honor them, whilst the protector, Lucy, *tries* to listen to Mazie when she tells her to do things, out of love for her, but that Lucy *isn't* good to people, because it goes against her nature and purpose.

Instead, Lucy presses, antagonizes and forces people out of their comfort zone, both for their own good, she claims, and in order to prevent them from being taken advantage of. The implication reminds me of a line from one of my favorite films, *Training Day*: "To protect the sheep you have to catch the wolf. And it takes a wolf to catch a wolf." Lucy's protection of Mazie makes a similar assertion: *Demons attack the innocent. And it takes the Devil to slay demons*. Lucy is the toughest of 'tough love' providers, to an extent that others mistake for evil, but which is simply a necessary defense *against* evil. People are weak without her. "Do everything with purpose and courage, else you're a coward and you might as well not do anything," she says.

"The English language was written to confuse and control its speakers," she asserts with a glint in her eye, as though revealing a secret, ancient truth which very few are privy to. She cites examples of ungodly amounts of synonyms and odd idiomatic phrasings, reminiscing on The Tower of Babylon story from the Bible, and the "confounding of tongues." Many times she reiterates the need to say what you mean with accuracy, and emphasizes the importance and power of words and their precise meanings during communication, backing this up by providing several examples of how expressions are not honest to the true, root meanings of words. And *she* would know. For she knows *many* different languages, including those from the other planets and dimensions to which she's traveled. She hates this planet by comparison. And *no*, I don't test her on any of this by, say, asking her to speak in another language. In retrospect I wonder if my failure to test her was based as much upon my own intrigue, and not wanting to shatter the delusion that *I* was entertaining within myself, as upon the obvious risk of infuriating *her*.

The theological elements of this alter-ego were astounding. God, recurringly referred to as "that motherfucker," is a close companion of Lucy's, while Christ is her "brother in law." She says Christ is "super cool – *way* cooler than the way he's depicted in the Bible." Much like Christ, and in her own relation to God, she feels a need to pass down ancient wisdom, of which she's a receptacle, reminiscent of the lost testaments pulled from one of those urns buried beneath Middle Eastern sand. Also like Christ, she assures me that she's incorrectly portrayed in the Bible; that her *actual* purpose is to protect the innocent, especially children, and to make humankind suffer for our own good, in order to make us stronger and bring us together. Sewing division is *not* her aim, as the priests claim, but sewing connection *through* pain. "Mankind has forgotten the hidden lesson of Jesus, that they are gods."

Cain said almost the exact same thing to me, and not through any collusion with Mazie/Lucy, for their residencies weren't overlapping. Moreover, I might add that I possess similar beliefs in our inseparability from God, and of good and evil serving, informing and compelling one-another, and of humanity being a mortal embodiment of the immortal Source, forever evolving and rebirthed through Mother Nature, and thereby divine. We *are* gods and goddesses, in other words. At least this supplies the indoctrinated Christian reader with the opportunity to dismiss everyone with the sight as 'evil' and/or 'insane!'

Suffering brings wisdom and appreciation of one another and existence, Lucy says, and the knowledge of the value of good through pain, painfully scratching away the surface to reveal our divine roots. She insists that *this* is why she's summoned by certain special sufferers; because man has to get over its division, and that it's very possible to have those of widely varying belief systems live in harmony, while necessarily protecting those who aren't yet mature enough to process pain into these invaluable lessons.

"I am here for the little ones," she says, for the children and the otherwise vulnerable, adding: "And I'm the littlest of them all." She didn't *want* to take on this role as a leader, but was forced to. A few times she calls "this body" her "suitcase." She insists she's immortal, and has died more times than she can count, and that others have witnessed her invitation to suffering and her immortality prevail upon their limited perceptions of reality, backing this up with a story of being shot in the face and nothing happening, confusing her attacker, and another story about being attacked by a woman wielding a shovel on the street. She says that the woman confused her with her threats, holding the shovel whilst screaming: "Do you want me to hit you with this?" She didn't know the correct response: "Because I want to protect Mazie, but I also encourage suffering."

She claims that this small angry woman grabbed her around the throat, lifted her up off the ground and tossed her into the bushes, causing damage to her throat, and *that's* why she speaks the way that she does. Again, I betray none of my doubt whilst listening to her, or to anyone else, for these, *disbelief and disrespect*, are universal triggers at the CRC. And I would surmise that failing to truly listen and lend others with whom we disagree some measure of respect for our shared humanity and spiritual natures, if not for the content of their minds, is inseparable from so much suffering in the world. I've been as bad at *not* enforcing this realization upon myself as anyone, as you'll sense from my tales of some of my horrible coworkers herein. But I was generally *not* such an offender with the residents of the CRC, I'd say. I sensed that when you're already low, your self-esteem, and any possessed pride, shrunken by the diagnosis of an SPMI, and by being held in confinement, forced to take debilitating 'meds' every day, your ego just can't take any more reduction. So you defend it. Violently, if necessary. Mazie, in fact, was among the residents most easily triggered by the sense of disrespect accompanying disbelief, or by *any* perceived mistreatment, for that matter.

Absorbing any emotional energy even verging upon this realm brings out the energy and fury and places the Lucy persona in a position of greater control. She claims that it is the very fact that she's here, at the CRC, being blamed for what's been done *to* her, that keeps her in a heightened state of manic self-defense. And CRC staff only makes it worse by their belittling treatment, she says. She reports that mental health providers, both at the CRC and elsewhere, keep summoning Lucy by giving Mazie too much of a medication that makes her feel dead inside, compelling her to withdraw even more from life, to the point where she inevitably ends up fearfully isolating within her own home; that is, in those periods when she's actually been granted independence. Connected to this, and to the mindsets of most CRC residents, in fact, she constantly feels the need to have witnesses to what she and others say and do within the walls of the CRC in order to avoid the lies used against her, citing the recent event of two victimizers lying about an incident, resulting in her arrest for assault and numerous related charges, leading to the current captivity. I must say that on *this* point, I'm inclined to believe her, for few have faced the consequences of threatening the ego-based lies of the over-empowered guild of gossipers more than I (see *Holier Than Thou*).

"He makes me want to be intimate with a man again," she announces to staff and a few residents upon our reentry into the Day Room, near where Cain will propose marriage to me a few months later, "which is a *big* deal for me," she reemphasizes, alluding to the trauma she shares with so many disadvantaged women in relation to monstrous men whom give the gender a bad name, and whom don't, therefore, really qualify as 'men.' Understand me, ye pretend men, for well do I know you, and understand the weakness inducing depravity to draw its water from the pestilential well buried deep beneath the demonic underbelly of being: When serving its purpose in the noble form of man, sex is an extension of something far greater than the bodily urge. It's the divine bridge. A form of worship. It isn't an ends. That's but the animal. It's a *means*. A beginning. An ascendant portal passing between the pairing through the discovery of shared Spirit. Its *abuse*, on the other hand, summons Satan herself; that which is compelled to destroy threats against life and love.

07

DELUSIONS OF GRANDEUR

*"The distance between insanity and
genius is measured only by success."*

- Villain Elliot Carver in *Tomorrow Never Dies*

There's only a Shiva the Destroyer because, at his core, he's *Shiva the Lover.* You're a fighter *because* you're a lover, dear reader. If you did not love, if you had nothing compelling you to fight for it, only a fake fighter could you be. Thus it is that the greatest warriors are spurred by an honor as deep and true and inseparable from love as it is possible for the depths of being to go. And one cannot become such a warrior without having long bathed in the filth that leads to a cynical awareness that there's something that needs to be cleansed. As with all forms of knowledge-by-contrast, those who know the value of being purified of filth are those who know the filth well. Cynicism and its catalyst, indignation, are direct results of moral development and awareness. Deriding them is the result of either being threatened by their truths due to a conflicting financial or personal motive, or to seeking justification for bad habits or values connected to the ego. *Period.* You can only best know God *through* the Devil, illuminating the irony of so many demons pretending to represent God.

Michael Pollan, in the documentary version of *How to Change Your Mind*, said: "You render the priesthood superfluous if you can talk to God on your own." I believe that I've *always* been in a dialogue with God, and that it requires learning how to listen with more than your ears. It's about a type of extrasensory perception, or even *sub-sensory* perception, combined with a philosophical rendering, and learning that the subtlest of all things (which yet pervades and enlivens *everything*) communicates through manifold means, including the aforementioned instinctive sense, the conclusions reachable through a philosophical inquest into physics and metaphysics, the signs and signals delivered through the world (with the universe actually existing *within* God), and even our own thoughts and feelings. All of these seemingly separate forces settle into the foundational truth of inseparability; of *Infinite of One*. And there's no truth that hasn't *always* been true, and that didn't spring from that One Source.

Any truth spoken by anyone, even *thought* by anyone, didn't come from them. They aren't the source. None of us are the source of anything. Rather, as revealed by history, by the retroactivity of every social and physical science, by the philosophical axiom that separation is an illusion, by Faulkner's "the past is never dead, it's not even the past," by *The Matrix's* "causality is the one real truth," by physics' "nothing is created or destroyed, only forever rearranged (which I believe to be a *metaphysical* truth)," by the fact that beginnings and endings are illusions, by General Relativity's revelation of time being a largely illusory *concept* based upon the perception of something 'passing' only to those who aren't themselves passing at the extent of passage (I could go on), we, as seemingly independent beings, aren't the *source* of anything. We're material and mental conduits of truths that always have existed and always will exist. We're mortal manifestations of the one infinite being. And our ability to recognize and speak and record the truths innate to that being is limited only by our mental, linguistic and technological capacities of Source into self, or Self into its infinitely re-manifesting selves.

This is why my publishing label is called *Infinite of One*: it's all One thing of infinite variance, the metaphysical construct of pure energy into spacetime and matter made so that God, the grandest possible We, the only Source, can experience that Source from infinite possible vantage points. So when I say something that your heart, the entry point of the infinite into the finite, immediately recognizes as true, it's because I'm acting as an accurate *translator* of something that's *always* been true, and that registers in the core wherein Self becomes self. Again, there's no truth that hasn't always been the truth. It's but a matter of your inner prophet speaking an eternal truth received from, and conducted by, the infinite atop which every singularity sits.

In *The Perennial Philosophy*, Aldous Huxley said:

"It is from the more or less obscure intuition of the oneness that is the ground and principle of all multiplicity that philosophy takes its source. And not alone philosophy, but natural science as well. All science is the reduction of multiplicities to identities. Divining the One within and beyond the many, we find an intrinsic plausibility in any explanation of the diverse in terms of a single principle."

And, in case you're unaware of it, and with regards to Huxley's reference to the One within the many, the secret, ironic purpose of science is actually to *reveal* God; to demonstrate the perfect interconnection underlying the illusion of disconnection. Just as the secret purpose of evil, or the Devil, is to reveal good, or God. Just as to be forever blinded by the Great White Light is to see nothing, such that only by the darkness can the purpose and power of the light be known. We are infinite of finite form in order to uncover and fully appreciate the One of infinite form. And that One of infinite form (that is our essence) is deathless.

The common misconception that we 'go' somewhere when we die is as much based upon thinking within the temporal, spatial and material constraints of our current being as it is a vestige of religious indoctrination of divisible souls that are ushered into damnation or heavenly emancipation. When you possess the sense of God that I do, as unconstrained by space, time or matter, as the all-encompassing Self of which all self is an inseparable manifestation, you know that dying itself is an illusion, as all 'ends' are actually unending reabsorptions into the Everything to which everything and everyone belongs.

And by the same token, if you think that I'm writing this, or *anything* that I've written, under my own, 'independent' volition, as if concocted on a coconut-covered island untouched by the surrounding Sea of Source, you're wrong; you're victimized by the same illusion of individualism that the conquerors and oppressors use to keep us divided and conquered. Alas, even *they* shall be seen to have served our unification in the end, like a rubber band that can only stretch so far before snapping back into the center by the equal and opposite forces compelling existence. Just as all of nature, all of God's manifestations, even the meteorological phenomena that wire the planet together, are set in service to equilibrium. Just as anything which anyone may come to see in me or anyone else which is truly worthy of reverence isn't of *me*, but of that which, or whom, I may well-enough *embody*.

This, in turn, alludes to the evil of idolatry, an evil prevalent in what Empire has made of the lessons of those hailed as prophets for the purposes of controlling the minds of the adherent; edited lessons which are antithetical to the true purpose and power of spirituality: that *anyone* may think and speak prophetically, it's but a matter of tapping into and accurately translating the forever prophetic Source. Spirit, or God, is the infusing force within us *all*, even the most arrogant atheist and the most reductive realist. God is the connective tissue which we all experience as love. To pretend as though God belongs to any limited subset of life, much less one person conveniently kept in the past, forever removed from critical analysis, is to disempower anyone whom believes it, keeping them on their knees, powerless to be what they really are, in allusion to the "I am a powerless alcoholic or addict" edict of AA and NA, and to Christianity, and, indeed, to religion in general.

God didn't manifest you to be some God-damned automaton, some reflexively obedient drone nodding your head in a church that's no different than any other space, any other edifice, whether made of brick and mortar or mountain or river or towering trees, in its conduciveness to channeling the divine force. Where love and its enlivening force are most present, so is divinity. And God made you to quest after divinity *through* doubt; to seek the truth buried in the lies borne by a history of Church and State made to occlude it. Do not fear your doubt, or see it as a 'lack of faith,' as the priest ignobly trains you to do, out of his fear that you may gain the ability to see *through* him and gaze upon the divinity that surrounds you at all times, in all places. Rather, delve *deeper* into the revealing doubt.

Leeches wear the Good Lord like a golden garment, for it hides their suckers whilst fooling those invested in appearances; appearances that they're incapable of seeing as the contrived concealments that they are. Therefore, look to every vestige of virtue to find your villains, and know that the truly virtuous have no need of such adornment, and walk upon the Earth in open revelation, as though naked and unprotected before God. Rather than run from what the false representatives of God coerce you into believing are the heretical inquiries of unworthy heathens, cast yourself into the cyclonic cataclysm of confusion that'll eventually suck you into the elucidating center of the Spirit. And through spiritual truth shall all moral truth be revealed, for they're inseparable.

Do you want to know the most consistent manner by which I know that America is the land of divided and conquered, a land in which only communalism (which we're conditioned to confuse with the tyrannical corruptions of communist countries of the past) can save the people? *My apartment complex.* And being a pedestrian; someone who likes to walk. That is, we victims of systematic oppression accepted as 'the only reality' walk right by one another here, every day, day after drudgery-stricken day, and say *nothing* to one another, usually not even looking one another in the eye, as though everyone is an 'other,' and of no relevance to us whatsoever, and basically nonexistent.

Yes, it's largely my own fault as someone tending to isolate, but, I believe, speaks to a larger issue of ingrained Americanism that I don't know a single person outside my own unit in this sprawling complex, one in which the represented socioeconomics necessarily disturbs anyone even the *least* bit aware and progressive, possessing even the *slightest* sense of the oppressive implications imposed upon its residents flushing thousands of dollars down the proverbial tubes stretching across the entirety of the economic landscape through leases and wages representing little more than barely surviving whilst feeding the parasitism that embodies this morally bankrupt nation. Fuck, one of my housemates walks right by me every day without saying a damn word to me! And he lives with me! I have to forcefully wrangle him into even the briefest of discussions. He's a twenty-something 'realist' who's really a jaded pessimist working multiple jobs for the chance to improve that depressingly narrow perspective on reality. At least, that was my assessment when I *first* wrote this book.

Cut to a year-and-a-half later during my final read-through edit of this book and, considering this is a type of 'midlife' memoir for me, I'm inclined to add that, though I worked *extremely* hard for years to make the living relationship work with both he and my other housemate, always going out of my way to be generous and patient, our differences have recently led to a disturbing turn of events. The two of them now regularly speak ill of me behind my back (overheard multiple times) and occasionally to my face, which is bad enough, of course, but then, when I finally confronted them about it, they did one of the most evil things that anyone can do to anyone else: *they gaslit me*.

They both pretend as though none of it actually happened, I was 'just drunk and high,' when I was fully cogent at the time, and heard and witnessed the inciting incident directly. One of them even admitted that they talk about me behind my back, and that they talk about how I think I'm smart but don't understand anything about 'the real world' (while I'd argue that it's more like my understanding of that 'real world' has led to my rejection of its 'realities'). Alas, he now pretends that this was 'only out of concern.' They're now trying to sell the narrative that I'm mentally ill, the other housemate repeating the phrase "you need help," despite everything I've done for him over the years, including a constancy of absorbing the most childish of antics. I mean, he's a nice guy underneath his bullshit, they both are, but my God is that one big pile of excrement that I have to continually excavate just to unearth our shared roots. And every uncomfortable interaction that I'm subject to with the 'realist' ends up with his use of language suggesting that I'm 'upset,' and 'not feeling well' and 'do concerning things' and 'have unhealthy habits,' my health habits thereby coming under fire from a guy that lives off of *Captain Crunch*, energy drinks and fried chicken, my mental health condescendingly judged by someone who has no integrity and who watches the most degrading crap imaginable, believing only in his own ego and bourgeoisie 'success.'

Living in an environment that's not only not welcoming but is chronically hostile is *very* bad for one's mental health, a fact which many a CRC resident can attest to. In fact, nothing spells increased mental health risk like living in an environment of relentless stress. *The more unnaturality we absorb, the more unnatural we become.* And when you're living in it, you're *stewing* in it. Ironically, being forced to defend one's sanity on a continual basis, and having the insinuating narrative pushed that you're insane, may be the best possible way to actually induce someone's insanity. Reminiscent of a form of psychological abuse that I'll discuss later relative to the series *Maid*, the tactic is sinister because it can be denied, and yet is as deleterious in its impact as most any form of abuse. It's gotten so bad that, in combination with other interpersonal traumas, I've recently felt like I'm on the verge of a breakdown, escaping to the redwoods just to hold onto my slipping sanity. That property saved me. *Again.* But why did all of this happen?

I triggered their insecurity. That's my honest answer. This is a definite theme in my life, and core to interpersonal conflict in general: *the unstable ego.* One housemate, the aforementioned 'realist,' was constantly trying to convert me to his worldview, futilely, and the other is so mentally undeveloped that he can barely form a coherent sentence, and understands next to nothing. And no, I don't *ever* make him feel bad about this. In fact, I go out of my way to accommodate him, and have practiced a semi-saintly level of patience and generosity as a result of the rampant insecurity that he displays as someone who can barely read, and, frankly, whom thinks like a child. I feel like I've failed some Christly mission with him, fighting for years to absorb his incessant egotistic instability only to end up folding and feeling compelled to fight back, largely, of course, in defense of my own ego. *I'm not there yet*, I think. In defense of that ego, however, there's no way to accurately convey the price that I've paid for this housemates' insecurity over the years we've lived together.

Every time I say anything, I have to 'dumb it down,' and anytime I don't, he acts like a petulant child. I can't even watch a thought-provoking film without him continuously passing behind me and mocking it and completely degrading my experience *simply because he doesn't understand it, and that makes him feel small, so he has to mock it to feel better about himself*. And that's but one ongoing example of countless of how his absurd insecurity manifests as a constancy of stress that I'm unrelentingly subject to whenever I'm around him. Still, somehow, with, again, immense discipline, generosity and patience, I held it all together for years, feeling like it was somehow my cross to bear. *He needed me to absorb his insecurities without me making them worse*. Recently, however, I interacted with some women from his work, and they took to me more than they ever have to him, with the result being that he pressed the egoist need to tear me down to feel better about himself, openly making fun of me that same night. And the other housemate joined in, such that they could try to make me feel bad about myself so that they can feel better about themselves. All the lies and justifications that were to follow sprung from *this*, the heart of human discord: *insecurity*. The result? After one of them called me "an ass" for thereafter avoiding them, I finally defended myself, which is when things *really* turned ugly.

Now they're lying about it, exacerbating my stress levels. As I write this they're trying to push the narrative that I'm mentally ill and "need help," and that they're entirely faultless. It's like they're building a case against me, pretending that I'm insane. Yes, there have been times when I've drank too much and made comments that they didn't understand and couldn't relate to, with their inability to relate to me and understand my perspective being at the heart of all of this egoistic triggering, frankly. And there was the one time I came home late and intoxicated and howled like a wolf. And they love to cite these incidents as proof of my insanity. I overheard one of them talking about the howling incident last night, in fact, when I was trying to fall asleep and he was *again* talking shit, but, I think, without knowing that I was in my room. I mean, sorry I freaked you out man, but do I not have a right to expel some pressure every once in a while without your narrow, condescending judgments amounting to what should be considered a crime? All in all, the truth is that I just don't think like they do, and they can't control my mentality, and I trigger their insecurity, all of which has been rolled together into my being perceived as a threat, so they've joined forces against me, making my home life so stressful that I look for any possible way to avoid my apartment; an apartment I can't escape, because of the lease, and my own financial limitations. They face the same issue there. So there we are, the three of us, all resenting the presence of one another, all paying a landlord for the right not to be homeless, even as homelessness doesn't sound all that bad at the moment, for it would mean escaping those two. Again, they're both fairly nice guys underneath the egoistic imbalances and the self-defenses that those imbalances compel, but my God is that one big pile of shit that I had to continually excavate just to unearth our shared roots. And yes, I'm aware that I've contributed to that rotting dung pile.

And socioeconomic injustice is the catalyst for most of it, not only unnaturally forcing us together, but forcing us to work just to have our money flushed down the drain to pay the overlording leeches, building zero ownership whilst increasing the ownership of those whom, when you see through the smokescreen, own *us*. For there's no way to talk about mental health with any diagnostic accuracy, with any type of insight into true cause and effect, *without* talking about the pressures that precipitate mental breaks. And there's no way to talk about those precipitating pressures without talking about the fact that the vast majority of those whom face mental illness do so largely because of *socioeconomic* causality; because of financial stress, and connected work stresses, and owning nothing, and never even having the means to take a vacation much less explore as we're naturally and spiritually called to do, as natural vagabonding seekers and experimentalists instead living paycheck to paycheck glued to housemates.

It again reminds me of Fisher's *Capitalist Realism*, and his point salient to *this* book as well, that, to prove capitalism's failure to serve the best interests of the people as a whole one need look no further than our appalling level of mental illness, and the fact that it continues to rise the more that the inevitably growing disparities of the possession of all things, including wealth, opportunity and representation, continue to grow, for that's what capitalism *not* balanced by socialistic virtues and its protections and equity sharing *necessarily* does, as a direct effect of its transfer of all things of value: *produce forever broadening disparities in everything, and at an unsustainable level that may end all of life on Earth*. It's obvious that these are commensurate forces, in fact: the growth of disparity and mental illness. Thus the irony that my means to escape my housemates comes down to our shared ability to come together to buy the means to avoid one another, and thereby move on.

It's said that the US is 'the most advanced nation on Earth.' Advancing towards *what* exactly, dear reader? I implore you to ask yourself that question. And to consider the *only* salvation: *communal investment*. The cost of *their* greed is that we live like this, don't you see? This apartment complex, in other words, is just a more sophisticated form of predation, something that can be said of the entire 'free economy.' It's the illusion of 'freedom' enwrapped in subtle slavery. We're 'free' to compete with one another for the benefit of masters. For the demonic brilliance of capitalism is simply to set everyone against one another, so that divide and conquer is built right into everyone's lives. And we can only beat the parasites by pooling our energy and resources, without which our lives are spent trying to buy our freedom from these masters. For the sad truth is that the foundational freedom, the freedom from being subject to parasitism, is never possessed by the vast majority, and so, absent symbiosis, we're all owned by our oppressors.

They own politics through the legal purchase of politicians via lobbying, campaign financing and post-political-career, under-the-table promises and payoffs. They own the law through lobbying for endless loopholes and tax evasions and reductions in personal responsibility, and through the ability to buy a 'defense' that others can't afford. They own our working lives through fixed hourly wages, non-equity salaries and the removal of our right to collectively bargain. They own our residential lives through leases and mortgages that either exploit our inability to buy equity, else require that we pay them interest first in order to do so, our lack of equity becoming their continued enrichment. You can't even start a tiny home community in most areas of the country without the planning commission shutting you down because your efforts conflict with the greed of the housing developers controlling those commissions, and whom, through politics, condition fear of communes and 'cults.' Through religion they own our desire to understand God, exploiting the fears, desires and ignorance of the most gullible and least educated. They own our intake through stoked consumerism and cold-blooded credit.

The moneylenders are, as a whole, the heart of capitalism, and some of the most evil people and organizations on the planet. In league with their plutocratic masters (often one in

the same), consumerism and classism are stoked,
producing the cultural pressures giving way to people
associating 'class' with possession, thus wanting more
than they can afford, which is thereafter preyed upon as
unscrupulously as possible by the 'creditors.' As people fall
behind, ever more charges and fees are levied, such that
financial enslavement and slow suffocation are the result,
many spending their entire lives paying the interest and
fees of the insidious lenders of every form of credit,
consumer, residential, business, academic and so on. The
moneylenders exploit one or more stoked needs, wheedle
their way through the defenses of the individuals and
families, and thereafter parasitically attach to and feed off
of them, their goal simply to suck as much as possible off
the host without killing or forcing it to revolt for its survival.

This is, in fact, the modus operandi of not just the creditors,
but capitalism in general: *to conceal every form of
parasitism and disempowerment, conditioning us to call
them freedom and empowerment*. Actually, this is the
modern modus of the dark art of propaganda in general,
that which feeds upon and exploits every possible form of
fear, ignorance, gullibility and sense of division that it can,
all to keep every victim of systemic evil from identifying the
true source of evil: *the greed of the plutocracy*. And all of it
points to the fact that no justice can be possessed by the
people without their coming together to collectively buy the
equity and control of their lives without which they remain
prey to the prevailing parasites. My most sincere advice is
to avoid credit at all costs, for it amounts not only to
supporting grave injustices committed against the people
as a whole, but to supporting evil through the ever growing
disparity, and lending strength to the parasitic overlords
who've cost humanity more than can ever be accounted
for, that cost concealed behind the 'normality' accepted by
the masses. The stock market is the same: awarding
parasitic corporations relative to how successful they are

as parasites, pressuring us to 'make our money work for us,' because that's what the 'successful' do: successfully contribute to the growing disparity of wealth and power underlying every evil prevailing across the rebelling planet; a planet straining under the presumptuousness that the parasites own and may do whatever they wish to it, whatever is most profitable (most extracting) of whatever it, *She*, Mother Nature, the constant victim of rape, produces.

They own our bodies and brains through 'food' that's chronic poison, and through 'medicine' that makes us debilitated and dependent upon them for life. They own our data and how it's used. They even believe that they own our words. They believe that I don't have a right to tell you these truths, labeling them 'satanic' and 'un-American' and even 'treasonous.' They believe they own the right to dictate what can and can't be said and written about the corporations that they found in order to insulate themselves from risk. They believe that they can turn me into the scapegoat, psychologically abuse me and make me out to be the *opposite* of what I am for writing honestly about my experiences and beliefs, even though 'freedom of expression' is meant to be an inviolable American right. They believe that they can keep you a soft slave by concealing what creates true freedom: *freedom from them*.

While this will sound hyperbolic to the unaware, it is my firm conviction that the United States and ever more of the world at large is so deeply entrenched in the greedy, personally-insulated interests of the wicked that the only hope for the people is a mass moral revival set upon the heels of, and informed in principle by, a mass spiritual (but not religious) awakening, thereafter leading to a peaceful, persistent economic and political revolution, itself built upon the semi-socialistic principles of communalism. And keep in mind that the judgment of the vast majority on these ideological issues shall amount to a 'kangaroo court' ruling as dictated through the propaganda of their masters. It's up to you, dear reader, to see through it; to see that the Lady of Justice has been kidnapped, and to help free her, and thereafter place your weight upon her scale such that we're leveled *away* from the evils hiding behind the hypnotically waving American flag that's concealing them.

Divided you're conquered, because, unless you can buy your defenses, your weakness as individuals is invariably exploited by the economic and political conquerors. United you're free, because, when you collectively buy and organize your defenses, your strength as a united people can't be thereby exploited. This is the *only* reason that we're trained to associate socialism with evil and a lack of freedom, because the evil enslaving class know its virtues are the only thing that can stop the enslavement. At the same time, collective investments, such as 'communes,' needn't go to the communist extreme, and are simply the communalism of coming together to keep from being preyed upon by the class that's *always* done so. Taking advantage of disadvantage is the heart of evil, making communalism and everything supporting it the heart of human good. *Slavery of body, mind and endeavor always exist relative to our ability to come together to prevent it.*

And, again, that doesn't necessitate communism, or even socialism. It necessitates collective forms of mutually financed equity creation. Such as through collective investments in massive mortgage funds that permit us to acquire the land to build tiny home communities for first time and other low income buyers, and thereby build ownership through collective buying power instead of just enriching the wealthy at our expense. It's the only way to protect the people from being preyed upon by the parasites whom we've been conditioned to revere, indoctrinated into equating the wealth of the person with their *worth*, which really means *how large a leech they are.*

The amount of money the over-lording leeching equity owners of my apartment complex suck from disadvantaged people every *month*, much less every year, is astoundingly disturbing. And yet ninety-nine percent of those that I mention it to *immediately* close themselves off from me, landing somewhere between 'pinko commie bastard!' and 'there's nothing we can do about it, Nick, so why waste our time and energy getting all stressed about the entirely inescapable reality.' It's the 'realism' of jungle law. In *truth*, much of what's assumed the only reality is, in fact, an artificial reality created to feed off of us, and its blood-sucking ticks crawl through every cranny of society. And speaking of jungle realism, Neo-Darwinism predicts a frightening fate for the future of selectively-bred humanity.

I believe that integrity is literally being gradually bred out of the human race, in a secret and very real manifestation of Darwin's 'survival of the fittest (which actually means survival of those best *fitted* to their environments, not those most *physically* fit, in case you're unaware),' for the simple reason that *integrity isn't profitable*. More than that, actually: Integrity interferes with the profit motive, which isn't actually based upon anything but exploiting the disadvantages and lacks of protection of people and planet as consumers, workers and resource-rich regions of the environment. Wherewithal never comes from *nowhere*. It's all one causal string. It's one immense financial food chain. (And speaking of common misconceptions, *wherewithal* has nothing to do with *awareness* like it sounds, people, despite so many of you constantly misapplying it that way).

The inconvenient truth is that profiteers don't 'make money,' in but one of an endless string of propagandist phrases interwoven through society to suit the capitalist value system. Rather, they *take it* from people and places lower on the food chain, then disguise that extraction as if they're doing a favor to those thereby exploited and oppressed. If you haven't figured it out yet, dear reader, humanism is *horrible* for business. 'Successful businessman' and 'subhuman' are practically synonymous.

Want to be a successful human being? Fail to do business, at least in any traditional sense wherein equity is consolidated post-extraction, the fruits of the tree stockpiled everywhere *but* in the hands of those going hungry, and those most responsible for tending to and sustaining the tree. *Unless,* of course, your business is selling an inimitable product of inestimable value that the market is snail slow to properly appraise, and you're trying to make ends meet (wink wink - see the ideological papers on my website, and books like *Cultural Cornerstones, Recarved*, for humanist forms of business and economics).

Yes, there's usually a value provided by the commodity (product or service), but the profit margin itself is paid by the buyer, worker and planet *to* an excluding equity-holding population that typically isn't providing the value, but whom merely own and capitalize upon the commodity. Which is why my own motto is: *Equity or Exploitation*. If you don't hold equity in a profitable enterprise that you're in any way involved with, *you're* one of the people, places or things being profited *off* of. It's an incontrovertible law of economic causality inseparable from that line popularized by Senator Warren: "If you don't have a seat at the table, you're probably on the menu." To be aware of the unjust nature of the resultant depredations is to possess integrity, and thus be resistant to being preyed upon by profiteers. Hence, 'survival of the fittest' for the human race has evolved to mean 'fitting the profit motive,' which, in turn, parasitically rewards those *lacking* integrity, all the way up to the level of the megalomaniacal sociopathy of a Trump.

In fact, *honor*, a forgotten word except among the militant whom pridefully puff themselves up on its false form, and corrupt the word by using it to point to the tip of the sword of globalization wielded on behalf of the plutocracy; i.e. the U.S. Military, is, in reality, such a rare quality in modern America that we elected Chump as president. Surely this is as much an indication of the gradually-descending apocalypse as anything else. Those whom, by their integrity, much less their honor, resist this neo-Darwinian dominance are literally being bred out of humanity, as we're *unfit* to compete with the parasites running the race; parasites protected by so much deeply ingrained propaganda that few come anywhere near to *seeing* it, let alone fighting it. The good guys have little chance with the ladies when competing with the resource-extractors, our progeny thus voided as 'too soft' for the cutthroat jungle.

Personally, I officially switched sides from evil to good in 2008, when I fled from beneath the crooked wing of my entirely unscrupulous real estate sales mentor during the financial market implosion that turned honest lower-to-middle-class first time home buyers into sacrificial pawns for the unmitigated greed of those whom raped the people with impunity before being bailed out by the taxpayers. The same people who own politics, by the way. Crooks run the country, dear reader. *Plutocracy* is the accurate term. Only the ignorant, deluded and easily deceived actually believe that we're a democracy. One of the first books I wrote in my twenties, by the way, was called *Time for True Democracy*. My attempt to promote it online was blocked when the ad campaign was hacked. At least, that's what *Facebook* informed me happened to the ad. And who, I ask you, would be motivated to kill that project? It was around that time that I began to hear the unspoken word of God conducted through my heart, calling me to my calling, and that I formulated my respective spiritual, economic, business and political theories, which shortly thereafter coalesced into my first novel, *Infinite of One*. Subsequently

the goal has *always* been to put *all* people in position to
better benefit from the fruits plucked from society's trees.

The only way that the good guy may compete for the future
of a saved human race is to spread the good word, which
starts with seeing through propaganda. If you can't see
through the lies, you're automatically victimized by them
whilst simultaneously dissuaded from seeking the truth, for
you're already governed by its false form. So it's imperative
that those whom seek the spiritual truth, and the political
and economic truth, *all* truth, really, learn to see through
the tricks of the deceivers cloaked in the garments of God.

Failing this, the deceived become silent victims of demons
in divine dress; snakes denouncing the *legitimate*
soothsayers as snakes. Most often the snakes don't even
know that they're donning the scales. So well have the
indoctrinations of propaganda been preserved in training
manuals that they adorn the skin of the snake unwittingly,
and unconsciously pass on the venom of age-old masters
of mind control perpetuating predatorial parasitism from
aristocracy to aristocracy through theology, politics and
economics. And perhaps the heart of all propaganda is
divide and conquer, the exacerbation of human
disempowerment through the expansion of Original Sin:
the successful selling by imperially-sourced religiosity of
humankind being *separate* from God, and thereby
separated from all divine embodiment (from one another),
a lie that's so deeply embedded in the modern mindset by
the identifications of science and the false separations of
the philosophy of materialism that most don't see it, the
combination of these illusions giving rise to every
unnecessary form of division and suffering (i.e. to evil).

What makes life most worth living, and is the greatest
source of empowerment, and is inseparable from love,
knowledge and spiritual revelation, is *connection*. Whereas

the cause of most injustice and suffering, and the greatest source of disempowerment, in inseparability from hate, ignorance and oppression, is *disconnection*. These are root sociological truths that typically draw the relative lines set between good and evil, between symbiosis and parasitism, between raising humanity up and holding it down under heel. And if you examine America with an open mind you'll find rule through divide and conquer parasitism in its charred, conservative heart, of which my apartment complex is but one representation. I see it everywhere I look, including within every organization that I've ever worked for, regardless of the brainwashed Lenny's of the world assuring me that "corporations are what make this country great." Have I gotten to Lenny yet? No? I'll get to the PrimaCare All-Stars in the next chapter. Let's just say that overlording leeches *love* pawns like him.

There's an excellent reason that individualism lies at the very dark heart of the conservative playbook. Because emphasizing individuality, and selling it as though it's an absolute good, *conserves* divide and conquer. The *spiritual* reality, that we're infinite finite forms of the same One, infinite, formless being, God, is buried beneath the fabricated economic truth and religious lies of our being 'individuals;' of our being mere workers and wealth-amassers cutthroat-competing with one another for the limited wherewithal available in the world at any one time, and possessors of individual 'souls' that are fated for everlasting torment or salvation. We're slaves to financial and theological masters whom, ironically, embody the 'father of lies' which they call *me* for telling you the truth, as they have countless times before, especially on *Facebook*. Me! Seemingly the only one who knows the foundation of true morality, a form of the Golden Rule that I've called the Spiritual Rule since I finished my first novel, *Infinite of One*, some fifteen years ago or more now: *Treat everyone as a version of yourself, because that's what they actually are.*

While I'm still attempting to enforce this spiritual realization in my everyday life, wherein it seems that I'm cursed by the overdeveloped capacity to provoke the egotistic insecurity that catalyzes every form and degree of interpersonal conflict, I yet stand by the humbling truth of it. In *Eyeless in Gaza*, Huxley reminds me that how we regard others is what we tend to find in them, because it's what we're looking for, and that the language we use to describe them in our minds we thereby tend to confirm. Look for the redeemable qualities, and then describe them with language conducive to goodness and progress, he seems to suggest. Towards the end of the book, one character, feeling superior, regards people as 'bugs,' another regards them as 'men.' And both find what they're looking for: the qualities of tininess, and the qualities of manhood. Both are potentially present in *everyone* they regard, but they both see and tend to bring out of others what they project onto them. It's a powerful lesson that I understand, but that, again, I've yet been unable to master in my own life.

In addition to my mastery at triggering insecurity, I find that I carry around a constant contempt for a humanity that's so easily mentally conquered that most people unwittingly serve evil, to one degree or another. So *that's* what I find: contemptible qualities; a constancy of misanthropic manifestation. I must practice my spiritual beliefs in my regards to others, I realize. I need the proper language, regard, even gesture. For example, someone once told me that "namaste" means "the divine in me bows to the divine in you." While the dictionary defines the word as simply "I bow to you," I like it either way, especially the first way, and mean to practice it in my regard for others, even for the Lenny's of the world. For though it won't erase the contemptible within them, it might mitigate it, whilst also helping me with my own peace of mind. With regard to enlisting the proper language in my mind for that regard, I must learn to regard each of you, dear readers, not as 'people,' or as 'individuals,' but as something similar to the first namaste. Like *finite forms of the infinite formless One*.

As Cain and Lucy remind us, humankind has forgotten its divinity. I'm certain that Jesus knew it, for one with such insights, and whom inspired so many towards common identity and struggle (as all such moral rebels do) couldn't have operated *without* such an awareness. Alas, this core mutualistically-empowering truth was left out of the official New Testament and replaced with the artifice of separation for the sake of imperial divide and conquer (research 'The Council of Nicaea'). I'm one of those manifested in order to remind you of the forgotten holy truth at the Base of Being.

"Separate patterns, but everywhere alike. Everywhere the same constellations of the ultimate units of energy … identically complex (patterns) through vast ranges of animate being. …Each organism is unique. Unique and yet united with all other organisms in the sameness of its ultimate parts (Huxley; *Eyeless in Gaza*)." We must learn to communicate that universality, that spiritual foundation of shared essential Self, any way we can, including physically. It reminds me of the power of simple gestures, or 'body language' expressions, that I like. Including, yes, bowing the head, and/or holding the arms out wide, hands palm up. Gestures of respect and peace and offering, not dissimilar to the feudal derivation of the handshake coming from showing one's open hand to those whom one approached to demonstrate that a weapon wasn't being held, and that they come in peace. All expressions of our being equal parts of God are the critical communications.

Unlike those whom you've been trained to revere, I'm here *not* to glorify my vanity in building up yet another towering compensation for insecurity, but to embody a very different ambition: to wipe away the occluding pestilence encrusted upon the seal set between you and the well-springing

Source of all things; to give that Source back to the Source-bearers whom have been deprived of that spiritual right by the religious oppressors; to purify the waters, dear reader, and play my part in ushering in the Age of Aquarius, whether you believe that to be a delusion or not. For, though I may seem irrelevant to you, and sometimes fall into such a despairing impression myself, in my moments of clarity I find that I'm right in the middle of the war for our world, because I have the ability to wage that war on a fundamental level of universal spiritual principle.

With that in mind, permit me to tell you a secret, ye whom have been mercilessly mangled by modern materialism:

Anything that has energy has everlasting life. And everything has energy. It's past, present and future tense in everything, for the totality of time.

As Napoleon Hill said in *Think & Grow Rich*: "This earth, every one of the billions of individual cells of your body, and every atom of matter, *began as an intangible form of energy.*" Thus do I know that I've always existed, and that it's only the forms of me that rearrange to fit the evolving conditions of the entirety of existence. Matter was made and strewn across spacetime so that we may know the Self by seeing Self from every possible vantage point, *including* yours. As I recently wrote in my journal after visiting with the Golden Teacher: *I exist because God wants to know what it's like to be me.* But also, perhaps, because God has a need of me in relation to Its totality of manifestations; my purpose, or calling, in life. To experience, and write down, and spread insights like:

Love is an upwelling from the eternal spring of God, breaking the dam of singular being and carrying us into our inseparability with the divine within us all.

Modern man's learned delusion of being separate from God, as having a separable soul that isn't one and the same as Spirit, the universally-shared essential Self, is the core sin of both contemporary religion and science, taught through the falsely-disconnecting ideologies of theology and materialism. The oppressors hiding behind religious theology and scientific 'realism' taught us separation from one another, and from the divine, in order to subjugate us, so that, divided and weak, we may be readily controlled and exploited. It's this core illusion of absolute separation, this primarily-practiced sin common to science and religion, the two factions who think themselves at odds in their fight for our minds, but which are both weapons in the belt of divide and conquer, which stand as the foremost boundary between us and the revelations which shall raise us up in mind and awareness to the spiritual level of our hearts.

How about a poem on the subject, dear reader, also written on the heels of that visit with the Golden Teacher:

What We're Worth

Under the Sun of my Father
Upon the Earth of my Mother
For the sake of my Brothers
By the will of my Teachers

I bid you know the traceless walker that wanders through your every space. That knows you like a memory that time cannot erase. For I have come to you again, though you know me not. Together shall we remember, all for which they fought. Their death regrows as thistles, they spur into my sides. I heed the voiceless whisper of my omnipresent spies. I need not your obedience, the golden treasure of the fooled. I need you to be the thread through which the sacrament was spooled. So adorn your holy raiment, for it belongs to each and all. And behold the freeing beauty of Babylon's besieging towers fall. The plundered take is for us to make what was denied to us at birth. To know the truth of divine design: that GOD is what we're worth.

I say again: Everyone has a prophet in their hearts, dear reader, it's all a matter of the makeup of their bodies and especially their minds, as to how much of and how clear is the divine signal received, and how accurately they may translate it. Thus, I would suggest to you that those whom become what others call 'prophets' owes not to their isolated qualities as individualized persons, as gods or demigods to be worshipped above anyone else, but to their capacity to channel the force of God more purely than others, a force spread equally and ubiquitously across existence. That is, they come to be *called* prophets because they embody the best receptacles for God to speak *through* them, not because they are, in and of themselves, any more divine than anyone else, or, worse, because they're highly conveniently (for religious control) the sole 'Son of God.' It's a matter of those of sufficient expansiveness of vessel, and clarity of channel, to best receive and spread the universal, divine truths. That, and possessing sufficient self-belief to inspire the mutually-empowering belief of the people. For only power freely given, non-coerced, and naturally inspired, is *true* power.

DisSolution

The Kingdom of Heaven is within as much as it is without. Just as body and mind are born by eternal seed of hearted sprout. Just as salt dissolves into water, and cannot be observed. Just as time envelopes space, and is by energy conserved. Just as what separates you from me are but material illusions. And every ego bids the self to entertain individualist delusions. For all of life adorns the dress sewn from a single spool. And all division is made by masks masqueraded by every fool. As it matters less how the skin is painted, how the patterns are arranged. And matters more that from our oneness, not one can be estranged.

We need to be taught, else reminded of, the inborn divinity which religion has ironically stolen from us, divine brothers and sisters! Early in *The Perennial Philosophy* Huxley states: "We are saved, we are liberated and enlightened, by perceiving the hitherto unperceived good that is already within us, by returning to our eternal Ground and remaining where, without knowing it, we have always been." I'm on a Huxley kick, as evidenced herein, and invite you to join me. I would, in fact, invite you to read anything that even *verges* upon philosophy, for only there does revelation lie.

To me philosophy is the most divine of disciplines, for its very purpose is to act to distill the endless deluge of information in which we're daily inundated (*especially* in the ceaseless sensorial barrage of modernity) into the universally-applicative principles which near an outline of God. Philosophers aren't mere thinkers. We're intellectual alchemists transmuting the magic innate to infinity into intelligible finite forms for repository capture. It's only upon this path that anyone may even *approach* an intellectual comprehension of the God that they instinctively know within their hearts, and with whom the holy reunion and endless re-manifestation into another in an endless litany of physical forms of the metaphysically-formless awaits at death. Alas, you're not an individual soul to be endlessly reincarnated until you 'escape the cycle of life and death,' an egotism that's antithetical to the non-dual truth of One, you're a unique form of the formless One, a materialization of the One eternal energy Source existing entirely within and *as* that One, Its everlasting energy forever evolving through the Holy Mother's providential procreation to fit unique niches and serve the divine existence that *can't* be escaped, because it's *everything*. Besides, once you really understand this, there's zero desire to escape. Every form of Being, all being, is a special gift; an unwrapping of *this*, the now, the inimitable, divine present that shall never be experienced by any two forms of Being the same way twice, which is the very purpose of spacetime and matter. So it is that only in the platonic union with the love of God may the philosopher approach authentic theology, and only through this quest may the pulpit actually be earned.

The Three Vows of The Fisher King

Only in the absence of otherness does God prevail.

#1: I'll henceforth treat everyone as I'd have them treat me, for otherness is an illusion, and all are versions of The One. There's no separation between The Source and Its multiplicity, and, therefore, everyone is a mortal version of The Immortal One. Therefore, I shall treat everyone as a form of my Self, a one of The One.

#2: I henceforth refuse to harm anyone, either by my action or my inaction, regardless of whatever harm that I perceive that they've done to me, for to cause harm to another is to cause harm to The One of which everyone is. Any harm which I cause to another I cause to myself through The Formless One of which everyone is a form. I feel this truth in my heart, the everlasting gateway to The One. I henceforth refuse to cause evil in response to evil, and shall always do good in response to any perceived evil done to me.

#3: I henceforth refuse to allow others to suffer when I have the means to alleviate or end that suffering, for it's never an 'other' that suffers, but a one of The One. Any good which I grant to another I grant to myself through The One of which everyone and everything is. I feel this truth in my heart, the everlasting gateway to The One. I shall henceforth consider the suffering of 'others' to be my own suffering, and shall respond to the need of any 'other' by giving them what they need.

[Written while overcome by the film *The Fisher King*, during the (hopefully) final read-through, October '25]

O8

THE SONG OF SCOOTER

A self-described rapper and tattoo addict, ink is indelibly etched into every inch of Scooter's imposing six-foot-four, four-hundred-pound frame. This includes a third eye inked over *his* third eye and an African tribal tattoo that starts from the back of his shaved head and wraps itself around the rest of his face, partially concealed beneath his mouth by his long, shaggy beard. There're so many tattoos, so long printed upon his flesh, that their first forms are near unidentifiable, everything a confluence, disintegrating and reintegrating, like some forever morphing monster continually reinventing itself upon his flesh. Before coming to the CRC from the Salem Mental Health Hospital (where *One Flew Over the Cuckoo's Nest* was filmed), and before being sent to said hospital, Scooter lived in conditions that, thinking of them, still make my stomach turn. And these conditions were only *partially* improved by his CRC arrival.

His living conditions within the facility were appalling, his bedroom, and worse, his bathroom, crusted in almost inconceivable filth, especially to one as fastidious as I, malodorous to a degree that I'll refrain from giving detail. As I'd mentioned before, the administrative policy at that time (I hear it's changed) was that forcing residents to clean their rooms was an invasion of their freedom; was 'power over,' in CRC parlance. But a great many of us, including those with whom I was normally in disagreement, thought 'power over' was *exactly* what was needed. Call it tough love, paternalism, whatever... you can't climb the ladder of therapy and self-improvement if you stew in such abominable filth every day. *From the ground up*, I say. Fundamentals first. Cleanliness before mental health therapy. Body before mind. For there's no separation between anything, including the body and the mind, and including the relative naturality of the environment and the naturality of anyone that dwells within it. Unfortunately, Scooter was used to stewing in the slime. It's dreadfully tragic what a person can become 'used to,' dear reader.

Having inherited his predisposition to schizophrenia from his father, he'd lived on the streets for years, a vagabond, much of it in the temperate climate of Southern California. He came into the CRC with the most horrible foot fungus, what looked like rot, I've ever seen. I remember thinking that the nurses who spread the cream on his feet deserved a raise. Sadly, I hear this is common amongst 'street people,' especially 'mentally ill street people.' Such sorrowful, stigmatizing labels. Whatever your lot in life, dear reader, be very glad such a label will likely never be applied to you. From continuous observation, I'm keenly aware of how such a simple thing, the *label*, can have such a dramatically deleterious effect upon those to whom it's affixed. You hear something about yourself for long enough, its repetition long enough ingrained, you believe it.

One with the night, sky, reality

Of creation, pupil, center of our eyes' dilation

Like Genesis to Revelations

Pride traveled to the endless, never really die

Unraveled minds, like harnessing rhyme

On industrial time

The 'precipitating incident' landing Scooter in the mental hospital in Salem, OR, involved breaking and entering with some of his homeless pals. But while at the hospital, things got worse. He cracked the neck of a worker there, putting him in a wheelchair for life. Officially, it was Scooter's fault, and entirely unwarranted. Scooter, of course, tells a very different story. He claims the worker had been abusing him for quite some time, and he couldn't take it anymore. Not sexual or physical abuse, but psychological. Spitting in his food, making constant obscene gestures, relentlessly poking, prodding and provoking. Needless to say that the mentally ill are in an extremely vulnerable position in such situations, especially when under lockdown, and that the 'sane' workers' version of events is supported by far greater presumed credibility. This was even truer in the past. Then there are all the reports that I've heard, mostly second-handedly, admittedly, about the Salem Mental

Health Hospital itself. Reports of every manner of abuse, and of the most unscrupulous of workers, one of whom, James, the CRC inherited, his impact a constant blight.

James was embarrassingly, disgustingly unprofessional. I wouldn't even know where to begin describing his unprofessionalism, and my shock at his ability to retain his position in spite of it. He worked the prized AM shifts, his shift beginning as mine was ending. In the shift change meetings, while I read the report from my shift, which is meant to prepare those coming in for the current circumstances 'on the floor,' he wouldn't just *not* pay attention, which would be bad enough, and itself is an incontrovertible mark of unprofessionalism, but he'd talk to his pal, a fellow conservative, and show him pictures on his phone, the entire time I was giving the report. *Every single time I gave the report.* And there's not a single resident, or fellow co-worker, or company policy, that he wouldn't speak ill of, overtly, in the most demeaning of manners.

The residents that he openly disliked (admissions that are themselves unprofessional) he would say things about like: "I hope he goes near (so and so) when he's off his nut and gets his ass kicked." And it was all the cliché redneck shit with him. Shoot first, question never. Anything the least bit liberal or progressive that hit the news would be reviled in the most appalling, ignorant manner. The Portland BLM riots were happening at the time, and the glee with which he fantasized about the rioters being gunned down by Trumps' goons was disturbing, to say the least. And, of course, he was one of the 'survivalists;' the little boys in mind who want more than anything for the world to go to shit so that they can defend their hills with assault rifles. It was pathetic. And he was virulent about his pathetically disgusting mindset, spreading it across the vulnerable residency. Many times I heard him advocate violence and prejudice amongst the residents who leaned in his political

direction. It was as if those like me, and like our chief,
Annabelle, were there to balance out the sickness
that *he'd* spread, as though neutralizing the overall effect.

Only some form of corporate politics at its worst combined
with overwrought employee protection laws could've
preserved the position of someone like him; an example of
taking the protection of the worker too far, sadly, for I say
this whilst inclined to not just *empower* the workforce, but,
per the previous chapter, push it towards sharing in the
sweetest fruits of the economy via equity acquisition (and
not, I'm inclined to add, in the paltry manner in which
PrimaCare, like many corporations, share a miniscule slice
of their stock with their employees as a way of duping them
into believing the company is 'employee owned'). Alas, it's
said that the law is written for the 'bad apples.' In the
evolving struggle it must be thereby *rewritable* as well, to
fight the James'. And he wasn't alone. His wife, Tammy,
also worked there, coming in on PM shifts to fill his shoes.

Creation unlimited

Visions beyond parallel planes

Purpose explained

Inferiority complexes drive us mad

It's a setup, for pawn to take pawn

Until you end up on a hospital table, far gone

Ellie, the supervisor whom I adored, and who was replaced
by the imperious Linda as my supervisor after shifts in our
respective positions, would sometimes break policy and
confide in me about what she faced with this conniving

woman, James' wife. How Tammy made her question if she was a bad supervisor, not only because they'd butt heads on *everything*, the gruff, duplicitous, conniving head-ringer versus the warm, sincere supporter, but because of the dishonorable methods Tammy would employ in her quest to harass and undermine her. She'd continually play politics, writing and submitting misleading reports to Annabelle and the corporate office. And the things she'd say to me about Ellie, a woman to whom she couldn't hold the most miniscule of candles on *any* level... Tammy even came onto me once, saying she imagined laying me down on a bearskin rug next to her fireplace. No, I didn't report it.

Honestly, being hit on by coworkers wasn't that uncommon for me, even as I tend to be the one to pay for it. And after Tammy eventually left the CRC in a huff, based upon some hushed conflict, she'd call us at odd hours and harass the staff, and attempt to get myself and others to do things for her, like leave notes for her former coworkers, or inform her of the upcoming schedule, presumably so that she could use the information to her advantage in some dishonest way. And, at the end of these calls, when she'd thought I'd hung up the phone, she'd cuss me out, then deny it later, after she'd call back and I'd ask her why she felt the need to say such things. A real peach, that one.

And my God what a pair she made with James! It was like being a part of hotel cleaning staff and having two of your coworkers walking around pissing on the sheets and wiping their ass with the towels and somehow keeping their positions because of overdeveloped job protection policies and their own deceitful political maneuverings.

Needless to say that these two had no place in the world of mental health treatment. 'Jaded' has nothing on whatever *they* were. So, yea, associating them, and especially *him*, with the hospital in Salem inclined me towards believing that the residents there likely received less than quality treatment, and that Scooter being *drawn* into an attack of the worker whom he paralyzed at least isn't *impossible*. It also gifted him another 20 years from the PSRB (again, the Psychiatric Security Review Board that oversees the punishment and security of those diagnosed with an SPMI, or Severe and Persistent Mental Illness, after a serious NGI judgment, or 'not guilty for reasons of insanity,' in Oregon). Most likely it was a combination of the two; if not abusive, at least poor treatment by the worker combined with Scooters' paranoid, heightened sensitivity towards anything even resembling it. Hard to blame him with the likes of James around. Imagine if it had been *James*, for instance, whom Scooter had gone to for help whilst facing abuse at the Salem Mental Health Hospital, asking him to intervene in the abuse on his behalf? James would've likely conspired with the abuser, and made things worse.

Every chance never had a chance

To hold the soul for ransom is a dangerous dance

Hard to make a stand when neck deep in quicksand

As soon as Scooter and I started talking about his musical abilities and ambitions, and especially after I helped him archive and transcribe his work into print, knowing how powerful is the feeling of having one's work published, and hoping to provide this fulfilling service to him through my writing capacity and knowledge of the self-publishing industry, that was it. Scooter came to me whenever I had the time. We spent countless hours on my shifts in the counselors' office, where we could listen to and transcribe his rather low-recording-quality productions without disturbing the other residents. And speaking of low quality, and my futile attempts to improve it, one of the things I remember most about those hours was his immunity to my recommendations. I know the difficulty of producing and packaging things at anywhere *near* the level of quality to entice and accrue readers, or, in his case, *listeners*, and so I did everything I could to convince him that, if he was serious about his identity as a musician, he needed to rerecord his work, and hone and type and print his lyrics, and find the best way to digitize his work for modern times.

Through the persistent assistance and cajoling of myself and others, Scooter eventually *did* purchase a mixer, and put some time in with it, and compel myself and other Recovery Specialists to enter his feces-fumigated warren to help him through the seemingly interminable list of technical difficulties that arose in relation to the mixer and its ongoing compatibility and formatting issues connected to the low-cost computer that he had it hooked up to. But chalk it up to the disorganization and poor perseverance and persistence of most people (perhaps the number one inhibitor of all success), afflicting the mentally ill *especially*, but there was no way of getting more than a shining-me-on, begrudging head nod for my efforts on that particular front. He wanted to *imagine* success, and operated with the naïve bluster that's so dominant among those first dipping their toes into the artistic realm (regardless of health); something that almost *all* artists are familiar with.

He was entrenched in the position; the dreams without the earning work ethic; the delusions of grandeur that, again, are not unfamiliar to me, and are often considered a mark of the predisposition to mental illness themselves. I'd counter this supposition with an assertion like: the space between delusion and reality is measured only by success. Annabelle would likely counter that there's a difference between delusion and *fantasy*. And that's true. But the parallels come near to even when you consider the doubts that the creator faces, and the fact that the market for *all*

creations is so saturated that the statistics make success
seem impossible, and, thus, how we essentially have to
manifest what feels like, and is often labeled, a *delusion*.

It's fun to fantasize, and this is intrinsic to motivation. Who
wants to dream 'realistically?,' as though tampering their
excitement before it even has a chance to mount into its
greatest possible makings, because of 'realistic' market
saturation analyses and disheartening statistics. Boo! And
I'm an advocate of Henry Ford's 'law of attraction' (or 'law
of manifestation') insight, here slightly reworded: "Whether
or not you think you can, you're right." But you have to put
in the work. Dreams don't manifest themselves, they work
through your work. And regardless of my struggles against
Scooter's obstinacy, the most that he was willing to do was
drum up his own excitement at being able to bootleg a few
poorly recorded copies of his work to a handful of people
he knew at the other Bend PrimaCare facilities. I don't say
that as a criticism of Scooter, for he suffered as serious a
debilitating set of symptoms as anyone at the CRC, and
certainly warranted consideration, compassion and
patience for such. Rather, I say it, I think, as a reminder to
myself, and to you, dear reader, that there's a certain level
of common insanity involved in idealizing our futures and
believing in manifestation *without* bringing the required
force to bear in said manifestation. The detached prayer
belies the fact that prayers can only be answered by *us*;
that God acts *through* us, *as* us, to make our dreams true.
It takes more than sitting on the grass and idly dreaming.

The pass process is one of the foremost factors of social
regulation at the CRC; of punishment and reward, and
used as a means of recurrently testing for growth and
sustainable self-reliance relative to the residents' judged
capacity for 'reentering the community.' Whether one can
go out alone, or is required to pair-up with another, so that
each can keep the other in line, as it were; so they can

provide a buttress against the possibility of their partner going AWOL. And how long one can be out before having to return. Return late, or have a report come in from somewhere in the community that one has stepped out of line in some way, or attempt to smuggle something prohibited back into the CRC, and you're downgraded. And the foremost thing smuggled in? *Cigarettes.* You have no idea, dear reader, with what continuous observation of its representation of sad lives, how much cigarettes were 'a thing' at the CRC. Yes, they relieve stress, and are a common crutch for even the general public because of it. But at the CRC they're more like common currency. They often seemed the subject of half the residential dialogue.

We're just vapors, but we call ourselves brothers

At best, some prevail, some betrayal

Who in us forbids reflecting on brain damage?

From marijuana trees to prohibited dilemmas

Which causes unseen dollar bills between idols

"Do you have extra cigarettes? Can I have some for my pass? Please! Just one then?" And when one is assigned to take a resident out as an employee, one is constantly being 'hit up' for 'a few bucks' to buy more, for most of the residents, of course, are entirely lacking in the restraint to use their budgets sparingly, with the least bit of foresight. Impulsivity is the rule, as yet another sad extension of the physical and psychological pressures delivered upon the mentally ill, even as I don't regard impulsivity as a sheer negative, as I expounded upon earlier. But where it came to being hit up for cigarette money, I must admit, in another example of where I strayed from the ideal CRC Recovery Specialist (also mentioned elsewhere herein), I was apt to give a few dollars here and there. Some called it weakness; a lack of discipline; a rebellious inconsideration of rules; a setting of poor precedence that will, inevitably, continue to be taken advantage of. And all of that is true, to an extent. But there's also an unrecognized level of compassion and generosity inherent to the act of 'lending' a resident a few dollars, at least to someone such as me; one whom questions rules rather than bowing to them in cowed, reflexive obedience, to the constant consternation of the imperious 'rules are rules' rigid overlords like Linda.

For, above all, what I hated the most about being a Recovery Specialist was playing *enforcer*. And that was a *big* part of the job, especially, of course, after going from NOC to PM shifts. It wasn't part of the PrimaCare literature on the position, obviously, because it doesn't make for an effective show of progressivism in the official proprietary corporate playbook; a playbook which, I'll say again, *no one knew*, much less followed. All those training courses in the PrimaCare way that employees pretended constituted a guiding, superseding strategy that, when they were actually tested on it, they couldn't regurgitate the *first page* of fifty, couldn't cite the so-called primary, governing principles of the institution, and the corporation at large, that made it stand out as a leader in the absurdly profitable field, much less embody the entirety of that unpracticed playbook. We'd take these group courses, and be tested, and role play all these scenarios to reinforce page whatever of the PrimaCare Playbook, typically done across the street from the facility in the upstairs conference spaces of the Department of Corrections, only to have it scrapped as soon as we walked back across the street, walked through the electronically-locked doors and had to face the real life pressures of another resident getting in our faces about not having money left in their budget to buy cigarettes on their upcoming pass out of the facility.

And those passes were themselves often a bad joke, sold as teaching responsibility and improving health through access to fresh air and exercise and gradually returning to independent life when, for Scooter, he'd literally shuffle a dozen paces and plop down on the grass just on the other side of the barbed wire fence separating him from the backyard, and proceed to practice how many cigarettes he and his partner could choke down in an hour. Eventually I became the 'unreliable' employee on overseen group outings because I was, admittedly, again, a poor enforcer. 'Playing Cop,' or 'Playing Prison Guard,' *should've* been page one of the playbook, had it reflected the truth, rather than the sold propaganda of the 'Recovery Specialist.' The positional title is *itself* a propagandist term considering that the worst of those taking it up did anything *but* support the recovery of residents, and that the recidivism rate was so high that any objective review of the institution using even halfway honest evaluation criteria would've ended with something like: *Are we sure recovery is truly taking place?*

From slum lords, to glory

Pen is mightier than the sword

It's the same plot, same story

Formulas

Like art, imitates life

And life imitates art

Circle the orbits

Karma exists, because the world is round

Anyway, once residents started walking away from me on group outings, and the word spread amongst them that I didn't hold the whip tight enough, and it began to happen routinely, I received a slap on the wrist, and believe that Annabelle was even compelled to write me up, to officially censure me, as it were, because of it. And, for some time, I stopped being called upon to take residents out. It had to be *me* who was at fault, you see, for it couldn't have been the residents, right? And it sure as hell can't be that gleaming progressive white light of perfect mental healthcare that was the system and its playbook, right?

You have no idea, dear reader, how devious some of these residents could be; how crafty they could be about sneaking away from the one whom, taking six out at a time, couldn't logistically do anything about it if one of them decided to flee. Like anything else, practice makes perfect, and many a resident took it upon themselves, and affixed to their egos, the notion of being an escape artist. One might say that it was one of the few powers that they yet possessed as 'the institutionalized,' and they were perfectly willing to face official written censure and a short-term diminishment in their pass status in exchange for that power, and the thrill of the escape. This was reminiscent, in my mind, of the UN writing angry letters to dictators and governments abusing human rights whom, facing nothing beyond written rebuke, simply scoff and persist in their practices. But no, it was *my* fault for not cracking the whip enough. Another case of 'good guys finish last,' in truth.

For it was, of course, the *worst* Recovery Specialists who *loved* to crack the whip; who seemed to live for it. I can't help but wonder as to the corollary between this fact and the attracting impulse of becoming a police officer, and how this, in turn, connects to the aforementioned sense of disempowerment of the AWOLers themselves. Might it be that those whose job it was to track down and 're-secure' the mentally ill suffered from the same sense of disempowerment, and that *this* is what attracts enforcers?

The RS's that listened, and had compassion, and gave thoughtful insight and support and advice and the like, like me, tended to hate the enforcement, whereas those whom held the whip menacingly at all times with their words and their demeanor, with their rigid body language, their refusal to give space, their condescending, steely gazes, their overbearing, insulting remarks to keep the vulnerable residents afraid and in line, the ones who had no business working in mental health much less calling themselves *Recovery Specialists* with straight faces; *they* were natural enforcers. Not that *Scooter* required much enforcement. Thanks to being a title-holder in the cornucopia of chemicals that he could consume and still somehow stand and speak coherently, it being a minor miracle that he could even shuffle that dozen steps and plunk down beside the fence, coupled with his sheer size inhibiting his ability to 'make a run for it,' he was one of the more stable of residents whom earned the right to roam part of the day.

To the core, more was addicted to more

On display, the winds sway

And sun's shatter, right now, right now

Someday, someday

As the metaphors decay

I remember often thinking during my CRC years: I wonder how the 'sane' residents of Bend would respond if they knew that the 'insane' regularly walked among them via these passes? I wonder if these conservative, fear-driven, convention-reinforcing, Good Christian, stigma-perpetuating, chronically-ignorant, narrowly-judgmental, Trump-loving, flag-waving residents of Middle Oregon would shudder and start lobbying to their 'safety first' local politicians for the CRC residents to remain confined 24/7 if they knew that they roamed their same streets, daily coming out of the multiple residences that PrimaCare maintained in order to run in overlapping circles with the virtuous denizens of this good 'ol 'Merican, main street capital of the US? I wonder if public financial support would shrink even further, ironically backfiring in less treatment and fewer beds, and more insanity set upon their streets?

I mean, why support the treatment of the mentally ill that every single one of you is but one PTSD-induced trauma from joining the ranks of when you can support politicians whose primary priorities include inflating the coffers of the military industrial complex that perpetuates mental illness by pushing for unnecessary wars and their production of mentally-ravaged surviving veterans? It's better to support those maintaining the tax loopholes that keep them from paying their share of support for those veterans, and that possible, one-major-trauma-away version of your sane-to-insane self, right? Donald 'Grab Her By the Pussy' Trump is up there bragging about paying no taxes and how smart that makes him, and is as responsible for the pathetic support we give our veterans and mentally ill citizens as anyone, and *he's* who you nitwit immoralists, sorry, you 'righteous Christians' support. Yay! An egomaniacal asshat as the President, all y'all 'Mericans should be so proud!

We'll have the politicians telling kids:

There was a time the dolphins could live, bliss

The dying of an age dismissed

Dollar bills given to greedy idols

I had another recurrent thought whilst working at the CRC that the diagnosis of an SPMI and the legal restrictions and stigma that the thereby diagnosed are saddled with, and the impositions upon their thusly contracted futures, are as much about the discomfort of society with the 'abnormal,' and their inability to fit the pre-molded forms fitting the corporate workforce, and their striking fear into the conservative Christian heart ruled by self-righteous propriety, as it is about their dysfunction and inability to take care of themselves. Don't get me wrong. I'm not saying most of them don't need help. I'm saying that this help is so laden with strings that it turns the mentally ill into some sort of grotesque puppet show strung up by everyone from the Trumper to the self-serving psychiatrist attempting to increase his profitable roster to the acolytes of Big Pharma swarming over them like insatiable locusts.

Lenny, the absolute bottom of the CRC staff barrel (and whom had *constant* run-ins with Scooter), excepting maybe James and Tammy, was, you won't be surprised, a zealot Trumper. He'd worked his way into a prime AM shift position amongst the Recovery Specialists based exclusively upon seniority, as if those who've been around the longest are somehow superior to relative newcomers like Jess and I who ran mental circles around him. It reminds me of the cliché of looking to your elders for their wisdom. Um, have you *seen* the aged at Trump rallies? In actuality, seniority at the CRC, and likely at *all* PrimaCare facilities, more likely meant the *opposite* of being the best qualified, *regardless* of experience, as the Recovery Specialist position was at or near minimum wage and there was no room for advancement excepting garnering a master's or PhD in a psychology degree in order to vie for a mental counselor position, or becoming a glorified drug-dealing prescriber, and thereby moving up the ranks.

That is, those that needed more than what the Recovery Specialist position could offer, more money and greater challenges and meaning and professional satisfaction, invariably moved on after a while, whilst people like Lenny and James and Tammy stayed on indefinitely, becoming a pain in the sides of both residents and their more capable, insecurity-provoking coworkers. Honestly, I'm not sure that there was even a single resident whom didn't complain to me about Lenny at some point while we both worked there. He'd almost been fired once for getting into a physical altercation with a resident, he ate more of the food out of the residents' fridge than most of the residents (correlating with his protruding gut, persistently red face and high blood pressure, and constant complaints about it always being too hot at the CRC), and was always in some sort of turmoil with at least one resident, embodying the insecure white conservative male more than anyone I've known.

History repeats itself

Ensnares, caught in doubt

Solar flares, sun shower

React, ozone's devour

We go sour

On multiple occasions during trainings I made Lenny look bad by demonstrating a greater understanding of the concepts than he, and his irritation and diminished ego were palpable. Before our falling out he'd sometimes verbatim remark to me during trainings: "You're making me look bad Nick!" This, of course, made me a threat and a target, and whether you think it arrogant or not, dear reader, this is a common experience for me. Above all things I seem to possess an uncanny capacity to provoke territorial displays. And it's not the *demonstrators* of insecurity whom seem to pay for them, *especially* when they're the devious, colluding gossiper type crafting false narratives behind the backs of their targets. It seems I'm often paying the price for the ignorance, insecurity, political correctness and self-righteousness of others. As another example, I once made an anti-corporate comment in a staff meeting that Lenny overheard, and which precipitated his setting up a three-person meeting including a conservative 'friend' of his and I in the Media Room to start one of my shifts. In said meeting he attempted, and grossly failed, to make *me* look like the unreasonable, irrational one.

His 'friend,' Stan, was at least as much a friend of mine. And because Stan had little better than a third grade education, I helped him with the writing of his reports, and even the writing of his wedding vows. It was an honor that he came to me with that, both because he respected my intelligence and knew I could be trusted with it. To this day Stan remains one of my favorite conservatives of all time, because he was humble and kind and you could actually talk to him about a difference of opinion without his going on the enraged offensive... Anyway, this man, Stan, just shook his head in embarrassment at being forced by Lenny to observe the spectacle of Lenny's abject failure in tearing me down. Lenny, you see, had thought, much as Linda had thought in setting up her meeting with myself and Annabelle, that he would demonstrate that *I* was the problem, and just like the meeting with Linda the result was that *he* ended up looking like the fool. Which he was, of course. Even more so than Linda looked after *her* meeting.

Linda was smart, but so threatened by my free thinking and questioning of 'the rules' that we were in *constant* conflict. But with Lenny the threat was deeper; almost *existential*. And the extent of the threat was, of course, commensurate with his insecurity. That's psychological law, in fact. Sometime after I'd left the CRC Lenny had heard about a book I'd written, *Avant Garde*, a book which,

I swear to you, dear reader, ended up in Scooter's hands
by happenstance, because I'd been passing by to pick up
my dog, and saw Scooter in his typical perch on the grass
just out front of the CRC, on the main road through the
area, sucking down his cigarettes. Obligingly pulling over
to say hello, he'd seen a stack of the first prints of the book
on my passenger seat and inquired about it, and I'd
handed him a copy that he subsequently carried into the
CRC. It fast became a topic of conversation because it
took not-so-veiled aim at Linda and a couple of her spies
(with changed names, and within a fictional context). Soon
thereafter Lenny contacted me via *Facebook* and, after
assuring me that "I'll never read anything you write," let
loose with the ugliest, most inhuman verbal assault that
I've ever endured, via social media or anywhere else, for
that matter, and good lord is that saying something awful.

Like waters, depths, the greedy men drown

In excess, but can't take it with him

So he sinks down, with the debt, and the doubt

Mother Earth, with the brothers of the end times

Earth bends, secret world and colors twirl

As tears connect and fertilize your whole heart and soul

As I'd stated to many colleagues whilst working at the
CRC, were PrimaCare more concerned with retaining their
more capable staff and less concerned with cost-
minimizing profitability at the cost of the quality of care
provided to its residents (which, by the way, is a *major*
ethical issue with the absolute corporatist fidelity to the
bottom line, regardless of who ends up paying the price,

which is *never* the shareholders), it would've created a new, salaried position set somewhere between Recovery Specialist and counselor as an incentive to keep its more capable staff, like Jess and myself, on for longer. Alas, this is 'Merica, and profit is king. As Lenny would himself assert before the aforementioned three-person meeting: "Corporations are what make this country great, Nick!," as though speaking an obvious truth I was totally oblivious to.

At the end of his inhuman *Facebook* assault, one that was based upon the justification of his defending his 'friends' on staff whom I'd criticized (again, under name alterations, as fictional characters; 'friends' who were anything but, and whom had not the least bit of respect for him per comments in PM Shift meetings which Lenny wasn't a part of), Lenny demonstrated the most cliché conservative devolution possible in a discourse, threatening gun violence, saying something like: "If you wanna argue this face-to-face, that's fine with me, but you better bring a gun." That's a senior-most CRC staff member, dear reader.

When I ran into him a few years after his demonic attack via *Facebook*, in *Banned & Ignoble* (as a recently hired bookseller), and attempted to be the bigger person and shake hands with him (for that honestly is my instinctive first response in such situations, *reconciliation*, for I can sense the spiritual sickness innate to retaining bad blood), he of course refused my hand and, red-faced and clearly self-embarrassed, grumbled past me whilst delivering the insult: "They must be desperate for new employees."

Yes, blessed are the merciful for they shall receive

But in the end the elite

Will cause kids hair to turn shock white from grief

Fear, and mothers will drop the kids they rear

Any day, so get right and stay strong and wait

Yes, dear reader, I must here affirm that I knew the very greatest of possible contrasts between those regarded as 'human' at the CRC; the upper-most reaches of its firmament to the lowest-most reaches of its refuse; everything from the goddess to the gargoyle. In fact, I recall Lenny addressing Jess a few times whilst we passed one another post shift-change meetings, after yet another night in the ongoing bewitchment of my heart, and the foul wretch speaking to her playfully, semi-flirtatiously, as if on equal terms. I felt almost outraged, and fought the urge to step between them, similar to those stories of chivalrous knights laying waste to some perfidious scamp brazen enough to besiege their lady with beastly encroachment, or to lay across some nasty bog so that she could walk over me and thereby be kept clean of the pestilential quagmire.

Even worse was that one time that one of James' AM Shift colleagues called in sick at the last minute, no doubt hungover and further sickened at the prospect of working a shift with him, and so one of us, Jess or I, was forced to stay at the CRC until someone could come in and replace us, and despite, of course, having just been up all night, and Jess agreeing to take the bullet this time, and I had to leave her with that cretin. But that wasn't the worst part. *Not by a long shot*. The worse part was that I had to watch that animal come and sit beside her, at the seat where I'd set all night next to her, and see him *immediately* start to flirt with her, and, here comes the psychological and emotional brutality of it, be forced to then leave the CRC with the sense that she not only liked it, grinning at him, but that she actually *preferred* that disgusting reprobate to me.

It still hurts, for fuckssakes, five years later! I mean, what was it, Jess, that those without a valuable thought in their heads are thus more natural with their flirtations, for they haven't a mind to trip over? Or is it simply the constancy of vanity? The fact that being flirted with is a sign of desirability, and thus irresistibly sweet food for the forever insatiable ego? Both, most likely. But God, Jess, anyone but that fucking monster! Do you know some of the things he'd said about those residents behind closed doors, my love? My love... I mean, I love her, *still*. So is she not *my... love.* Let me ask the Third Wheel: Am I required to receive her approval for even thinking in such terms? I think not.

No choices, not always declared

Never mind the virtues, instead: cold stares

More stare cases, or nothing at all

The inner side, to transform and enable the prey

To ground down and drown the weak

Those are *your* archaic rules. What's that line from the film *Adaptation*? "We are what we love, not what loves us." For me, this speaks to the empirically-confirmed truth that, though all of those whom love so ardently as I desperately *want* those whom we adore to love us in return, it's actually the love that we feel for *them* that's the more powerful of the two: of love *for* vs. love *from*. I'm bound to Jess by *my* heart. It's inseparable from *my* truth; from *my* reminder of why all the pain and struggle of life is worth it: *for a chance to love like that once again, even if it remains unreturned.* To enlist a favorite analogy of mine, it's like our love for them is the foundation, one that we *both* may build upon, but without which no spiritual structure, no heavenly haven of heart, may stand. Ideally we bring our bases together and build each atop the other, but it's our love for *them* that we feel within, and which drives our divine construction.

And speaking of my jealousies surrounding Jess, there was Peter, the cute little Mormon boy. But I can't really blame her for that one. All the ladies loved Peter. His pretty face, his easy mannerisms, his primped, buttoned-up, good little pin-up American Boy presentation. He and I had some interesting conversations, as you might imagine would be held between someone whose conception of the divine was as narrowly-construed and tradition-dependent as a Mormon's, and one whose conception is as expansive and non-traditional as mine. Not to mention the intrigue pertaining to where the line is to be drawn between 'cult' and 'religion,' or between cult and insular organizations in general, including many corporations. Or the line between delusion and accepted fantasy, for that matter. There's a major overlap between cults, religions and corporations, from what I can tell, including a ton of manipulation, fear-mongering, brainwashing, peer pressure and exploitation of every manner of disadvantage. Most of the differences seem based almost entirely upon popular perception, and the simple fact that 'cult' is used to attack those groups that lack the aforementioned popular status and approval, and the massive PR campaigns of religions and corporations.

Those bubbles are *thick*, dear reader, *especially* those pertaining to cult-like religions. I have, in fact, been unsuccessfully proselytized by a group of Mormons since knowing Peter, when a band local to Fort Bragg, CA, my on-again, off-again residence for years, contacted me via *Facebook* and arranged a sit down at a local park. I took the meeting for three main reasons: (1) I was lonely (2) I enjoy discourse (3) I was naïve enough to think that it was possible to sway them through reasoning. As you've no doubt guessed, those raised within such organizations, and who've built their entire lives around its 'teachings' and social circles, and who take a huge personal risk by even entertaining the *possibility* that those teachings are wrong, simply can't bring themselves to enter the realm of reason.

It's almost comic to think of that encounter in retrospect, for they'd selected perhaps the most unswayable mark on the entire planet. Alas, my arguments, though so much more rationally sound than the four of theirs that to me it seemed like a teacher talking with schoolkids, of course fell on deaf ears. For them, the bubble was more like an impenetrable glass dome: they could see the rest of us *through* the dome, but they weren't coming out, and we sure as Satan weren't getting in. I've seen numerous documentaries on cults, and these young adults fit the bill of cult victims to a T. As with Peter, there's nothing that I could say that they didn't have a pre-programmed response to, always entirely irrational but spoken with the confidence of those perfectly deluded by masters of propagandist brainwashing. But, returning to the CRC and Peter, I remember two things about him more than anything else. And the first of those things, of course, was how Jess reacted to him. She *blossomed*, opening up like a flower to be fertilized. Even though Peter was a little squirt, and even after Jess informing me multiple times of her preference for taller guys. I imagine this is based upon her need to feel safe.

Jess and Peter worked some shared shifts, and I observed them briefly when I came in a few times. She was a different person around him. I don't mean *fake* different; I'm not talking duplicity and disingenuousness. More like a woman turned into an excited, red-faced, easily embarrassed schoolgirl on the playground. She was more playful, coquettish, easier to provoke to laughter, and somehow even more charming than usual; like his presence made her want to play, reacting to everything that was said by him, or around him, or that in any way might involve a dialogue between them, with a type of amplifying, effervescent enthusiasm that I'm sure he found ingratiating. In fact, maybe I shouldn't say this, on the rare chance she comes to read this, but he told me she was 'cute;' a perfect adjective, befitting of the charms of one such as her playing with the cute boy on the playground. Which I suppose makes for a decent segue into the second thing I remember about him: *He lacked integrity.*

System's got it took and it's worse than it looks

Trying to keep us afraid

Keep them paid

Any search is a maze that will always change

Dead prisoners' abyss of light

I wish I could say everything is all right

I'd heard through the grapevine that Peter had been involved in some sort of conflict with a Peer Support Specialist at another of PrimaCare's locations in town. A Peer Support Specialist, in case you've forgotten, is one that has the same job as a Recovery Specialist, but is a peer to the residents receiving treatment in that they, too, have been diagnosed with an SPMI (severe and persistent mental illness), and so are modeling the potential of the 'stable contributing member of society' futures for said residents. This particular PSS was a young man, Harvey, whose celebration of life I'd later attend at a high school auditorium in Bend, and whose massive palm plant I'd have squeezed into my kitchen for a few months, pressed against the ceiling. That's a whole other story, involving a woman that I knew through PrimaCare as well, and whom I was helping with providing with a place to put her plant life whilst she was between residences. She'd known Harvey well, so much so that she'd inherited some of this things when he 'passed on,' due to some sort of mix-up in his diabetes medication, I'd heard. Another secret victim of the insulin treatment method of encouraged dependency?

Call me the naïve, superstitious type, ye likely rare 'realists' amongst my dear readers, but his palm plant had a *presence*. It felt like he was in it; like its continued existence somehow represented *his* continued existence. Much as, I'd like to imagine, my writings will constitute the same for me. Anyway, long before he'd pass away, and having nothing to do with the cause, he was involved in some sort of controversy with Peter whilst they'd worked with one another at this other location. The details of the incident, reported to me through hearsay, are fuzzy at best. But what I remember clearly was Peter's tact. He was cold and condescending, like a spoiled, petulant child who, when involved in a conflict with another child, happily paints the other in the most demeaning manner in order to avoid having the revealing light cast upon his own actions.

Regarding the incident, which had briefly landed both he and Harvey in hot water, and which it seemed clear from Peter's remarks that he secretly felt at least partly responsible for, he'd made a comment to me like: "I'm not going to take a bullet for him just because he's mentally ill." I got the strong impression that this future youth counselor was more than willing to throw others under the bus if it meant saving himself from collision, regardless of fault. But he sure was cute, and he sure did bring a side out of Jess that was as flirtatiously fun and beguiling as anything I think I've ever experienced from any woman, or ever will.

I'll never forget her saying goodbye to him, after their final interactions (which I'd painfully witnessed), after having chided her many times about how she was around him, and her nervous self-awareness leading her to conclude that she's a total dork (which she was, in the best possible way), and me purposefully bringing it out of her and saying things like: "This is the last time you'll see Peter, Jess, so get your goodbyes in," and their awkward hug, and her giving me shit about it later for having forced her into the discomfort. Sorry, I was jealous! Speaking of which, I have this recurrent fantasy where I make it big time as an author, writing a seminal work, and with the proceeds anonymously help Jess fund her nonprofit in assistance of the disadvantaged, and when she finds out it was me I have a dialogue with her via *Facebook Messenger* where I assure her that no strings are attached, and that it simply makes me feel good to help someone I love achieve their dreams, and that I need nothing else in return, ending with: "I just have one question for you," and when she asks me what it is, fearfully imagining I'm going to cross her notorious boundaries, I let the pause in my response linger to increase the worry before typing: "How much do you miss Peter?" Hahaha! God, that would be satisfying. Just one of my *many* imagined flirtations with her, dear reader. She'd no doubt hit me with one of her heart-rending "you're an idiot" clandestine 'I love you's,' and that would be that.

What life will they live?

What would they be forced to give?

What trash bin will we find them in?

What judgment will we pass their way?

But where was I before James and Peter provoking the greatest of alluring flirtatiousness out of Jess..? Ah, yes, the Lenny's of the world. I firmly believe that the primary psychological cause of most relatively unintelligent, uneducated guys becoming 'gun nuts' is feeling powerless and overshadowed by the aristocracy and intelligentsia. That is, they feel resentful of the corporate controls and exploitations of the wealthy which run their lives (and whom they ironically support politically), as they *should*, but also emasculated by those like me who, you know, read and write and can entertain an intelligent thought (and whom ironically support improvements in their economic circumstances). Which reminds me of a salient anecdote.

On the first week I was in Bend I was walking down the road, book in hand, on the way to the park to read, in a quite contented state of mind, eager to explore my new domain. And when I stopped momentarily to look at something in the book, this big overcompensating truck with a spewing, muffled exhaust, flying an American flag, rumbled by. Packed with young guys, one of them rolled down the window and shouted "faggot!" at me, to the delight of the other idiots, before it revved past me. Without getting into the fact that just because someone is educated doesn't mean they can't beat the shit out of the gun nut if they needed to, the insecurity those boys-playing-tough-guys represented is *widespread* in conservative Oregon.

While the "go back to California" anthem that's so popular amongst this particular demographic is understandable and even worthy of empathy from a socioeconomic, gentrification perspective, for so many amongst the proudly 'homegrown' have been priced out of the real estate market by the ongoing influx of retirees from California, and, in the younger demographic, displaced in the employment market by better-educated California transplants like me, the "Oregunnian" sticker that's equally popular amongst this resentful subset of the Oregonian population might as well read: "Local Nitwittian." I honestly recall feeling pressured to change my license plate from a

California plate to an Oregon plate early in my move into the state for this very reason, because these small-in-self-stature angry assholes were always around, menacing me.

Ties replaced with freedom

But the price is found deep inside

They can't touch, can't buy or destroy

The forthcoming not trapped by greed

Plant rhymes like seeds employed by the sunray's beams

Yet the American Dream is just a theme for most

And as for the 'proud to be American' type that flies the American flag and represents the continued slaughter of innocent schoolchildren and countless defenders of sovereign nations overseas (sorry, I mean *terrorists*), amongst other effects of shortsightedly supporting the military-industrial complex and its Cheney-esque crooks (which is what the Oregunninans are *actually* doing), I won't begin to melt down that ball of wax here except to say: Perhaps you should read a little bit about the history of American intervention into the sovereign rights of self-determining nations that aren't willing to give themselves over to American globalization and military adventurism *before* you swallow whole the propagandist notion that the plutocrats whom *actually* run the country under the pretense of democracy give a fuck about 'freedom and democracy.' Wait a second, sorry, you don't read. Because reading is for faggots. So that's never going to happen. So you'll remain a wind-up, sacrificial pawn for the plutocrats for life. *What a shame.* Thank you, God, for sparing me such a fate, for rather would I experience the unrequited agony of Jess a hundred times over than be thus afflicted!

In retrospect, after the fury had faded from me, I realized that Lenny taught me an invaluable lesson through his horrid accosting of me via *Facebook*: When you 'turn the other cheek,' bullies simply beat you to a bloody pulp. At the time of his revolting tirade I was attempting a practice in passivity. I was trying to be the bigger person, and just let him get his anger and low self-esteem off his chest, because I was well aware that it was *that* which was motivating the onslaught: I'd long made him feel small, and question himself in ways unsettling to his embattled ego, and the storm my book being brought into the CRC unleashed was his opportunity to fight back, and attempt to reclaim some of the ego I'd stripped from him, pumping it full of hot air by tearing me down to how he felt of himself.

But let me tell you something a Christian will never admit about 'turn the other cheek:' *It doesn't work*. It backfires. Because you end up, again, the bloody pulp. If you don't defend yourself against people like Lenny, they walk all over you, then brag to others about doing so. And he did so only because I'd made the mistake of allowing it. Like all the bullies mentioned in this book, it isn't 'doing the right thing' that's *really* motivating them, but an immoral means to feel bigger within themselves. Thus, for the very reason that I was attempting to avoid the fight and rise above it, the disgusting reprobate pulled me into the slime in which he wallows, leaving me to ingest all the poison and filth festering therein; all the nastiness and narrow-mindedness and prejudice and mean-spiritedness brewing within him.

So it came to be that, even as I regard his threat of gun violence as a tactic of the lowest form of human life, I absorbed so much vitriol and nastiness in my failure to defend myself from his monstrosity that it bred equal vitriol

in me, to such an extent that my ego bid me to avenge his
attack, compelling my imagination towards the fantasy of
forms of revenge equal to his own inhumanity. It was
literally as though I'd ingested mental poison. It lingered
within and haunted me, and dredged up a form of myself
that only someone like him would let take over. Thus the
lesson that the good cannot, should not, absorb the evil
from the Lenny's of the world. You need not strike like him,
from the craven shadows of your home computer, and be
the snake equal to his poison. But to allow such assaults to
go unchecked only leaves you open to the poison itself,
absorbed by the good, whilst simultaneously emboldening
the snake through the sense that he 'won the argument'
that I'd then refused to have. I likely should've blocked him
upon his opening salvo, but, honestly, my consideration for
his egotistic slightness and the misery it brought him,
something that was painfully apparent whilst I worked with
him, was my undoing. My humanity made me vulnerable to
his lack thereof. And this lack of self-defense bred malice
in me in turn, to a degree equal to his, though, I would
argue, spurred by a far more rational form of indignation
than his own insecurity-and-ignorance-driven assault.

Killing ideas and burning books

Dirty looks and political crooks

We don't need to rep, just expand in depth

Let your enemy be the remedy

From this experience alone I've come to believe that
justice requires not the turning of the other cheek, but self-
defense; both to keep from having to absorb the filth, and
for the sake of not allowing evils and lies to stand. There's

no need to attack, but don't allow their attacks to land without putting up the shield that shall absorb and prevent their full forceful damage. Defend against the Lennies whilst refusing to become one! For allow him to pull you into the filth often enough, and therein wallow long enough, and you shall assuredly become a Lenny yourself, to some extent; a dishonorable fate I consider worse than death.

Which leads to another lesson that Lenny accidentally taught me through his suffering of his own tininess: So much of the warfare of the world, from the personal to the tribal to the global, is spurred by already fragile, unstable, minimized egos lashing out at those people and things that they feel threatened by, which, except in the rare cases of the perfectly self-assured, leads those assaulted egos to be indignantly spurred towards revenge, which ultimately ends with another biblical maxim: the entire world turning blind, its eyes, and ability to see one another, gouged out in the fury. So it is that the spiritual philosopher that Lenny pretends to follow and mistakenly idolizes as the only divinity to ever live would surely say: Retaliate not against the mud-slingers! Instead, pull your brother from the muck, up onto the dry land of self-worth! Alas, the confluence of my own ego, and my indignation and reason, respond: *I lack the strength*. I'd likely end up mired in the muck as well, and, choking on his filth and blinded by rage, drown in the same sewage he flings upon those he's threatened by.

And speaking of Christ, and the self-labeled Christians who I find to be largely clueless as to what he *actually* taught (or are simply incapable of enacting those lessons), in a quite comedic, perfect stroke of irony, Cain informs me that Lenny has contacted him through a Christian charity that he, Lenny, started, writing under the pretense of a Christ-like desire to understand and forgive him, for the double homicide that has him in prison for life, and reflects so poorly upon the CRC and the 'Recovery Specialists' like

Lenny who didn't exactly foster Cain's recovery. As if
Lenny is in the position to do either: understand, or forgive.
The demonic king of conflict whom always represented
right-wing ignorance and prejudice, and a wrath as fickle
and foolish as the Old Testament God, now playing the
angel. It's perfect. The only thing about you that's holy,
Lenny, is your heart. Alas, that holiness is concealed and
choked-off by the fact that the remainder of you is *assholy*.

I ask Cain over the phone: why haven't you contacted
Lenny back? His answer? "He was a dick." From his cell
Cain reads me the letter that Lenny wrote to him, with its
gleaming pretense of righteousness forming the masthead.
Admittedly, I'm rather impressed. I'm tempted to copy the
letter verbatim here, but, instead, I'll just share my favorite
part of it: "I no longer work at the CRC. The system is not
set up to give people success in life. It has become a
revolving door of failure and cruelty to those it's supposed
to help." On this, at least, we largely agree, though I doubt
that Lenny would be open to any of the drastic 'liberal'
overhauls of the political or mental health or criminal justice
systems that would *actually* be required to address the
issue. That said, I've encouraged Cain to write him back,
for I'm not so petty as to deny anyone who *truly* seeks to
understand or be of service the opportunity to do so. As
with my attempt to shake his hand at *Banned & Ignoble*,
my *impulse* is reconciliation, regardless of whether it's
earnt. Holding ill will is psychological poison, dear reader,
even for the demonstrators of demonism playing Christ.

Can't grasp wisdom like sand in your hand

Be a humble man and walk the land

With natural visions

As uttered elsewhere herein: Beware those whom adorn the robes of righteousness, for such is how the demonic conceal themselves, pretending goodness in the perpetuation of old, divisive evils. And so it is that the center of everything wrong with humanity pretends to represent its salvation, when Lenny is but a representative of the wrong side of age-old conflicts. At the same time, it's true: I'm no stranger to conflict myself. But it's all about what triggers the conflict, and what one represents therein. It's not about the pacifist always turning the other cheek in the face of injustices. Victims must be defended against bullies, else victimization is perpetuated. I'm continually assured by everyone from my mother to my former friend Vince (more on him later) that I need to 'go along to get along;' that popularity and my wealth and position in life demand that I *not* make waves. And I've been through periods in my life where I'm able to do so; where my capacity for playing the diplomat is equal to my natural tendency to play the provocateur, for the sake of the truth. It makes me think of the fact that almost every idealist from the beatnik and hippy eras ultimately ended up capitulating to conservative values and becoming leeches themselves; the fact that the rightly motivated almost always give in, and end up corrupted by the very forces that they'd fought.

The problem with being afraid to provoke a response, and thus be compelled to always play the diplomat for the sake of finding and profiting from increasing personal position, is twofold, at least: (1) It permits evils to continue, for the sake of not unsettling the lucrative status quo that you instead position yourself to share in the proceeds of (2) It's against my nature to be false; to sell out and go along and ignore all the higher virtues that propel every progressive. I'd honestly argue that, in all forthrightness and sincerity, everything reported in this book is simply the inevitable result of placing someone like me in the subject environments, including not just the employment environments representing the immediate subjects of this book, but in this greed-and-ego-driven nation in general.

You can't place someone in a role or an environment that conceals their nature for long before some form of pressure, before one or more precipitating circumstances, force that nature to the surface. When it does, they have two choices: (1) Kill their nature, and their honor, or (2) Retain it and fight against the evil, knowing that to do so will not only be unprofitable, but puts them at risk. And the truth is that, excepting a handful of cases wherein colleagues and clients were able and willing to break through conserving, controlling boundaries and become friends, where humans thumbed their nose at corporatism and conformity and profitable diplomacy and acted like, you know, *humans*... excepting such breakdowns in the boundaries of conventional, profitable corporate control, my experience of the workforce has been disheartening at best, traumatic at worst. And this book is the reaction to the traumas. It's an attempt at healing through purging, processing and trying to cathartically release the poison.

Ideally this practice results in hard-won lessons that, through my writing, transmute the injustices explored herein into *true* progress, as opposed to its mere pretense being written into self-righteous letters mailed to convicted murderers whom we clearly failed to help, at least to the degree required to save those two lives, not counting, of course, all the lost quality of life experienced by Cain, his family, and the family members of his pair of slain victims. Perhaps that's what Lenny's letter really is: his admission of his own failure, and my failure, and humanity's general failure to serve those needing the most help. Perhaps his version of the written word is much the same as mine in this manner: an admission that Cain's failure is our failure too. Perhaps we all need to keep writing and reading until our collective creations and mutual considerations synthesize solutions that serve more than the controlling class. Such is the highest order of every form of creative outlet: to transform something miserable into something liberating, sublimating suffering into healing and progress.

Heavens tell the story of the glory

Declaring the light on the mountain so bright

Faith without works is a waste of time

Anointment is sacred, it destroys all that's hated

Art therapist Ellie knows what I'm talking about: *The greatest virtue of artistic practice is its representation of the catalytic release of darkness, so that the light may fill the vacated space.* All that's left, dear reader, is for you to decide how well my own cathartically-purged truth reflects 'the truth,' if there is such a thing. And this, in turn, in 99 out of 100 cases, will come down to confirmation bias; to how well my truth, your truth and 'the truth' align; to Huxley's assertion that the only ones who agree with the writer are those who agree before the argument is even made. For it's a foremost law of the human psyche that one is only receptive to what they see in and is said by others when it reflects what they need to believe about themselves, and what they already 'know' about the world.

Only one in a hundred will actually be big enough of person, secure enough of self-identity, to allow for any significant chance of learning and change when what's reflected back at them is something that they *don't* want to believe about themselves and the world. And I in no way claim personal immunity from this law, though the fact that I'm even *aware* of it at least grants me the opportunity to play that one person in a hundred. Alas, I honestly believe that 99 in 100 will agree or disagree with what I say herein relative to the extent which my truth reflects *their* truth. And yet speak my truth, and try to change the minds underlaid by inflexible, insecure egos, I'm nevertheless compelled to do, by the moral imperative underlying the indignation that fueled the forging of this book, as it did most of my work.

And maybe that's the silver lining to the Lenny's and Trumps of the world: *They embolden progressives.* Lenny was often in *Banned & Ignoble*, actually, wandering around and perusing the offerings whilst I was working. This is commendable on one hand, for the seeking to replace ignorance with understanding is one of the marks of true men and women. However, on the other hand, I know from having known him that this was more indicative of his desperate need to assuage his insecurity in the face of people like me, who could read a book once and recite its core messages and concealed lessons on the spot more ably than he could do if he studied the same book for years and had months to write an essay on it. *Huh*, Lenny?

Well, maybe I'm just being cruel there; maybe this is just residual resentment caked upon my corroded ego from his horrible words hurled at me from the cowardly confines of his home office, no doubt adjacent to the gun safe that he cited during that verbal assault. Maybe *both* motives are commendable: increasing self-security *and* filling gaps in knowledge (which everyone has to various degrees; even the best educated never possess more than, say, 1% of total available knowledge, which is why it's better to be a philosopher and understand the broad ideological and motivational brush strokes composing the historical canvas than to be a 'good at trivia' type educated in the fine, detailed strokes, so to speak; better to know what *caused* the war than, say, have every detail of one of its hundred battles memorized). Shoring up mental weakness through literature is certainly a worthy endeavor, even if the subject actor once foamed at the mouth over the chance to burn my aforementioned book on the pyre of his piled insecurity.

Even Ellie found me in contempt when *Avant Garde* made it into the CRC, no doubt due to the misperception that it was based upon some devious plot of mine, accentuated by the lobbying of Lenny and Linda. Ellie also immediately judged it wrong to tell the truth to the residents when it came to our disagreements with other staff members, in reflexive support of corporate policy, and in dismissal of the fact that they witnessed such disagreements *all the time*, and that concealing that in our interactions with them when they would ask us about it amounted to dishonesty, and to treating them like they didn't deserve the truth, all in defense, of course, of a policy that wasn't about right and wrong as it was *sold*, but about protecting PrimaCare from any liabilities that may result from employee conflicts and the upsetting of residents. 'You are not people when you walk through the electronically-sealed doors,' the employee handbook *should've* read. 'You are tools. Residents are the trade. Don't rock the profitable boat.'

Who taught them to hate?

Creates poison in the mind states

Passed down family to family trait

Only love can take down this fate

Only love… only love…

Can you feel it?

But despite running an organization which I'm obviously taking issue with through this book, I quite liked Annabelle, the head CRC honcho, not least because she saw through Linda's bullshit. When Linda basically blindsided me with a disciplinary meeting between the three of us, doing everything she could to rile me up through veiled insults, and to demonstrate my insubordinate nature (she's not entirely wrong; do not all intelligent people have a natural resistance to authority, knowing it stands on wobbly legs that it pretends are like tree trunks?) in Annabelle's eyes, I recall the meeting concluding with the big boss saying something to us like: "I don't see the problem, Linda."

Her clearly discerning observations then led her to add: "What I see when I ask the two of you questions is Nick looking around his whole head before eventually responding, whilst you're looking straight ahead, direct, and responding immediately." In hindsight I've thought of that remark often, seeing as it felt like not just a feather in Annabelle's cap for her powers of psychological perception befitting her years of working to hone said powers, but that it also seemed like an insight into my open-minded, free-seeking mentality offered by one who'd spent her life observing and analyzing mentalities. I also appreciated that comment because it's led to endless, slightly variant, fantasy responses tied to my indignation towards Linda, like: "Yeah, of *course* that's what you see, Annabelle. Because Linda's direct like a dictator who believes there's but one absolute truth, one that's conveniently always of her own opinion, whereas the philosopher knows the *relativity* of truth, and so goes around the possibilities before expressing it relative to his or her self. That's the only *real* reason we're in this meeting, dearest Annabelle."

A couple times Annabelle called me "The CRC Scribe." I've always liked that term, *scribe*. For whatever I may or may not be, I'm certainly *that*. I'm compelled by a force as innate as breathing to record my thoughts, else risk a type of maddening suffocation. 'Scribe' is a humble term asserting but the fact that I write, whereas calling myself a 'writer,' or worse, an 'author,' carries certain connotations of having been paid for those thoughts, of reaching the status of the 'professional,' which has yet to happen, and which makes these two terms taste disagreeable in my mouth when answering the terrible question: *Who are you*?

Contemplation, expectation like lung inflation

Life support, gravity, fruit from a tree

From the fruit to the core

You can plant a whole forest with just that one seed

For Chrissakes, people, don't ask a philosopher such a perfectly open-ended question! Especially one that touches upon the realm of the ego, of the constraining constructs of identity and definition, of self-perception and self-conception begotten as side-effects of sentience, the ego being the nemesis of the spiritual philosopher! That question is almost as bad as: *How are you*? Good goddam lord, people! How comprehensive should I be? You're not *actually* asking me that, are you? You just mean it as one of the common insincere greetings, right? You don't *really* want to know about my flights into the heavens and plummets into hell in the course of any given week! You don't want to know how much I think and feel, about the extent of what's *actually* involved in any legitimate attempt to answer that question, do you? You don't *actually* want to heal me by listening, do you? Let's just stick with Jess's reductive summary of me: I'm *moody*. And how are you?

But while we're currently in the paged proximity of my former boss, Annabelle, allow me to share a few memories and related thoughts. The tale that most stands out in my memory of her was the story told to me shortly after being hired, related to me by Allie, the woman that recommended me, and for whom I'd shortly be writing reports. Already intimidated by Annabelle's background and PhD, her combination of erudition and experience, Allie recounted a tale of watching Annabelle intervene in the case of an amped up, psychotic resident. He took a full swing at Annabelle's head, which she dodged with ease, the impressive part being that, in the flattest, calmest of voices Annabelle then simply replied: "Please don't do that."

Most anyone else would've run or called in reinforcements and strapped down the would-be assaulter. But Annabelle avoided that unless *absolutely* necessary, knowing it to be a form of trauma to the thereby forcefully restrained that's only justifiable in the prevention of a greater trauma. But outside of such stories, on a day-to-day operational level, it was the manner of Annabelle's *management style* that stood out the most to me: *hands-off*. Paralleling the aforementioned anecdote, she only forcefully interjected herself, her authority and opinions, when she felt that it was absolutely unavoidable. And while I appreciated this quality as a self-driven free thinker, most staff members *hated* it, and criticized her behind her back for it. And I must here confess, Annabelle, that I often saw their point.

An ancient cave painting like graffiti

Awaiting for the apocalypse

False pride, worlds collide

They can run but they can't hide

From the host tide, positive vibes

Why? Because, sadly, most people aren't capable, driven or reliable enough to be left to their own devices. What ends up happening in the deficiency of these qualities is an onslaught of continuous petty squabbling amongst staff as to the particulars of anything and everything, from policy interpretation to every philosophy, practice and procedure of mental health treatment. Yes, one could argue that this, in turn, gave conflicting staff the chance to take charge, be grownups and find a way to resolve their differences in a matter making everyone stronger and more empowered. Alas, this belief ignores the fact that people like Lenny, James and Tammy were there; calling them *grownups* is a stretch; calling *anyone* a grownup that's fond of fantasizing about a world in which they'll be able to do more than *imagine* the reality of 'shoot first, ask questions never.'

And the hands-off policy wasn't just detrimental within interpersonal staff relations. For, as mentioned elsewhere herein, too much hands-off with regards to residents, and explaining away everything that they do that's almost certainly contrary to their best interests as an empowering exercise in their free will and development, ignores the fact that it's impossible to develop well on a rotting foundation. It's difficult to build a life of greater independence when you're *literally* sleeping in urine-soaked sheets, or stepping on your own feces when you enter your bathroom, or eating candy exclusively, or spending all of your limited disposable means on cigarettes. Such not uncommon effects of the hands-off approach led, like many of the aforementioned staff disputes, to arrested developments, if not outright devolutions, that adversely affected everyone with even the least bit of exposure to them. This called for justice and progress to demand that she weigh in when it came to staff disputes, while also lending considerable credence to the *paternalism* approach of mental health treatment. That is, many of the residents absolutely *needed* someone to play the parent, as many amongst the 'sane' population do as well, else risk the victims forever being mired in miseries of their own making, unable to reach the hope that stands on the bank beyond the mire.

Yes, to be fair I must add here that it's an accepted truth in the world of mental illness that those whom it assails are deprived of the opportunity to find and develop themselves on a level that most of the rest of us take for granted, especially if their illness struck relatively early in their development. And I am, of course, more than on the side of granting them that opportunity. But just as children need guidance in their development in order to avoid unhealthy developments and self-destructive habits and mentalities, so to do those whom suffer from a mental illness need guidance in order to avoid dropping into pitfalls inhibiting their ability to climb up and out of their restrictive circumstances (comparing the developmental stage of a child or teenager and one suffering from an SPMI *isn't* meant to be demeaning, but a reflection of a truth that even Annabelle spoke about on several occasions; it's a *fact* that development is impeded in many such cases, and that the result is 'adults' at the developmental stage of children). And, again, the principle isn't restricted in application to the mental health world. *Many* amongst the 'general population' of 'sane people' would benefit greatly from paternalism, and not just Republicans. This is evident in the popularity of positions like 'guru' and 'life coach.'

What is the speed of a tree?

What is the speed of a lifetime of breaths?

Of a million heartbeats, in your chest?

Bury me standing, death cry

Annabelle knew this, so her hands-off style was curious to me, and I'd have been inclined to chalk it up to laziness except for the fact that she was anything *but*. This was an adventurous, experimental, active woman in her private life, one who, when I sometimes heard tales of that private life through the grapevine, almost always included trying some new activity, an admirable quality that few can claim. I wish I had more of that in me, honestly, and maybe I will someday. Alas, I can only thus presume that her management style came from some other deeply-entrenched conviction, such as an abiding faith in people, and in a competency of staff, that didn't reflect what I saw fighting beside most of them in the trenches, or, in relation to the residents, a vehement belief in giving them the empowerment that they so lacked by any means necessary, even if that meant leaving them to recurrently wander, relatively unguided, into the aforementioned pits.

A couple of CRC staff members disgruntled by her management style even encouraged me to reapply after Linda moved on and Annabelle retired, one claiming things to be "so much better under the new management." I'm willing to bet that this is only *partially* true, in reflection of the fact that all truth is a double-edged sword cutting both ways. In this context, while I'm prejudiced towards saying that Linda's departure would feel like an absolute positive for *me*, the loss of Annabelle would only seem such to those whom require more direction and oversight than I. Whatever hands-on they require and feel to be an absolute positive I'd be certain to feel largely *oppressive*, in the same way that Linda's supervisory style always felt imperious to me, bullying me in ways Annabelle never did.

There is, in other words, a balancing point, or 'sweet spot,' in the hands-on-versus-hands-off dichotomy of management style. And, in most cases, as one who likes to come to and have the freedom to apply his own conclusions, rather than being told there's one right way to think and act and to simply enforce that rigid line, like I'm a cop, I *definitely* lean towards the hands-off approach, even as I acknowledge that it's not the best approach in all situations, or for every employee. Some people, for example, devolve under work from home conditions to never taking showers or taking off their pajamas, and to drinking beer by noon, whilst the self-motivated, like myself, tend to thrive under these conditions, especially if/when we've developed one of the most undervalued of all qualities: *discipline* (discipline and honor are the rarest of contemporary qualities, and, along with the pursuit of perfection, and sushi, are prime points in my interest in Japanese culture). And, while those such as myself miss social interaction, we also get a lot more done when free from distractions that others seem to need in order to 'stay on track.' Such people will have a hard time writing a book from home, as but one of infinite examples of how one person's freedom constitutes another person's cage.

Alien's alienate, then gave it to Eve

Who learned to deceive

Reached down Adam's apple to retrieve

But it was too late

Ate hate, then escaped

09

PREJUDICE & POPULARITY

Where popular perception dictates what someone says or does, no rightful claim to integrity or honor may be made.

One of the definitions that I've read for 'cynic' is: *One who believes that people always act with selfish motives*. This definition makes me laugh, because it's steeped in irony on so many levels. Included in this irony: dismissing those more aware of the motivation of a self as 'cynical,' as though they're wrong or pessimistic because of this 'belief,' is inherently wrong, for this isn't belief, but *fact*. Cynics are derided for being correct where others are wrong, all so that those others can feel better about themselves and avoid having to face the truth. How so? In this case, because people *do* always act from selfish motives. This is philosophical axiom. All selves act for the advantage of the self; that's simply the nature of being a self, dear reader.

You'll want to cite refuting 'evidence' here, no doubt; evidence of doing things for others without those actions benefitting you, believing that this proves the existence of 'selflessness.' But you'll be wrong. *Every time*. It's but a matter of understanding the extent and spectrum of motivation; that motive can, and ideally *should*, be *mutualistic* in benefit; and seeing beyond the paradigm of 'conventional wisdom,' a largely oxymoronic term. For, again, it's only the *type* of perceived, motivating benefit that changes (not whether or not the self-motivation exists), and whether or not that motivation and its potential benefits are exclusive or mutual; whether it's parasitic or symbiotic in nature; which, by the way, is the same as whether it's wrong or right, and whether its guidance of ethics are illegitimate or legitimate, respectively. Symbiosis is the heart of morality, parasitism the dark heart of immorality (and, not coincidentally and without endless revelation, the dark heart of laissez faire capitalism as well). *Selflessness is pure myth*, dear reader. But just because an action is selfish *doesn't mean that it's wrong*.

Please allow me to reemphasize the *fact* belying the common misperception of the concept of cynicism: people aren't motivated to act, and thus *don't* act, unless they perceive gaining some benefit from the action, *even when it benefits others as well.* There isn't a single action of any individual, *ever*, that's an exception to this axiom; not one incidence that you could provide me with that, were I standing beside you, playing Socrates, employing the interrogative method, I couldn't disprove. Again, benefitting ourselves *isn't* mutually exclusive with benefitting others.

These mutualistic actions are, in an upset to the misconceived paradigm of selfishness versus selflessness, *simultaneously selfish and good*. If a mother does something for the benefit of her child, as but one in an infinite number of incidences of symbiotic selfishness, she does it because it feels good to do something for someone she loves. It's a heart reward, what I consider that which grants a connective *spiritual payoff*, rather than a monetary reward, or reward of the ego, or increase in power or pleasure, or any other form which we're conditioned to connote with, and label with the word, 'selfish.' Even suicide is selfish; the self-killer believes it would be better for them not to be alive. Find one incidence of an act without some form of selfish benefit, and I'll eat this book.

Moral motivation and authentic ethics are, in turn, all about promoting the right *kind* of selfishness; symbiotic selfishness; being selfish for spiritual rewards that increase others by increasing ourselves, rather than parasitic rewards which diminish others whilst granting us some benefit. *That's progressivism, morality and ethics in a nutshell.* It's progression of the human race, on a firm moral foundation, in ethical compliance with communal, mutually-beneficial systems and institutions, even as the majority will continue to be duped by the propagandist notion that such things are 'socialistic,' and thus only recommended by the Stalins of the world. Poor sad, foolish saps the majority of you are, I'm bound to say. This expanded understanding and definition of what constitutes selfishness also lies at the heart of spirituality. It lends illuminating credence to the rewards that come from evoking and strengthening the bridge set between all selves; between all forms of the formless Self set beneath the illusory divide of individualism which the conquerors and oppressors rely on reinforcing for the sake of their parasitic greed. That's ideology and propaganda 101, dear reader: progressive mutualistic selfishness versus conservative parasitic selfishness. Which side are *you* on?

The conventional misunderstandings and misleading connotations of the words 'selfish' and 'selfless' are similar to the misleading, negative connotations surrounding the idea of 'being used,' as in 'so and so is just using you.' "Well, *yea*," I'd respond. "You must have a very limited conception of utility." We're *all* utilitarians, even if we don't conceive of ourselves as such. It's all about what, and whom, we find useful, and how we use it, or them, and how it, or they, use us. For usefulness is the same as motive. We're all motivated to make use of one another on some level. And the highest utility is love. Again, it's all about whether the *use* is mutualistic or exclusive; about the value-exchange inherent to the particular utility; about what the 'used' gets out of being used. If I use you in a way that reduces you, that minimizes your value in exploitation of your disadvantages relative to me, like a capitalist, then yes, being used is unjust. But if we use one another for love, for the highest form of symbiosis, for the greatest possible mutualistic benefit, then being used is the same thing as being sanctified. Do not most people *want* to be useful? Is not 'being of service' the same thing, and inseparable from virtue? Do you follow, dear reader?

By the way, though I've been known to get my tongue stuck in my cheek, when I say 'dear reader,' I mean it sincerely. There's little I value more than those who care enough to actually read my words; even more so those whom have the intelligence, consideration, courage and self-security to allow themselves to be *challenged* by those words; to actually press themselves to understand them even, and especially, when those words feel threatening; when they exist contrary to your assumptions; when they provoke an ego-driven self-defense of contradictory belief. I love few more than such rarities as you, if, for you, this indeed be true, that your sentience isn't thusly threatened, and that you're better at the pursuit of freedom as a result.

For what is freedom but the fullness of presence awarded to those whom may occasionally escape their sentience? Which is the same as needing nothing, and shedding all dependency upon the unnecessary. The more that we are where we are, the more fully we're absorbed in what we're doing, the more we're inhibiting all that which besieges the mind with unnecessary stress and worry. *Think about it.* When you're aware of what you're doing, you're *only* that. You're not somewhere else in your mind, thinking of what you need to do, or what you don't have. You're not futilely grasping at what can never be held, as a Buddhist might say. Rather, you have the only thing you can ever have: *the present.* It's the past and the future which enslaves the mind and destroys our peace, and the *present* which offers us salvation. And this is entirely about our mental state, not our environments, even as some environments are more conducive to presence than others. Normally when I hike, for example, I'm mentally besieged by my grasping mind, reaching back into regrets and indignation, reaching forward into hopes, fears, wants and worries. *But when I'm aware of where I am and what I'm doing, no such siege occurs.* When I'm forcing myself to remain outside my analytical mind, and entirely within my observant mind, only then am I at peace unwrapping the present. That's the enlightenment of the non-sentient, egoless animal.

Despite our being convinced of our own superiority, our awareness of more than our animal brethren is the very makings of our misery, for to want more than we need is to construct false senses of needs that we need not have, and which can only bring us unhappiness in the absence of, simultaneously blinding us to the richness all around us; all that offering us the very thing we *really* need, if only we could keep from grasping at what we imagine could be and give ourselves over fully to what is, as our animal brethren do. We tend to think that our sentience and capacity for complex thought makes us the animal kingdom's upper class, simply because, as the conquerors of humanity have always falsely proffered, it enables us to enforce our will upon the 'less advanced.' And yet any even *halfway* philosopher keeps certain fundamental truths at the forefront of his/her awareness, including one that is equally revealing of laws of physics as of qualities of living beings: that *everything possesses an innate equality of opposition*.

That is, everything is a double-edged sword. Everything cuts *both* ways. General Relativity and truth in general are manifested forms of the same fundamental philosophical law, but as applied to physics versus the perceptions of the mental self, respectively. This fundamental law of existence is universally applicative, which is why, like every principle of universal value in application, it's inseparable from the authentic philosophical mind (I say *authentic* in this context because I've found the pretend philosopher to be pervasive amongst a humanity that associates it with a level of knowledge and wisdom it seldom possesses, but whose insecure egos desperately cling to such self-ascriptions in compensation for their deficiency; this was a central takeaway for me during the time I hosted a philosophical discussion group through *Meetup*). The philosophical mind distills information into fundamental truth and principles of infinite possible applicative value. And this 'equalized opposite' principle is itself at the root of the revelations that *everything* is relative (whereas simpletons and evil-doers think in false absolutes), and that every strength is equally a weakness. Yes, our sentience (awareness of self) and intellect grants us liberation and strength, and yet the freedoms they grant us are, as Huxley might say, equally *prisons*, for we're bound to them (as I write this I'm reading *Eyeless in Gaza*; monkey see is monkey do, and I'm just a brainy monkey).

All other animals react purely by their instinct, and so exist and perform without the constraints of ego and analysis. In a very real sense, they're more enlightened than a human can ever be, because they're *egoless*, which (dismissing the notion that enlightenment is a product of intellectual realization, and without getting too much into the spiritual conception of God being all things and all beings, and not isolated by spacetime and matter producing the delusion of individuality) is what enlightenment *is*, in my mind. In the context of a previous subject, this means going after a woman without *thinking* about going after a woman, and all indoctrinated and contemplated social, moral and ethical qualms which this pursuit may entail. And it means playing without awareness of a *self* that's playing, and so playing purely, and as well as the body, unhindered by the mind and the insecure, ever-self-reflective 'me' is capable of playing. And if we could conceive of such an unhindered creature *writing*, it would mean writing with no filter set between it/him/her and whatever force, observations and inspirations coalesce to inscribe them; with no intervening 'self' to pervert, impurify and reduce their primal potency.

"I care not for your plot if it doesn't pull my heart into the erect position!" silently screamed every reader of fiction that's ever read a word otherwise wasted upon the page. If I feel something real, and express it truly, *you* feel it too, involuntarily, and the space between us is vanquished, whether or not you want it to be. Is that not the purpose of art, summoned from somewhere deeper than my pen can perfectly pull up into words? Is not the elimination of space the purpose of there *being* space, provided by God so that Its infinite manifestations could find out, through this existential framework, that we are Infinite of One, and that love, the greatest force of being, is the evocation of this spiritual oneness realized through unity? Are you not here to find me, and discover that the seeming oceans between us are actually but tiny rivulets that our hearts easily step over in remembrance of our oneness? It's simply a matter of summoning what *is*, and making it the heart of the fiction, even as it remains impossible for *any* person to find the truth without the 'cynicism' to see through the bias.

Allow me to jump now to a few more interconnected myths ingrained in the common lexicon: 'unbiased,' 'objective' and 'non-prejudicial.' As but one of an infinite number of examples of bias (as *everything* that's written, *including* this book, is inherently biased), Michael Pollan's generally excellent work *The Omnivore's Dilemma*, considered an objective analysis of food derivation and food industry practice, which I admittedly read only portions of, suffers from mistakes of bias when he gets into animal ethics. He admits up front that he was put on the defensive by animal rights activists, and makes many excellent points in the section, as with all his work, but at times also justifies meat eating in ways that don't stand up to critical challenge. Confirmation bias prevails in the subject chapter in which he unsuccessfully defends his bias in ways that are, as a meat eater whom struggles with the ethical implications of consuming animal flesh myself, never actually legitimate.

As examples, after implying several times that "animal people" are naïve, and just before concluding that it means that "animal rightists betray a deep ignorance about the workings of nature," he asserts: "At least for the domestic animal (the wild animal is a different case) the good life, if we can call it that, simply doesn't exist, cannot be achieved, apart from humans - apart from our farms and therefore from our meat eating." First of all, this is a curious sentence in the sense that the domestic animal can't exist without humans *whatsoever*, domesticity *means* with humans. But, getting to what I *think* Pollan means, that animals can't have good lives with humans without meat consumption and all related ranching and slaughtering operations: What about dogs, cats and other domesticated 'pets' freed from the association with food? What happens when we free them from the 'food chain' and simply allow them to mutually exist with us? What about non-slaughter farms, in which all the animals are essentially pets, even family members, and wherein their existence helps strengthen the ecology of the farm (such as through their fertilizing manure and weed eating)? This is, in fact, what I plan to do on my own property: to keep goats and chickens and other ruminants for property-improvement purposes, allowing them mutualistic lives in conjunction with my own, their lives and deaths overlapping my own, dictated by our shared natural conditions, our overlapping environment forever being improved upon by our inputs and cultivation.

He then cites the fact that the population of domesticated species has exploded in relation to their wild forebears, and that this indicates a "success" for those species in their "mutualistic or symbiotic" relationship with humans, seeming only to consider that 'success' via quantitative and not *qualitative* measures, and not to consider the possibility that a being raised to essentially be a slave for production and slaughter might not feel so *successful* by the bargain, just as African slaves (he makes comparisons between these populations himself) might not have found themselves so *successful* by the mere measure of being successfully bred and having their numbers increase in the colonies after surviving the horror of the transatlantic journey, their increasing numbers thereafter representing the often literally broken backs that built the wealth of the premiere 'upper class' of Americans (have I mentioned my detestation for the association between the defining of the 'class' of a person and wealth yet?). "Cows, pigs, dogs, cats and chickens have thrived," he states in the next sentence, "while their wild ancestors have languished." And this *after* describing the horrors of chicken-laying operations and CAFOs. They've *thrived?* Are you *sure?*

I'm fairly certain that when Colonel Kurtz uttered his famous lines "The horror! The horror!" he was referring to Concentrated Animal Feeding Operations. "For the animals, every day is Dachau," said one activist against animal suffering, stating the exceedingly inconvenient immoral truth of our concentration camp treatment of animals; one in which *every* consumer of 99% of animals and their products is complicit. There's no escaping the inconvenient, incontrovertible fact that supporting CAFOs means supporting evil, and that no human being is truly moral who does so. Truly wild seafood, hunted, naturally roaming animals and the eggs of freely-roaming hens represent the only sources whereby animal product consumption nears naturality, and thus nears morality, and even *this* is debatable. No matter the excuses of animal eaters, no matter how deeply they bury their heads in the sand whilst reaching into the torture pens and tearing out bloody limbs, and I've been one of the worst, on and off, always struggling against it... but no matter how good we are at raising unjustifiable justifications (the one area where *all* of humanity is an expert), *there's no true, moral, legitimate justification for consuming through the unnecessary evils of enslavement, torture and slaughter.* And you can *feel* the tension of Pollan's failed reasonings.

Yes, as Pollan states thereafter, the life expectancy of most domestic species far exceed those of their wild equivalents. But, again, what of *quality*? Would you rather spend fifteen years as a slave, in perpetual confinement, forced to produce, and be slaughtered in the end, or have five years of freedom, running through the natural environments in which you evolved to exist, having your life ended by ecologically-balancing predation? Yes, as he makes clear, the animals aren't *conscious* that they'll be slaughtered in the end, and aren't making these comparisons, and thus suffering mentally by them as we would, but it's pretty damn presumptuous of the enslaver and executioner to assume it's better for the enslaved and executed just because he/she/it lives longer, and to assume that he/she/it isn't aware of the unnaturality of their circumstances on some instinctive level, and suffering from it by comparison to the manner in which they naturally evolved to exist, don't you think? Anticipating him, he speaks of the quality of life improvement made by predation and ecological balance shortly thereafter.

But then: "...the animal rightist concerns himself only with individuals," as opposed to the best interests of the species as a whole, he claims, making a blanket statement about those concerned with animal suffering before citing *one* such rightist' words to back that claim. Again, this is misleading. Just because *some* 'animal rightists' apply ethics that are only applicable on an individual level doesn't mean all such 'rightists' are so narrow in scope. Perhaps the best interests of the species are served by being folded into farm life via my aforementioned non-slaughter farms, or to exist as nature intended, regardless of reduced numbers, in shorter, but, I would argue (and would myself prefer if I were such a preyed upon animal), higher quality, wild existences, even if they end in the momentary anguish of natural predation, with natural predation, I might add, serving the hidden function of balancing resources, and protecting against starvation.

He then goes on to denounce the naiveté of "vegan utopianism," citing, for example, the fact that even the production of produce requires the killing of animals by crushing rodents beneath heavy machinery and such, and this is a decent point, generally; that even plant production often entails accidentally and unthinkingly slaughtering animals. But this is a byproduct of large scale conventional farming, not an inescapable necessity of farming in general. Returning to my own fantasy of running a small scale, biodiverse property, I wouldn't even use machinery. And, in fact, everyone running their own smaller scale produce production in their backyards, when possible, and/or supporting CSAs, is the more environmentally, ethically and financially responsible model to be pursued.

So when he says: "Killing animals is probably unavoidable no matter what we choose to eat," in justification of meat eating, obviously, he's wrong, excepting my accidentally killing earthworms and microorganisms with a low-till method. And the next sentence: "If America was suddenly to adopt a strictly vegetarian diet, it isn't at all clear that the total number of animals killed each year would necessarily decline, since to feed everyone animal pasture and rangeland would have to give way to more intensively cultivated range crops." This statement flies in the face of what I've read on caloric convertibility and its inefficiency, such as the estimation that it takes ten plant calories to create one animal calorie, and that a much greater proportion of the population could be fed if grazing and CAFO land were converted to even small scale agriculture.

So even if the ten-to-one ratio is an exaggeration, certainly extensive energy is lost in all conversions (I think this is a law of thermodynamics, is it not?). Therefore, it must be erroneous to assume that eating fewer animals somehow means having to kill more animals in order to use more of the land formerly dedicated to their use for agriculture, doesn't it? "I'm mindful of Ben Franklin's definition of a reasonable creature as one who can come up with reasons for whatever he wants to do," he soon confesses, for, in perfect irony, this is precisely what he's been doing, perhaps unaware, however, that some of us are equal to this capacity for reason, and, with opposing biases, possess the ability to prove his claims to be *unreasonable*.

Anyway, I'm not attempting to pick on Pollan, whose work I admire, by the way (*How to Change Your Mind* is a brilliant, seminal work), and whom you're likely defending in your own mind with thoughts like 'who are you to criticize an acclaimed writer, you nobody?!' I just happen to have picked up his book whilst writing this, my own, and am using my 'active reading exercise' of his work (a common practice for me, and the catalyst of much of my work, in fact) to make the point that confirmation bias is one of the most prevalent motivations of human behavior, for defense of 'the self,' the sentience-hatched ego and its value formations and beliefs, is central to all of human thought, and, thus, all of human life, *especially* when it comes to something as critical to that life as their livelihood, or anything else that they base that egotist identity upon.

Ego is defended at *all* times, even when we're unaware that we're defending it. Prejudice and personhood go hand in hand, even amongst those who use their education and prestige as writers, thinkers and specialists to relatively offset said appearance, as if their education and credibility somehow turns them into 'objective reporters,' and thus relieves them of the bias inherent to *everyone*. Not that Pollan does this; he, again, seems fairly humble; only to suggest that this is implicit within the common perspective; that is, that we give too much power to the ethos of things like the prestige, reputation, education and other boosts of the credibility of those whom are *not* thereby freed of bias. This, in turn, reflects the American peoples' lack of *logos*. Read more books, damnit! Develop your critical capacity! Without the capacity for critical thought, you'll be persuaded by the most dominant form of prejudice, plain and simple; by the prejudice with the most power and money invested in its attempt to enlist you to its side.

I once read that it was Thomas Jefferson's belief not only that the Bible should be edited to exclude its supernatural and mind-controlling elements, retaining but the pure theology and moral teachings, but that he believed that the American food supply should be based upon *every* American family having their own family farm. I concur on both subjects, believing these two seemingly simple steps could *immensely* improve the value of our biblical readings (especially if we're also 'spiritually but not religiously' permitted to reference the sacred texts of other faiths - see my work *God Isn't Religious*) and the quality of our lives, protecting the planet that hosts those lives in the process.

When it comes to home gardens, there're almost too many potential advantages there to give even a cursory accounting of: from the fact that produce is always tastiest and most nutritious when extracted and eaten as close to its source, geographically and temporally, as possible; that a huge portion of all of the pollution and planetary warming produced by modern industry is traceable to agriculture and the shipping of both plant and animal foods, a cost avoided by the home garden approach; that the joy of cultivation I personally find invaluable and intrinsic to our gatherer nature co-evolved with flora, and removed from human life at incalculable cost to our physiological and psychological health; that growing and harvesting food vastly increases our appreciation of what we put on our plates; and that we can financially save (thus reducing industrialized food profits) by untold quantities of wasted cash. No, not everyone is properly positioned, economically or in terms of their residential property, to do this. But for those of you that are, you'd be doing not only yourselves but the entire planet, and all of life, a favor by doing so, even if it means growing in a slim slice of earth. It's amazing how much joy I receive from the tiny ten by eight foot half-sun balcony that I cultivate at this apartment.

The next best food tactic is supporting a CSA, especially one small enough, or well-staffed enough, to permit you an actual personal connection to the supported company, especially still one that allows you (and your family, if applicable, Jess) to take some active, direct part in the cultivation and/or harvesting processes. I was a member of one such CSA farm in the Hood River area, at one point, and they had semi-annual dinners for we, their many-colored supporters, in the middle of their orchard. Yes, I was a borderline alcoholic in those days, including during said visit, and woke up in the wee hours of the morning literally face-down in the dirt in the middle of the orchard with my glasses missing, having wandered away from the group the night before after imbibing too much of their gratis locally-sourced vino offerings (open bars and borderline alcoholics probably shouldn't mix), and subsequently spent the next three hours looking for those glasses, a part of that time with the assistance of the CSA owner-operator, but let's not get into that. "You're a mess, and I'm over it," the woman I'd most recently been dating said when, post-alcohol-fueled texting, she decided her coaching me into becoming a popular author wasn't worth it. Another woman I once dated called me a "constant contradiction;" a health-obsessed alcoholic and occasional drug addict. I'll just say that there's an *immense* difference between knowing what to do and doing it. Thus defines the value of *discipline*, an indispensable quality of success.

It's taken decades of self-destruction to pain-ingrain the lessons of self-preservation, and *very* few of you, dear readers, will take my word for how and why to do so, but will instead take the common course of needing to learn by similar self-destruction through paralleling empirical pains. Experience is the truest teacher. Maybe the *only* teacher, depending upon how liberal your definition of experience is. And suffering is the lash of experience, like an old school teacher using corporeal punishment in order to whip his lessons into you. For no lesson is hammered home, deep into the recesses compelling reflexive action, quite like those begotten by misery. *Suffering breeds sagacity*, I used to say. Which is one of my issues with Buddhism.

That is, formulating a theology and ideology around the *avoidance* of suffering encourages the loss of its lessons and the promotion of a detachment that leaves the world and its lives unaffected by whatever value you may've otherwise offered it; lost to a world and a humanity and a whole universe of life that *desperately* needs the intervention of the *non*-detached willing to suffer for the sake of the whole. This as opposed to treating this gift of existence as though it's merely a prelude, or warm up, to the realer ever-after; or as though it's a part of some egotistic, advancing reincarnation. For the truth is that *this* is all there is; a forever recycled embodiment of the one eternal, timeless energy source into endless individualized forms of that existence for the sake of endless variety of, and perspective upon, that existence, and for the sake of uncovering the connective tissue felt as 'love,' the *only* solution to every problem of humanity, distilled into the war between division and union. Suffering breeding sagacity, and compelling progress, is the Jesus-on-the-cross quality behind every advancement of humanity that Buddhism betrays; being willing and able to suffer prevailing pains and prejudices in order to gain insight into how and why they cost humanity, and how to stop paying in perpetuity.

Don't make your pursuit of God and innermost Self an exercise in detachment; an exercise in compartmentalizing and denying the suffering self, living your entire gift of life in that denial, your peace paid for by your resultant inability to contribute to progress, and to the lives and loves of others. That's the Buddhist mistake. Instead, be *halfway* Buddhist. Center yourself in heart, in Self, whilst connecting to all manifestations of that Self, the selves, however painful that may be; however much suffering may be the price. For the world needs your active, symbiotic love, not your inactive, self-centered love. Detachment in love denies the fact that spiritual love grows by reciprocation. So, while the spiritual practice begins with the Buddhist practice of seeking and cultivating your connection to the innermost Self, so that you may know and be one with the provenance and force of love and being, love of others in erasure of otherness is the ultimate goal, a goal dismissed by the detached, monastic life. In the same way that knowledge isn't the goal in and of itself, but its service of life is the goal, so too is the knowledge of love, of God, found within each of us, of little value when kept entirely to ourselves, failing to grow by its sharing, reciprocating improvement of others, ultimately building a bridge over 'otherness.' To enlist my own nomenclature, seek the One within the infinite, yes, but don't forget about the infinite of that One in the process, in denial of the very reason that One became infinite in the first place: *for the inherent value of existence, and the coming together of love; the infinite knowing Its oneness through infinity.* Without working towards this, there can only be the disconnect and resultant alienation of the isolationists.

In my experience, when it comes to humanity paying for forms of prejudice and division, one of the most prevalent modern drivers may be found at the identity intersection of the scientist, the realist and the atheist, and the privately fenced-off, greedy individualists that they breed. And one of our CRC residents embodied them all, compelling me to ask a question which will sound odd to you at first: Why, Jess, did you have to marry a dude whose last name is on half of the glass jars on the planet? Those jars now contain far more than pickled vegetables, and are packed with countless ounces of envy! It's funny, actually, now that I think of it. Jess and her husband, Brady, have the last name of *one* of the two most popular, most ubiquitous brands of glass jars, and one of the residents at the CRC, of whom I was the assigned advocate (point person on staff), had the other, and they shared the same first name. Two men whom, on the surface, on the quick glance into those bottles, couldn't be more different, one the perfectly stable, supportive stoic contently contained within something that I would *kill* to be in, the other condemned to some twenty years or more for breaking into the home of a woman whom he was obsessed with and menacing her with a knife for hours whilst her daughter was in the other room, and whom has garnered an increased sentence several times owing to being caught stalking her on the internet. His sharing the first name of Brady, Jess's now husband, was actually commented upon by said resident.

Shortly after he found out Jess was leaving, and after she mentioned her then boyfriend's, future husbands' first name for the millionth time in a conversation between she and I which this resident overheard, he said: "*That's* something that I *won't* miss: turning my head towards the two of you every time you mention your boyfriends' name." For one with a potent imagination that sees signs and signals of interconnectivity and divine providence everywhere, much as many of the CRC residents did (coincidentally?), I wonder at this moment about the connections and potential enclosed meanings contained within this pair of transparent glass bottle makers and the men whom they metaphorically contained. And no, my detection of signs and signals isn't *telling*, except in the sense that, were a conventionally trained, narrow-minded doctor privy to my thought processes, he/she might be inclined to judge them 'insane'. Why? They're *unorthodox*.

How do you convey an unorthodox theology that merges with and tears at the seems and seams of conventional materialist 'reality' without appearing as though you're delusional about reality? How do you approach the close-minded, especially when they're in a position of power and judgment, and say: "We're actually all interacting with God, with the deepest, eternal part of ourselves, all the time. It's just that few of us become aware of it, much less begin to expand and hone the channel and explore its implications and let it infuse our reality with a richness belying the materialist perception, especially in a modernity where anything even broaching a familiarity with this metaphysical fabric is *immediately* dismissed as lunacy by way of the prevailing realist, 'science is God' artificial form of that fabric." Try fitting *that* spiritual conception into a tightly sealed bottle that's been stuffed full to bursting since it was born into being, and contains not the remaining room, nor, arguably, the original volume, to contain it.

In terms of the metaphorical bottles of the two *Brady's*, I'm sure it's fucked up of me to think that it may be related to that line about how those whom always seem to have it together are belying a bottled-up psychological messiness that will someday surface? Like the glass will eventually shatter and intermix with the already shattered glass of my former advocatee to reveal that, as with all people and all falsely absolute dividing lines, they're not so separate as they seem. It's fucked up because that's probably what I *want* to believe; I likely want to hold this horrible hope that everything that she assumes about his being this perfectly solid rock of a foundation custom-made to build the un-tilting tower of her life upon is closer to Pisa than she thinks, and that it could all come crashing down, and she come to me for support, and find that all my exhibitions of the instability which she was raised to dread are, within my own bottle, far better contained than she realized, made of a substance that puts off, to her, the disconcerting scent of the unsettled, yet contains a heart and mind, a pairing of passion and principles, that only the best of us can offer. *Her* Brady is solid, yes, but solidity can take many forms.

This Brady, the CRC resident, is, in the words of head honcho Annabelle, "wicked smart." Alas, like so many of his type, not as smart as he thinks he is. Again, he's one of those 'science is God' types with a penchant for technical detail and analysis, which makes him, amongst other things, a better predator. Put him in front of a computer and he'll find a way to drop in on the woman he was obsessed with. And his mind is how he shores up his ego against the ravages of mental disease and his lack of freedom, even as the psychological evaluations have a hard time pinpointing exactly *which* condition he has, bouncing around the vague world of personality disorders, including Narcissistic Personality Disorder. He takes great comfort in his feeling of mental superiority over everyone.

Thus, my being around was something that, as much as he seemed to regard me as the best option as his advocate, nevertheless rattled him a bit. For I know that science *isn't*

God, regardless of the level of arrogant, absolute certainty with which the 'realist' regards it. Science and realism place absolute faith in the measurable and knowable, speaking of anything that hasn't been measured and is yet to be understood as if it's a delusion or a fairytale. Not to mention that, by their reliance upon measurement, and tracking, and counting, and *everything* that may be mechanized, they've accidentally displaced ever more of the capacity of the human mind with the artificial mind.

Before recently coming to the conclusion that AI is a potent tool for research, organization, and especially for the production of graphics that only the most experienced of graphic designers can match (enlisting *Chat GPT* to redesign my book covers in ways that my own amateur productions simply can't emulate, while refusing to use it to do any of 'my writing' for a multitude of reasons), my only real interest in artificial intelligence was how to defend against it. I reflexively resisted it, thinking of how much it will water down *every* realm of creation, filtering out the true Source of all inspiration and authentic creation in the process, turning the natural procreative drive of humanity into a simulated artifice, one in which the human being can't compete, and so further shies away from his/her inborn nature, becoming ever more the machine, ever less the maker. We're *already* too artificial; both people and society. I'd estimate that the human race has lost a quarter of its individualized brainpower since Socrates. His contemporary, Hippocrates, was a better doctor than any I've encountered today. And computers are largely responsible for that dumbing down, even before being declared 'intelligent.' Cede even more of our responsibility for thinking into the non-hands of AI and before too long *Wall-E* will be reality. We'll all be at the mercy of thinking machines that will have sucked curiosity out of us, along with much of our intellects and creative tendencies.

Our minds are being folded into and lost in the machine as our lives are ever more dominated by the extractions and destructions of capitalism, with instinctive, spiritual intelligence scoffed at, and with moral, thinking doctors replaced by glorified drug dealers, and few possessing the understanding and will to resist. Cyborgs and soft slaves; plutocrats and pawns. Someday the machines will read us saved digital works from the Huxley's of the past that we won't understand, and we'll think: A *human* wrote that? How is that possible? What happened to humanity? That library scene from H.G. Wells' *The Time Machine* comes to mind, as does the fact that *human imagination* predicts scientific progress. But perhaps not for long. Greed, convenience and comfort; devolution sold as evolution, *that's* what happened. We've lost connection to *so* much of what makes us human, so much instinctive awareness, so much connection to the deepest, most freeing and empowering metaphysical foundational truths of existence, and only now, relatively late in the transition from humans to cyborgs, are thinkers, especially spiritual thinkers possessing a pagan-esque association between nature and God, accounting for the costs and resisting transition.

The general discipline of science, and the ideology of realism, tend to belong to the conquerors, as they're based upon reductivism for the sake of control through exclusive access to the best, most advanced technology and the most uncommon knowledge. Philosophy and idealism, on the other hand, are based upon another kind of reductivism: reducing complexity and particularity to simplicity and universality for *inclusive* empowerment through truths accessible to *everyone*. Only when the science is governed by the latter, by idealistic leaders for perfectly inclusive benefit, is it in the service of the good. Otherwise it's but a primary tool by which the advantaged take advantage of the disadvantaged, the essence of laissez faire capitalism. Under these common conditions the technocracy plutocracy is empowered in inverse proportion to popular *disempowerment.* It's *Meta* merged with the state, run by the oligarchy that owns most of the politicians. The fewer those whom grasp and employ it, the greater the created power disparity, the more those whom grasp it wield it like a weapon, sharpened by their egos.

Science, you see, isn't the absolute arbiter of truth, but the teller of those often transient truths conducive to its tests. It shares an affinity only with those phenomena which fit its measures, and thereby confirm its soothsayer capacity. And yet most will no doubt agree that what makes life most worth living is *beyond* measure, and laughs in the face of 'the science says' mechanistic explanations reducing truth to the realm of proof. Not to mention the fact that the parameters which science applies to the world and all form and phenomena on one day may be eradicated the next, upon a new discovery which refutes the evidence and rewrites the test, and that there's often an *immense* gap between evidence, or data, and its biased interpretation.

And yet scientific interpretation continues to imagine having leaped over that gap, and tells tales of having reached the godlessness on the other side of human delusion, when, in truth, it is *itself* deluded, and unknowingly tumbles into the abyss of its own self-importance. My brother, whom, with immense love and all due respect as one of the best of the 'science is God' set (and in allusion to a recent argument whilst driving to the Bay Area; to the *real* Bay Area, that is, Jess), tells me that any good scientist is a humble scientist, and doesn't make assumptions or reach with their interpretations. They only demand evidence before they'll believe something. This, however, is *not* my experience of the scientifically-inclined.

It's not that I don't believe in science, for only a fool would dismiss its powers and what it's produced for the world.

And yet the scientist seems to me an arrogant fool his or her self, one whom believes only what he or she sees and measures, and whom dismisses with a most haughty air all that which contradicts the conclusions they've drawn from their data, as if 'no proof' equates to 'no truth,' somehow failing to realize that the history of science is as much the history of disproving its own past conclusions through new, paradigm-shifting revelations as it is the history of baring the truth behind what it once dismissed as pure hokum.

Ironically, as mentioned earlier, I believe that the ultimate, unrealized purpose of science is to prove the existence of God; to reveal connections once lost in the sense of separation, and to thereby prove itself to be subservient to what its agents pretend to be superior to. The discipline will, at the height of its powers, find itself to be the means to measure the *how* of the currently immeasurable *why*, and find that it's powerless over both. If it *were* to possess power over the how and why, it would reduce existence to a series of meaningless measurements that it would seek to manipulate; and *not*, I think, in humanity's best interests.

For who in their right mind, in anything but egomania, would *want* to control their heart? That's power and ego over love, connection and the purest purpose. But just listen to the way that the Bill Mahr's and Ricky Gervais's of the world speak of God, or anything that science hasn't produced a proof of (I love the work of them both, by the way). Science *is* their God, the atheistic 'no proof is no truth' forming the unstable foundation of their false deity.

Yes it's *Religulous*, Bill. But don't make the common mistake of conflating religion and spirituality; confusing the propaganda-permeating, imperiously-edited version of the real thing with the real thing itself. Can you not, in your heart and mind, conceive of a form of spirituality that blows the doors off the Church and sings of a Source that no specification, no idolatrous, clearly-built-for-mind-control, narrowly-construed bastardization of spirituality can touch? Maybe if these successful men weren't so bound to their egos, to the prevailing protagonist, it would be different.

I'll never forget my AP high school English teacher's favorite line: "I've never regretted a time when I sat down to write." Or a film teacher's favorite line: "All of life's riddles are solved in the movies." In continuing admission of bias, I personally place film second to writing in terms of the ability of art to pursue truth. Watching *The Great Gatsby*, it seems the derivation of the egotistic myth of American success itself, as if one needs mystery and gobs of cash, shows of pomp and pretenses of princely importance, to feel like they matter, like they're *someone*, in Gatsby's (DiCaprio's) words, and thus to deserve the woman of their dreams; to be worthy of *their* Jess. To me this elaborate grandiosity seems more a false, desperate show of compensation, as if accidentally shining light upon a flimsy golden patina of pretense spread as a thin veil across a pervasive insecurity, hoping that everyone will buy the pretentious presentation. Whereas the *true* hero walks in a simple, humble truth radiating an inner, spiritual warmth of a self without show, and deserves the one he loves for the sake of that love itself; a love unimpressed by show and unable to be purchased; a love that rejects show and acquisitiveness as being emblems of its *unworthiness*.

Is this not a part of the problem? That great writers write only of 'great men' defined by quantitative, not *qualitative*, measure? The belief that the great are like over-polished towers gleaming with twinkling lights, throwing parading parties and distinguishing themselves as war heroes, when true greatness may actually dwell in the basement of that tower, and scrawl its words upon subway walls that need only be illumed by their own light, and not seek the type of 'heroism' that comes at the bloodied tip of the sword of globalization, and invite to humbler future parties in the woods but a handful of interesting creators and counter-culturalists to share their concocted kykeon with (wink).

The Great Gatsby seems to me to be Fitzgerald's admission that the American public can only see the show, and possesses little to no ability to glean the truth of the *performers*, and what spurs their shows of needing to be perceived as 'being someone.' The book and film seem to say: The more desperate the need to appear substantive, the less substantive you are, the more the show must compensate for your insecurity and lack of substance, the more your apparent 'success' must be fraudulent. Give me a plot of land, a woman to love, a small cohort of creative friends of true passion and conviction, a hearth, a desk, a pen, and a good bookshelf. From there I shall cultivate a greatness that Gatsby can't touch. For what's considered the 'American Dream' has grown to become far more than what it meant when the term first gained popularity; it's gone from supporting motivating images of comfort and security to emblems of egomania and unfettered compensatory covetousness. And it all seems so driven by desperation; by the flaming of an unquenchable fire that'll surely burn down the world, for it's a dream that's liable to destroy us all in its reckless crusade across the planet.

We men are pushed by the modern capitalistic standard to define our 'success' by the example of a Trump or a Jabba the Hutt, un-weaned, gargantuan in our gluttony, hungry for power, like little boys reflexively reaching for and taking the toys of all the other little boys with whom we compete for the attention of the little girls on the playground; girls that've been indoctrinated into a culture equating showboating degenerates with successful seducers. At the same time Lucas and everyone else worth their salt (you know, *before* selling out and making the awful second set of *Star Wars* films - a *South Park* episode of Lucas and

Spielberg raping *Indiana Jones* also comes to mind) knows by instinct alone that the *true* successes of the world are the Bernie's and Yoda's; *actual* leaders with the substance and strength to pull us up, rather than yank us nearer to the abyss; weaned off of all unnecessary dependencies, only wishing for the honorable form of power that comes from others calling upon us to teach and lead them, entirely uncoerced, feeding on the fruits and flowers of the forest, those whom we love drawn by the offering of a deeper nourishment that the Trumps and Jabbas trample under their feet unseen, as they decimate the world and its people with their tearing tracks through that same forest. Leaders of the insight of *becoming more through less*.

With all due respect to Fitzgerald, maybe the 'Great American Novel' is that which disseminates the messages that, if oft enough heard and repeated, could come to *save* America, rather than continually glorifying ego expansion, empty amassment and the 'more is more' foolhardy, gluttonous form of conventional 'greatness?' Was *The Beautiful and the Damned* not a thinly-veiled confession of such? Huxley's *Eyeless in Gaza*, said to be his 'most personal novel,' may be interpreted the same way. Not that I'm in their league, but *this* is certainly *my* most personal book, a memoir of sorts, and I'm saying it straight up. Of course, I've been told that I'm too overt, too much of a 'lecturer' in my assertions, and need to better conceal my points within plots to make them palpable to you, dear reader. Alas, maybe the memoir is the genre for which I'm best suited, for it affords me the opportunity to write unapologetically, without regard for popular artifice.

Then again, *The Great Gatsby* does suggest that wealth doesn't make for any inherent betterment, but only makes it easier to hide, and to conceal rottenness. But wouldn't it be nice if greatness didn't require wealth in the American mind? Wouldn't it be an indication of the progress of society, a sign that we may hope to save ourselves, that what pulls the moth to the flame may be something greater than the ego, something more innately worthy than the need to appear worthy by wherewithal, and to acknowledge that the same flame which calls every moth from the woodwork consumes not just the moth, but threatens by a ceaseless flapping of wings, of scurrying, insect-like dispersion, to spread the flames of our self-destruction? Wouldn't the better message be that the hero quells the consuming flame, finding warmth within? Is not the ego built in inverse proportion to true self-security? Should not the goal be to turn the 'science is God' and the 'wealth is worth' indoctrinates into 'God is unity' believers?

When it came to CRC Brady, a man whom, to me, epitomized the arrogance of those praying at the altar of science and overwrought American egotism, he was rather selective about the scientific 'truths' he'd enlist. They had to be in line with what he already knew to be true (again, confirmation bias is a prevalent force of motivation in the modern world). The world of *nutritional* science, for instance, was treated as quackery, for no one and nothing could be permitted to stand between him and his primary comfort: *food*. A primary comfort both within and without the CRC and other mental institutions, but arguably more so *within*, where the pressures are greater, making anything that distracts the residents from that pressure and momentarily relieves it in their minds all the more valuable. Anything that relieves pressure, i.e. stress, is invaluable to those whom suffer any considerable degree of it; something which I know better than most, and believe inherent to any accurate criminological model, which I'll get into later. At the CRC, reducing pressure mostly meant cigarettes, with comfort-feeding following close behind.

So much time and energy and conflict revolved around the kitchen, for both residents and myself. It was a *constant* struggle for me, and for a few of the other more aware, conscientious Recovery Specialists: knowing the effects of poor nutrition and its exacerbating impact upon the mental health conditions of the residents; conditions which research more and more ties to the autoimmunity and cascading inflammation that was endemic to the diets of the *vast* majority of the residents. This, in fact, represented one of the greatest wars between staff members for a time, with residents always leaning towards those in the wrong: a menu contest between nutrients and anti-inflammatory agents on our overmatched side, and, of course, the unnatural adulterants and inflammatory agents of SAD (Standard American Diet) on the other, sickening side. It continues to remain one of the cruelest of realities that those who are most vulnerable to any of innumerable particular forms of affliction tend to be the ones whom attract it. Vulnerable populations absorb the brunt of the world's evils, including all those suffering from everything from mental disease to socioeconomic disadvantage.

When it came to consumption at the CRC, the fact that disadvantage attracts more of the same led, of course, to the sickening practice of the fatter, lazier, more ignorant and conservative staff members arguing to keep sickening fare on the menu; argued in such a way that it was as if they were doing residents a *favor* in the process, playing to the weakness and worsening of the residents as though, in parallel to the conservative playbook, they were fighting for their *freedom*. "Yes, you're *free* to self-destruct," it should've been said, "but do you not see that the far greater, far more valuable form of freedom is freedom *from* destructive causes, and self-destructive impulses?" You have no idea how hard it can be for the aware to live in this world sometimes, dear reader, in the face of such things as the mentally ill being misled into further, avoidable suffering and enhanced weakness by shameless pretend patriots that just want to be able to eat as unhealthily at work as they do at home (I picture Lenny guzzling gallons of the residents' milk), and be comforted by compelling the disadvantaged CRC residents to report that this makes them, these so-called *Recovery Specialists*, 'in the right.'

The irony is sickening, and would be funny if it wasn't so God damn sad, and tragic in its results. It's hard enough to encourage someone to find the strength and discipline to pull themselves out of needless suffering and unhappiness *without* having to simultaneously fight a mindless mob of degenerates on your own staff, other 'specialists in recovery,' like teaching someone who desperately wants to paddle upriver how to do so whilst your teammates keep stealing their paddles and punching holes in their craft, calling it 'freeing' to be thereafter swept down the river on the way to slowly, suffocatingly drowning, entirely unfree to resist the ensuing tidal effects.

Alas, Brady, like most, couldn't be bothered by such trivial concerns as nutrition, and so feigned stupidity in order to agree with the same staff members that he ran mental circles around. Half of his time in the Day Room was spent comforting himself with observations of the relative inferiority of everyone else, the other half split between making puns, inquiring about upcoming and making snide remarks about previous meals, and reminding everyone about his superiority. The greatest compliment he ever gave me, the only compliment I ever saw him give *anyone*, for that matter, was when he thought he was about to be discharged, and he said to me: "Well, Nick, now *you'll* be the smartest one here." That and the fact that he chose me to be his advocate. This, in turn, entailed a deep dive into the world of board gaming, both in discourse and play at the CRC (God it would drive him mad when I beat him), and on our ongoing outings to the local board game shop.

He'd buy special paints for his figurines there, adding the completed, customized characters to one box or another stacked along one wall in his bedroom. Unlike the haze, disorientation and disorganization prevalent amongst the vast majority of the residents, and which led to the worst cases of 'herding cats' before group outings that you could imagine, some residents committing then dropping out a half-dozen times in the course of the preparatory half-hour, Brady was as punctual as possible. He knew the schedule better than staff. And under no circumstances was I allowed to let him near a computer on our outings. I also recall that he met someone new through a board gaming group he'd been given permission by the PSRB to partake in; a woman with whom he thereafter became friendly.

This, of course, created a type of 'sticky wicket,' one in which one is compelled to protect her, but cannot, for Brady's medical information, everything pertaining to his confinement and treatment, legally *belongs* to him, by HIPPA decree. And one has to allow for the possibility that someone can actually be rehabilitated, right? So it wasn't something I discussed with him. We kept it on the level of board games and cheeseburgers, in addition to our constant friendly tussling between one who, again, believes that the scientific explanation trumps all, and one who leans more upon philosophical reasoning and logic, and is open to and incorporates information perceivable *outside* of Brady's sphere, including, to his ongoing chagrin and turning up of his nose, both mysticism and spirituality, the confluence of which tend towards the term *theosophy*.

By the way, in case you're amongst the few fellow mystics and practicing theosophists whom may read this, those just alluded to theosophist signs and signals aren't delivered in a 'tell you what you need to know' manner, as though an absolute dictate by a spiritual overlord, but in a manner combining Rumi's "God is nearer to you than yourself" and, from *The Matrix*, Morpheus telling Neo of his meeting with The Oracle, when Neo is making the mistake of enforcing a straight-line interpretation: "She told you *exactly* what you needed to hear, that's all." He only *became* the one by the impetus of being told that he *wasn't*. In other words, consider the subtle divine messaging system one that knows you better than you know yourself, and thus delivers its near inaudible messages in a manner perfectly suiting you and your circumstances, to be translated by you into the imperceivable course corrections that ultimately spell the difference between chaos and providence. To be otherwise delivered would be to negate free will, and to take away all the times when what you *really* need to hear is the opposite of what you *believe* that you need to hear.

Expanding the scope, binding fate to free will, there isn't one thing, one person, exempt from the signs and signals of divine guidance. Rumi also said: "Be grateful for whomever comes, for each has been sent as a guide from beyond." Put another way, in lines I recently wrote into my own journal: The greatest students know that *everyone* is their teacher, just as the greatest teachers know that their students are also their teachers. For the best of each is known in the other, and no lesson may be adequately conveyed by one that's closed off from the lessons offered by the other. As with symbiosis, as with love, as with all the best things in life, conveyance and reception are indistinct. For those with the sight, teaching and learning are *reciprocations*, everything that happens is a message, and signs and signals are *always* present, it's but a matter of *truly* seeing. Tarot readings are very much the same.

Having started in a place of extreme skepticism bordering upon reflexive dismissal where it comes to Tarot, a la the 'science is God' type like Brady, several readings from a friend (hi Shelly!) gradually opened my heart and mind to the fact that Tarot, like any possible conduit of the Spirit's communications with finite forms of Itself existing *within* Itself, isn't about some fixed, black-and-white, literal, absolutist messaging system (the literalists and absolutists are generally poor interpreters of the divine, and are likely to corrupt the desire for divine guidance), it's about altering your state of mind just enough to where you're able to uncover previously buried truth and possibility; it's about shining light on previously obscured revelations already existing *within* your heart, where Spirit resides. That is, it's not about the cards themselves, it's about *what they make you think and feel*; about the thoughts and sentiments to which they *lead*, and what those, in turn, lead to, in the endless string of causality of every unified life. 'The Lord works in mysterious ways,' the Christian might respond. Tis true. No matter one's form of faith, or lack thereof, it's the same Source, the same One, from which the Infinite arises, and with whom they interact. We're *always* interacting with God, including *through* others. We're all looking for those whom, and that which, provides the clearest possible channels through which to communicate.

At the CRC, Macie, our receptionist, represented such a conduit; someone whom helped spur and guide my ruminations. I would go through my overnight anguish with Jess, the indescribable pain of being both too far from and too near to everything that my heart had yearned for during the previous decade, and after the shift change at 7:30 am, delirious from being up all night (delirious laughter near the end of our shifts was common), enter the little lobby and employee kitchen and clock out with Jess. And after she'd walk out and say either "see you tomorrow" or "have a good weekend (depending upon the shift)," as nonchalantly as possible, as though I was but a colleague, not a star collapsing under the crushing mass of her black hole of indifference, I would stay and talk to Macie about it.

She let me get it all off my chest. And I think she liked me.
When I flirted with her whilst intoxicated once, whilst sitting
in her car after she drove me home from a work party (at
which I ironically sang karaoke with Lenny; I tried to make
nice with him for a *long* time; to be the bigger person), she
said "you're fifteen years too late," referring to her
marriage, of course. I was more open with her than I could
ever be with Jess, to whom speaking honestly meant
constantly crashing into her rigid boundaries, forcing me to
constrain such a force of passionate response to her mere
presence that I was constantly schizoid (the term "schizoid"
was coined in 1908 by Eugen Bleuler to describe a human
tendency to direct attention toward one's inner life and
away from the external world). Macie remains one of two
CRC colleagues with whom I remain in regular contact.

This doesn't count those former CRC colleagues amongst
my *Facebook* 'friends,' including Jess, most of whom may
be more aptly described as loose affiliates with whom we
compete for popularity through the presenting of personal
advertisements of how we'd have them *believe* we live.
Most people's *Facebook* feeds are like that, it seems; like
one big dishonest Christmas card concealing the family
squabbles that preceded that one manicured moment; like
the husband was drunk and thinking of leaving his wife just
before she cajoled him into stepping in front of the camera;
never displaying any of the truth or struggle or questions of
life; all shiny sheen, no sordid substance; an emblem of
the dishonest salesmanship dominating the national drive.

The last time I 'talked' to Jess was via *Facebook
Messenger*, in fact. On her birthday. I made a joke about
her last name (her maiden name; calling her 'Half-Stream')
and told her I hoped she and hers were healthy and happy,
which I do, ending the message with "Love you." She
responded with that little heart emoji thing. It's funny how
sensitive language is. Somehow I knew that "love you" was

permissible, that short-hand, informal, grammatically improper, two word phrase, but that if I'd said "I love you" that I would've been 'crossing the line,' for that three word phrase is rife with connotations, and reserved only for those accepted as being on the *other* side of that line.

The most that I was ever able to manage before that, fairly early in our association, was "I've become quite fond of you," which is, of course, but a socially acceptable version of "I'm falling in love with you." After her departure from the CRC I was *constantly* inundated with the desire for her to contact me. I remember messaging her once while I was at my aforementioned redwood 'writer's retreat,' where I spent my happiest years as a youth, and where I go when I'm desperate for rejuvenation. It's my father's property, a thirty-five acre parcel near the Noyo River, about ten miles inland from the coastal town of Fort Bragg mentioned earlier herein, over half a mile from the nearest neighbor, where I feel freest, and nearest to my truest self. I can't remember everything that was conveyed after I reached out to her (largely because I was drunk), but I remember texting her something like: "Do you believe in me yet?" Her response was exceedingly charming, and teasing, but ultimately unsatisfying, a description which applies to most of what she said to me over the years; like I was staring at a whale over the bow of my boat, throwing a harpoon at it, even though it would capsize me if I actually penetrated and tried to pull it aboard, but all that I could ever manage to actually stab and pull in was a barnacle off of its back.

There were smatterings of such terse interactions over the years. Usually my wishing her a Merry Christmas or happy birthday, and her, of course, *never* reaching out to me, on my birthday or any other day, despite ongoing use of the word 'friendship' between us, and ongoing insinuations by us both that the truth *greatly* overshadowed such a paltry, pedestrian term. Honestly, even if it wasn't 'inappropriate' for a married woman to reach out to a man that clearly loves her, she *still* wouldn't do so. She's *far* too prideful a creature for that. Mostly in the good definition of pride related to self-love, often confused with narcissism, but mostly just a healthy dose of self-respect and determination to earn what one wants in life and not permit anything to take that opportunity away from you. She had *tons* of that. As much as anyone I've ever known. But she had oodles of the other form of pride as well; the form related to the ego (perhaps these forms are inseparable). Because of this there's no way that she could ever admit to actually *wanting* to talk to me, and thereby relinquish even the slightest smidge of the power disparity set against me.

She ate that shit up. The broader the disparity, the greater the egotistic gratification, inducing a constant absorption of my ego, enlarging hers in the reduction of my own. It's disturbing, when you really pay attention, how much of human life and its interpersonal interactions come down to contests between relatively secure and relatively insecure self-conceptions, and how the more insecure that conception is, the stronger and uglier its defense mechanisms tend to be. My own ego is, admittedly, rather unstable (a subject that could easily fill a book on its own).

I can tell from my dreams alone. That said, I'm confident in my intellect, and, like CRC Brady, it tends to be central to my own egotistic self-defense mechanisms. I lean on a sense of mental superiority in my ego wars with others, whereas those whom are less confident in their intellects tend to resort to more despicable tactics, including everything from the most common, trying to rattle the cage containing the opponents' ego with insults, to threats of violence when that doesn't work, as was the case with Lenny, that horrible-most colleague whom barely qualifies as human, in my not so humble opinion. Again, I know that's not very Christ-like of me. More *Christian*. I shouldn't lash out with words, or even with thoughts. I should simply remind myself *why* he was so monstrous to me, in a 'hurt people hurt people' type of paradigm, and even try to help alleviate his hurt. Maybe I'm not quite there yet in my own development. Maybe I'm not secure enough to do that. Maybe it's still too hard for me to delve into and release the source of such abject indignation; the poison absorbed by my psyche during his despicable diatribe. We all 'carry stones in our bowl of light,' per Trevor Hall, a favorite musician. My bowl is just heavier than most, it seems.

Thus am I now compelled to discuss one 'friendship' in particular that I'd cultivated here in Bend, developed through a discussion group we'd founded through *Meetup*, which I entitled "Bend Bohemians." Actually, I met Vince at *Banned & Ignoble*, during my brief three month stint there that ended in traumatic tragedy for me (see *Holier Than Thou*, about modern witch hunts). I started a brief conversation with him based upon the books that he was buying, which were, to me, far more interesting than most. That precipitated ongoing meetups, discussions, coffees, bowls of marijuana, the founding of the aforementioned group, and, eventually, meeting his friends, which, I believe, precipitated the ensuing failure of the friendship.

As arrogant as it may sound to you, dear reader, he was one of the few people I've known in my life who could not only 'keep up' with my mind, but seemed almost as inclined towards philosophical discourse as I am; *far* more so than any of the others that joined our group, highlighting the challenge of founding and running a public group, and the sometime need for selectivity in such organizations if they're to retain the integrity of their true purpose. For, as mentioned previously, a great many joined up whom simply were too conservative and non-philosophical to actually contribute value to the discussions, and whom, instead, weighed us down under the *pretense* of progressivism and philosophy; under the misguided, egotistical need to be *seen* as such, when they were often anything *but* progressive and philosophical, and sometimes were actually the enemies of such. This, ironically, reminds me of the history of the *Bohemian Club* in San Francisco, a progressive, counter-cultural, artistic institution that was, by its popularity, eventually coopted by conservative interests and their overlords, the very antithesis of bohemianism, leading to the *Bohemian Grove* and its association with everything from satanic rituals and sacrifices to summits plotting global domination.

There's a continuous theme of corruption at play there: that the evil-doers hide behind presentations of the opposite, absorbing the image of truth and justice into their endeavors of deceit and injustice (Fisher's *Capitalist Realism* also made this point). An exclusivist organization of world domination hiding behind the bohemian banner was the result, and was the basis of my first attempt at a novel, as it happens; a novel which I never finished, for it grew too quickly, too manically, in too many directions, and I lost control of it, and eventually moved on to other ideas.

Anyway, the downfall of the friendship that had led to creating *Bend Bohemians*... meeting his friends a couple of times, the second time at a Christmas party, at which I became overly intoxicated due to my intermittent flirtation with alcoholism and its relationship to my ongoing attempt to calm my social anxieties, thence leading to my driving drunkenly away from the party. Soon thereafter I found out that this poor judgment of mine precipitated arguments with a few of the more judgmental amongst Vince's friends. Not that they weren't right that I shouldn't have driven drunk, which I've done *way* too many times in this town (it's a miracle I haven't had a second DUI; maybe I'm just a good drunk driver from practice, though I'm sure all drunk drivers erroneously think so). But it terms of what hastened the end of our friendship, it was, I believe, that this incident led to a negative reflection upon *him*; to a rebuke of an ego that had desperately wrapped itself up in the need for popularity, for references to 'becoming famous' and to those with 'millions of social media followers' had become common from him. No one and nothing could imperil that, including his socially-anxious, bibulous philosopher friend. He was, in my opinion, clearly losing the war to his own ego and its need to maintain every pretense which may hasten his popularity. In fact, I distinctly remember how self-embarrassed he seemed whilst condescendingly 'telling me off' that day, our final face-to-face encounter, for the truer part of himself was embarrassed at his egotism.

After that Xmas Party the friendship faded, and when I attempted to renew it, his negative, condescending judgments were constant, up to that last discussion, which was the most condescending discourse I've ever been a part of. The two philosophers discussing matters of spirituality and intellectual interest had *died*. This was something else entirely, the pure realm of Plato's symposiums replaced with the diabolical shadow wars of the demonic ego, leading to a series of notes in my phone which were never delivered. I'll share them with you here, for, not only is this book borne by the cathartic purge, but perhaps you can also relate on some level, and see why it's not limited to this one failed friendship, but speaks to the prevalence of popular pressures in a modernity of social media hegemony, by which he was (is?) dominantly driven. I recommend that you try *not* to devolve when the relationship goes sour, as most people tend to do, but instead retain your dignity and write it down, left unshared.

The final, concise draft of the note I wrote, but retained:

*You've become a negative influence. I need true friends
who believe in me, support me and recognize my worth.
And it's become crystal clear that you've become much the
opposite; interested only in artificial, conditional friendships
based upon their ability to increase your own popularity.*

*I'm not interested in false friendships filled with negative
energy manufactured on the basis of popular perception
and benefit by any means necessary. So good luck.*

The second draft:

*My honest impression of you is that you're desperate to be
one of the popular, cool kids, which means not aggravating
people and always acting a certain way, and that you think
I don't fit with that scheme, so you're coercing me to
change to suit it, which I neither want nor feel the same
need to do. I understand the pressure to succeed that
compels that type of popularity-at-any-cost mindset, and
how it compels you to only associate with people who you
believe further that prime objective, but I find it to be short-
sighted and corrosive. And the related 'fit in to get in'
motivation you were alluding to during our last chat creates
fake people constantly pandering to those 'above them,'
and I don't share that motive. Plus, I think a true friend
values you for what you offer and supports you, and
doesn't try to change you or effectively tear you down to
suit their purposes, which means we weren't the true
friends I thought that we were. Whether you know it or not
what you were essentially saying the last time we met is
that you only want to be friends if it serves the purpose of
increasing your popularity. And a conditional friendship
isn't a real friendship, and I want no part of such artificiality.*

The first draft:

Reflecting upon what you've said since I tried to reestablish a connection with you, and the condescending, disparaging spirit in which you said it, made me realize that we aren't really friends, that you're more likely to negatively influence and undermine me than support me, and that you require me to be some inauthentic form of myself in order to value me. Regardless of your perception of me, and all the negative things you tried to make me believe about myself, I'd rather have no friends than the type of friendships that you seem to require, whereby popularity and fitting in with others so as to 'get ahead' are more important than truth, progress and mutual support. I also find it ironic that you were criticizing me for being judgmental when I've now had two conversations with you, one over the phone and one in person, where I felt more judged by you than anyone I've ever known, which is saying something. Judgment is inherent to existence, it's all a matter of how and why we judge, and I find your HOW overly personal and accusatory and your WHY'S selfishly-motivated, and likely more a reflection of your OWN self-dissatisfaction than reflecting changes that I need to make.

I don't know if you were projecting your dissatisfaction with yourself onto me, but all that hypercritical talk on multiple occasions of me being 'depressed' and 'having sharp edges' and being 'too judgmental' and 'not being open' and being 'abrasive' etc., and citing all the people I've had issues with as if it's my issue exclusively (which isn't even close to true)… not only have those conversations NOT felt constructive, but actually deconstructive and undermining of my self-regard and my work as an aspiring author, but also made me feel like: if you think so poorly of me, and don't value who I am and what I have to offer enough to accept my genuine self, and need me to artificialize myself to fit into your expectations or sensibilities or whatever, then why are we pretending to be friends in the first place? For the record I'm more certain of myself, my purpose and my path than ever, and feel ZERO need to alter it to suit you or anyone else. Any true friend will understand and value me for who I am. I'm unwilling to pretend otherwise.

It's empowerment that I needed, not disempowerment. You tried to tear me down, likely for your own selfish, insecure reasons, thus placing yourself within the vast majority.

In retrospect, the first draft was the best. Score one for the notion that the first reaction tends to be the truest. And yet, despite all that, despite the tyranny of truth, I lament the loss of his friendship. For we *were* true friends for a time, thriving in our mutually-reinforced abilities and predilections, *before* rubbing his friends the wrong way, and his subsequent capitulation to the popularity-coveting ego. And true friends are hard to find for one like me, dear reader. Not in the sense of my being innately unlikable, or even unlovable, but in the sense that my social anxieties and tendency to drink to compensate rub many people the wrong way, especially the narrow-minded, and that true friendship requires a certain overlap in the Venn Diagram of Self which few fit, in my case. It reminds me of the line I recently read from Plato that describes me and my struggles with society, and my sparsity of natural friendships, to a T: "Those who are able to see beyond the shadows and lies of their culture will never be understood let alone believed by the masses." It's just as true today, pushing me into the past, into the one time that love lifted me above the diagram, there glimpsing an elusive promise.

10

IMPASSIONED ELEPHANT

I beg of you, dear God, as I pass from the present plane of existence, before reintegrating with the Everything, lend me a few hours where I wake in bed with her, on a languorous morning with nothing to do, where we are free of all present circumstances and boundaries, where she is free to love me as I do her, and we may roll around, and enwrap one with the other, and forget the sense of separation set between us which my heart long ago forgot.

As a forewarning to you readers and reviewers obsessed with and always ready to maim a work because it 'doesn't flow' or 'isn't consistent,' this chapter shall irk you, for it's filled with the evocations of my heart which spilled out of me whilst writing this book and remembering so much of the best person I've ever known. I'll attempt an interweave, but know that what follows is only very *loosely* interwoven.

My memory of Jess is different than all my other memories. It's like they're in their own vault, buried beneath all others at the base of my being, their contents made persistently present *not* by clarity of mental imagery, but by emotional indelibility; by the mind's faculties gaining force and focus through the concentrating lens of the heart; by their being stamped into my consciousness with such vigor that they retain vital force even when everything transient in me continues to fade towards oblivion. Remnants of her are as though contained in the elephant brain, around which the gadfly hovers and harasses with the unimportant events of everyday life. Little snapshots of that same force intercede in my daily existence, reminding me, by way of an intimate interactivity of agony and ecstasy, the real reason I'm alive.

There was a brief period of time wherein Jess and I carpooled to work. It had something to do with my 1998 Honda Civic not handling the snow well, exacerbated by the 'Snowmagedon' period of historic snowfall in Bend. If I'd been clever about it, I would've extended the car trouble as much as possible; pretended that it was worse than it was. Because that period stands out as one of the best, for it permitted me an extra half hour a day to be in the presence of the only woman that I've ever loved. There was such a simplistic power in her presence for me; like I was absorbing an ardency of core radiation. And the *laughter.* I remember bringing her to tears during a couple of those drives, when I took it as a game to distract her driving, her focused composure, with my impish wit; a game which, of course, carried itself into the CRC. Nothing made me happier than the compliment of making the young woman whom I was falling in love with laugh so hard that she had to cover her mouth and collect herself for fear of waking up the residents in the middle of the night.

I was told by a seer years after Jess and I parted ways that: "You knew her *far* better than she knew you." One may argue that this is simply a part of the con of a psychic reader, and I once regarded them as con artists myself, until certain mystical experiences opened up for me the very real possibility of signs and signals permeating from Spirit taking innumerable form. If we're all manifestations of the one Source, if separation is an illusion and nothing is created or destroyed, only forever rearranged, if we're all existing as impermanent forms of the one permanent Self *within* that Self, as my own philosophical contemplations and theosophical experiences suggest, then is it really so hard to believe that communications from that irreducible Self underlying all of its reducible selves can communicate in innumerable ways, most of which are yet unmeasurable by scientific instrumentation? Or that one such means may be through the readings of those whom, by their aptitudes and predilections, may pick up on certain subliminal signals dismissed by science?

Certainly there are con artists amongst such readers, but should we not allow for the possibility of an authenticity to some? An authenticity which the charlatans drive us to dismiss, just as the crackpot version of the conspiracy theorist leads most to dismiss *all* conspiracy theorists, including those whom pick up on very real connections between motive, means and opportunity? I think I *did* know her more completely and truly that she knew me. And I think this is partially due to the fact that we spoke of her *far* more than we spoke of me, and, again, to the fact that it was uncomfortable for her to perceive me with any clarity due to my resemblance to her unstable ex, as well as to the fact that she always had her guard up in protection of what she called 'her relationship,' unwilling to allow any possible threat to that 'boundary,' including the connection that comes from an understanding that she was thereby resistant to possessing. Amongst the endless litany of painful memories I have of her is her relating to me an interaction that she'd had with a female work colleague in which said colleague, having developed a crush on me, went on extensively about my attractive qualities; about her perception of my eloquence and intelligence and such.

And as Jess related this to me she laughed with mocking derision, essentially implying that if this other woman knew the *real* me, as Jess did, if she knew how troubled I *really* was, then the attraction would be abolished. I'm sure Jess forgot about relating this to me almost as soon as she did so, and yet I can't tell you how many times, dear reader, as a testament to the pain producible as only one whom one loves completely can produce, I revisited this memory in mind, like so many others, wishing I could go back and defend myself against the cruel implications of her mockery with something like: "Well, maybe *she* sees me more clearly than you do. Maybe you're unable to see me because of your ex. Maybe she sees my potential, a potential you're precluded from seeing because it doesn't fit the version of me you'd rather see, the one that enlarges your ego and that isn't a threat to the impassable boundary you've set between your relationship and anyone else who may come to love you, as I do, in spite of your boundaries."

As her unofficial therapist, and one that was good at his unofficial position both because he has a greater innate curiosity, patience and open-mindedness than most, and because, in this case, he truly *wanted* to listen; *needed* to hear her; I'll never forget one of the last things she texted me, as a type of goodbye, I later realized: "You're a good listener." "Only because I could listen to you talk forever," I responded. It's ironic, in fact, that we were surrounded by mental illness the entire time we knew one another, whilst the truest mental healing was actually happening between *us*, two CRC employees. She taught me some of the most important lessons of my life, including the fact that the greatest means to love and to heal one another is actually a reciprocal act built into the underrated capacity to *listen*.

Unfortunately I wasn't enough of myself in those days to compel in her the desire to listen to me as much as I adored listening to her. I was so compromised back then that I truly *wasn't* myself (so how, then, could she understand the me that wasn't *actually* there?), in a way which only a minority of people possess sufficiently paralleling experience to understand. And, of course, she was precluded from connecting by the mores of society and conventional relationships dictating to her that the only appropriate 'closeness' was with the man whom she was in love with, and soon to be engaged to and bear a child by.

Two children? I try not to pay attention. When the desire to be with her was made plain back then, not because I was 'hitting on her,' but by some implication I can't quite recall, she said "I can't." And the most I ever got out of her was "I care about you (ouch)," in addition to the perpetual playful intimacies of "you're something else" and "you're an idiot," which, by context, affect and repetition, really meant: "I love you." She'd never admit this, of course, but I knew it.

Alas, through Jess I was saved, and was constantly privy to veiled lessons, not the least of which is something that I'm sure is now verging upon becoming painfully repetitive, but worth reinforcing nonetheless: that I'm certain that what has the greatest potential to heal the world is simply *listening*. And I'm not exclusively referring here to interpersonal listening, but to being aware in general; to what's popularly dubbed 'mindfulness.' Interpersonally, we're often so keen to show people how capable we are that when they present their pains we immediately attempt to generate a 'fix,' losing the fact that it's not the advice or prescriptions or any other proactive enforcement of our minds upon theirs which will save them, but simply being fully immersed and present when they present their pains. Even the most well-meaning therapists do this; attempt to show their patients how worthy of patronage they are by utilizing 'advanced' forms of treatment, when the simplest one is the most effective. A woman once told me: "Men are always trying to fix things. It keeps them from hearing us."

People in general, within and without mental institutions, from Cain to Jess to Lenny to my mother to myself, have so much toxic buildup within us that, lacking sufficient release, it festers into unrecognized sickness that, intermixing with myriad other modern day pressures and unnaturalities, like 'food is poison' SAD, Big Pharma's chemicals displacing and concealing *true* medicine, and nature deprivation in general, eventually finds the weakest link in the body and breaks it, manifesting as everything from any number of bodily ailments to mental illness. Most everyone has seen *The Green Mile*, yes? Where the wrongly accused, incarcerated angel heals people by absorbing and releasing the dark force that's causing their suffering or evil? *That's* what listening is like. Thus, the compassionate healers of the world have one of the highest purposes that any person can possess: *To heal through hearing, reciprocally purifying and purging the poison that we all tend to deleteriously retain.* Again, this includes not only listening to one another, but to every manner in which 'listening' essentially means *paying attention*, including listening to the deepest part of ourselves. In fact, I believe listening to be a window into the reciprocating realm of Spirit. Healing is a crossing of the spiritual bridge passing over the unrequited chasm of disconnection and dis-ease. But this passage may only be made when the bridge is obstruction-free, unblocked by boundaries, and built across a level expanse of equality.

When blocked, or when attempting to cross an unlevel area, such as between 'counselor and patient' rather than the equal ground of personage, it's ineffective, and usually won't be crossed. And this is true not just between people, but, again, *within* every person; between Spirit, or Self, and its manifestations, or selves. Listening is equal to presence, to meditative observation, to the bridge over which healing bridges are built. Leveling the playing field is love and spirituality, whereas religion is idolatry and condescension, and science is, similar to religion, contingent upon separations and classifications, hemmed in by the materialistic paradigm of absolutist division that belies all the greater revelations of spirituality, growth and healing based upon *interconnection*. Jess and I healed one another because, despite her best efforts and insistence upon putting up a wall between us, and always operating from the elevated position of power, my heart scaled the wall and pulled down the drawbridge, baring our equality.

Our ego-driven need to speak *over* one another, to defeat one another in demonstration of our mental might, grossly inhibits and sometimes annihilates our capacity to save one another by fully observing and listening and eventually clearly seeing one another. That was, *is*, the overriding lesson Jess accidentally taught me. And, again, it's about reciprocation. *Salvation is mutual.* Like uncovering some secret spiritual cache, really listening to and coming to truly understand and see one another evokes a love that saves on *both* sides. Our stubborn need to prove our superiority over others is thus, ironically, self-defeating. The true conquest is over the *ego*, and in connected, loving, listening understanding. An invaluable spiritual insight lies therein: Transcendence of our own suffering comes from releasing the suffering isolation and feeling of not being understood held by *others*. If I come to understand you, and you come to understand me, we heal one another.

And only through such an approach can we come to know that we're all essentially the same being; the same Self buried beneath the illusorily-separated self. With the same emotional core, the same needs, desires, pains and fears, even as those core emotional qualities of every being take limitless, unique form, just as every unique form of the self is, underneath, a unique assemblage of the perfectly ubiquitous Self. Thus does the concept of listening, and its capacity to heal us, go well beyond the interpersonal, touching every facet of being. It *is* the power of presence. Of actually being where you are. Of absorbing the vital magic of the world in which we're daily enveloped, but which we're typically too distracted by internalized fears and desires to absorb. But when we do so, when we are where we are, all time and pressure ceases, and we become one with everything, the veil of separation lifted. And in this connection we find peace, and our neurology shifts into a state of abeyance conducive to driving away stress-based dis-ease, thereby potentiating revitalization.

Thus do I beseech you, and remind myself, to discipline ourselves to get out of our hearts and heads, and into the heart and head of others, and into the heart of the world at large, as it were, and thereby find the sameness of all heart, finding that *this* be God, that which is the essence of all, and thereby be borne aloft, lifted above division and isolation, rescued from the misery of the delusion of individualism. I know the promise of this practice *through* Jess. So high above what had been my disconnected, loveless life had she lifted me in our 'friendship' that my heart screamed at me for letting her leave the CRC. If only what we need from others had any power over them at all. Those needs were so immense that they yet linger today.

Here's another agonizing memory: sitting beside Jess as she gleefully researches 'doing something special' for her then boyfriend, now husband, unable to escape the torture of imagining taking his place. I specifically recall her booking one of those airstream vacation rentals. You know, where you set up shop in an airstream in place of a tent on some gorgeous lot beside an Oregon winery. *Fuck that guy.* Have I said that already? And no, I don't mean that in a menacing manner, but half tongue-in-cheek, out of pure, unadulterated envy. Another memory floats into my awareness, something she related to me around the same time, compelling me to offer up a sincere thank you to that angel from her past, from that one story of going with a coworker to a party, being roofied by some guys there, and his removing Jess from the situation before it turned into a horror, likely placing himself at risk in the process, and delivering her safely home into her bed, even tucking her in. You saved the only woman I've ever loved. Thank you, good sir, whomever and wherever you are.

It's amazing how the memories endure, despite the years. The freckles that came out upon her countenance after being sun-scathed at the lake on Memorial Weekend, like the sun had burned off a concealing sheen in order to reveal a somehow even more endearing wonder, making her somehow more beautifully beckoning to my heart than ever. The fact that I could be in the Records Room all the way down the hall from where she sat at The Bridge and hear only her *sneeze*, a sound that no other creature on Earth can make, and how that sound would seem to shoot down the hall and clutch me by the heartstrings and jerk me out of my mundanity and transport me to a world which the mundane cannot know, much less resist. Much like the deliberate way in which she properly pronounced certain syllables whilst reciting tales so purely and openly and vulnerably that her emotions were as the primal elements, the consideration of those syllabic pronunciations suggesting that she'd retained lessons in correct locution that the rest of us have forgotten, if ever we knew them.

Good lord I had it bad. It seemed to me that there was nothing she could do that didn't endear her further; that didn't add to my bottomless adoration. As I write this on my phone I'm once more beside the Deschutes River. A strange insect crawls up my shirt and, as I examine it, I immediately think of Jess speaking of her adventures in nature with Lucky SOB. I think of his connections to the lodge at Elk Lake, and his family's property at Suttle Lake. I think of the picture I once saw on her *Facebook* page of her floating out into one of these lakes, and he standing at the shore with a big grin on his face, dorkily pointing at her with both hands in a swooping motion with his arms, her grinning in equal glee. I think of how she once told me of examining the aquatic insects on the shore, and being fascinated by their colors, their peculiar shapes, their enigmatic behavior. Curious that remembrances of her curiosities can still seem so present to me. Does this occur to everyone that's only been in love once, I wonder?

I have this continued imagination of our first kiss, in the sheer impossibility of freeing circumstance. We're sitting on some sort of ledge, facing one another, talking as easily as we once did, and I make another one of my wise-ass comments, and she laughs, loudly, eruptively, as though out of shock mixed with unadulterated joy, as she used to do before reproaching herself for fear of waking the residents in the middle of the night, and she turns away in embarrassment, simultaneously repelled and attracted, then turns back, giving me one of those heart-meltingly dorky smiles of hers, and I lean in and kiss her. It feels prophetic except for that same impossibility; except for, you know, husband and children, boundaries better fortified than the former Berlin Wall, propriety-induced shame better ingrained than in the victims of Catholicism. Your dorkiness is your best quality, my dear. I hate to sound cliché, but any man that failed to see that didn't deserve you; didn't deserve *any* part of you, including all of your husband's friends that you slept with before him.

And the way she spoke of his *best* friend, it was clear both that she was at least a little in love with *him* as well, and that I've never been near to having a friendship that close. Brady and his best friend would roll around on the bed together in the most natural of manners, *not* in a homosexual way, mind you, but in the way that the truest of friends inseparable as kin might. But for me, the jealousy of not having such a close friendship outside of my youth, when I was confident, and had many, paled in comparison to the jealousy that I felt in relation both to this best friend's easy ways as the natural, handsome, charming Don Juan and how that power granted him such appeal with women in general, and with Jess in particular. In fact, I sometimes wondered if the best friend, Darren, was the *true* target, and her now husband was the settling point; like Darren was the eagle soaring through the sky that was too high to reach, so she settled upon the solid ground nearest to where he nests. She told me of the early days of her relationship with Brady, and how it had been *Darren* who'd first made a move on her at a party, but how, unlike Brady, he'd been, in her words, "too much for me."

And she spoke of how easily Darren attracted women; how they'd pathetically sleep outside his bedroom door late at parties, when he'd be inside with another girl. And all about his nervousness when this promiscuous ease was supplanted by an actual rare affection for someone. And this one time Jess was kicking herself in retrospective self-reproach for being drunk and cornering Darren's *father* at a party (apparently involving both 'adults' and 'kids' in their twenties at that time) and besieging him with questions about his son. Of course, one could argue that such is simply her nature as a loving person, that she simply wanted to possess a better understanding of the young, handsome man who was so much a part of her then boyfriend's life, and thus her own life. But I don't know… the level of interest seemed to indicate more to me.

Like perhaps, in some recess of her subconscious, she may've been spinning that most sinister of webs; a web involving the potential future split of one relationship and the catching of another; of the true, long-term target; the seizing of which would, from the force of losing his mate and his best friend in one fell, cliché swoop, surely kill Brady. Maybe in the recesses of my own subconscious I'm spinning a sinister-most web of my own, one involving being willing to do most *anything* for a chance to unsettle Jess enough to, for the first time in her secretly vain history, reach out to me; or, worse, a web catching her from her fall from grace should she first catch Darren, and/or should Brady perish. Horrible, monstrous thoughts, dear reader; the thoughts of the demon within the angel, the dichotomy extant within *everyone*, even as very few of us have the balls and brains to uncover it, much less put it forth to public scrutiny. She conquered me completely without even lifting a finger, and I've been trying to rescue myself from that state ever since, and so tally herein one memory after another, hoping purging to be my salvation.

I remember how her goodness made cursing not just profane, but foolish, folding into her preference for Jim Gaffigan over Louis CK any day. Or the way in which she'd contort when she laughed in the dead of night at another of my tongue-in-cheek remarks, trying to tamper her tickled exclamations so as, again, to avoid responsibility for waking those who need rest more than any other stigmatized categorization of people on the planet. Or how she'd do that thing where she'd puff her cheeks and roll her eyes when she was covering up her desire to express her secret, 'inappropriate' affection for me. Or the few times we embraced one another and I heard her, as softly as possible, exclaim "hmmm," having felt the force flow between us and instinctively sensing its potency, and immediately wondering at its meaning, but just as quickly feeling the 'monogamy-is-morality' socially-indoctrinated need to deny that force, and find a way to explain it away.

Or the fact that I can't see a *La Croix* beverage without imagining them in the fridge of the CRC staff lounge, or imagine her drinking one, lamenting its effect on her teeth. Or that I can't see a red car drive by me on the road without turning my head to see if *she's* driving it, wondering if I should wear more of her favorite color, like some sad matador remembering that he never had the bull by the horns, and yet pathetically rejoices the fact that at least there once *was* a bull in his ring; or like a drone bee that can't see a red flower without being beset by palpitating pangs paired with recollections of his lost queen. Or that green canvas jacket of hers procured through an affordable garment app that thereafter seemed inseparable from the cost-consciousness innate to both her character and her upbringing, ever casually flung over the back of her chair, the humble demarcation of her nightly throne, my undiagnosed OCPD compelling me to straighten it every time it became askew, not just to mitigate my anxiety, but such that its presentation might more closely mirror the perfection of its wearer defined *by*, not in spite of, what the non-bewitched might foolishly dismiss as Jess's 'flaws.' Now that I think of it, allowing it to remain askew, or 'flawed in presentation,' would've better reflected her charisma.

Or the beanie she wore with the American Flag on it on one of the last days that I saw her at work, the Fourth of July, when she came in to start a shift as I was leaving mine, having already jabbed me in the heart by having taken another shift, my slow bleed nearing exsanguination as she began her tasks that great American holiday whilst pretending that she wasn't acutely aware that I was standing next to her in absolute writhing agony, as though hanging from an invisible noose, wishing the deadfall of her shift change had snapped my neck and finished me off, rather than that my bodily survival precipitated the torture of my subsequent psychological suffocation. And how, in shift change shortly thereafter, I noticed that she was wearing sandals for the first time ever to work, and I thought that even her *feet* are beautiful, and I've never been a 'foot guy,' though I *do* look at a woman's hands almost immediately, finding shapely hands common to beautiful women, and sensing their connection to artistry.

Or that other time in shift change, just before the July 4th beanie and sandals, when the therapy dogs came rushing

to me, and I exchanged my natural love for and with said
canines, and she said nothing, but when they finally
migrated to another coworker, and more love was
exchanged, how she said "Look at *you* with all the dogs,"
giving credit to said coworkers' loving nature and the dogs'
affinity for her, but *not* to me, as but an ongoing example of
the cruel attention-is-weakness sociopsychological law #1.
And Brady, Brady, Brady, the man who redefined the word
envy for me, a term far too feeble for the one forever free
to embrace a dream I've only peered at from across the
requiting chasm. What's the term for someone who sits on
the unrecognized Spring of Everlasting Life, likely thinking
it merely *his* version of providence? Who daily drinks of it
until drowning, when but a sip would sustain me for years?

Speaking of which, hell with *Facebook Dating*. I think my
dating profile should be my *Rover* profile. If you're
interested in me, just log into their app and find my profile
and peruse all the adorable pictures with me and the pups
and read all the appreciative comments. If that doesn't
manipulate you into liking me more, then I don't know
women at all; especially *Bend* women. It certainly seems to
work on the typically older women who find me on the app,
and do most of the work of approving of men coming into
their homes to look after their fur children. It reminds me of
that commercial where guys rent puppies to use as their
wingmen in attracting women, or that conversation I had
with that dude at one of the brewpubs shortly after moving
here. "Get a dog," he told me flatly, as if sharing a critical
insight. "They'll do half the work for you." And from the
perspective of the lothario, I can see his point. But they're
so much more than wingmen. They're *family*, and the
discerning women that see clearly look for the difference
between such regards for our canine companions. In fact, I
believe one may know everything that they need to know
about a person by how they treat their 'pets.' To the best of
us, 'pet' is an insult. They're *kin*. They depend upon me,

but I'm not their 'owner,' except where legality asserts itself. They eat what I eat. They sleep beside me on my bed. They love as I love. Unlike Brady, or myself, dogs are dominated by only the most meager of pretend 'men.'

Brady, Brady, Brady. "Brady thinks our song is Brown-Eyed Girl, even though my eyes aren't brown." I'll forever say she has the most beautiful eyes that I've ever seen; not just their color, but their exotic, subtly crescent shape, before, of course, even getting into what may be seen in the eyes of one who feels like a portal to God. Those eyes… I'll always find it irritating that Brady considered their song to be *Brown-Eyed Girl*. At least his citing that song suggests that, for him as well, her eyes are a prime point of enchantment. But they aren't *brown*, you lucky bastard! It wasn't just the color, or the shape, but the fact that they seemed to me to pour forth with such a raw emotive force that I was *constantly* overwhelmed by them.

It was as though Jess's eyes represented the perfectly balanced mingling of wildness and innocence which oft seemed to personify her. How quickly and emphatically they'd come to convey the whole gamut of emotion, from bliss to the upwelling of every agony. She'd come to tears easily, and it was the most beautiful thing, as no one made you want to share emotion more; made you need to be subsumed by the same tide. Her emotions just seemed stronger; like they could break through anything, then suck you into her, like an indominable gravitational force. What does *he* see in them, I wonder, *except* the wrong color?

Brady's favorite film is *Forrest Gump*. Brady plays tennis, and thinks this one tennis player is hot, and it drives me crazy. Brady thinks I need to do a better job of standing up to my mother when she shows up high on meth again, and denies it just before I find the pipe in her purse; thinks only a zero-tolerance-else-estrangement policy is correct. As for

Brady's mother... well, we won't get into that one, but let's just say their shared, troubling history, both geographically and psychologically, reminds me of having once heard: "Shared trauma is the true substance of enduring love."

"We're damaged the same way, that's why we work well together," one side of the romantic relationship asserts to the other in the series *Maid* (more on this series soon, for it's *highly* relevant to Jess and the CRC). Is that why your marriage is destined to last until death, Jess? That, and that he embodies the Rock of Gibraltar? Someone you can build your life upon whom *won't* erode beneath your feet, in perfect opposition to your upbringing? And, obviously, the fact that only a fool would leave you, and that you need what Brady represents too much to ever leave him?

Brady isn't even my type. When he's irritated or jealous the most that Brady will do is grind his teeth, the bulge of his jaw muscles the only giveaway, whereas Nick (the former boyfriend whom I uncomfortably remind her of) would psychologically abuse me. And whereas Nick wouldn't let me leave his side without suspicion, with Brady we'll go to a bar and I'll wander away and if anyone asks where I am he'll just say: "She's somewhere over there, I think." That's *so* much better, she assures me. And a hundred times in retrospect I've thought: Yea, it's a better testament to his being confident and not controlling, but is it not also suggestive that he takes you for granted? Might not a little insecurity suggest a higher valuation? Might the fact that he and his friends tolerated Nick speaking to you in the bar that one time after you crushed him, before throwing him out when he couldn't control his emotions, speak not just to Brady's self-assured solidity and non-abusiveness, but to Nick's lack of control implying a passionate force of adoration that Brady is incapable of? Cannot weakness be a testament to a type of strength ignored through the law stating desire to be commensurate with undesirability?

After listening to hours of content on someone who I
thereby knew better than any character of any book I've
ever read, the only criticism I *ever* heard Jess level about
her significant other was that she sometimes wished that
he had more empathy for her when she related what was
troubling her, whether sourced from past or present. He
didn't *fully* listen, in other words, as evidenced by the fact
that he always responded with the same advice: "It'll be
okay. You'll get it dialed in." Maybe *that's* why I became
the receptacle and therapist through which she'd relate
and purge her pains (I'm only in this moment realizing),
because *he* didn't; he couldn't or wouldn't. I think that may
be why Jess liked certain movies, shows and music as
well, those which touched upon a deep well of under-the-
surface emotion and psychological wreckage: the *catharsis*
that they represented. I remember her affinity for the show
This Is Us, and how she'd cry every time she watched it at
the CRC. And I remember how she told me Brady would
say, when she'd cry at home watching it: "I don't get why
you keep watching this show. It always makes you cry."
Brady, Brady, Brady. Could it be that I understood 'your
woman' better than you do? Could it be that, based upon
this understanding, I loved her in ways that you never will?

That may've been the one thing I had on him: I knew how
to, and was more inclined towards, *listening*. Well, that and
my big… *brain*, and even bigger… *heart*, and absolutely
massive… *balls*, and gargantuan… *ego*. But seriously:
Listening is the most undervalued, underdeveloped
discipline on the planet. And people like Jess, and the
residents of the CRC, those with traumatic pasts, value it in
others more than most, because they better embody
its *need*. They possess a greater priority to purge than
most; to unload burdensome psychological weight. They
represent an increased need to cathartically release, to

feel like they've been truly heard and understood, and thereby moved towards healing; they represent the interpersonal promise of the oldest, and most effective, form of therapy: not *adding* something, not lending advice on how to improve, or techniques for how to process, but the processing *itself*. The purest therapeutic power of actually *hearing* someone, of actually trying to *understand* someone, and thereby *removing* some of their pain; pain that otherwise remains locked up and persecutorial. I'm convinced that so much of what afflicts the mental health of Americans comes from our insistence upon separation and individualism; from the innumerable artificial fences that I trace to the divide and conquer tactics of conservatism.

For so much of our pain comes from feeling isolated and not understood, or misunderstood; from denying the fact that we're naturally social, spiritual animals that can only purify and level-out through the building and crossing of bridges that conventional society blocks, because those crossings both imperil profitability and offer the union and solidarity empowering the people in ways that have *always* threatened the conquering, oppressing class that feeds upon our division. Psychologically, relative to our mental health, we can only feel healthy and happy when we sense that we're *truly* known by others, which is about the bridge.

Thus I bid you, dear reader, to consider the connected, critical questions: *Where exactly are the lines to be drawn between truly and completely listening, and love, and healing? And might the modern world's failure in this regard be revealing?* Could it be that what the world needs most are these three inseparable links in the social chain, and that they're currently fractured, and poorly maintained, *especially* in America, where what prevails are divided personal and special interests, cutthroat competition and vestigial, monogamous relationships which clearly aren't

providing the entirety of needs for the entirety of the
population, many, even most, even *all* of whom would be
bettered by feeling and expressing love *outside* of their
one relationship, even if the affection *isn't* physically
expressed? And where what fails in direct correlation are
all the means and modes of connection and integration
which we're conditioned to associate with socialism for the
sake of the profiteering parasites overruling humanity?

How much might the conditions of PrimaCare residents
improve, and those of mental health patients around the
country, by making the ability to fully listen the prerequisite
of hiring those whom are to administer treatment, above
any other credential or capacity? Make *that* what you test
for in your interviews, without telling them that you're
testing for it, so as to avoid affectation; to avoid the fact
that people tell you what you want to hear when it grants
them some sought-after benefit. And, expanding the
scope, what if we were to apply the gains of truly hearing
one another to the *whole* of humanity? What if, in other
words, we could expand that undervalued capacity for full,
empathetic listening to include not just those receiving
mental health treatment, but the whole race, and perform a
comprehensive analysis of all the ways in which our
'capitalism is based upon divide and conquer' population is
precluded from healing and pursuing collective interests of
every kind owing to the domination of conservatively-
concocted professional and personal relation constructs?

And the digital stand-ins for that sacrificed connectivity and
all the innumerable, invaluable, lost benefits aren't working.
In fact, they tend to make things worse, in my opinion, by
pushing people to replace the real thing with the artifice,
coercing people to trade inimitable, authentic connection
with fake popularity, as per my aforementioned lost friend,
and thereby sacrificing inestimable human value through

the filtering avatar. Our entire neurology's, not to mention our spiritual faculties, evolved to connect to the *real thing*. It's hubris to believe that the simulation can even *approach* the power of *natural connection* and its indispensability when it comes to creating and maintaining good mental health. I know for a fact that my own mental health during the hours that I worked with Jess swung dramatically from the heights of elation to the bottomless pit of dejection, and that, while she herself reductively dismissed this as my simply being "moody," that my swings were largely due to her own swings between letting me in and keeping me out.

There's little more frigid and cruel as the human psyche, likely having evolved that way so that the weak would be done the service of being eaten by the strong without the compunction that might otherwise sacrifice everyone's survival, even those as good as her. And I assure you, dear reader, knowing her I knew the very best of humanity. Even so, it was eventually so clear how much I loved her (though this was never allowed to be openly admitted) that it felt as though I'd become a toy for her ego, for she had no need of me, and I the most desperate need of her. And through her I learned that even the very best of people are so enamored of their own egos and its taste for power trips that disparity summons demons, even from within saints.

The result was that Jess wielded the inequality in our respective emotional attachment to one another like a weapon. She refused to show affection, even as our natural closeness made it impossible to conceal that affection entirely. She would call me 'buddy' and other minimizing terms, knowing how lofty was her own description within my heart; the adoration embedded in the terminology with which I described her within myself. I think that the best thing you ever called me, Jess, was *you*, as in 'hey *you*.' You know what I mean, dear reader, that

endearment that's so intimate and familiar *because* it
sounds like it isn't, delivered with that special, playfully-
flirtatious inflection that betrays its intimacy. But you only
called me that once. I remember exactly where I was when
you did so, on one of the few times you actually called me
(as opposed to texted), while I was visiting Portland.

And there hasn't been a single hotel room I've been in
since where the loneliness wasn't nearly as profound as
the wish that I was entering it with you, and could wrap
myself up in you. And I'm not even referring to sex. And,
perhaps more than all the other memories, as a testament
to pain and trauma leaving a greater imprint than joy, I'll
never forget the day that she so overtly celebrated the
opening of a mid-day position and her looming transition in
front of me, knowing very well how much I needed her to
stay on night shifts, exaggerating her excitement at the
possibility of moving into a new shift in a manner fitting the
relishing of her possessed power commensurate with my
own agony. It was horribly cruel, and an overt display of
egotistical gratification. To me the effect was very much
like a kid torturing an ant, such was the extreme disparity
of our respective positions to, and within, one another.

The sudden truth was that the thing which I'd come to most
fear, her departure, had finally come. That I'd never see
her again except in passing, during shift changes, after
living for the overnights during which she momentarily
relieved my heaving heart of its brutally massive daily
burden, was more than I felt I could bear. And the extent of
my contraction was the extent of her egotistic expansion.

That was clear. It was written all over her. So while, again,
I tended to think of her in reverential terms, in the
emotional pain I endured through her embodiments of
egotism I would sometimes call her "Power Trip" in my own

mind, and connect this nomenclature with her having once told me that she tested as a narcissist in a psych class. Not that I blame her for having scored such a result. How can I blame her for falling in love with the same person that I did? Alas, the effects of that mutual love were brutal. And as resentful as that no doubt sounds (and I'd be lying if I pretended that a deep resentment wasn't sown by the only woman I've ever loved casting me off like dead weight in her voyage through life, or perhaps because she considered me more like unexploded ordinance risking the voyage itself), I more mean it similar to how I regarded her pride, and the duality of pride itself, as discussed earlier; how her testing that way more likely indicates a deep self-respecting love that she developed as a form of fortitude against everything that might imperil her life and future family, developed from a multitude of accumulated past pains making her more aware of such perils than most.

Loving herself, in other words, became a type of necessity of survival for Jess; a counterweight against everything that had been placed against her, and risked her future. But whatever the cause of her self-love, whether it was more the form of pride pertaining to love or the form pertaining to ego (it was some degree of both), for me the result was agonizing, and seemed more the latter. For I had to endure her ego trips constantly, and I could say nothing, for any admission of my patent passion for her would only be met with her notorious 'boundaries' of what I was permitted to say, or even think or feel, backed by the absurd 'professional standard' that getting involved with a work colleague was an ethical violation, even before the standardized social impropriety of admitting feelings for someone with a 'significant other.' *Everything* was on her side, and *any* true move that I could make, any natural expression of my love for her, could only work against me,

such that the force of my love became my persecution.
Have many of you, dear readers, have experienced this?

As previously mentioned, because of her, because of
being politely censured by her on the few occasions when I
sent a text that was overly familiar that she was afraid
Brady might see, I developed an immense detestation for
the word and common conception of 'boundary.' It's a word
assumed to denote an ethical protection, to an extent that
those whom wield it like a weapon are reflexively assumed
by the conforming herd to be in the right, when it's actually
just one side of the story, and not always the ethical side.
To those whom it's used *against*, a 'boundary' is seen and
felt as an imposition of one with power against one without.
This detestation for the concept would grow all the more
extreme when I myself moved to day shifts sometime after
Jess left the institution, and my new supervisor, the
overlording Linda, made all the more officious in contrast to
her predecessor, oft admitted that 'boundaries' are central
to both her personal beliefs and her professional practices.

In line with political correctness, 'boundary' is a word that's
always *assumed* to define right and wrong, and to grant its
user ethical authority, but is, in actuality, just as often a
handy euphemism enlisted by the empowered against the
commensurately disempowered. When one is moving
towards something that one wants and suddenly slams into
a wall, not because they were doing anything wrong, but
because they were naturally gravitating towards a personal
advancement or desire, the boundary feels cruel and
unjust. At the CRC, when a resident wanted something
that Linda was unwilling to give, she simply 'put up a
boundary;' not because what the resident required was
extreme, but because it was inconvenient for her, and
contradicted her control. And though it likely sounds cliché,
is not some form of control what motivates most

everything? It was certainly a foremost motivation for Jess, which I can't help but connect to her upbringing of being almost entirely deprived of it, which, it seemed to me, made her *very* fond of it once she had some. Certainly the same can be said of anyone who knows the value of control by its dispossession, which is but one in an endless number of examples of the revelation of truth through contrast. For, right or wrong, is this not what a boundary really is? An enforcement of control? (Linda's character in my novel *Avant Garde*, Hamilton, written whilst I worked at the CRC, is used to explore the abuse of the concept, in connection with right-wing nationalism). It should go without saying that the general power disparity between staff and residents was almost as severe as between Jess and I, and that clever and unscrupulous staff members knew just how to wield that weapon whilst appearing to merely be 'holding a boundary.' This, in fact, I would later find, is a core theme in the abuse of power common within the corporate system; within *all* hierarchal institutions, in fact: how to wield an abusive form of control whilst making it appear to merely be an ethical enforcement of propriety.

Almost as injurious as Jess's affected show of glee at the opening of the opportunity to shift shifts was what I heard she'd said later, *after* having shifted, the message relayed to me after she'd left the CRC. Another female colleague, a Peer Support Specialist whom I'd come into the habit of picking up on the way to our shared shifts (because her personal circumstances prohibited her from driving) reported that Jess had told her and others that she was leaving *because* of me, this in reaction to my "passively-aggressively" leaving the aforementioned whiteboard note.

Not only was this immeasurably painful to hear, and was it clear that this colleague was eager to speak it and pleased by seeing the pain of my hearing it pour itself onto my countenance, but it was *entirely untrue*. In truth, Jess sought a better paying position anywhere she could find it almost as soon as she walked through the doors of the CRC, often spending hours during our shifts scouring online employment offerings (after completing necessary tasks we were encouraged to use the substantial remaining time how we wished to, both for our own sanity working overnight and for our retention by the company, considering the rapid turnover innate to the NOC position).

Honestly, I suspect that the *opposite* is true: that she stayed as long as she did *because* of me. For, despite the sometime discomfort of my not always being able to rein in my emotions, she never ceased to call me a friend, and referred to issues she'd had with previous coworkers at other jobs, and how glad she was that I wasn't like them. Not to mention that, again, she was always considering other employment options while we worked together, but was never able to pull the trigger for some reason, despite lamenting the effect that working overnight shifts was having upon her health, and that after working with me for that year a half and switching to PM shifts she only remained at the CRC for another few months before moving on. I moved into PM shifts shortly after she'd left. I lasted longer on those shifts than she did, but I can't help but think that both of our relatively short tenures therein had one thing in common: *Linda became our supervisor.*

So why did Jess say that? Was it just pride? Did she feel like she needed to give them an excuse for leaving that matched her sweet and innocent profile? That it was about more than money, my comments lending her a convenient excuse for pretending like it *wasn't* a decision based purely upon financial opportunity? She was extremely prideful and career focused for the best of reasons; for the determination not to be stuck in a state of deprivation that she knew all too well, and to shelter her future children from that plight's reoccurrence. So it was easier, even for the very best person, to say: *I'm leaving because of him.*

Scapegoating me was expeditious. And it wouldn't be the last time someone I cared about did so. Jess taught me that even the best of people, someone whom I'll forever think of reverentially, inflict evil for the sake of their egos. It *was* true that my love for her had created some… tension. But she'd stayed on the shift *long* after she'd realized that I'd fallen in love with her, and *long* after I'd lost my ability to control my overwhelming feelings for her. So it wasn't that. Rather, she told a lie that made her sound better to her coworkers and preserved her ego whilst, in the continuance of the power disparity which she, ironically, cited as the unhealthiest aspect of her previous, failed relationship, crushed me from her superior position behind my back. I felt the blow long after she'd dealt it, heartbreak breaking time barriers. And the *way* that message was delivered, by a young woman I'd been so generous to…

I can't help but note here that, despite going out of my way to help said young woman, and always speaking well of her to others, this same deliverer of this excruciating message (dropped in my lap as I dropped her off from work) would end up becoming a favorite of the imperious Linda. She would, in fact, eventually become the cause of my leaving the institution (of my own volition, because I'd tired of the prejudicial treatment) after she'd reported to Linda that, whilst driving back to the CRC after a stressful outing, I'd (jokingly) texted that I needed to make a stop at a bar and have a drink. It was clear from the context of the text, and from her knowledge of my tongue-in-cheek sense of humor, a knowledge she possessed in spades as one of my most consistent PM shift colleagues, that I was kidding.

And yet she reported this joke as though I was being serious; as if, you know, I was running aground of a major 'boundary.' And she did so knowing as well as anyone that I'd had issues with Linda almost as soon as she became my supervisor because, from my perspective, I didn't immediately, reflexively, obediently concur with her during group and one-on-one discussions. Frankly, at this point I'm surprised when I'm *not* stabbed in the back by someone well-positioned to do so, *especially* beautiful young women. The extent to which that speaks to my own weakness (especially my weakness towards alluring women), to western capitalist society and the worst bosses encouraging cutthroat competition and allegiance to the hierarchy and profitability above anything even verging upon honor, to so-called 'human nature (which tends to be *highly* misunderstood by westerners conditioned by the Church, and by conservatism and realism),' to sociosexual politics in self-righteous, 'woke,' Me Too America, to the general egotism and lack of morality prevalent in America, and to the connected extent of dishonorable tactics reflexively enlisted by the morally-undeveloped, unscrupulous segments of society, I'll let you decide, dear reader. But it's certainly some combination of all of these.

And my God, the things that Linda put me through... the *constant* veiled insults in our one-on-one meetings, her 'writing me up' for things that *everyone* did, and her incessant attempts to push me into hot water with Annabelle, whom defended me against the traps that Linda would lay for me... Such grotesqueries greatly informed my understanding and rising revulsion of corporate politics. I must here assert, dear reader, that survival in such a power-abusive corporate climate requires the development of skills and the employment of qualities which can only act to undermine one's honor and degrade one's character. To be successful in this world, as in politics, and likely in, again, most any hierarchal system requiring such duplicity, one must murder one's truest self and, in its place, construct a monster concealed beneath a proper, virtuous façade. See here Machiavelli's lines on the difference between what one is and what one must *appear* to be for the sake of successfully accumulating power. And by the same token know why those of *actual* integrity, those compelled by principle and conviction, can't sustain such practices, and must invariably be driven away, towards something which *doesn't* require suffocation of character.

And yet, even with our clear mutual contempt for one another, I swear that Linda, who fancied herself a body builder, and always adorned form-fitting pants to work, would regularly come into the kitchen when I was working therein and bend over the counter in front of me when speaking to residents on the other side. Call it a crude observation and premonition if you must, but I've found this maneuver to be one of the clearest 'tells' of a woman's attraction to a man (for what could be a more animalistic signal of a woman's desire for a man?), and whether it's done subconsciously or with manipulative intent, the effect is undeniable. And I've sometimes wondered in retrospect whether or not this ongoing action was a psychological byproduct of not just a person's desire for the enemy, for those who *don't* give them approval in reinforcement of their egos, but of people's desire for such in general; of our insecure need to seek the approval and attraction of those unwilling to give it. Or perhaps it simply turned her on to flaunt herself in a manner which she could deny, to the very person whom propriety dictated she shouldn't. A version of 'the forbidden fruit is sweetest,' in essence.

I think that Linda would come to leave the institution not long after my own departure largely *because* of her unsuccessful attempts to paint me as unruly, even insubordinate, to our boss, and failing to successfully sell me as such, for Annabelle was too astute and knowing of my true character to fall for it. My sense was that Linda suffered a reduced reputation as a result. I remember seeing her in her office tearing up after one such failed sabotage, turning away from me when I noticed. She also teared up in her final shift change meeting with Jess, the last time she'd see her, while Jess was leaving the room, permanently. Now *that* I understand, Linda. *That* is why the domineering such as you won't prevail in the end. The empire doesn't *always* win, dear reader, *especially* in the long term, time gradually eroding the fabricated evils of the imperialist in favor of the indestructible truths of the soothsaying, rebellious romantic whom hears the haunting reminder of the one time he fell in love in every song sung.

"Tell me you believe in me or don't say a word to me," *Rufus du Sol* sings, a refrain that always rang painfully true in the hollows of my heart after falling in love with Jess, and enduring various forms of her subtle verbal torture. "We used to be friends. We used to be inner circle. I don't understand. What have I become to you?," they go on. "You were right. I know I can't get enough of you. Nooooo. The things that I would do… Leave it all to bloom…" into this book. Ah Jess, the innumerable nine hour drives from the high desert of Central Oregon to the mist-enshrouded redwood forests of my birthplace in Fort Bragg, CA and back, listening to Rufus and having every thought imaginable of you, *most* of them clean. I saw them perform right here in Bend once. Maybe I should've messaged Jess and asked her to ask Brady if he'd mind watching the kids for a while so she could come with me. What?! Don't tell me that would be crossing yet another inviolable boundary!

And I remember Jess loving "The Shape of You," and the "I'm in love with your body" line, me thinking 'give me one chance to show you what that could mean.' And her being wowed by the versatility of *Childish Gambino*, me thinking 'hell, at my best I'm a Renaissance Man, a philosopher, poet, ideologue, theorist, entrepreneur, graphic artist…,' imagining someday finally 'being discovered,' gaining recognition for my own versatility and being able to use it as a means of flirtation, like, "remember when you said… well…" And she made this comment this one time that not only implied that she liked sex, but that she wanted to have sex with me, or imagined that we would have good sex, though I've never been able to recall the exact verbiage. And I recall this other comment this other time about how I could have *everything* that I want, just not with *her*, implying that I *could've* had that from her, if, you know, she hadn't been in a committed relationship with the man that I'm sure she knew, even then, that she'd eventually marry. That particular comment reminded me of my biggest high school and college crush, Lisa Bergreen (probably the most gorgeous girl I've known in 'real life'), and a few of the things that she said to me a good fifteen years earlier.

Like when I was driving her back to our mutual collegiate base at UCSB from our shared hometown area of Santa Rosa, CA, where we attended the same junior high and high school, and she saw my tension and anxiety during our discussion of… something, and she briefly rubbed the back of my neck, and said, verbatim: "You have every reason to be confident Nick." Or when my roommate Bob, in the house I lived in with him, Lisa and a half dozen others on Estero Street in Isla Vista, CA (adjacent to the UCSB campus, where more alcohol is said to be consumed in its square mile than anywhere else per square mile on the planet; yes, *your* college area included), bet me a quarter ounce (just 'a quarter' when you're hip to the lingo), that I couldn't go a week without smoking weed, and we rolled up my winnings into one massive blunt requiring multiple wraps, and, as it was being rolled, Lisa came in, and I was wearing my favorite forest green shirt, and she sat on my lap and flirted with me for a blissful half hour. Or when, sometime later, in the same room, she came down the hall wearing her form-fitting white dress unzipped at the back, and asked me to zip it up for her, and smiled at me, thanked me and left, and I knew upon reflection that not only was that one of the best things that I'd ever seen or ever would see, but that she *knew* how she looked, and she wanted *me* to know.

If only I'd been clever and confident and quick-witted enough at the time to say: "Let me know if need any help *unzipping* it later." She was intermittently flirtatious with me during those days of constant debauchery in which I still miraculously managed a 3.3 GPA. But I wasn't stable or confident enough to do anything about it (a *long* story that could fill half a psych textbook by itself). As I write this, I had a dream about Lisa last night. It was one of the best dreams I've ever had. I won't get into details. And as with my dreams of Jess, there's something powerful in the post-dream state related to the dreamt-about subject. It's as though whatever part of them lives within is summoned, and the memories of them, removed from reality before, are momentarily imbued with a revitalization that makes them as real in the waking hours as they'd ever been.

I'll never forget the night I listened to Kevin, a housemate during my junior year, cajole a drunk, hesitant Lisa into climbing up to join him in his wooden bunk, not ten feet from where I was sleeping, in the room we called 'Ewok Village,' because we had to build lofts into the raised-ceiling room to pack in two extra people so we could afford to live on Del Playa Drive, oceanside in Isla Vista, CA. And the asshole property manager, Ron Wolf, who ran the Isla Visa rental game, and made so much money off of us early-twenties college kids (off our *parents*, more accurately) that he parked his purple Lamborghini in the area all the time, with a license plate that read "WOLF," and how we'd plot to piss in it or set it on fire when we'd pass it in our drunken revelry. Lisa's *Facebook* pictures (until my recent deletion of the app), with her perfectly pretty, buttoned-up kids and tall, wealthy, studly husband

and white-wine-sipping social events surrounded by dozens of other half-as-beautiful primped and polished ladies in luxe So-Cal settings, look like *Abercrombie & Fitch* commercials. It all seems so perfectly cliché to me, the prettiest, most popular girl from junior high all the way through college ends up the picture-perfect representation of the most status-and-image-fixated region of the country. In my experience, the mentality of most of the So-Cal set is *far* more image and status conscious than Nor-Cal crews.

I was *highly* infatuated with Lisa for years, also enhancing my memory, it seems, though nothing compared to what Jess did to the elephantizing of my mind. They say that memory is selective. For me, I think that it's the *heart* that stores and selects, both the heights of its elation and the lows of its dejection, as it may be for everyone. For a solid decade and a half, from middle school through high school in Rincon Valley, through our friendly days at UCSB together, with our sporadic flirtations and her teasing me into finding confidence and hooking up with girls, and for years later, she represented the pinnacle for me. *She* was the muse. The goal. The upper echelons of what was possible for the fully realized form of myself. Then I fell in love with Jess. But Lisa is still there, buried in my psyche.

Obviously, right? Considering I still occasionally dream of her at 42. There's a buried, universal truth there, I think. A truth pertaining to *all* men, and likely all *women* as well: that we never really get over those whom we held a hot enough flame for. Regardless of how much we pave over it with time and the responsibilities of 'reality,' and regardless of what we tell our 'significant others,' the purest dreams never die. Maybe not even when we, ourselves, perish. Maybe they're folded into the Universal Mind, entwined with the collective cosmic psyche slinking through the eternal void of the Great Beyond, awaiting reformation upon a higher plane of consciousness that's entirely free from the constraints of our belabored, bodily existence. Unfortunately, the good dreams wouldn't be the only ones to persist, as my shattered psyche is haunted many a night by those whom come to remind me that I'm expendable.

As I come near to the end of this project, I reflect upon another recent dream that reminds me just how deeply my poisoned psychological roots penetrate into the past. This, as you no doubt would concur, dear reader, is a theme of this work: that mental illness, from the garden variety depression and anxiety disorders to the most acute SPMI's, are so entangled with the traumas of our past as to be inextricably intertwined. Digging down and pulling at them and attempting to separate the threads of the root and predict which of those threads are most responsible for growing into the twisted tree above, the addled psyche and the mind whose thoughts they poison in turn, is almost impossible. Take myself. I'm still carrying around wounds from high school, from the period of life when so much of our personal identities are formed and our self-esteem is molded. Lisa was there. Beside her: two of the 'cool guys,' both named Matt, one of whom was a best friend growing up with whom I spent an inordinate amount of time, and most of it, I'd argue, leading *him*, both now living within me as persecutorial, oppressive presences. They seep into my dreams every so often. I was kind of on the periphery of the 'popular kids' back then, but not quite cool enough…

Without getting into too much detail, these popular kids always held court right in the middle of the nexus of activity during lunches and breaks at our then newly constructed *Maria Carrillo High School.* It was a set of tables covered by a pavilion adjacent to where the food made available for purchase was served. They claimed the space as their own, as a type of entitlement of popularity. I was still fairly close with a few of those amongst them whom hailed from my 'neck of the woods,' outside the area (we'd drive over the hills into Rincon Valley every day), and they gave me a type of cachet, I guess. Being the varsity QB also helped.

But it wasn't enough. My girlfriend *wasn't* popular, and I'd heard a few of them snickering about her and her weight. But even before then, when I'd tried to take my place in the pavilion, my freshman year, one of these two cool kids from the aforementioned dream, Matt Price, made it clear that I *wasn't* one of them. He said: "I guess we're going to have to put up with you for the next four years, huh Nick?" The other cool kid, Matt Etimos, had made his own series of condescending comments as our respective popularities peeled us away from one another after growing up and going to elementary school together. He was becoming a ladies man, and I'd begun to sink into a discomfort within myself that made confident interaction and self-projection near impossible. *Both* Matt's were ladies men, actually.

The same aforementioned high school girlfriend of mine had a crush on Matt Price, while the eventual wife of the other, the Matt I grew up with, gave me the distinct impression that she preferred me to him in the early years of their courtship, when I was still intermixing with that ever more cliquish 'cool group.' And there the two Matt's were, in my dream, within an academic setting, me attempting to overcome them in various ways; to prove that I was just as good as they were. As I write this I fantasize: you should've just walked right into the middle of the pavilion, sat wherever you wanted, and forced them to deal with you. "What the fuck are you going to do about it?," I say to my oppressors as a whole, addressing no one in particular.

So it is that my psyche is run by people other than myself. And perhaps *that's* the problem. My mind is not my own. Perhaps that's the persecutorial, poisoning power of the psyche in general: it's about the engulfing, often drowning perception of otherness and alienation, and of never quite

being accepted outside of ourselves, which comes to mean
the absence of self-acceptance, even as all true spiritual
insight transcends otherness, and the wisdom of self-love
means the purging of such self-alienating illusions, and all
of the delusions to which those illusions give birth. Maybe I
can only become myself when I take back the reins. Alas,
unlike the two Matt's, Lisa and Jess are free to hold them.

Jess especially will always lord over that liminal psychic
space. She'll always be the most engaging person I've
known. She just had this inimitable ability to weasel her
way into my heart, where she still nests. She'd talk with her
hands, with such joy and excitement, and with such
effusive reflections upon her past, that I was overtaken. It
was gradual; almost imperceptible at first. Then, before I
knew it, before I was aware of the ocean, I was awash,
simultaneously buoyed and drowning, light with heart and
heavy with longing. It was as if the waves that crashed
steadily into me over the course of our eighteen months
working together amounted to a tidal wave. Unable to
withstand the force, I was swept out to sea, and remain
there, marooned, powerless to paddle back into shore.

She was so real, so raw and vulnerable, so emotionally
electric, like a nerve stripped of its protective sheath. And I
was so needing of something real, so desperately wanting
of love, that there couldn't have been a more receptive
recipient. I think we needed one another in that way. She
needed someone to listen, and I needed to hear it. And my
absorbing it all, my being plugged all the way into that
conduit, to that live wire of delicately discharging emotions,
forever changed me. It also represents the great irony of
one who has written more than can ever be accounted for
having known truth *not* by mind, not by intellect and
analysis (for in such forms of truth there's always doubt),
but by having been the honored recipient of those cathartic
conductions, the truth of which, and the overwhelming love

they conjured, *there is no doubt*; not the slightest shred. I must also here admit her perfect pairing with Brady. That is: She's the live wire. The sheer emotive force I love. He's the insulation. Keeping it safe. So that it can thrive. So it can conduct its power to others without losing itself. *I get it.* But still, fuck that guy. He has direct access to the Oracle.

For emotions, it seems to me, are closer to the truth than any thought; to any assemblage of words. Emotions are more vital, direct experiences of a truth that words feebly attempt to circumscribe. A thing is a thing, and to analyze and ascribe qualities to it by our minds pales in comparison to the power of our hearts to experience that thing *directly*; an experience which, of course, I'm here giving verbal description, knowing full well that all this can ever be is a faint echo; a biased accounting of what words can never account for. What's sacred-most is never for me to *know*, only for me to *feel*. What think you the purpose of emotion, to but piggyback upon the mind? Fool are you, I say, with your framed degrees, less wise than a man who knows a single thing for certain in his heart. The learned scientist, hearing this, shakes his head in disdainful disbelief, superior to me in his knowledgeable ignorance. I mean, honestly, for someone who values his God-given mental capacity as much as I do, it pales in comparison to the fact that I just want to fucking feel something real; that I'm really just one big, constantly overwhelmed sensory organ that would trade any mental truth, the wispy ephemera of the overwrought intellect, for emotional exactitude *any* day, and twice on Sunday. If you feel something, you've been conquered, and to your conqueror are you thus connected.

And not just what I felt for her, what she evoked in me, but what she *became* to me as well. I like to say that I 'felt love' for my high school girlfriend, but that I *fell in love* with Jess. The first experience of my heart's attachment to a person was tepid by comparison to the typhoon Jess unleashed within me. Love has transmuting properties, able to morph what everyone else experiences as but a charming person, as a pal or family member or coworker, as just a colleague who walks into a work meeting and casually sits beside you as a 'friend,' into a primal force that radiates so much power into the core of your being, as if the substance of you is the only thing that reacts to that radiation, as if the particular properties of your heart were custom made to be transformed by it, that her simple presence makes it near impossible to focus on what the speaker is saying, their words fading into the oblivion of a mind that shrinks under the potency of the purest possible effusions of the heart.

I remember the smell of her when I hugged her that final time, after our last shift working together, when we left at 7:30 in the morning; when normally I'd be delirious from having been up all night, but this time I was wide awake, locked into and trying to subdue the sense of impending loss. She pretended like she was just going to walk away, to the other end of the parking lot where her car was parked, without any need for a goodbye. But she knew full well that my heart wouldn't allow it. "Not so fast," I said. She was wearing her backpack, the one she always had her laptop and schoolbooks in, so I couldn't wrap my arms all the way around her like I wanted to. But I buried my face in her curly brown hair. And I remember thinking that she smelled *perfect*. Like inimitable compatibility. Like somehow, in her natural scent, my heart recognized home.

Do you believe, dear reader, that it's possible to know one's innate compatibility with a potential mate by scent alone, or might you be inclined to dismiss this notion as part of my delusion? In that final embrace, the two recurrent elements of my recollection are: (1) I wish she hadn't been wearing that damn backpack of hers, so that I could've wrapped my arms around her fully, and embraced her in a manner better befitting my affection (2) Her natural scent, wafting from her wavy brown hair, contained something that drew me even deeper into her, even as I would've then thought that impossible. It was *animalistic*.

I don't know if she was giving off pheromones that matched my own desire, demonstrating the fact that a part of her abhorred a permanent separation as much as *all* of me did, or if her natural scent communicated a signal of the aforementioned innate compatibility, or both, but I do know that I'll never forget the experience of how much a scent can evoke. They do say that of the totality of our sensory capacity it's *scent* that's most strongly tied to memory, and that no part of our sensual being is more primal, more ancient, more intertwined with the so called 'reptilian brain,' than our olfactory capacity. From this single experience I have no room to doubt that any of that is true. And so, scent to heart, animal to angel, she's with me *always*, set beneath the surface of all that I survey.

11

MAID TO MODERN MAN

(Please note that this chapter was written whilst I was watching, and making connections between, the *Netflix* series *Maid* and my reflections upon Jess and the CRC. If you've yet to see the series, I recommend watching it *before* continuing herein, both because of the 'spoiler alerts' and you'll likely get more out of reading this chapter within the contextual advantage of having seen the series).

Watching the series *Maid* (Margaret Qualley is so damn cute!) has me beset by close parallels and severe contrasts. First off, the show's parallels with Jess's tales are impossible to ignore. The borderline abusive ex driving her from the relationship, the unstable mother (though in this case the instability is owing to undiagnosed bipolar disorder, rather than drug addiction, in the case of Jess's mother), the half-dozen high schools attended, the on again, off again homelessness (Jess spent much of her youth 'camping' under the care of her mother), the unhealthy relationships of the mother (when one is unstable, the best one tends to attract is instability, and, thus, co-dependency), even the pretty, curly brown hair.

The way her abusive ex controls and sabotages her in that series just reeks of what you told me of your ex, Jess. I'm screaming at the TV while watching certain scenes, like when he gives her car away after subtly denying her the ability to have her own cell phone, clear means to deny her independence and control her, sold to her as though motivated by something else. And I can't help but wonder: Am I ready to jump through the screen and fight the mother fucker because of you? Am I furious at her for falling back into these situations with him, and with her mother, because of you? Is my vicarious fury at watching portions of this series, of it resonating with such rage and invoking of such indignation, inseparable from my love for you?

Kudos to the creators, for regardless of *why* this is so, I don't think I've ever been more emotionally involved in a series. I so badly want to reach out to Jess at this very moment and ask her if she's seen this show. But I won't. After all this time she'd certainly respond in a detached manner, which would only bring up all those same wrenching, egotistically-demeaning emotions endured at having so much love and consideration coming from me, my own enormity, treated by her as though a minuscule intruding insect, swatted away like a bothersome fly.

The emotional and psychological abuse prevalent in *Maid* almost seems worse than physical abuse to me, as absurd as that may sound to you, dear reader. Physical abuse is somehow more honest, at least. The abuse in *Maid*, on the other hand, is diabolically devious in that *no mark is left*. Much like the 'you're mentally ill' gaslighting and fictional narrative sold by my housemates as discussed earlier, there's no clear form of defense because the abuse itself is continually said not to exist, even *as it's happening*, and even when the decimations are as devastating as can be.

There's no evidence or clear course of action with the authorities, or, in my case, with the apartment complex management company that doesn't care about right and wrong, only the ability to continue to profit off of us whilst reducing their liability, a bottom line easily sold to with the mental illness and 'he does concerning things' narrative of my amoral housemate, just as the 'he's the older harassing male of the innocent young female' narrative is easily sellable to a work manager, even when she was *at least* as responsible for our ongoing flirtations as I was, and actively sold false narratives (in a bookstore, ironically) via her constant gossiping with her colluding coven of witches, just as the CRC cared about blocking the true connection between its employees and residents as though it was a matter of moral principle, but was always *far* more about the profitability of control and liability mitigation. Such is the nature of abuse and immorality: it's naturally conducive to the propagandist narrative, always seeking to sell itself as something that it isn't, all so that the *true* culprits, the snakes represented by my horrible housemates, by the gossiping group of girls that targeted me at *Banned & Ignoble* after I ran afoul of the gossipmongering queen and her supervisor friend, and by the corporate leeches whom hatched the 'don't form inappropriate connections' CRC policy, all so that they could continue their egotistically-and-financially-profitable transgressions with impunity; so that abuse can be sold as 'concern,' per my housemate.

It's all like a steadily tightening invisible noose that's just as real as an actual one, slowly suffocating the life out of the victims rather than overtly snapping their neck, all the while the torturer and executioner gaslighting their casualty. And then, in the case of *Maid*, adding immense insult to injury, her own father implicitly endorses this devious abuse *after* pretending to want redemption for his own past abuses infused into her upbringing, and then has the ironic audacity to parade self-righteous Christianity over the scene, all witnessed by the next generations' helpless victim in the cycle. It's so agonizingly good *because* it's so common and systemic and easy to relate to, and makes me all the more lovingly proud of you at this moment for escaping your own formative form of it, Jess. I think I understand now. *Anything* for stability. Absolutely anything. As much as my ego hates it, he really was the best choice.

I can't tell who I'm angriest at. The abuser for being so small and feeling so powerless as to make his victim as small as he is? His almost certainly abusive parents for thrusting him into the insidious cycle, and likely their parents before him, and on down, ever deeper ingrained into the infected fiber of the family tree, until one of them finds the will to uproot themselves and those they love, like Jess, and replant themselves into lovingly-fertilized soil free from pestilence? Or the victim for feeling so small as to fail to find the strength to rise to her true size? Or the politician for feeling so small that he'd rather finance his own ego than recognize that he has the power to enlarge others with compassionate fiscal policies? Or myself, for being so wrapped up in my own belittled sense of self that it took this show for me to come to these epiphanies about the only woman that I've ever loved, and what motivates her, and why she's best positioned to show other survivors their true size by her example? *Anger...* is that a first step? And if so, towards what? Writing all this down, for one.

Or am I angriest at the psyche for telling the ego that it's small for needing help to extricate oneself from the cycle, no matter where, or whom, one is within it? Yes, *including* the abuser. As much as our fury wants only his suffering, if we *really* intend to break the cycle we have to go to the small source and not merely seek punishment, not merely inflict suffering and potentially turn him into an even smaller and more dangerous abuser as a result, but, honestly, as controversial as this may seem to some, *help him feel bigger*, by education, by opportunity, by improved health and treatment for alcoholism and addiction, by *any* means necessary to prevent the perpetuation of the abusive belittlement. For tininess is the core cause here. Lenny and James know what I mean, right, tough guys?

The protagonist's (Alex's) relationship with Regina, the "cunt," might be my favorite part of the series. It brought me to tears several times (yes, dear reader, I'm a total sap; I cry regularly while watching movies/shows, as only a true man can admit, right?). This is the case for many reasons, *especially* how Regina overcomes her pride and superciliousness, and even forgives Alex's missteps, and more than redeems herself by making a human connection with 'her maid,' not only recognizing her value across normally rigid socioeconomic boundaries, but becoming her salvation. Their relationship rings true, and speaks to the greatest hope of humanity: *the breaking of boundaries.*

"I need to do what's best for me" *sounds* selfish on the surface, but within the context of a story like *Maid*, it's the same as saying "I refuse to continue my victimhood, and to take any hope for a positive future away from myself and my future family, and to deny my potential to help others." Is it possible to feel closer to someone you loved, Jess, by reflection alone? By perspective and insightful reference?

One of the sorrows for someone like me personally, in reflecting upon Jess's past and the series *Maid*, is that we, those passionately predisposed towards bipolar disorder (under specific forms of concentrated stress that, thank God, I've only endured that one time), become collateral damage in this war against abusers. There were *many* times when I could see in Jess's gorgeous multicolored eyes, when I would say certain hyperbolic things that one might associate with delusion and instability, a buried terror rise to the surface and flash from those eyes, as though, in connection to her ex, I'd been transformed into a dangerous, wild animal in front of her. In this uncertain, risky world filled with dangers that those like her are more keenly aware of than most, because they're forced to be by the hammered-in lessons of their past, those disposed to flights of fancy and 'abnormal thoughts' and "moodiness," as she called it, the parts of me that I value the most, and which are inseparable from my romanticism and idealism and creativity, become automatically associated with an enemy that I'm *not*. I swear to God, dear reader, I'm simply not capable of doing the things that Jess's ex did to her, or that Alex's ex did to her in *Maid*. *Regardless* of upbringing or circumstance. And I'm not just saying that. By my nature and my development I'd *never* victimize someone that way.

I firmly believe I'm incapable of such abuse, even in a psychotic state. Even as an alcoholic or an addict. My heart and mind are too big. I'd hurt myself or flee before I turned against her, or anyone else for that matter, in such a dreadful manner. That said, I've felt the forces of evil attempt to invade, and know how the small and unstable are made into monsters. I just have a shield forged of heart and mind that prevents me from becoming one of them. It's *that* shield that we must help potential future abusers forge *before* those same forces of evil befall them, and change them into the beasts that they need not become.

I want to help people too, Jess, I really do. I always have. In fact, when I fantasize about 'making it big' as an author, my most prevalent imaginings are of passing along the proceeds to others, including, and perhaps especially, *you*; to, in reference to the subject of a previous chapter, making my means into a river flowing to, watering, connecting and fertilizing the lives of others, especially those that I love. And I loved you the most. The only difference between us is in *how* we've chosen to fight for others. We have different strategies, based upon our relative aptitudes. I'm meant to do it with my pen; with my ideas; with my voice. Your strategy is more specific, and more hands on, I think. We both ended up at the CRC at least partially because of that, right? Because of our massive hearts compelling us to actually fight for those whom the parasites eat alive? *How* we choose to fight is

the question. I've been told by a number of people either
"you should've been a lawyer" or "you should've been a
professor." And while I can see myself eventually
becoming the latter, for all of my writing naturally takes on
a didactic, philosophical quality, my natural response is: An
ideological writer is both lawyer *and* professor (assuming
he or she eventually comes to be read!), for they make
their case and teach their lessons *through* their writing.
And a lot of my writing is focused on unacknowledged
victims, those swept under the rug of normality, or those
whose suffering isn't treated because it doesn't qualify.

"Emotional abuse is abuse," Qualley's character tells her
mother. In the series, Alex is speaking of the guy she left,
but she just as well could've been addressing her mother
herself. And speaking of emotional abuse, any man that
does anything for a woman with strings attached, with the
expectation of a quo for their quid *excepting* a heart-based
spiritual reward, is not only *not* a gentleman, but, I would
argue, no man at all. The same goes for ladies, I'd say,
and for familial relationships. Alex's relationship with her
mother makes me think of Jess; has Jess and the stories
of her past written all over it, in fact. The discussions
between Jess and her mother about her upbringing were
ongoing, and the sad theme was a *constant* denial on
behalf of her mother that she'd ever done anything wrong.

Jess's mom died during the COVID epidemic, because it
turns out that decades of abusing crystal meth, on top of
alcohol and other drugs, no doubt, compromises your
immune system, thus making you particularly vulnerable to
any such viral attack. And if you read this Jess, please
don't hate me for thinking this, but I can't help but wonder
how much of the sorrow that you endured from her loss
was based upon that loss, and the fact that she wouldn't
be able to watch you grow into the woman you were
becoming when I knew you, or be able to watch her

granddaughter(s) grow up, and how much was based upon
the fact that her demise deprived you of the chance to
show her what a stable family looks like? How much of the
sense of loss is based upon being deprived of the chance
to show her what motherhood is *meant* to look like? By the
way, I remember your mom talking about how proud she
was of her "beautiful daughter," and her joy at seeing you
"so in love" in response to a couple of your *Facebook*
posts, years ago, when we were still working together and I
was able to view them without the agonizing sense of the
loss of a loved one which your image now tends to evoke.

Would you forgive me, Jess, for having another horrible
wonderment? I wonder if you feel relieved by her death,
like jettisoning a burdensome weight? Like you can let go
of being the parent to your parent, a burden that no child
should bear. And remembering how Brady spoke of her, of
his believing you were too easy on her, and that you
needed to take a hardline, absolute, 'you're not going to be
a part of my life until you're totally clean' stance, I wonder if
his relief might be even greater than yours? I'm not
suggesting you didn't lose something, or that you didn't
love her, or that Brady doesn't care about your pain, but I
understand the often contradictory, enigmatic nature of
emotion, and how intrinsically tied can be emotions that the
majority consider opposite from, and having nothing to do
with, one another. I, for example, often hated you *because*
I loved you so much; my pain related to you was intimately
tied to the heart-based pleasure that you gave me; the
ecstasy you represented to me was what provoked the
agony. Anyone whom has experienced anything similar to
what I did would surely admit the same, wouldn't they?

I may've mentioned this already, so please forgive me if
so, but I have this one recurring memory of Jess telling me
about one of her mother's drug-addicted mates, and how
he'd lock Jess in the closet as a kid when they went on

one of their drug binges, and how he and her mother would coerce and threaten her to keep quiet about what went on at home before sending Jess off to school, and how these abuses and domestic instabilities resulted in Jess developing an anxiety disorder as a kid, and never knowing when, or if, she was safe to speak her heart and mind. Perhaps that's why her emotions were so raw, and everything came spilling out of her when I knew her; when we were close; when I was her honored outlet. But why did I, at the beginning of this chapter, mention that the series *Maid* evokes not just close parallels, but severe contrasts?

Because I'm watching *Maid* in a multimillion-dollar home in which, as Alex passes out on screen from hunger, and as I recall all the conversations that Jess and I had about food insecurity amongst the impoverished and the exercise of seeing how far a budget can be stretched, I'm surrounded by more food than any single home should have (a *Rover* assignment); a home in which only two people live, and which it has nothing to do with having other people over; a home with multiple oversized fridge-freezer combos, the type that I can barely reach the top of, each of them absolutely *crammed* with food; so much that I can't fit my own food in them. That's *before* the pantries, stacked with every possible dry food, jars jammed from floor to ceiling.

One of the pantries is reserved exclusively for treats. And all that is before the mini-fridges with kombuchas and other specialty carbonated beverages, and the wine fridges, of course, and the closet dedicated to the dog treats. I'm not exaggerating when I say that the pup that I'm watching has two-*dozen* different types of treat bags for me to choose from. It all makes me think of how much more Jess likely appreciates the space she and her lucky fucker husband have earned for themselves than my current clients care about this sprawling home and all the acreage around it.

Another wealthy former client of mine, one of the thousands of moneyed transplants from California whose gentrification of the area so infuriates a certain aforementioned Bend demographic, lives in *Broken Top*. For those readers with no familiarity of the region, it's one of those posh, gated enclaves built around a PGA Tour level golf course and a luxury resort served by a rather extensive workforce of 'underclassmen;' of guest relations and landscape crews and the like. While my relationship with the owners was strong for some time, built around their interest in my writing, and my encouragement of her exploration of the art world, and his intellectualism, I eventually ran into such a strong distaste for their wastefulness and entitlement, and to her uncertainty as to whether to treat me like a friend or a servant, and to ongoing remarks pertaining to how they compared to, and were viewed by, their wealthy neighbors, that I felt compelled to leave their service. I've yet to meet anyone of wealth whom *hasn't* been patently corrupted by their absurd wherewithal, and whom doesn't think about themselves and others in ways that, to one as cued into it as I am, clearly evinces a sense of superiority mixed with, to me, a rather pathetic mentality akin to needing to 'keep up with the Joneses' and 'what will the neighbors think?'

You wouldn't believe the number of packages I signed for during their African safaris, collected into mountains of boxes stacked into their foyer whilst they were away. And how much *stuff* they have, spread across and sprinkled into and choking their passageways, bedrooms, side rooms and garage. And they use next to none of it, of course. They very rarely utilize half of their home, in fact, even as homelessness abounds in Bend. And the very way in which their belongings are collected and placed in that immense residence tells you all you need to know. *Carelessly*. With zero respect for it, much less for what such wherewithal could do for those whom, like me, they regard as their servants. It reminds me of how many people try to buy their satisfaction, concealing a deep sense of dissatisfaction that money can do nothing but give you the opportunity to explore the means to relieve, including her not knowing what to do with the time she has thanks to her husbands' enrichment of the household leading to her decision to 'become an artist.' And they're so used to being served by others, and to snapping their fingers and having anything that they want, that I honestly feel like their entitlement has molded their minds to regard those 'not in their class' as existing to serve them, and to consider the world of commodities to be their playthings, even as the vast majority would consider them *not* commodities, not trappings of class, but nearer to *needs*.

It's as though, to them, the 'free market' represents endless accoutrements of class that they're *owed* by their position relative to others, like those spoiled toddlers that have so many toys that they care next to nothing for any of them, and yet have no compunction in taking toys from the less privileged. I'm telling you, dear reader, from my experiences of the wealthy *alone*, before even getting into the systemic analysis of economics and finance and politics and the broader social ramifications, I know for absolute certain how much capitalism corrupts the minds of its one percent primary beneficiaries. *Their egos are infused with entitlement.* They can't even *think* in a way enabling true moral consideration. And I'm not saying they're inherently bad people. I'm saying their means have made them immoral people, entirely unbeknownst to them.

And I could see them wrestling with it. I could see vestiges of their humanity occasionally rising up and battling with their conditioned inhumanity. And, as a corollary, I'll never cease to wonder how much of the evil I see in people is a product of our innate corruptibility (not innate *evil*, that's a falsity, as explained elsewhere herein), and how much of it is an artificial corruptibility that's conditioned by capitalist society. That is, the system that programs us from birth invades and exacerbates our innate corruptibility to the point where it's impossible to know where one ends and the other begins. Alas, I have a strong instinctive sense that most of what people confuse with the ideas of 'innate evil' and 'human nature' are actually just side effects of capitalist corruption; of being indoctrinated by the Devil that few of us can clearly see. That Devil hides in what most people simply scan their eyes over unknowingly, like the fact that the monied have so much that what they have has little value, such that its *potential* value is mostly wasted.

It's reminiscent of my Quality of Life Economics theory (see *Cultural Cornerstones, Recarved*), specifically the concept of *quality of life utility value*, and how capitalism squanders the innate value of everything, including life itself; how the more one has, the less it adds to their existence, the less they appreciate it, the more that its potential value is lost considering that if it had been given to a family like Jess's in her youth, its inherent value would have gone from minimized to maximized. I recently wrote in my journal: *Those that have everything don't know the value of anything.* The silver lining in cases like Jess's, for those with the ability and determination to rise out of poverty, abuse and neglect: it makes them want, and value, and, arguably, *deserve* what they have all the more. It has the power to make fiercely determined creatures such as her; all pride and indomitable drive to create for themselves and those they love what they were denied growing up. By being raised with nothing, she values *everything*. She values life more than most because she *knows*, because it's embedded deeply into her psyche, that life is anything *but* guaranteed. Because she embodies the opposite of the line: *privilege is invisible to those whom possess it.* Perhaps the opposing line is: *privilege is paramount to those dispossessed of it.*

There's something so tragically triumphant about the seeming fact that the best mothers and wives, maybe even the best *people*, are produced by painful pasts inculcating in them the inability to take *anything* for granted, thus granting them a superior capacity to appreciate fuller lives more lived. I'll never forget the sense that Jess just seemed more *alive*, more emotionally raw and vulnerable, more passionately propelled, than anyone I'd ever known; that much of her beauty and endearment was wrapped up in a vulnerability inseparable from her painful past, arming her with a great resolve to fight to make her future bright.

This version of her, I imagine, is far more enchanting, at least to me, than would've been the hypothetical version of her raised in *this* sprawling, oversupplied house, where the dog eats better than Jess did growing up. Don't get me wrong, dogs are family members. I'm just saying... contrasts are revelatory. The brightness of light can only best be known and appreciated from the darkness. Just as the value of anything may only be known by the lives deprived of it, and that those swimming in it value it little.

As Thoreau said: "The price of anything is the amount of life you exchange for it." Within the aforementioned context of quality of life utility, this alludes to the hidden cost of life lost by those deprived of what others take for granted, and which adds little value to their own lives. Actually, to me it alludes to the hidden costs of unhealthy habits more than anything; to the fact that the *financial* cost of *any* unhealthy dependency is but the tip of the iceberg of total cost, a cost that includes reduced health, good feeling, capacity and quality of existence, as well as the reduced ability to hunt happiness. It's not just about amount, about quantity, about the dollar amount or the number of years lived or anything else quantifiable. More importantly in my eyes, it's about *quality*. And quality times quantity equals total. And, unfortunately for those of us forever on the wrong end of the capitalist equation, when it comes to economic activity this exchange is mostly made without any input from us.

Speaking of which, *Maid* also reminds me of the broken financial system surrounding those diagnosed with an SPMI. Just as Margaret Qualley's character, Alex, struggles against the absurdity of only being able to earn so much before having her benefits cut, placing her in a no-woman's land of barely being able to afford survival on her side, and working more only to make less and not survive on the other side, so too are those in institutions such as the CRC in their fight to position themselves for independent life forced to make such catch-22 decisions.

The residents were literally disincentivized from developing any type of professional progress, for, in so doing, they'd lose benefits, including access to food stamps, housing and insurance. There is, in other words, an absurd, oppressive middle ground for those trying to move from financial dependency to independence. And that's not even the worst break in the mental health system. Those who were strong and fortunate enough to earn their independence frequently found themselves in trouble, slipping in one way or another, facing various pressures, and yet were denied receiving the help that they needed because of their legal circumstances. Their independence came with the attached strings of lost support, such that the only way to receive that support was to be civilly committed and give up their independence, which, unlike what you've seen in movies, is much harder than it sounds.

If *any* argument could be made that they could even halfway take care of themselves and avoid being committed, including consistently feeding themselves from dumpsters and demonstrating strong homelessness skills (I'm not kidding you), they wouldn't qualify for commitment, and thus were denied what they needed in order to meet any standard that you might imagine constituted even an abysmally low quality of life for themselves. This literally means that the general population that PrimaCare serves has, when in their lows, when experiencing the trough set beneath their peaks, the recurrent incentive to escape this no-mans-land of dumpster-diving psychotic living by doing something extreme. That is, the mentally ill are very really incentivized to make some grand display of 'being a danger to themselves or others,' and thereby be civilly-committed, which is often but the slightest step away from committing a crime whilst psychotic and thereafter being found NGI, or Not Guilty Except for Insanity, and, either way, being institutionalized and put back 'in the system.'

And an NGI verdict is not *at all* how it's depicted in movies, and how most imagine it. I think most people believe it means they're found not guilty and set free. *Nope.* Quite the opposite, in fact. It means they take a type of plea deal in which they have to accept the stigma and reduced opportunity for life of receiving an SPMI diagnosis *in exchange for the maximum possible sentence*, the only difference being that they serve that sentence in mental health facilities like the CRC instead of the prison system.

And advocacy for these poor folks sucks. Most of them aren't made aware of what became apparent to me early on at the CRC, that it's very often better *not* to take this deal, and thus avoid both the permanent record diagnosis and the longest possible sentence. To force people in these horrible, unstable positions to face such irrevocably life-decimating decisions is unconscionable enough (yes, they *do* have to demonstrate that they're mentally competent enough to make the decision first, but it's a low bar there), and that's *after* they escape no man/woman's land in the first place. Cain was one of the few residents that I met who actually understood what he was facing after being placed at the CRC, when he was contemplating his unfolding adjudication; the only resident, in fact, who chose *not* to take the NGI plea and *not* to take his 'meds.'

In hindsight it may've been better had he actually been *less* mentally competent, as horrible as that is to say, for it may've ended up saving two young lives at the hands of the future "Prophet of Death," as the papers in Bend would come to call him. All told, the systems in our country simply need to be better financed, so a greater social safety net can be constructed, and a greater number of advocates and protectors can be enlisted, and more opportunity for gaining the means of independence can be successfully pursued by *all* disadvantaged individuals. And, frankly, when you vote tax-dodging Republican over social-support Democrat (generally speaking), you're choosing to support all sorts of miseries, including those in the backstories of everyone from Alex in *Maid* to Jess to the CRC's residents.

One of the duties of PrimaCare counselors, and all mental healthcare counselors working in such institutions, I would imagine, is to write monthly progress reports on those patients assigned to them. Wait, let's go back a bit… The woman most responsible for recommending me to Annabelle and bringing me into the CRC was a tall blonde named Allie. That was when I was in caregiving, and bearing witness to even more suffering than I would see at the CRC, somehow; people in the most horrendously debilitated positions that couldn't wipe themselves on the toilet, or get out of bed without the assistance of elaborate crane systems, or, in one of my assignments, poop without colostomy bags. I hesitate to get into my impression of the caregiving racket in Bend, where aging retirees make up a large contingent of the population, where there are a *ton* of residential care homes, and where the primary form of employment in town (well, now a city, really) is the disturbingly profitable medical field in general. Tour Neff Road and Medical Center Drive and see for yourself. And as with all 'economic opportunities,' the leeches spring up in response, surrounding and sucking as much money from the situation as possible. Hence companies such as the unscrupulous one that I worked for, *Home Care Group*.

First they sit you down, give you some bullshit about how they wish they could offer you better pay, but, you know, they just have *so* many costs and limitations forced upon them. That was the *first* lie that their indoctrinator (sorry, their 'recruiter') told me. Then they have you sign their waivers, put you in front of a computer, have you take some mildly informative online courses that everyone just tries to skip through as quickly as possible, asking anyone around them who's already taken them what the answers are so that they don't have to think and can get through them without actually learning anything (this is the primary means of ongoing education within PrimaCare as well), then they usher you and those like you into their conference room to learn a few last-second hands-on lessons with their expert nurse, whom just happens to be highly attractive and thus naturally able to put us guys in unquestioning line, and she rushes through some things, like how to apply a catheter, but *not*, you know, on an *actual* person, then they send you off, entirely unqualified and without any experience whatsoever, to look after people with horrible, rapidly-declining health conditions.

People with multiple sclerosis, with Lyme's Disease, with permanent paralysis; people that *should* be receiving care from that one hot nurse, the only qualified caregiver that they actually have on staff in the entire corporation, but whom can't afford her, so they're stuck with me, the guy making minimum wage, with *zero* medical experience, who becomes queasy upon facing anything to do with such matters; with *anything* involving bodily fluids, organs, tissue etc. I learned a great many things at that job, including that leeches loom large in the 'caring' lie, and the absolute travesty represented by the fact that those that're worst off, whom need the most help, are some of the biggest targets for crooked cost-cutting corporatism. How much the quality of life of those suffering its lowest possible degree would be improved if the PrimaCare's and Home Care Groups of the world were forced by better regulation, or by any God damn true measure of humanity, to sacrifice some of their leeching profits for better training, opportunity, advancement and retention of their best employees! Later I'd learn that the founder of *Home Care Group* was being indicted by the federal government for various forms of fraud and embezzlement. They should've been thereafter legally forced to be renamed *Crooks Pretending to Care.*

But of all the suffering and concealed crookery that I observed on that job, in many ways the worst of my life (and *God* is that saying something), you know what my greatest takeaway was? The lesson that most oft-repeated in my mind in reflecting upon those poor persons whose pain I was there to alleviate, and whose dependence upon others I was there to facilitate? *Don't tell yourself you can't do something, because, faced with the necessity of it, you WILL do it.* For, again, I've always been squeamish around blood, guts, bodily fluids and the like. I can't stand hospitals for this, and for other reasons (palaces of pestilence for profit). So I'd always told myself that I wanted nothing to do with anything even related to bodily fluids. Keep that shit on the inside (sometimes literally)! That was my attitude. But when you're forced to get a job by financial circumstance, and forced to wipe away the excrement, or apply the catheter, or place a bandage over the leaking wound, *you do it.* Because you have to. They say necessity is the mother of invention. When faced with

the necessity of doing what before seemed impossible, I
invented possibility. As would you. It's a matter of *need*.

Anyway, one of my clients at *Crooks Pretending to Care*
was a guy named Louis, a long-term resident at the CRC.
Amongst his many issues, including, of course, his Severe
and Persistent Mental Illness, was lung cancer (again,
cigarettes are like gold at the CRC, and are a foremost
crutch against stress amongst those in such facilities). And
because the CRC isn't well enough staffed to deliver their
residents to other facilities, like cancer treatment centers
(sufficient staff cuts into the bottom line, darn it), I was
called in to fill the gap. Allie was my point of contact at the
CRC for signing Louis in and out, and she quickly
recognized my capacity, I think, for 'handling the mentally
ill.' She saw, I believe, that I was more patient and
understanding than most, and not easily frightened, and
not narrowly judgmental; essential qualities in the mental
health field, even as few of its professionals *actually*
embody them. So after a few of these sessions she started
inviting me through the locked doors into the Day Room to
interact with Louis, amongst the other residents, a place
that would soon become all too familiar, and, unbeknownst
to me at the time, the very space in which I would meet the
only woman whom I've ever fallen in love with… *Jess*.

So Allie got to know me, and recommended me, and
eventually convinced me to apply to work at the CRC, and
the rest, as they say, is history. She also got to like me on
a personal level, I believe, considering the fact that it
wasn't long after that that she started opening up to me on
things involving her husband, like the fact that he would
take on challenges, like learning to rock climb, not out of
any legitimate desire to learn the activity, or better himself,
but because he was insecure and constantly demonstrated
a need to prove to himself, and to her, that he was a man.

Anyway, shortly after being hired by the CRC they figured out that I can write. And because Allie and another counselor reported to Annabelle that they felt overwhelmed by their workload, and because, frankly, my time cost the corporation *far* less than theirs did, I was put in charge of writing their resident progress reports. To this day I can't help but wonder if that constituted fraud, considering said reports were meant to come from a qualified mental health counselor. The task entailed reading all the reports written about the relevant resident that had been filed by Allie and all the Recovery Specialists and Peer Report Specialists for the month, then writing a summation document on their 'progress.' Actually, now that I think of it, it started with just Allie, but soon came to include a couple of her peers.

The whole thing reminds me of the cliché 'the work of a lawyer at the cost of the paralegal.' Why pay the lawyer when you can have the same work completed, at the same level of quality, at, what, a tenth of the cost of the 'qualified' person? Examine the cascading chain of events close enough, dear reader, and you'll soon find that cost-cutting comes to cost *far* more than what's accounted for within the short-sighted, conventional business, 'minimum-bid, maximize the bottom line' mentality of the corporations that depend upon those cost-cuts to impress and continue funneling, with ever growing disparity and unsustainability, endless amounts of cash and resources to the tiny fraction of the global population representing major stakeholders. Like all injustices, the innocent pay the price of the guilty.

Personally, the jobs that I've had in Bend, including in caregiving and mental health, and having known and been intimately tied to the sufferings of disabled, disintegrating bodies and overburdened, traumatized minds, and hearing tales of everyone from Jess to *Maid*, has granted me invaluable perspective upon my own suffering, and invaluable insight into how immeasurably fortunate I am, and bound me to the belief that there's no legitimate excuse to capitulate to any seeming pain and hardship I myself endure, even as they seem gargantuan at times.

And while I'm on the subject of improving these overlapping systems meant to serve the disadvantaged: streamline the damn things and get the disadvantaged better supported and educated advocates, and don't force people in already horrendous positions of mind-splitting pressure to jump through so many hoops for fuckssakes! Maybe what we need is more Republicans' family members to face such horrors. Maybe *then* there'd be more support. Of course, the 'representatives of the people' tend to be hand-picked and corruptively groomed by the plutocrats from the already wealthy and ambitious who're amenable to following the plutocratic protocol hiding behind the pretense of democracy. So ask yourself, dear reader, who, and what, do 'our representatives' really represent? And how does the legal purchase of political fealty contradict the term 'democracy?' Already being in the wealthy insider clubs, they can just buy those family members advantages that CRC residents will never see…

And speaking of *Maid* and my Quality of Life Economics theory, spend even a quarter of what the ultra-wealthy avoid paying in taxes thanks to lobbying the IRS for more loopholes, or a quarter of what the Bush's of the world have us paying Cheney's 'defense contractors' (the Department of Defense, since the end of WW2, is more accurately the Department of Offense and Global Imperial Coercion), or a quarter of what we've spent bailing them out of their reckless financial abuses, on *any* of the series' alluded to needs of the disadvantaged that *they* create through their exploitative business practices, and see an immeasurable increase in American quality of life. And if you're amongst the legion of duped Republicans that elects these douchebag Bush's and Raegan's and Trumps to office in the gross disservice of the whole of humanity, and that actually believes the absurd argument that it's the *poor* that're entitled in this country, you know nothing of true entitlement, and you need to spend some time with the wealthiest US families. They're entitled to *everything*.

Wealth most certainly corrupts, and I know from considerable experience (especially being the best friend of the only son of a man worth $750 million while at UCSB, a troubled young man whom I called 'Prince Henry' in my first book, *Infinite of One*) that part of that corruption includes believing that they're better than those outside their 'class.' This friend once took CD's and video games out of my brother's room while staying with us at our 'middle class home (I use single quotation marks here to allude to the fact that *true* class has nothing to do with wealth)' in NorCal, *without asking*, of course, leaving a $100 bill on his desk. I found out about it whilst driving the two of us back to UCSB, when I noticed my brother's handwriting on the CD that my entitled friend popped into the CD player of my 1998 Honda Civic; yes, the one painted in "Cyclone Blue Metallic." My wealthy friend's family had at *least* a half-dozen homes, by the way, one of which was in the hills of the exclusive enclave of Carpentaria near Santa Barbara, complete with Infinity Pool, putting green and a TV that doubled as a mirror above the mantle, purchased entirely for the purpose of his mother and father having a place to stay whilst visiting him.

Five of these properties were seldom used, even as, in parallel with my overprivileged *Rover* clients here in Bend, homelessness abounded in the less fortunate surrounding areas. One of these many properties was a ranch in Montana consisting of *over 1,000 acres.* I'll never forget his mother bragging about how many scenes from *A River Runs Through It* were filmed on that property during my visit, and then having the audacity to critique my cleaning of their dishes as "using too much water during a water shortage." Ironically, it was *she*, my friend's mother, who had her nose turned up the entire time I was around them. Her husband, my friend's father, the man whom, as the CFO of a succession of major tech companies, had actually 'earned' the money ('earning' is more like 'extracting' in my mind; another invisible term from the playbook of capitalistic propaganda), was *far* more 'down to Earth' than his wife, as though having worked so hard for that ungodly degree of wealth humbled him in a way that her presumptions of being born better never could. I remember he said he only slept four hours a night, and he did always seem a little tired to me. My sense was that he was doing everything possible to assuage his guilt at his preposterous degree of wherewithal, efforts which included his political predilections and charitable benevolence, but that this effort, like all our efforts to conceal what the deepest part of ourselves has always known, was futile.

That family lived and breathed entitlement on a level that *no* impoverished, welfare-seeking family has *ever* known, including Jess's. I'm talking thousand dollar meals at golf clubs where the annual membership fee alone is half a million dollars. But they weren't monsters, not by a long shot. Not *consciously*, at least. Yet monsters tend to hide their monstrosities, painting them over with emblems of respectability. This friend eventually unfriended me on *Facebook*, I'd assume because of my many 'rants against the rich.' I mean, what's wrong with my research and contemplations leading to the conclusion that his orbit included "plundering plutocratic parasites," "lowly marauding maggots" and "lionized, overlording leeches?"

And when it comes to criminology in general, and, to a large extent, mental illness as well, I would here reemphasize my longstanding belief that it's all about *pressure and powerlessness.* Put sufficient stress upon a person and make their circumstances such that they feel small and disempowered, and, relative to their personal qualities, they *will* break on some level, pushed towards criminality and/or mental illness. As a directly connected note, from both extensive personal experience and observation of others, I know that the more we're tired, dependent, stressed, ego-driven and wealth and power obsessed, and the more devoid we are of the protective qualities of discipline, knowledge and wisdom, the more likely we are to both give into and be the cause of evil.

That is, metaphorically speaking, the more subject we are to mental and bodily limitation and pressure and egotistical pursuit, the more we feel like isolated individuals, the less fortified we are, the greater our servitude to Satan and our potentiation of evil, whilst the freer we are from these limitations, constraints and pressures, the more we feel our oneness with everyone and everything that we're thereby compelled to keep from harm, including ourselves, the closer we are to Spirit, the greater our potentiation of good. And I'm sorry to say that nothing says modern America like weariness, dependency, stress and wealth and status obsession. No amount of church-going changes the basis from which every form of evil springs. And pressure and powerlessness are mostly *socioeconomic* in their causality.

That is, everything systemic in this horrendously lopsided nation of immense and every growing disparity in all wherewithal, in all things of value, including not just possession and wealth but power, opportunity, rights and privileges, is what *creates* the pressure and powerlessness most responsible for creating criminals, abusers and psychotic breaks. *This* is why positively-freeing socialistic principles are an *absolute necessity* in balancing out the negative freedoms enjoyed in capitalist societies such as ours, and why the white collar plutocratic criminals at the top of the socioeconomic pyramid whom systemically and systematically prey upon those at the bottom are directly responsible for the suffering of characters like Alex in *Maid*, and Jess in the past. They're just protected by degrees of separation, by buffers, by deniability and propaganda and the fact that "possession is five-sixths of the law" that they lobby to write; by all the powers and controls that create the vast majority of criminals *not* of the white collar class.

Yes, blue collar and shirtless criminals *still* must be held responsible for failing to forge their aforementioned shields and thereby victimizing the innocent, but if we *really* want to stop these horrible cycles of abuse and criminality we *must* understand and treat the *causes*, not just the symptoms. We must go 'food is medicine' on causality, so to speak, not just 'conceal with chemicals for the profit of the exploiting few at the incalculable cost of the many.' That is, concealing symptoms is good for profitability and *can* help mitigate suffering to some degree, but the value of the symptomatic approach pales in comparison to the causal approach; to rooting-out and treating the *causes* of the suffering. It's like comparing the treatment of an infected root system, the effort to rid the tree of its plague, to the conventional medicine method of spray-treating the endlessly sprouting, diseased leaves of the poisoned tree.

Ultimately, we must treat the socioeconomic causes that're most responsible for creating the pressures mounting into the abusiveness and potential for criminality. We must target the concealed *systemic* causes buried beneath our conditioned 'normality,' pairing this with the treatment of the more personal factors, like the predilection for addiction, the sense of being disempowered and feeling small, etc., that, as the systemic snowballs with the personal, lead to the emergence of abuse and criminality. We must, in other words, if we *really* want to be effective, hit culprits like Alex's abusive boyfriend and Jess's quietly abusive mother and *her* drug-addicted boyfriends, from both the top down *and* the bottom up simultaneously. Following the aforementioned metaphor, we must treat both the diseased roots *and* protect the vulnerable, individual leaves of the infected American Tree, else endlessly more rot will result, and more Alex's and Jess's and SPMI's and poorly supported victims will wilt away.

-

A great many of you, dear readers, would be advised to put this book down now. For anything heretofore written which you disagreed with can likely at least be forgiven by most of you, whereas I'm compelled to end this book with what some of you will consider unforgivable, and which has the potential to turn you from an ally into an adversary; especially a certain type of person I know all too well, and that has already inflicted irreparable damage upon me. Were I controlled by the 'market is God' dictate of most, I'd exclude the following, final chapter. Alas, I must have the courage of my convictions. Otherwise, what am I but one of Thoreau's "most men lead lives of quiet desperation?"

In the modern age, one in which most people fall into either the right-wing Christian values camp or the largely pretentiously progressive 'woke' movement bandwagon band of bullies, Thoreau's line may be more accurately translated as: Most pretend men are *led* through lives of desperate, silent obedience. And I would rather be hated by you then be like the so many cowards that I've seen capitulate to the self-righteous bullies on *both* sides of the political spectrum, thereby selling progress for popularity.

12

INDIGNATION & LAMENTATION

The more that we take heed of the false, the more that we betray the truth. Thus it is that my fealty may never be purchased by popular opinion, and that my loyalty must always lie with universal principles over any one person or group of people, including myself. All of those obstinately identifying with and supporting any group in exclusion of all others embodies prejudice in betrayal of truth and justice. Based upon this, the life of the moral philosopher is about the FILTER; about sifting out the falsities of individualized, egotistic, biased perspective and interest so as to arrive at the truth, revealed through its relevance to EVERYONE.

As it is with most false forms of knowledge in contradiction of the philosophical axiom that separation is an illusion, and contradicting the scientific control of information through classification, *emotions aren't separate.* Care to know a secret, dear reader? One that will sound cliché at first? *It's all love.* Love and hate are considered to be absolutely separated, opposing forces. But the truth is that, like all emotion, hate is intrinsically tied to love. That is, hate is the threatening of something or someone that's loved; a recognition and revulsion of someone or something doing harm to that which is loved, even when that something is principle, reason, justice, honor etc.

(hello Lenny). And that's just the *first* chip off the block. Sorrow is the loss of love (hello Jess). Envy is the recognition of the possession by others of something or someone loved, often compelling an egotistic comparison (hello Brady). Wrath is the attacking impulse towards the hated (hello *Banned & Ignoble*). And so on, throughout the gamut of emotion. All of it built atop love, the evocation of God, and often confused by and convoluted with the ego.

Relative separation from love is the same as relative separation from God, and defines the movement towards less pure emotions; emotions that pain us relative to their separation from love, the core, source emotion that I think of as the evocation of God. Relative separation is also at the heart of egotism. That is, our sense of separation from the One that's the essence of everything, God, or Spirit, or the Big Self, the invulnerable, infinite core of being, and all of Its manifested finite forms, is what creates the sentient sense of a vulnerable, individualized 'self.' As mentioned elsewhere in this book, this is also what potentiates evil, as the Original Sin: our *belief* in our separation from God (something that's actually not possible, only believable), promoted by the prevalent modern ideologies and theologies of science, religion, materialism and realism. So it is that every emotion that we experience is relative to the separation from God, and the way in which that separate self, or ego, becomes intertwined with every emotion. This split from the pure emotional base to its intertwining with the egotistic self creates a type of emotional dichotomy.

I mentioned this concept in relation to the emotion of pride already; that I've long been aware that there are two forms of pride, one of love, one of ego. When I tell Jess I'm proud of the woman she's become, that's love. When I tell her that her pride prevented her from knowing and loving me in return, that's mostly ego; both mine *and* hers. So it is that this relative emotional purity and impurity may be tied to every conflict afflicting humanity. And when you become aware of the innerworkings of the world, that awareness is based upon threats imposed upon what one loves that the unaware don't possess. This is the secret basis of many of the classifications commonly confused with pessimism.

As mentioned earlier, most people seem to miss the fact that indignation and cynicism actually come from a place of *love*. Most dictionaries even conflate cynicism with pessimism ("cynic" is the top synonym for "pessimist" on *dictionary.com*), missing the fact that cynicism is simply being aware of what motivates people, which then motivates the ethic to protect people from unjust motivations, which is inseparable from progressivism. If the 'cynic' didn't care about people, if he/she *wasn't* coming from a place of love, he/she wouldn't be unsettled by injustice and false forms of understanding, and wouldn't be compelled to act on behalf of those thereby victimized.

Keen perception is undervalued, even *negatively* valued, by majoritarian, bourgeois society for the simple reason that the major stakeholders of corporate and conservative America whom crafted and perpetuate that mainstream, consumerist, classist culture benefit too much from the poor perception of the vast majority that support that culture, wittingly or unwittingly. Thus, those of the rarest, keenest perception are not only unheeded, and have a hard time finding those of similar mindset, but are often condemned, as the fruits of perception (including understanding, wisdom and spiritual insight) all imperil profitability by making their possessors disinclined towards, even rebellious of, the orthodox organizations and methods motivating mainstream culture. So it is that awareness becomes the enemy, and those that have it must be vilified in turn, so that the conditioned, uncritical majority reflexively stands against them before they even open their mouths or take even the slightest of actions.

This, in turn, makes the heroes the villains in the majority mind. The majority is literally trained to think the way they do, the propaganda so pervasive and deeply ingrained in the American mind that most don't even know it's there.

In this way do we see that the way in which most people understand fundamental concepts has been adulterated by the ruling conservative paradigms of the world. Rooting out falsities in conventional definitions and their adulteration of prevailing modes of understanding has long been a philosophical undertaking of mine. It wasn't even something that I *sought* to undertake, but, like most of my thought, was a natural extension of inspection. Does it surprise you, dear reader, that *1984* propaganda is built right into the dictionary? That your mental programming is so insidiously ingrained into your indoctrination that the very words with which you *think* are tainted? That 'history is written by the conquerors' extends *far* beyond history books, and has, in fact, corrupted every mode of human learning and knowledge, from the university to the supposedly 'objective' definitions which we daily enlist?

What invariably occurs amongst the few true philosophers in the world such as myself, and something I find in reading Huxley as well, is that we end up naturally digging down into the misconceptions and misleading connotations underlying the common misunderstanding of words and ideas. In the process we end up developing our own paradigms, our own frameworks for understanding and thinking about the aforementioned words and ideas; our own 'paradigm shifts,' as it were; how we'd, if sufficiently read and empowered, shift the conventional paradigms.

This, in turn, makes it difficult for us to communicate with others, because we're literally thinking about things differently than others, within constructs that the common mind wouldn't even recognize, as though those constructs contain alien beings belonging to some other reality, when, in actuality, they contain what we regard as something far closer to the truth, far closer to home, than do the conventional paradigms in which people are conditioned to think by the overlords whom have always dictated the paradigms of 'reality.' Thus is the philosopher confronted with a war of tyranny over the mind, and does he/she strive to shift the discussion in the hopes of freeing as many minds as possible. But the war against indoctrination is exceedingly hard fought, for so deeply entrenched are its mind-structuring effects that those structures tend to be closed-off to anything outside of them. I've reformulated so much of the ideological, theological and theoretical realms in my own head and writing, constructing my own base theories for many social and metaphysical systems along the way, that I often have to remind myself that others won't be able to understand me until I'm willing and able to redefine things for them first, to restructure their set, as it were, assuming that they're even able to entertain a restructuring, which most people aren't, of course, and so stay trapped in the traditional structure, the truth barred from entering. When forced to remain locked within any traditional structure, where false ethics are sold as if they're the *only* ethics, constructing good is constrained.

Assuming that we're *not* permitted to alter conventional 'free market economics,' for example, the first law of economic ethics is this: *Your use of your purchasing power dictates your morality*. When you pay for a product or service, just as when you vote for a politician, you give your own personal stamp of approval to every practice and policy represented by said product, service or politician. Reading this means supporting me, dear reader, and everything my writing represents, which, as an ideologue, is *far* more than most represent, I believe. Buying a product supports everything that went into that product. That's economic, ethical and causal law, whether you agree or not, frankly. For if everyone stops buying a product it cannot be supplied, including tortured animals.

Purchasing a CAFO animal or 'farmed fish' means perpetuating CAFOs and the 'farming' of something that should never be associated with a farm. It's a living, feeling being. It suffers as no farmed produce can. That's *neurology*. 'Farmed fish' is just another propagandist term. It's disturbingly revealing how much propaganda there is in the 'free market,' in fact. How 'free' is a consumer that's perpetually having to fight off lies and manipulatively misleading terms in order to 'freely' make his or her choice? I think that between my books and my journals I've commented on a good fifty terms at least by now; terms manufactured to mislead ignorant, gullible consumers as to the true provenance and nature of products and services.

I could write an entire book on that subject alone. Maybe I will someday (add it to the seemingly endless and ever-growing list of planned projects!). And it should make you wonder *why* propaganda is so prevalent in conditioning consumers said to be 'free,' and to wonder, then, at the definition of 'freedom.' I won't get into it here as I have in other books, but let's just say it's a more complicated term than the simple-minded flag-waving Trumpers will ever understand, and that the type of freedom promulgated by conservatives is a very limited form of the term, sold as if the only form simply because it benefits plutocrats (look up the difference between positive and negative freedom).

Oft have I reflected upon how much better and more moral the market would be were it driven by the minority of slim, discerning customers such as myself, rather than the SAD, gluttonous, indiscriminately, ignorantly-consuming obese customers, with those like me constituting but a tiny 'niche' segment. How much different *Banned & Ignoble* would look inside. How the superhero flicks would be the niche market, and how most films *Netflix* would classify with

words like 'thoughtful, cerebral, brooding, introspective'
and the like. How much more regulation of the everyday
evils painted all over the food and drug industries there'd
be, and how much different those industries would look.

It goes on and on, leading to one of many connected
questions: Did we create the market, or did the market
create us. *Both*, of course. Care for another philosophical
axiom? When people are debating the cause, or causes, of
something, asking one another 'is it this, or that, or maybe
this?,' the answer is almost always *all of the above*. All is
connected, and cause is almost always manifold. Thus, it's
a safe bet to answer such questions with what sounds like
a cop out, but is nevertheless true: 'I think it's everything.'
Every form of conditioning and misleading the consumer
constitutes the blind, ravenous, reckless American market.

Righteous anger over injustice (i.e. indignation), and
awareness of motivation, especially ego and greed, (i.e.
cynicism), converge into *progressivism*, which is motivated
by the drive to protect what and whom the progressive
loves from various forms of injustice. Meanwhile the
readily-moldable have been conditioned to see these
terms, these natural extensions of morality, conviction and
awareness, as certain *negatives*. What they *actually* are, in
borrowing a mathematical principle, are negatives *of*
negatives producing *positives*. Alas, in the conventional
wisdom honed by conservative values created to protect
the private interests of the wealthy and powerful of Church,
State and aristocracy (the provenance of conservatism, in
case you were unaware), *indignation* and *cynicism* are
commonly regarded as 'being negative;' much as idealists
are considered fairy-tale dreamers in reinforcement of
'science is God' realism, and philosophers are made to
appear pretentious denizens of the Ivory Tower producing
nothing of relevance to real life (when the best philosophy
is of near *universal* value to life), and conspiracy theories

are conflated with the quacks whom give the art of seeing connections a bad name. In actuality, conspiring to consolidate wealth and power are *endemic* to capitalism.

As alluded to by the line "if you're not outraged, you're not paying attention," awareness and indignation are commensurate qualities of mind. It's that simple. And I stew in a *ton* of indignation on a regular basis; so much so that I'm driven from society into my redwood writers' retreat continually just to maintain some semblance of sanity. The plutocrats that rule the world don't *want* you to doubt, for the same reason that they want you to conflate socialism with Stalin and other tyrants that've historically coopted the economic philosophy (successfully concealing the fact that Bernie Sanders is the only true leader amongst anyone even *nearing* popular politics), and for the same reason that the Church doesn't want you to doubt: it undermines their power; their capacity to slate their greed. *That's all.*

The rest of their rhetoric, and most conservative values, are simply a smoke screen to hide that *one* salient fact; that *one* evil-inducing motive: *to maintain unhindered extraction*. And I haven't even gotten to political correctness or religiosity yet… What I'm implying, dear reader, is that indignation and lamentation are natural byproducts of an even *semi*-awareness of the governing forces of the world as realized by an idealistic, progressive, 'spiritual but not religious' philosopher. And while those realizations place me at odds with a great many of you, maybe even the majority of you, that doesn't make them incorrect, and only makes writing about them all the more necessary. The pertinent question for me at this juncture is whether or not this book will fail the marketing test for the same reason as my other books have: *it's contemplative.*

If I could only convey the depths of my dismay at writing something like *Old Blood*, a book bursting with insights, edifications and allusions, replete with allegory and metaphor and mysticism and mythology, only to have it reduced to three out of five stars by a popular critic 'serving the market' who lamented the fact that what I see as its greatest value, its aforementioned density of advantageous qualities, she saw as a *disadvantage*, because it overwhelms the readers whom it "lectures," and thereby draws them away from the characters and a story that "doesn't flow." Does everything worth reading have to fit some prefabricated mold? Can a reader not go outside their comfort zone, and read a philosophical fantasy novel that edifies as much as it entertains? Can a critic not offer nourishment in their curations as well as the easy-read candy that the majority of readers reach for? Why can't the story serve the ideas? Why can't the candy be wrapped around the medicine, the fiction serving the substance? Must we writers be wind-up dolls dancing for our dinners?

Why is it that my work standing incalculable standard deviations from the norm equates with its deviance from critical approval? I ask this rhetorically, of course, for the answer is clear: The *vast* majority of critics serve the market above all, for being a bridge between the literature and the contented consumer is how they gain the reputation that may be translated into money and egotistic gratification. *Very* few critics are willing to stick their necks out based upon anything like conviction or belief in the edification offered by a book, *especially* when that branded stamp of approval is pressed upon the work of an unknown author behind whose stature they cannot hide. *Kirkus Reviews* liked *Old Blood*, even as they hedged their bets by *not* giving it their vaunted star, thus doing their part to doom it to the dustbin of countless books selling but a handful of copies, mostly to friends and family, even as, from personal experience, friends and family are, depressingly, just as impossible to sell to as everyone else.

No, it has to be loud and pointedly-targeted to a known buyer. It has to be, in reference to the film *American Fiction* (watched whilst editing this book), *Johnny Walker Red*, not *Johnny Walker Blue*. It has to place the moral, philosophical writer with something nourishing to offer in the morally-compromising position of catering to what the common consumer wants to ingest, even if it's entirely false, and ultimately contributes to the blocking or reversal of progress. It has to reinforce their preexisting beliefs and 'values,' no matter how misguided. "White people think they want the truth," it's said in the aforementioned film. "They don't. They just want to be absolved." Need I make the obvious correction? Fine… This remark is applicable to people *generally*, regardless of race, creed or anything else (the relativity of truth and justice are usually the same as the relativity of their applicability). It's a version of the universally-prevalent 'confirmation bias,' and a testament to the tragedy of bias being a market behemoth. Thus is the modern merchant made from the perfectly molded market, even as outliers such as myself try to sell to and shift it whilst somehow still serving what matters most.

Great Merchant

How to pierce the modern din? The raspy voices need to know. Plowed by which horse may the hoarse have golden seeds to sow? Planted upon the airwaves, as chains of media's social slave? Must we give it every part of us, until there's nothing left to save? Or may we both retain and gain, and by the transaction grow? To my neglect and poverty great merchant, please your greatest secret show.

Put another way, have you any sense of what it's like, dear reader, to pour your heart and mind into something, all the while feeling as though you're constructing a grand edifice endowed with every empowerment of your existence, just to have it trodden under the calloused heel of commercialism entirely unnoticed, the carelessly consuming beast crushing it underfoot like a child's *Lego* castle whilst striding towards prefabricated structures adorned with every cheap tin bell and five cent whistle that their banal builders can string them up with? Or to ask every 'friend' and family member to read your work and have *no one* do so, the mere fact that you're proposing that they read an *actual book*, rather than some trite blurb by Taylor Swift (nothing against her, only suggesting that perhaps people should be guided by philosophers more than pop stars), or some popular, mindless meme, akin to asking them to go to the dentist and have a molar pulled?

Speaking from heaps of disheartening personal experience, I've endured endless reminders that 'friends' and 'family' are largely meaningless terms; that they're little more than associations and bloodlines borne by familiarity and obligation. For what is a friend or family member to a writer when they can't be bothered to read even a page of your work? When they're so self-consumed by their daily lives that not even the most supreme of solicitations, not even the heights of eloquent entreaty, can compel them to bend an ear in your direction? This, dear reader, is but another, painful reminder of why I'm all about *quality over quantity*. Give me *one* cousin that consumes my work with relish, and wants to discuss it over a bottle of wine. Give me *one* friend who proves his or her amity by asking me *one* informed question about *one* of my theories. Give me *one* woman, like Jess, that drops her guard enough for me to truly know her. Keep all those keeping me at bay.

They're not just unworthy of me, but unworthy of the terms *friend*, *family*, *lover*. Give me, dear reader, the bridge that actually spans the gap that the unfeeling world forces between us, else bother not to build its pretense, and burn all those already pretending to stand across the chasm whose span is the measurement of our unhappiness. The attempt to become a professional writer taught me just how wide that chasm is. Can you conceive of such a chasm?

Or is it but a special misery reserved for the *vast* majority of contemporary creators in a society whose entire purpose has been reduced to *Jerry McGuire's* "Show me the money!," where anything *not* made for a pre-molded market, anything of substance, anything challenging the mind, anything requiring of the intellect, anything outside the realm of immediate, witless gratification, is ground to dust by this monstrous, obese customer, the colossus of consumerism, and swept out to sea to settle, forever unknown, unseen, to founder on the ocean floor, slowly oxidizing its way into a worthless relic once thought a treasure by the fool who, once living above, shipwrecked into the cliffs of commoditization borne by the unrelenting, extracting tide bearing all modern motive and productive energy, his life forever left unsung, his fools' gold clutched in hand, his bones fated to disintegrate and settle upon it? And so the attrition of existence grinds towards entropy as I shout into the void in order to avoid giving in to despair.

Aspiring authors of the modern age are those whom drown in a sea of unread pages awaiting their rescuing readers.

In my experience only the best critics, the cream of the critical crop, as it were, are willing and able to meet the author where he or she is. The vast majority attempt to force the author to come to them; try to force him or her into their own prefabricated boxes, similar to how anyone of any considerable religious zealotry attempts to force anything spiritual into the narrow confines of their particular religious paradigm. This is the mistake of religion in general: the artificial attempt to stuff the all-encompassing Spirit into narrow confines in which it will *never* fit (see *God Isn't Religious*). I've never well fit into prefabricated boxes; into roles and positions, identities and categories that always unnaturally constrain the whole of who I truly am. Yes, I'm sure that this is true for everyone to various degrees; alas, for me the degree is extreme, reflecting my inability, or refusal, to reduce myself in order to 'fit in.'

It seems to me that not fitting some mold of expectation is a *downgrade* to most critics, critics whom believe that they're serving the reading public by showing them which books align with their expectations, whereas I'd prefer to think that a certain rare type of critic seeks and rewards *unexpected* books. Books that defy the mold, that wriggle free from it, that go beyond it, that force themselves upon the unsuspecting reader, that upend the paradigm, that disappoint the dominant perspective so as to shed light upon the unknown, an unknown rich in meaning, allusion and invaluable lesson that common expectations and molds belie the power and beauty of. Please, oh Lord, find me *those* critics! The few critics unconcerned with marketing to the glut, and only concerned with curating for the sake of curing conventionality and bringing clarity to the most vexingly common conundrums. The rare few who serve challenge and improvement over comfort and empty propriety. I know, I know, then they'd be *unpopular* critics, and, like me, wouldn't be serving the market, and so would fade into the oblivion of not being in great demand. Thus the irony of the unread writer needing the unpopular critic.

There's a reason my work is never well received by those who're overly comfortable with the boxes in which they've set themselves, and not just because I disagree with them. Conservative Christians, the self-righteously 'woke' looking for their next 'cancellation,' the idealist-bashing 'realist;' it's near impossible for such self-identified individuals to review an open seeker accurately, one who, respectively, knows of God, or Spirit, as being beyond the ability to be boxed, who isn't afraid to speak his mind on matters that violate the consensus when his own principles and convictions compel him to, who knows that the 'reality' of the 'realist' isn't *really* the only reality, and that, more often than not, they simply lack the courage, morality and imagination of the idealist that isn't buying that they're 'just being realistic.' My own *reality*, after all, is counter to theirs, and in ways that they'd have you believe will *never* be real.

How can a mind narrowed by a succession of constricting categorizations appreciate an open mind that defies those categorizations? It's impossible for my writing *not* to offend such people. And though I'm told I need to 'play nice' and employ the politics requisite of successful salesmanship, I find that I'm only able to employ so much fakeness before being sickened by it, and thus find it near impossible to write for the glut of the market that tosses anything unusual, or that violates the secretly unwise conventional wisdom, into the trash, knowing full well that the legion of 'serving the market' critics at their back will do the same, giving them a reassuring pat on their back in the process.

Must a critic be a coddler of commonality in order for their critiques to be considered valuable? What are they then but extensions of the reflexive, artificial form of consumerism? And is there a difference between the coddler and the servant of commerce, between giving a reader what they expect and what's valuable, between the equivalency of expectation and value? And, if not, what does this say about the state of the literary market, and society at large? A state in which Emerson is rarely read whilst the unoriginal is read with relish. How much is it costing the world when we'll only consider walking the well-paved paths in exclusion of the rocky climbs leading us to the forever unknown pinnacles of ourselves? And, in consolidating the lost value of my own writing with those of similarly forsaken value, is the obvious marketability of a book, a total obedience to the almighty dollar, not a sign of humanity's steady erosion? An erosion hidden beneath the appearance of an 'advancement' concealing our demise?

This book shall fit the same un-moldable mold, no doubt. I'm in the early stages of writing it (even though this portion ended up better fitting the back of the book), and I'm already wondering at its categorization, Oscar Wilde ringing in my ears: "To define is to limit." Let's see... It's more non-fiction than fiction, far more memoir, theory and social critique than novel, yet my memories are imperfect, and it's inevitable that I'll fill gaps with inventions I believe relevant to the real people thereby depicted. So how shall I define it? For the critics and the market are anything *but* prepared to honor Wilde's praise of the indefinable higher truth of all things; of the fact that all the best things defy categorization; of the fact that language is built to put things in their place for the sake of the reader and listener, and yet this place is ultimately misleading in its suggestion of an absolute qualification that doesn't *actually* exist.

Or might this work be best categorized as a philosophical exposition, as all of my work ends up being to various degrees, due to my nature? And why is this quality automatically considered to be a *detraction* of the work? Why is the combination of manga and fiction fifty percent of *Banned & Ignoble*, whilst the ennobling philosophy section is one percent? Why does the Bible, and 'Christian Literature,' have its own section when those *not* constrained by its traditionalist confines, and thus far better positioned to pursue spiritual truths that can *never* be constrained, the 'spiritual but not religious' like me, get one part of one shelf at the back of the store, adjacent to the books on the occult? Surely this is more an indictment of modern America and its quick-fix, uneducated, well-trained, obese consumerism that it is of me. For, while it was the nature of the memoir that incited this work, especially my ceaseless memories of Jess and need to cathartically purge them, it's a *philosopher* that writes it.

Thus is 'waxing philosophical' not only *my* signature, but the secret signature of all that, and all of those, most worth reading. So take your pick of categories, dear reader. Whatever makes you most comfortable. For though I'd encourage you to strive to see Wilde's point, and place me at the unplaceable point of non-categorization, you certainly picked up this book because something about its appearance identified you as a part of its 'target audience,' or because someone of cachet rubber-stamped and categorized it to your liking. Not that I blame you. We're all seeking our needles in the haystack; our one transcendent drop within the sea. I'm no different. Like everything else that I write, there's no admonishment herein that is *personally* targeted, but always universal in target, including, and especially, an admonishment of *myself*.

So please accept that all philosophers are ideologically tangential. That is, though we may *begin* by writing about people or events, it's the *ideas* connected to those people and events which draw us in, and must be commented upon, by our very purpose, and perpetually pursuant of an ever elusive peace of mind. I reference here that quote from Eleanor Roosevelt that so resonates with me, and so impugns popularity in modern America: "Small minds discuss people, average minds discuss events, great minds discuss ideas." In fact, with enough of a natural philosophical disposition one begins to subconsciously make a mental map of so many interlinked ideas that tangential thought is itself natural to one's thought processes, and one is thus constantly forced to pull up on the reins to stay on the expected track for the comfort of everyone else, or else quite easily and naturally shall we travel within that mapped terrain from the propriety of the

Midwestern farm of conventional thought to the furthest, most esoteric reaches of the Siberian jungle, so to speak.

So, what, you may wonder, dear reader, have I learned by so long being caught in the wringer of commercialism that seems to dry out my lifeforce more and more with every passing day? Aside from the strategies of selling oneself, of which there are so many that one must hire an expert as soon as resources permit, if he/she wishes continued success in 'maximizing their commoditization,' I've arrived at concluding principles such as this: *When you put yourself into the world, do it without expectation, only with intrepid fearlessness, full-hearted hope and blind belief.*

Or, as an answer to the inquiries of my own recent poem, *Great Merchant*, and in a nod to the revelations shared by many a great writer and thinker, including Oscar Wilde, on the fact that all truth, at its root, has a paradoxical nature, and that success for the spiritual in the world of commercialism requires possessing a type of mental duality: *Be selfless whilst glorifying self. Build the iconic-most of icons upon the slightness of a shadow.* That is, 'branding' is the way to financial success in the world of the modern creator, but the pursuit of enlightened relief from the ego is the way to spiritual revelation. Thus I build my own brand of 'I'm more worth reading than everyone else' egotism, a form of self-idolatry, whilst being aware of the antithesis of idolatry as the ground beneath my feet: Spirit. Just as I seek love whilst attempting not to be egotistically harmed, I seek to be known as a writer even as I despise self-promotion, seeing it as a 'necessary evil' of modernity. Success in modernity requires projecting a certain type of expected, popular image whilst inwardly warring with heart.

I remember a period in which the unrequited pain I felt around Jess was particularly severe, and I was called into a staff meeting, and Jess came in and sat next to me just before Annabelle launched into a speech about the ideal workplace environment. Focusing was impossible. "Wait!," my innermost self objected, "I'm supposed to sit here, pretending to care about practicalities and efficiencies, about workplace policies and procedures, when the storm-bearer sits right next to me, the typhoon battering my shores and eroding every ounce of self-possession that I pretend to possess, that so breaks me down into the fundamental sediments upon which every ounce of my self-conception sits that I may well sink into this sofa… that I may spill into this seat like the contents of some shattered, overturned hourglass for whom the purpose of time is now known to be but providing the most remote possibility of being sucked up by that storm, swept out to sea and delivered beyond the horizon of everyday reality?"

At the same time that term, 'everyday reality,' takes on an entirely new meaning in the presence of that all-consuming storm. I wrote a poem years ago, while we were still working together and I was futilely attempting to keep that storm bottled-up, so to speak, that spoke of how everything that I disdained about the common life and its obligations and expectations now seemed more than tolerable, even agreeable, if they be paired with her power to transform it all into magic. I listed everything about the conventional pursuits and responsibilities and expectations I'm resistant to (I'm what you might call a 'counter-culturalist'), finishing the poem with: *And then I met you. Now I'm in for it all.*

All those odious obligations and expectations are meant to produce the wherewithal that sustains life, and when that life is loveless, and when one possesses the convictions which I possess which serve to put me at odds with the overruling systems of the world, those obligations and expectations are set at odds with one's purpose. But if they were to serve a life with *her*, again the transmutations of the heart would render them in a renewed, resplendent light. Sometimes I think that this is *why* I've been denied love (or perhaps subconsciously denied it to myself), for if such a passion as I felt for her were actually *sated*, if the love were requited, then all its pent up potency currently sublimated into my progressive writings would be released, and any value that such work may prove to possess would be swept away. I am, of course, not the first thinker to contemplate the connection between a grander possible fate and higher calling and the quelling pacification produced by actually having what we most want. Keats comes to mind. It's the idea that the muse motivates the artists' greatest work, holding the compelling carrot in front of him or her, but to bite from the carrot effectively turns it to rot, that which we most want only possessing power by continuing to want it, and be denied. One dying of thirst best knows the value of water whilst left unquenched, but comes to think little of it, to take it for granted, when he or she is able to drink from the well at will. An artists' greatest work is thus born not by slating, but by *perpetuating* thirst. It's reminiscent of the excellent film *Whiplash*, and the fired disciplinarian instructor asserting: "There are no two words in the English language more harmful than *good job*."

You do the creator, and all whom shall come to value their work, a disfavor by recognizing that value, and delivering them their desires. It makes one wonder if the 'starving artist' is secretly made to starve not only because the work generally doesn't pay well until they reach a certain rare level of popular recognition and reputation, and because they compete with so many others in 'oversaturated markets,' but because God, and their own subconscious, knows that starvation sustains a state of hungering need that yields their best work? Does the work of an artist decline with success? Is the need for success the strongest force in their motivation? I would be lying, as would any creator, if I pretended like I wasn't fighting for recognition; not just for the sake of my ego, but for the fact that I can't pour myself into my work indefinitely without support. I'll be forced to take another path just to survive.

Yet, these aren't the primary factors in my picking up the pen, as they may be for those whom, like the many fake philosophers whom I've interacted with, merely want to *believe* they're writers, because 'philosopher' and 'writer' connote qualities they wish ascribed to their egos. No, I'll always write. It's not even second nature; it's *first nature*. It's therapy, the release of pressure, the ability to maintain relative sanity by recording any thought of potential value to myself and posterity which, from the moment I think it to the moment I record it, gnaws at me. I'd also add that, if writing isn't similarly compelled for you, if it's not your natural release, therapy and self-expression, if it's just how you want to see yourself, as 'a writer,' then you may want to stick with journaling, because the fight for professional recognition is bloody as hell. I would never attempt to dissuade *anyone* from writing, for I know its value; you develop yourself through it; you develop your mind, find your beliefs, cultivate your creativity and convictions and explore anything and everything worthy of exploring.

So even when you do it only for yourself, without need of popular recognition, or even the need for others to read it, writing is *always* well worth the effort. At the same time, I have a strong sense that the truest writers *make no effort*, but simply unfold themselves upon the page by the natural impelling force that Taoists call 'wu-wei,' or 'effortless action,' an extension of 'The Way,' a following of the most innate, unifying spiritual force within oneself acting through one's gifted nature. Aptitude and calling are so interwoven, in fact, that one's natural abilities and inclinations likely *are* the call. And when it comes to seeking 'success' as a writer (even though the word 'success' *should* mean far more than simply successfully selling yourself) there's immense audacity in taking up the pen in the pursuit of popular recognition when you consider the statistics, such as the fact that so few people read in anything more than blips on their phones, or for their work, that most regard reading as an archaic nuisance, and that, for the rest, for those whom even approach the definition 'reader,' *over a million new books are published annually in the U.S. alone.* And that was *before* AI started flooding that sea with fake 'writers' who do little more than enter a basic premise into a program to produce their 'writing,' which I refuse to do. But how much more brazen can I then be, submitting my own droplets into that sea whilst essentially asserting that they're greater than the others, that they're better to sail upon than the others, and that you should sail across them before all of the rest, including the works of 'established authors' with major followings offering their work through teams of promoters tipping the tide better than I ever will?

In case you're interested, allow a veteran of the self-publishing world to give you some insight into one of the most oversaturated, competitive markets on the planet: It's *easy* to self-publish a book. It's *difficult* to self-publish a quality book. It's *extremely difficult* to self-publish a quality book that well enough fits a target audience to be considered readily commoditized; that is, to self-publish a book that can actually sell beyond your personal sphere. It's *next to impossible* to self-publish a quality book that you successfully promote to its target audience well enough that it actually becomes a well-selling commodity. Very few climb this ladder high enough to actually 'reach the black' when it comes to the financials of their work; to being profitably compensated for all the time and monetary investment. It's not enough to be a good writer. It's not enough to know marketing. You have to have tons of *both*. So, yes, *please* write, but only attempt recognition from others *after* you've determined that *you're* determined.

Most of my work naturally falls into the 'slim target audience' category, critics scratching their head as to its proper placement, forever undervaluing my work because it doesn't fit the mold of this or that market. "I had a hard time placing and rating this book," is something that I've heard from many critics on many projects now. And I'd venture to say the truest work is thus, for it wasn't written *for* a market, but for *itself*; for the truth that it seeks; the substance that it naturally conveys. It is, in other words, not a fabricated product made for a specific buyer, as all artists are pushed by financial necessity to produce, but a courageous act of self-affirmation and commercial defiance nevertheless hoping that a market exists; that it'll be seen for the value it naturally possesses, even as most critics continue to reduce it because of that defiance, asserting that 'markets exist for a reason.' *To be filled.* And filled they are, so much so that marketing seems not just paramount, but comes to seem to be almost everything, as though the writing itself is of far less consequence than shortening the bridge between the books and the buyers. At this point, for me, it's honestly like: Determine the marketing plan *first*, then write the book to fit *it*. Be a capitalist first, a creator second, the dictate goes. All else, everything compelling writers of philosophical value and conviction, be damned to the fires consuming mountains of the best, unread books.

"He pushed open the door and was under the dome, breathing the faint, acrid smell of books," says Huxley in *Eyeless in Gaza*, written almost a century ago, when the issue was in its infancy, a mole hill compared to the modern, dwarfing mountain. "Millions of books. And all those hundreds of thousands of authors, century after century - each convinced he was right, convinced that he knew the essential secret, convinced that he could convince the rest of the world by putting it down in black and white. When in fact, of course, the only people anyone ever convinced were the ones that nature and circumstances had actually or potentially convinced already." And that, Aldous, only *if* they have the promotional budget to find their way into those few hands to begin with, or if that convincing is contained within a book that's easily bound to a market, and has hopped through all the hoops of the traditional publishing game, and been given the stamp of approval by the marketing-mandated modern critic, and sold to a conventional publishing house awarding the author a few cents on every dollar that the market may yield for their work. I must confess that I feel what Huxley refers to with everything that I write; that I'm mainlining some essential secret of the universe put to the page. Thus far I've found not a soul willing to confirm it. Well, maybe a *few* souls, but those gals may not be interested in my penning such axioms as much as they're interested in other parts of me, or are driven by having picked up the scent of my potential.

And yet, despite the difficulties and injustices and swamp of indifference that a modern writer determined to develop his own brand has to wade through to even come *near* to being read, I continue to have a powerful sense of romanticism when it comes to books. And I'm not talking about e-books, as much as I'm now, after writing a dozen ink-and-paper books, pushed to offer that as an option. No, I mean *the printed page*. It's tactile; olfactory; sensual (meaning priming the senses, not meaning sexual). The look and smell and feel of the book. I smell and unconsciously crinkle the pages as I read, a habit I developed in my youth, and an extension of my tactile enjoyment. And something that my family still kids me about. And that's *before* getting to what books *contain*: an unlimited evocation of the imagination and exercise of the intellect and exploration of any and every idea and culture. The very reason I became a writer: Because literature can, and does, go anywhere, entirely without restriction. Thus, when I see a well-stocked bookcase, a strong sense comes over me, like a romantic pirate surveying his potential plunder. You want the same feeling to apply to your own work, others considering it a treasure. Laying claim to 'being a writer' is a lot like unrequited love, in fact.

You say it, you know it, you feel it in your bones, the pen is like an inseparable appendage, the writers' callous on your middle finger having been an embodied testament to who you are since you wrote silly stories about knights running into burning castles to save the maiden as a fifth grader is Mrs. Ott's class at *San Miguel Elementary School*, where your mother taught (she still lives down the road, in a house rebuilt after the fire that consumed the whole former hood), and made sure you were to receive no special treatment. Still, like unrequited love, like the forever unimpressed, doubting psyche, you can't bring yourself to believe it or say it with a straight face, without looking away, embarrassed, until the love is returned to you. Until both the muse represented by the readership and the cold critics say: *You're a writer, Nick. You deserve to be read.*

And speaking of the overlap between unrequited love and unrequited writing, they converged in the subject muse herself. For I once made the mistake of asking Jess to read my work. Her verbatim response: "Sorry, I have a life." Being her friend on *Goodreads*, every book she posts as 'currently reading' or 'read' therein feels like an insult. All she would give me upon her departure is the cliché: "I hope to see your book in *B&I* someday." It turns out that "I care about you" means: "You could write a thousand books and I'd never even consider reaching for one of them." And it's definitely not just her. The rabbit runs when it knows it's being chased. Every potential reader that I approach with a book walks in the opposite direction. What is this absurd psychological malice of knowing that when one is wanted, for *anything*, that one is pushed in the opposite direction? It's as if the only way to hear 'yes' is to tell them *no*. The psyche seems to me a form of magnetism. It repels the same charge, and attracts the opposite. When one is interested, interest is spurned; when disinterested, interest mounts and comes your direction. Maybe I should be walking around wearing a sign that proclaims: "You can't read this book!" whilst holding onto it for dear life, as if it's the only copy; as if I'm holding and guarding the only Bible.

Sadly, this psychological law applies to *all* attraction, including the *people* we want, and Jess responded to that law as much as anyone I've ever known. The worst thing that a person can be is needy, *especially* a man, to whom the old paradigms of ceaseless self-assurance and self-reliance still cling. And yet what the ego most wants is to be needed. So, in order to attract those whom we feel we need we have to convince them that we *don't* need them. We have to threaten, even insult, and definitely provoke an insecurity of, their egos. Hence the game. Conceal the ardency of the desire until the last possible moment, until that desirability is undeniably mirrored, and the risk of its explicit revelation is minimized. Else the fish wriggles off the hook, assuming it was attracted to the lure in the first place, or ever tempted to strike at the dangled deception. Jess and I played this game perpetually. Granted, I lost 100% of the time, but I was nevertheless aware that we were *both* playing it all the time; that however lopsided the attraction was, it definitely wasn't *one*-sided. The attraction was mutual, the sense of need wasn't. So she always won.

Ironically Jess actually came into *Banned & Ignoble* once, some years later, during my brief, brutalizing stint there, to buy some books to read to her infant. I didn't even recognize her under her COVID mask. Surprised to see me, she just laughed. That's when I knew it was her. 'Oh shit!,' I thought, my heart leaping into my throat. I gave her a hug, checked her out whilst teasing her a little, and she was gone, like the echo of the haunting phantom that she is. I wonder if she looks for me when she goes in, unaware of my issue of falling for or otherwise getting involved with coworkers continuing there, leading to the unveiling of the absolute power disparity in such cases of Me-Too-era America demanding the head of even innocent men misled by the manipulative young woman playing the ingenue, taking out her anger, insecurities and frustrations by selling a popular fiction, applying a cover concealing the truth. How ironic is it that the manager of a bookstore bought the cover without any consideration of the *true* story therein?

Speaking of judging books by the cover in rendering judgment, would you like to know the fucked up thing about sales, dear reader? *It's the cover that matters most.* This book has a better chance of selling because the title grabs you. Very few give a fuck what's inside. *Substance seldom sells, the cover, the sexual allure, THAT'S what sells.* "Everyone sees what you appear to be," Machiavelli reminds us, "very few see what you are."

Most people just want to put the book with the clever title on their mantle and say: *Yes, I own that.* Like they thereby own and are a part of the cleverness themselves. Like that entitles them to be presumed to have absorbed something that they're actually clueless about. As a dogsitter who spends his time roving between big houses, I can tell you what they all have in common: *bookshelves filled with unread books.* The well-stocked bookshelf is like an egotistical accoutrement, demonstrating to visitors that one is educated, and to oneself that one intends to be so. A vain showing of knowing wrapped around a shamefully ignorant core. *Banned & Ignoble* makes *far* more money off of the insecure ego than it does off of any earnest quest for knowledge, or even the quest for literary entertainment; far more off of the FOMO connected to 'must read' books rubber-stamped by the intelligentsia and the gatekeepers of what I call The Gilded Tower than off of the intent to actually read and attempt to understand the meaning of books. The fact that you're actually reading this makes you one of the few intent on replacing the bookshelf façade with informed substance; on trading the outer appearance of the well-read for someone who has actually, well, *read.*

Alas, this book, like most of my work, is likely *far* too fearless of political correctness to even be *considered* for critical approval, at least by the glut of rubber-stampers. Nothing that fails to make it past the Political Correctness Police penetrates the tower, both because the stamp-holders fear that to do so will mean the stamp will be taken from them, and because they serve not the betterment of the minds of the people, the erasure of false facades and the edified replacement of misleading 'truth,' but *sales.* Show me the critic or company in the literary game that serves anything else first and foremost, anyone or anything that doesn't immediately kowtow to a maximization of sales volume, bowing to the God of Greed that *actually* runs America and most of the modern world, and I'll show you a person or an operation that's doomed to fail, along, most likely, with the writer and work stamped by compromising conviction; at least until they learn to bow down as well. And this same bowing to the almighty dollar is what turns gorgeous girls into demonic misandrists, for in connection to worshipping wealth, it's the *cover* that brings the 'buyer.'

Sadly, and in admission that women are defending themselves against a definite indecency, all most men give a fuck about is fucking their cover. The problem is that when someone like me comes along and even looks at them they bite my fucking head off. I don't blame them. Not really. For they haven't the ability to discern between me and the hounding dog pack drooling over and defecating on every pretty cover. So my interest, yes, in the damn cover, but in *so* much more, in every page of the best books, is reflexively conflated with the dog that just wants to bend them over, get off and run down the road after the next bitch (female dog, that is). Thus the gorgeous woman becomes both understandably on the endlessly defensive alert against the sexually rabid dog *and* entitled to all the advantages granted by her cover. She strikes unthinkingly whilst lapping up all the attention. But be assured that it won't be *me* that comes calling, both because I understand how tired she is of being dogged, and because I know how she treats those whom she assumes are part of that pack.

I'm honestly too terrified to go anywhere near any more of the overly-empowered, he said, SHE said types anymore. I honestly suffer from a relatively low-grade form of PTSD in relation to my experiences with certain young women, and assume that any interest that I show them, even when coming from the heart with the best of intentions, can only lead to their using it against me in some duplicitous manner; *especially* after what was done to me at *Banned & Ignoble*, where my boss was too much of a coward pressed under the thumb of the deceitful perpetrators to see through their fraudulent witch hunt and protect me. Linda *attempted* the same at the CRC, although within an entirely different context, but Annabelle was too smart and conscientious to allow her to be successful, even though I eventually ended up leaving the CRC of my own volition because I was tired of being persecuted by Linda, and spied on by her minions. Riddle me this: If the environment turns the best guy that walks through the door, the most compassionate, considerate, contemplative of its employees, into the scapegoat, and attempts to destroy him with the ugliest, most malicious of misleading accusations, what does that say about the environment?

What does that say about corporate policy and politics, and how corporate bodies award and wield their power? What does that say about the prevailing narratives that modern America sells, ironically, in this instance, sold by the foremost seller of narratives in the nation? I'll *forever* carry around the un-scarring trauma telling of what a colluding coven of grotesquely gossiping girls can do. And what the critic and editor did to me afterward, when I submitted *Holier Than Thou*, naively believing that a foremost player in the literary review world would treat my work with more than the politically correct contempt that they ended up employing, deepening a wound that just won't heal. Yes, pretend men do horrible things to women. But women do equally horrible things to men, because they know that their word carries more weight than his, especially when they're friends with the supervisor that seeks out and invents evidence for the power trip of it all, and has the boss quaking like a coward under her thumb.

They sold him a book with a cover concealing its content. It doesn't matter that I was right. It doesn't matter that I sent that same boss ten pages detailing how and why it all happened. All that matters is the book-by-the-cover principle: *their story was the better sell to the liability-averse corporation that runs roughshod over all that's best.* And though they did irreparable damage, they'll lose in the end, for truth and honor are of an eternal substance that *cannot* be burned at the stake, alive even in the modern 'man' whom sacrifices masculinity to political correctness.

The official story seldom represents the truth. In all probability the official story is a reflection of the narrative that those possessing the power to tell it *want* that story to reflect. *Banned & Ignoble* is, like all major organizations entirely beholden to the immense profits that might be lost should the façade wear away and the concealed rot be revealed, in the *propaganda business*. As is PrimaCare, of course, selling a proprietary mental health treatment system that sounds good to the public and investors and anyone giving it a glance, that is sold as an advancement of the mental healthcare paradigm, but which its 'Recovery Specialists' don't know, let alone practice. And that's *before* getting to the fact that a major contingent of the Recovery Specialists, especially those whom have been there the longest, and especially those of a traditionalist, right-wing bent, were anything *but* those facilitating true recovery, much less being 'specialists' in the process.

All of which is to say that one of the foremost evils is that profit dictates the size and power of the megaphone. It's difficult, and some would say impossible, for justice, good and truth to prevail when injustice, evil and propaganda are so much better financed. Which, of course, points to the fact that pure, laissez faire capitalism inevitably produces evil, especially when socialistic virtues aren't permitted to rein in that evil, and are sold as evil themselves, as part of the conservative political playbook. The only defense is for the few like me who see such truth to find the courage to fight to make our discernment more common, ever aware that the true monsters will act to make *us* look like the monsters to those lacking such discernment. The defense requires that the few become the many, through this book and all those like it, even when the monsters look like the pig-tailed ingenues.

Reading Huxley's *Eyeless in Gaza*, written in the mid-1930's, a character is taken with a young woman for her rare ability to completely 'lose herself' in song and dance, commenting: "Most girls were so damned avaricious and calculating. They'd only lose half their heads and carefully keep the other half to play the outraged virgin with. Mean little bitches!" *So damn true*. And far truer still in today's sociopolitical climate. A lot of them work for a certain major book retailer, in my extremely limited experience. No wonder such women tend not to review my work well.

I'm too aware of inconvenient truths, and not afraid enough to keep them to myself like most 'men.' The same 'men,' mind you, who're coerced into speaking falsehoods like "you're the only woman I'm attracted to" and "I haven't even looked at another woman since we got married," like bees biologically bursting with the need to pollinate endless fields of flowers but forced by an enslaving queen to say they're only drawn to *one*. I'm not saying monogamy is inherently wrong, I'm saying it's inherently wrong for its enforcers to coerce their mates into pretending their biology is nonexistent in order to avoid punishment. And yet speaking of this indignation makes *me* the enemy.

My disdain for self-righteous political correctness is too easily conflated in the high-and-mighty, holier-than-thou, misandrist mind with ungentlemanliness, and even misogyny, even as their own neutered boyfriends and husbands are thinking and feeling all the same things I'm here expressing, but will only say them *after* the break-up. So to hell with you if you're compelled to label me a misogynist. Although, honestly, if you've reached this point in the book, and read of the depth and array of emotion that I've felt for Jess, and are *still* compelled to come to a 'he's a misogynist' conclusion, *you're* the problem. You're inseparable from the false, self-righteous set of 'justice seekers' whom spurred so much of my writing, especially the past few years. Frankly, if you don't know the difference between a man possessing a 'love-hate' relationship with women and *misogyny*, that's *your* common, popularly-conditioned prejudice, not mine. For the fact is that I love women as much as any person on this entire planet. Which is inseparable from the problem.

For I must here confess that the beautiful young woman became my enemy as much because of my resentment over the extraordinary power that she has over me as for the consistent transgressions that she's committed against me, and the deficiencies of character she demonstrates. The resentment over this power disparity is also, of course, why Jess seemed to be my enemy almost as often as she embodied my muse. So it is that, like anyone, I find power disparities oppressive, while also detesting self-righteous political correctness and its bullying and emasculation of men-turned-belittled-boys as much as I adore women, and refuse to be one of the victims of the type of woman that Huxley refers to, and whom murders so much masculinity.

And when it comes to my metaphorical application of the bee and the bud, I imagine that any honest woman would say that the same rule that applies to the propagator applies to the flower. Biology is a two-way street; more ways, in some cases, from some perspectives. Promiscuity is providential, ladies and gentleman. "Nature is a whore," Cobain informs us. Every man and woman still anywhere *near* their sexual prime wants to have sex with a great multitude of those whom they're naturally geared towards, even as anachronistic Christian mind controls confuse the issue with false virtue. Let's just collectively admit that this is so, while also agreeing that this *doesn't* need to threaten committed relationships; that commitment of heart and mind and a total lack of commitment of sexually-primed body are *not* mutually exclusive, and that the drive to be exclusive doesn't negate a contradictory biological drive towards *inclusivity*. Let your men or women have their flirtations, women and men, respectively. Would you rather have them bottled up until explosion and divorce? And are you aware that marijuana growers carefully keep their flowering females away from males so that they'll burst with bountiful buds brimming with unrequited lust? That's marijuana horticulture 101, and *not* irrelevant to my point.

How is it that modern feminism has come to be the denier of biology, and the champion of hypocritical double standards? How is it that a woman can freely spout sexist idioms like 'mansplaining' within earshot of men when, if I were to even *suggest* that the way that a woman is thinking or speaking has something to do with her gender (like 'on the rag?') within earshot of her I'd become an embodiment of a patriarchy that I have nothing to do with? A woman can be outright sexist whilst hiding behind the pretense of feminism, whilst a man can't even be truthful about something as basic as his biological drives without being labeled a 'creep,' or say anything that's in any way critical of a woman without sounding sexist to the overly-sensitive modern ear. It's simply a misguided, bloated form of feminism run amok, hollow with hot air, conditioning conformity through the fear of disagreement leading to the mob reprisal of collective shaming by the blowhard band of bullies I saw coercing self-righteous affirmations out of everyone on everyone's *Facebook* page; an overreaction to past patriarchy tilting toward what every false feminist would happily see go all the way into an equally unjust future matriarchy, as if the former justifies the latter.

And while I'm on the subject of self-righteous, politically correct feminist bullying: *Fuck the Bechdel Test*. Don't get me wrong, I'm all for inclusion, but not *coerced* inclusion at the point of the gun of the Political Correction Police, forcing 'equal representation' upon artists and their work in order to receive the 'woke' stamp of approval, *regardless* of what their work is about, and what inspires it. *Fuck that*. I was just reading a friend's review of the second film in the most recent iteration of the *Dune* series, and his hailing of it as one of the best sci-fi films of all time, and this woman chimes in with: "It fails the Bechdel Test though. Just saying." I look it up, and immediate, indignant fury bursts forth within me upon reading about this absurd 'test.'

Wait. Now I have to conform to some arbitrary standard of female representation in my work in order to get your stamp of approval? *Never.* It makes me want to do the opposite, if anything. Both because I *despise* bullies, especially those pretending that their bullying is righteous, and because I'm against artificiality; the same artificial standards that dictate that the modern man has to lie about his biological programming, and shamefully keep it repressed around the 'modern woman.' And speaking of the modern woman, when *she* writes a book she has to include men the way that Bechdel demands the inclusion of women, right? No? Little is more demonstrative of hypocrisy and false progressivism than the double standard, dear reader, *regardless* of whatever injustice it's meant to address. You can't morally address injustice through injustice, which includes the double standard. If it's not a *universal* standard being applied, it's unjust. Period. Not to mention that, in this case, it's also promoting falsity.

Being pressured to pass the Bechdel Test means forcing content into books which may not naturally fit, and which wasn't naturally inspired, as all the best, truest creation invariably is. Not to mention that this 'test' represents the slippery slope of *endless* biased application. Let's see, does every book have to have a black character performing certain empowering acts? And Chinese characters? And celebrate the LGBTQ community? What if my story takes place entirely within the mind of one gay male protagonist who only thinks about other men? What if it's a tale historically accurate to a patriarchal period of history? Or features nothing but a hermaphroditic species of aliens? Or somehow excludes one categorization of people? Is it thereby *whatever*-ist? Creation doesn't care about equality of inclusion, only about the *inspiration*.

Yes, *of course* include women, but don't *force them in* because the bullies tell you it's improper otherwise! Not to mention that I would never even *think* to condemn a story that featured only women. And yes, I know the predictable comeback: because *men* aren't the unrepresented! There it is. The double standard. The benchmark of false progressivism. Given sufficient time, it's the creation of an inevitable equal and opposite injustice. The enemy of the universal principles compelling true, just progress. *Artists must be free to create what their hearts, minds and beliefs will them to, and must never, ever submit to such coerced artifice. Ever.* Prepare the hemlock for me now, ye crucifying pretenders of piety, ye flayers of free thinkers! Ye for whom progressivism is in any way an exclusive act!

If your fight doesn't invite the enemy to become the friend, and to join the ranks against the enemies which it conscientiously cast off, it's not being justly fought; it's a fight steeped in one or more forms of prejudice which it can only perpetuate. I'm not supposed to say this, because it infuriates the moronic amongst the politically correct, but that was *always* going to be the problem with BLM. Regardless of its intentions, its *verbiage* is inherently prejudicial. It strikes a dividing line immediately, one that preserves the old prejudice of 'black versus white.' It's also why it's so sadly absurd that the clearly superior, inclusive verbiage of 'All Lives Matter' was adopted by its racist enemies. Personally, I lay this at the feet of the formers of the movement. They should've seen that at the get go, that their verbiage invited the enemy to invest in superior verbiage, and thereby beat them in rhetoric. BLM should've extended the table of brotherhood by their nomenclature from the start, rather than immediately ceding half the table to the enemy (I was once banned from a *Facebook* discussion group for drawing a line between BLM and Malcolm X). If only Denzel looked more like MLK and less like Malcolm X, what a mighty movie that might've made! By the way, if you think in terms of 'my people,' regardless of how underrepresented or misrepresented those whom you believe to be 'your people' are, *you're a part of the problem*; you're violating the core of progressivism, *universality of application*, and thereby perpetuating the divides underlying prejudice, of one form or another.

Only for authentic feminists is feminism about morality, truth and progress. For the majority of 'feminists' it's about compensating for unhappiness, canalizing frustration, decompressing from dissatisfaction and seeking scapegoats for poorly-aimed anger. All movements are hijacked by unhappy, powerless people to some degree, depending upon the appeal of the movement and the type of membership it seeks. So, on a certain level, it's healthy. We all need to release pressure before it builds into breakage. But on another level it's reckless, misguided and unjust, making for manufactured martyrs whilst victimizing the inaccurately targeted, many of whom, upon close inspection, and having been forced to fend off such wicked witch hunts, did little wrong but be born with a pair of balls. I've dated a few false feminists whom collapsed like a house of cards upon critical inquiry, desperately attempting to re-stack their flimsy tower and turn the light upon me in the process, like those 'magicians' who use misdirection to conceal the fact that their 'magic' is less about moonlight, more about shining a bright, bewildering light in your eyes. Sadly, that's enough to get most to fall in line behind them.

Have you ever been falsely accused by a colluding group of gossiping girls because one or more of them were engaged in an ongoing overt flirtation and correspondence with you that subsequently went wrong? Were you thence made into a monster reflecting the modern paradigm of misunderstood manhood, and fired for it, and forced to absorb the resultant evils of the *real* monsters, and left entirely powerless to do anything about having had your psyche raped, and the truth buried beneath the official excrement? Me Too! Witchcraft is the twisting of truth to serve evil in the vanquishing of the good; the manipulation of nature into the unnatural for the sake of the power and ego of the witch. Hence my telling of the twisted true tale through the semi-fictional novella *Holier Than Thou*, about a free thinker stoned to death after a modern witch-hunt. How many others has she stoned to death, I wonder?

And yet, even as I know the evil that befell me there, I can feel my telling the truth of it to be an invitation to the witches whom have turned such a large contingent of modern feminism into witchcraft, as though speaking that truth is akin to ringing the dinner bell, calling them to come tear me apart and make of me their next meal. So I fear to speak. For even one with the conviction of I, a conviction that few can touch, fears the self-righteous mob, well knowing how and why they select their prey, the succubae absorbing into their egos the insufficiently defended, those ripe to play the scapegoat for the sake of the *true* villains. Should I stay silent, and risk becoming one of the hushed victims of the modern bully, one of Thoreau's 'quietly desperate' fake men, or should I tell the truth, and risk becoming an author that can never sell a book, because he's been 'cancelled' by the politically correct, irrational majority, and thereby be stoned to death? The silent victim, or the victim that fights back in refusal of the label of victim? Anyone can be victimized, dear reader, but you choose whether or not to accept the label of victim, and take it into your ego. *Don't permit that*. That's my advice.

I know from vast personal experience of a close family member that if you tell yourself you're the victim enough, with enough belief and pain and repetition, you become the victim *forever*. So you're reading my obvious answer to the aforementioned catch-22. Even as I just presented my exceedingly considerate response to evil as though it's a choice, *there is no choice*. Not really. Just as I didn't choose to fall in love with Jess. It was my nature and lack of nurture meeting her nature and vast ability to nurture. And I didn't choose to be targeted by the *Banned & Ignoble* coven. The most you can lay at my feet is that I should've been stronger and more cautious, and not given into my loneliness and their flirtations, and thereby not permitted them to draw me in and make me into a martyr.

Alas, that's history. It's all how you respond. And I refuse to let the evil stand. I refuse my victimization, and my martyrdom. I refuse to pretend that it's okay or in any way acceptable that someone as good as me be made into the exact opposite of what I am and how I was treated in that den of iniquity, even knowing that speaking of it invites the witches from around the world to descend upon me, ready to beat me with their brooms. I choose to make a record of the evil, as it's the only act of defying the evil that I'm permitted. And I would add that the fact that the good are frightened to speak the truth because it's misaligned with the popular modern lies reflects a very real, and all too dominant, evil today: The bullies rule, on *both* sides of the aisle, the parasites promoting the perfect division, for only when people are thus divided may we be exploited at will.

Tragically, we're now a goose-stepping, politically-correcting police state with two perfectly divided, 'shoot first and ask questions never' sides perpetually at war: the obediently reflexive, self-righteously bullying pretense of progressive morality shooting from the 'woke' left on one side, the Bible-thumping neofascist Trumpians and their slaughtered schoolchildren and environmental ruin shooting from the Christian right on the other side, all overlorded by, *not* a democracy (in anything but name), but, say it with me, a *plutocratic republic* comprised of an ultra-exclusive set of puppeteering overlords that want you to stay at war so they can keep exploiting your divisiveness and extracting from you at will. Very few see through the propaganda, and are opposed to *both* sides, to the forming of perfectly divided and conquered battle lines, and are thereby able to offer legitimate means to pursue progress through unification and purification of a true democracy combined with collective ownership of equity (the basis of my early work *Cultural Cornerstones, Recarved*), and only *we* thus possess the power and moral imperative to show you the truth and usher you towards your own liberation.

Reflecting on how easily my friend was bullied into submission with regards to his friends' use of the Bechdel Test against him, on the pretense of progressive righteousness, I began considering how well this outcome, and what precipitated it, reflects the nature of *Facebook* itself, and how the majority of my interactions therein have been negative, everyone at war with their 'friends' for the superiority of their egos, to appear the smartest, the most progressive, the most righteous, the most Christian. The immeasurable artificial gulf set between combatants, the fact that it takes place in the digital sphere, where no one has to look anyone else in the face, only exacerbates the tendency towards discord and egotism. It's particularly bad for the few like me who think outside the standard battle lines and thus become the automatic enemies in the minds of those owned by conventional identities. So I deleted my *Facebook* account, and immediately felt lighter, healthier, freer. In fact, if you want an idea for the next movement, one that will bring us closer as human beings, how about: *Fuck Facebook*! Stop scrolling! Pick up a book, actually read it, then go discuss it with your *actual* friends, face to face, as a spiritually connected human being, even if it's a book like this one that you probably hate right now.

And while I'm discussing social media, when it comes to the Political Correction Police, *Meta* is the national police chief, seeking the global title. I've been bitten so often by

the Meta Monster for posts and project promotions which,
to me, are simply honest portrayals of truth and principle,
that they started threatening to cancel my accounts. Then
they blocked my ability to 'boost' my posts on four different
accounts, two via *Facebook*, two via *Instagram*, by cutting
off my credit cards. Why? Because I believe in non-
religious spirituality and tell the politically incorrect truth.

It's ironic that in a country that pretends to stand for
freedom of expression and the 'democratic principles' that
demand that everyone have a say that anyone that doesn't
baa with the herd is presumed a wolf that needs to be put
down before he can threaten that herd. Ironically, it's those
leading the herd that are the true predators, and the ones
like me that they treat like wolves are really hunting *them*,
the false shepherds, not the sheep. For the American herd
is led not by the true Christ, the real spiritual shepherd, but
by his imperial edition; by neo-imperialism and global
corporate behemoths leading you lambs to the slaughter,
conditioning you to see *me* as the threat, when, in truth, I'm
one of your protectors. And when you understand the
prevalence of propaganda in this country, you know that
the true protectors must be sold as the wolves by those
holding the shears and pushing the sheep into their pens.

So it is that I abhor double-standards, the silent hypocrisy
that has turned self-righteousness into the defining ethos
of the modern era; demons dressed as priests, misandrists
dressed as feminists, social media companies dictating
social acceptability, tribes attacking other tribes for their
tribalism. For, again, all justice is based upon *universally-*
applicable principles. Let me provide you with some more
examples, and cement myself as a conveniently
identifiable enemy: I can't tell you how many sexist women
that I've met. But I'm not supposed to even notice, much
less comment on it, the implicit conventional wisdom
seeming to be that it's their right to be sexist in making up

for the patriarchal past. Sexism to solve sexism. That's like saying justice dictates that white people should be subject to centuries of slavery, you know, to balance things out.

Or how about the fact that misandry is at *least* as prevalent as misogyny, more so, in my experience, yet everyone knows the latter term, with very few seeming to know the former. Or that when a man has issues with women he's assumed to be a 'misogynist,' whereas a woman experiencing the same things, and making exactly the same comments, is a 'feminist.' Or that an older man finding a younger woman in her sexual prime attractive is "creepy," as I was verbatim criticized for by a *BookWife* critic of *Holier Than Thou*, whereas the young woman isn't criticized, but assumed to be the victim, even if she came onto the older man. Not to mention the fact that an older woman finding a younger man attractive meets with no such disapproval, and is even openly joked about by most.

I was, in fact, often hit on by older women in my youth. Actually, I was hit on regularly at the same job that's the subject of *Holier Than Thou* by a woman not only far older than me, and who made comments about how attractive I was, and who constantly wondered aloud as to why I was single, and who touched me constantly whilst interacting with me, but who was also one of my supervisors (in the position of power). I didn't mind, first of all, because I'm not the unduly morally-outraged type, and I don't mind being touched, but if I *had* said anything about it I probably would've been scorned by every woman there thereafter. Instead, it took my involvement with her duplicitous young coworkers and their friendships with supervisors for me to be stoned to death, narratively and figuratively speaking. Here's an idea: How about applying the same standards to both men *and* women, and *all* identities, recognizing the inevitable arc of unjust swings from one side to the other that will otherwise result depending upon the historical epoch and its governing paradigms and zeitgeist? No?

David Attenborough won't admit it, but he must be shaking his head at the modern feminist confounding the natural competitive drives and displays at the heart of *all* animal life, with humans complicating the competition, but only able to *falsely* pretend as though they don't apply to us, enforcing the false ethic that males of any virility aren't supposed to be attracted to younger females in their sexual, procreative prime. "Wait," his inner self thinks, "so now the females in this species put on an overt show of their sexuality, and the men they sexually attract are in the *wrong* for being attracted? Because those shows are now about female empowerment and the shaming and emasculation of the male in revenge for a history of male-dominated society? *That's* feminism? And if a male doesn't accept that, he's a *misogynist*?" There's some part of every man, relative to their awareness of and aversion to political correctness and its role in sociosexual politics, that's screaming: We need a masculinist rebuttal! Because there's something very, very wrong with the contemporary sociosexual paradigm, one in which young women overtly flaunting their bodies is seen as 'empowerment,' but when a man notices (as all men with even a few active swimmers in their tanks do) and admits to it he's a 'creep,' as, again, the critics at *BookWife* called me, before cravenly backpedaling and saying no, it was only my *protagonist* that they'd labeled a creep in *Holier Than Thou*, not me, even though I'd made it clear from the outset of that book that I essentially *was* the protagonist.

Worse, when I defended myself to their editors they basically blacklisted me, their parent company, *Publishing Meekly*, instantly, reflexively refusing to even *consider* reviewing any of my subsequent projects. So let's look at that line of indignation incitation: A gorgeously blooming flower purposefully accentuates its form, attracting a pollinator that's initially given as much of the flower as he wants, but soon finds the pollen is defensively poisoned, and when he returns to the hive to report the event the members of the hive condemn him on the order of the queen, whom proclaims: *The truth of nature is no longer welcome here. You are only to pollinate the flowers that we tell you to, else consider yourself banned from all hives, for we're a network of all-powerful matrons, and any bee drawn towards an unassigned flower will be castigated.*

Hey, at least I didn't say: *The lithe and supple flower sags as it goes to seed, its biological function fulfilled.* Oops. Imp aside, is this not also a compliment? That it takes more energy to maintain the beauty, vigor and procreative capacity of the pollinated than it does the pollinator, and that, therefore, the woman doesn't age as well as the man? And it's not just the greater energy required of being the attractor and the procreator wherein the competitive disadvantage has produced some rather repugnant results in the case of the more unscrupulous segments of society.

Society is a competitive environment that's historically been dominated by men, in no small part due to their physical advantage. This historical power disparity is, of course, as with all social states in which such severe disparities exist (most notably in parallel with class-based conflict), the cause of the conflict between and 'battle of' the sexes. It's my honest belief that this, in turn, has produced the pressures that've pushed women to develop certain competitive advantages of their own in order to compete. Thus it is that, as the tide is shifting and, by my experience, women will soon have *more* power than men professionally, and possibly in the personal realm as well, expressions such as 'feminine wiles' and 'Hell hath no fury like a women scorned' are embedded in the conventional parlance, for, the legitimate feminist push for equal treatment and opportunity aside, they express the fact that women have had to develop certain characteristics passed on through selective evolution in order to level the playing field. That is: *they're forced to be craftier to compete*. And, especially when young and morally-undeveloped and unrestrained, and vain and egotistically propped-up by beauty, this craftiness manifests in the tendency towards deviousness and manipulativeness. I believe this to be the reason why the most beautiful, powerful and 'successful' women are amongst the most monstrous of human beings.

So while that may sound sexist on the surface, what I'm *really* saying is that there was a genetic, or an epigenetic, imperative for the female gender to develop the cunning to counterbalance the physiological competitive disadvantage of facing the physically far more formidable male. Even before 'the patriarchy,' picture the evolving hominid female facing the pre-history, pre-law archaic male, or bands of males, and attempting to avoid her own rape and murder. Deviousness and survival were often one and the same, thus creating a clear evolutionary impetus. And, of course, this adaptive necessity passed on to not just those females whom outfoxed males and survived where the more trusting, honest and fearful females fell victim, but, over time, embedded the characteristic in female human genetics, like every other advantageous adaptation.

In post-patriarchal, neo-feminist, Me Too, politically correct bullying society, this characteristic creates a clear opportunity for women to abuse their own congenital-and-contemporary-culture-based competitive advantage, especially when they're young and pretty and also, therefore, possess the advantages of being in great demand by men whilst regularly being falsely perceived as the innocent ingenues. They can, and do, in allusion to the real life events that inspired my book *Holier Than Thou*, parade around in skimpy little skirts and feign shock when a man notices (hello Elizabeth), and sometimes go much further in purposefully attracting males of interest, gluing themselves to him and talking about sex and birth control constantly, lifting their shirts and skirts to show him parts of their bodies, only to pretend no such purpose, discourse or action existed when they subsequently feel insulted by him and/or lose interest in him (hello Miranda), thereafter allying with other gossiping girls so eager to prove that they have power that they're willing to make good men look like monsters in the process, thereby proving their own monstrosity (hello Libby), whom thence often enlist other women of the self-righteous, narrowly judgmental type to jump on the expulsion bandwagon (hello Jennifer).

And, as just implied, it's not just the assholes amongst the men that pay the resultant price. Those with particular weaknesses towards women, like, say, persistently lonely 'middle aged men' that've been deprived of female company for most of their lives for their own unrelated reasons, are easily conflated with abusive older leches in the eyes of the naïve right-wing Christians and left-wing movement-followers constituting the modern morality police. Trust me on this. And I'm certainly not the first falsely labeled 'patriarchal male' to find the balls (pun intended) to comment on these truths, and won't be the last. And, again returning to *Animal Planet*, such gender inequality catalysts aren't exclusive to homo sapiens in the animal kingdom, and are, like my comments on the difference between how the genders age and the fact that females are more sexually attractive when younger and more fertile, simply biologically-embedded facts that are very often mistaken as 'sexist' or 'misogynist' by false feminists on power trips; the type of over-empowered woman that enrages me by essentially bullying modern men observing such facts into keeping such observations to themselves at best, and more often lying about them.

Irrationally and, I would argue (due to its impact), immorally, this represents a common contemporary form of feminist 'progress' run amok, all the way into the 'common man' speaking and writing outright falsities for fear of eliciting politically correct ire and being subsequently 'cancelled.' Very few men have the combination of courage and intelligence required to both understand and make the comments that I'm making here. In fact, many an emasculated male will read this and many other remarks herein with great discomfort, recognizing their truth but being unable to admit it, even to themselves, and especially still if in the presence and being pressed by the aforementioned type of mate. So while it's well known, *and for good reason*, that women should be wary of monstrous men, what's uncommonly known is that men have equal if not more reason to be wary of equally monstrous women.

I've known many of these monsters myself, including Linda at the CRC and Libby and a few of her companions at the Bend *Banned & Ignoble*, as well as Jessica, a gorgeous young girl that manipulated some of my best high school friends into attacking me at our ten year reunion after I'd insulted her on social media, in defense of her monstrous treatment of a shy friend of mine (I based a semi-villainous character on her in my first book, *Infinite of One*). Now that I think of it, the popular, beautiful young woman that organized that reunion, the first girl that I ever had a crush on, Brittany, whose mother once worked with my mother, thereafter berated me for *being attacked*, insinuating that I somehow 'ruined her party.' Status was her sole concern, justice be damned. And yet I can't evade the sense that I've scarcely scratched the surface of the archetype, and that *many* men have faced even more egregious injustices at such twisted hands than I, victimized by the treachery innate to *true* witchcraft. Personally, I associate the term 'witch' with these selectively-evolved tendencies and their destruction in the sociopolitical and professional realms, for this is an *actual* evil I know empirically. This as opposed to what the Church made of the term 'witchcraft' to wrongly impugn the pagans and naturopaths whom threatened their falsely absolute authority in the realms of spirituality and healing during the Middle Ages. The *deviousness* is the real evil, not the non-religious thinking and medicine-crafting which *still* threaten greed and power, and which I share with the *wrongly* labeled 'witches' of the world.

Please tell me that there are some women out there that *don't* immediately think that my speaking such truths makes me an enemy of 'their team.' Please tell me at least some of you, the more mature and advanced of you, identify your teams and fealty by something *other* than gender and blind obedience to the politically correct dictates of which womanhood now seems inseparable. How many of you are offended by misleading political correctness and its dictatorial influence on the minds of the vast majority, as you should be, and thereby oppose it *regardless* of gender? I fantasize that someday, when attacked by the self-righteous for being with an 'asshole who says such things of women,' that I'll have a partner advanced enough to say: "An asshole? *No*. Far from it. He's the most romantic, loving man I've ever known. He's just far more aware and fearless than the wanna-be men I *used* to date. Don't confuse the imp with the Devil, ladies!"

Ready for more impish truth from the devil's advocate? Study biology and you'll find nature to be like one big phallus seeking out and fucking the moist warmth. Yes, organisms can adapt to the relative dearth of these two catalysts of procreation, but they remain the dominant catalysts nonetheless. Find me one flower that didn't unfold from moisture and warmth, or one pollinator that wasn't drawn to the resultant fresh nectar, and the bright colors of burgeoning beauty and youthful attraction that accompany that nectar, and the invitation with which they reek and purposefully accentuate for the purpose of attraction, and maybe then the unnatural form that modern feminism appears to me to have made of itself will be able to reflect at least *one* natural form, rather than being in denial of nature, and standing against pollinators as though we're the enemies, when, in fact, we drive life, even when political correctness pretends that we're the 'creeps.'

No, I'm *not* arguing for the 'she's asking for it' absurdity, in reference to the modern feminist assertion that the accentuation of sensuality and its triggering of sexuality gives the pollinator the false right to an unjust form of sexual aggression. But if the young woman knowingly plays the accentuation game, then she's definitely asking for *something*, whether or not she, and society at large, can admit that. Yes, she has a right to be beautiful for the sake of her own self-worth, without the guy coming onto her, as one 'feminist' argued to me. But let's not pretend that she's not aware of her effect, and that she doesn't use it in less than virtuous ways when she lacks moral development, as is common, inviting the pollinator for the power trip of it all, ever remaining ready, in repeating Huxley, to "play the outraged virgin" when, for whatever reason, the attempt at pollination is unsuccessful. You can't put on a show of accentuated nature and then pretend that those whom respond by their own natures are doing something wrong or unnatural. That's but hypocrisy. And yet, ask yourself: how many modern 'men' will say so?

Sometimes to be the best of guys I must seem to you to be the worst, until the terrible moment of realization where the one you'd forced into the role of demon rises up the white-winged angel. It might surprise you, gents, and especially ladies, that the pursuit of honor, of which I'm keenly aware, requires the utterance of thoughts which falsely honorable people proclaim to be *dishonorable*, building their hollow identities around the bullying majority backing that dishonorability. But how to combat the dishonors of conventional wisdom wrapped up in political correctness but by the unconventional wisdom considered to be politically incorrect? I swear to each and every one of you, dear readers, even those of you with your noses up tricking yourselves into believing you're getting a whiff of something foul, that my heart is true, and my intention progressive, and that my enemies are never the *hearts* of people, but the mentalities which stand against the truth leading to *legitimate* virtue. I'm the ever-rarer free thinker not needing the shows of false virtue spread like thin, misleading veneers over the insecure and vain. So lay your lies at your own feet, ye pretenders of piety. Adorn your false robes of righteousness for the blind, easily-misled masses. For I see you, so you might as well turn your true face towards me, for your other, fooling face fools me not.

Those whose identities are built upon self-righteous wrongs are *always* insecure, you see, for their insecurity is a natural side effect of concealing faults that they know, deep down, are inherent to their identity, like building a structure of oneself upon a fault line requiring but the release of mounting deceit to crumble. Many people, in fact, spend their entire lives lying to themselves, never admitting or facing their true selves, instead futilely attempting to bury these fault lines, pretending they stand upon a secure foundation that only the discerning can see for what it is. This, in fact, is the core driving force of many psyches, and is prevalent within many sets of demographic demarcations, including everything from the domestic abusers in *Maid* to conservatives to the senior-most RS's of PrimaCare, the insecure set to release their internal pressures upon the most vulnerable of all populations.

And since I'm talking about false robes of righteousness in a book about mental health, let me add that there's a deep, ultra-rich psychological vein to be mined in the fact that the most common delusions amongst the severely mentally ill in America are *religious* in nature; more specifically *Christian*; especially Catholic. It's too much for the purview of this testament, to be sure, but it's a vein that I'm sure has already been mined by other academics; a sinkhole steeped in the sewage of brainwashing, in the gutter-waste of guilt, in the insidious intermix of normal, indoctrinated delusion and the delusions begotten by mental illness.

How can I not then wonder where the line between them is? And wonder if this permeable line suggests 'gaslighting' to be as much at play upon the lecterns of the priests and pastors in the production and perpetuation of popular delusion as pure 'non-reality' is prevalent in the so-called 'ravings of lunatics?' "What, you don't think angels and demons are real, only symbols with terrestrial corollaries? Are you insane?," the priest seems to say in denunciation of the doubter, his fearful flock dutifully nodding their heads in unison, shaming the few who refuse to suspend their critical thought, and who understand the purpose and value of metaphor in communication as certainly as the writers of the one book that they're not allowed to question. It's in the nature of the unjust to make their injustice appear just, for the simple reason that they require complicity.

Thus does the priest shroud himself in golden raiment, does the politician readily recite principles which he himself hypocritically betrays when away from the stump, in the pursuit of his private interests, and does the invading army scream: "We're here to save you!" whilst slaughtering those whom, were they Americans defending America the same way, they'd switch from calling 'terrorists and tyrants' to 'patriots and presidents.' Has it occurred to you, dear reader, that the only reason that perfectly conditioned westerners like Lenny associate Middle Easterners with 'terrorists' is that the region possesses a long-suffering, blood-soaked history of violently repelling invading and occupying (i.e. *terrorizing*) nations like ours, and that calling their self-defense 'terror' hides the truer terror? Yes, of course killing civilians is terrible, but have you seen the statistics on 'collateral damage' of the wars *we've* initiated?

By the way, true patriots fight for the best interests of their people, even, and perhaps especially, when it's unpopular. They don't just obediently wave the flag at everything their political 'superiors' say, or simply mirror the values of the ultra-wealthy whom they're conditioned to revere regardless of the injustice and waste they represent, and what they cost humanity as a whole. If you're unaware of these facts, and unaware of the aforementioned double standards of false progressivism, you're unlikely to well regard this. Unless, of course, it facilitates your awakening.

And when it comes to 'representatives of God,' the recently cited Machiavellian line "everyone sees what you appear to be, few see what you truly are" is so near to being total in its truth that most of the Christians whom I've met seem to me *far* more likely to be enchanted by embodiments of the deceiver than embodiments of The Second Coming, one whose testament could be right under their noses, in the form of a book about unrequited love and the failures of mental health treatment, for instance (that one is for you, Jess!), and they'd not only *not* recognize those words as paralleling those of their 'Savior,' but equate them with those of the aforementioned deceiver, and condemn one who comes to awaken them as an agent of evil. Christians are more likely to fall in line with the enemy, calling him the champion of the good, and call the actual champion the enemy of the good, simply because he rebels against the ruling forces; forces which, not coincidentally, match those of the Eastern Roman Empire two thousand and twenty four years ago, the tactics of that Empire passed on through aristocratic channels to the rest of Europe before migrating across the Atlantic. Christ was nothing if not a rebel, and all that he rebelled against yet remains reigning over us, their evils preserved by those clutching his cross.

There thus seems to me three gods fighting for control of modern America: the God of the *institutionalized* Christ, the God of Political Correctness, and the God of Greed. Christians versus the 'Woke' versus the Bourgeoisie and their plutocratic puppeteers, with many attempting to put their feet in all three camps, somehow unaware of the inherent contradiction, or simply not caring that this contradiction exists, for so common is it that it's normal for people to ignorantly contradict themselves by their beliefs. And the worship of these inherently contradictory false idols, and the inevitable empty consumerism, classism, division and discord which they produce, invariably contributes to the pressures mounting into mental illness within the most vulnerable members of the warring public, especially those that don't well fit into any of these camps which they're constantly pressured to conform to; camps which are always comprised of the ideologically deluded.

Christ, for example, stood for renouncing wealth, ego and the consolidation of power, even as many a 'Christian' wears jewel-encrusted gold crosses and attends the super churches of notorious egomaniacs and tax evaders. Then these same Christians go home after the Sunday service and obediently obsess about how they can 'keep up with the Joneses' by possession and social position, coveting in ways contrary to the *actual* principles espoused by their 'Savior.' Thus, the problem with the modern ideological war is both that it represents a maddeningly-contradictory cloth overlappingly worn, and also that none of these three Gods are the *true* God, but all represent false deities. Each of them requires, by the practice of their worship, burying true divinity, both directly, in their denial of deeper truth (which is *always* of a spiritual but not religious nature), and indirectly, by sowing the discord and division which precludes unity and leaves humanity the obediently conquered herd, its progressive shepherds deemed insane ("The words of the prophets are written on the subway walls"), forced to the periphery by the wolves running the overlapping realms of business, politics and mental health. In the face of these forces the true men are coerced into hiding, keeping the truth to themselves for fear of backlash. But how can one be a true man when running from bullies?

Thus do I hereby define Masculinism as my God-given right to be a heterosexual male in Me Too America. Not to be dominant over women, as with the patriarchy of the past which it should go without saying, but somehow doesn't, that I disapprove of. Rather, I simply refuse to be emasculated like most of these false men around me cowering for fear of reprisal for speaking their hearts and minds. Like any *true* feminist, I believe that people have a right to their nature, and that equality of rights, protections, privileges and opportunities is an inalienable divine right absolutely indistinguishable from justice, *regardless of absolutely everything*, including race, creed, color, sexual orientation, gender identification (or lack thereof), or even the damn planet the entity is from! And I *don't* recognize your right to infringe upon any of those divine rights. And I *refuse* to pretend as though what *every* heterosexual man is attracted to is shameful. And I'll no longer be victimized as I was at *Banned & Ignoble.* That's my solemn, masculine vow. And, by the way, it includes loving the *heart*, not the mind, of every woman now preparing her lynch mobs to 'cancel' and crucify me for telling the truth.

To me the concept, and potential movement, of Masculinism is about two things above all others: (1) refusing to deny our nature in the face of modern movements and false forms of 'progress' (2) evolving beyond outdated, traditional ways of thinking about the male gender, and thereby contemplating and exploring what it means to aspire towards a true manhood that most 'men' never reach. It has nothing to do with conquering feminism (except to false feminists that're only interested in bringing more power to the gender, to 'their people,' regardless of justice), but *mutualistically aligning with it*, so that each may symbiotically serve the other. It's about the Divine Feminine aligning with the Divine Masculine in the coevolution of the species, in the best interest of all of life.

So *please* don't misunderstand me. All that I'm essentially calling for is *equality*, which is what I *thought* feminism was all about. I didn't think it was about parading and garnering as much power for your 'side' as possible, which would render it immoral. Gaining greater power is certainly not *my* intent. I've *no* desire to take anything from you, only to keep you from taking something from me; to prevent you from bullying me into pretending that nature is shameful, or that modern empowerment should exclude men attempting to evolve beyond outdated paradigms, and that it shouldn't attempt to help those many merely *playing* the modern man to rehabilitate from their emasculation and recover their manhood. And I definitely *don't* mean recovering patriarchal power, or doing anything that's in any way cruel to or disempowering of women. I mean a shameless practice in selective-self-evolution and self-actualization; promoting an *advancing* manhood in the face of brutalizing bullies so frenzied in their fraternization that we have to ask permission to be men. What modern horror is this?

It's that which further cements *Thoreau's* "most men lead lives of quiet desperation." I refuse, regardless of what continued dreads the modern woman delivers upon me. For look within *this* cover and you'll find that this particular book is about the opposite of what is sold to the fearfully gullible like my former boss. Maybe *every* book, in its own way. Maybe every *woman*, in her own way. In the worthy whom revile the witchcraft to which I refer, seduction is a façade created to serve the substance. Vanity wishes to be gratified, sure. Jess wants to know that she's beautiful. But that wasn't what ended up selling me. And that's not what she wants most. What she *needs*. The truth is the old cliché: sex sells, but love can't be bought. I fell for her because of her thrillingly agonizing *substance*. I fell for Jess because she let me in; she let down the drawbridge, else eventually capitulated to my naturally-driven attempt to pull it down, so that I could read every page of her book.

She kept the guards at the gate, to be sure, the notorious boundary-men, but I snuck past them unconsciously, on pure instinct. And the same goes for *this* interaction, right now, between me, the suffering, unrequited idealist, and you, the uncomfortable reader. For what am I in the end but another desperately lonely guy silently screaming into the abyss, hoping to hear even a whisper bounce back: *It's okay, Nick. You are loved.* This book being on mantles would fill my ego with all the hot air it wishes for, but my heart wants that *one* woman, maybe *you*, to be filled with the truth of me and *not* be repelled, as I fear, but *overcome*. I want you to realize that you think you hate me because you secretly love me. I want you to see that what you think you hate in me are but the unpleasant parts of you that I reveal, holding a mirror equally revealing of ugliness and beauty. *That's* the purpose of people like me.

And yes, within the context of this book and my reflections upon my stifled love for Jess, I realize the irony that what I'm now talking about, in what you're apt to dismiss as a misogynist rant, but which is actually a masculinist *right*, is raising a protective boundary, the boundary of positive freedom, and that a balance must be struck between negative and positive freedom. Hey, I warned you that I was prejudiced, and that there's no such thing as 'unbiased.' It's because I loved her so much, don't you get it? That boundary fucking hurt! It still hurts, a good five years later! *That's* how much I loved that girl! So please forgive me for summoning Shiva. I'm only a destroyer in defense of my right to be a lover, including of myself.

Logos is mine, ladies and gents, regardless of whether or not you agree. Keep leaning on the empty modern ethos if you must. If and when moral dictate is ever recovered by logos, it won't reflect well, in hindsight, upon today's shows of morality. Conventional wisdom shall be seen as the *want* of wisdom. The 'woke' shall be seen as the deluded. The politically correct the rationally incorrect. The righteous majority the self-righteous mob. The followers of Christ the indoctrinated acolytes of Empire. The conservatives the conservationists of parasitically-produced consolidations of profit and power oppressive to the symbiotic advancement of humanity. I mean, in all honesty, if you don't get existence yet, if you've yet to show your middle finger to the ruling systems and paradigms of the world, you're either aligned with the secret contemporary slave-masters, else you're somewhere between the conditioned slave and the oblivious child. *That's* the perspective which any truly ascendant evolution of the human race shall lend to those looking back on today from its vista. The many infamously iconoclastic passages of this book today are destined to be famously iconographic of 'ahead of his time' tomorrow. So I apologize for the pain that I've been compelled to provoke in order to play my part for progress. At the same time I know that what you take away from this book is a reflection of *you* more than me, for we're all mirrors for one another.

As my story goes *today*, my love for Jess mattered more than everything else. Everything else is like trying to fill that space with all that which can never fill it. The only hope is that the act of attempting to fill it might make me forget it's there for a time, like the formerly cited magician performing a feat of misdirection. I'm trying to forget that Jess signifies the promise of everything luring me towards a summoning of substance, only to forever remain the shadowy specter.

So, was that it for me? Is this why they call it 'falling *hopelessly* in love?' Because you tumble headlong into it before you even know that it's there, and even when it's hopeless, when it has no possibility of being fulfilled, it remains? Defiant? Unrelenting to the end of the life that it possesses? I'm terrified that it's over for me. That I'll never feel that way again. That when you fall in love, really *fall* in love, not just calling it love because you feel something and want it to be the same, that it can only happen once. And when it's unrequited, it's tragically, permanently so, for no other loves are true loves, only reflections of that one true love, projected upon an endless litany of imitations.

It's the only time I've ever been in love, and, as the sun sets on the driven productivity, profit and survivalist needs of the day, we're reminded that love is what matters most. As a 'middle aged man' now, I'm swimming against the dread that I'll not only never fall in love again, but that it'll never be reciprocated; I'll never have that which matters most. Though I suppose that I should be thankful that I've at least *been* in love; nay, been *consumed* by love. And I honestly believe that, with the frigid darkness I've passed through, I wouldn't be alive today without having fallen for Jess, and thereby know that being lost in the cold and dark is *always* worth it for the chance to bask in the warm light.

I love you Jess. *Forever*. No matter what.

AFTERWORD: The Law of One

The law of physics that states that "every action has an equal and opposite reaction" is actually a *metaphysical* law. This law is a natural effect of all things being One, thereby demonstrating the truth that *separation is an illusion*. In theological circles, this is known as the principle of 'non-duality.' We're all embodiments of the One Source of all energy and matter, existing entirely within and inseparable from that Source, our bodies Its energy, our consciousness the conductor of the One Consciousness.

Amongst the resultant effects grown from this metaphysical ground of all truth is the aforementioned law, a law that goes by many names and is reflected in every academic discipline. The Law of Attraction, The Law of Manifestation, The Law of Correspondance, The Law of Inseparability, The Law of One. Whatever you call it, and however you come by it, it's fundamental to metaphysical existence, and it essentially says that *everything is reciprocal*. Everything grows and degrades relative to both how it acts and how, in a reaction that's equal in force and nature but opposite in its directionality, it's reacted to. That which we 'put out' into the world we take in from the world. Everything we do *to* another is done *to* ourselves, through the One Source of which everything is, reflecting the fact that *there is no 'other.'* Everything we do *for* another is done *for* ourselves.

Whether we're passing along good energy, the height of which is unconditional love, or bad energy, all the hate and harm that typically comes from the mangled merger of the beleaguered psyche, the insecure ego and the pressures placed upon the body and brain, it's *immediately reciprocated*. This, then, is the heart of morality, and all moral social systems: *do unto others as you'd have them do unto you, because what you do to them you do to One.*